Successful Supervision

SUCCESSFUL SUPERVISION

JOHN H. JACKSON
University of Wyoming

TIMOTHY J. KEAVENY
University of Wyoming

PRENTICE-HALL, INC., Englewood Cliffs, New Jersey 07632

Library of Congress Cataloging in Publication Data

JACKSON, JOHN HAROLD.
  Successful supervision.

  Includes bibliographical references and index.
  1. Supervision of employees. 2. Personnel management.
I. Keaveny, Timothy J., joint author. II. Title.
HF5549.J25   658.3'02   79–21205
ISBN 0–13–872796–1

Printed in the United States of America

10 9 8 7 6 5 4 3 2 1

Editorial/production supervision and interior design by Joan L. Lee
Manufacturing buyer: Harry P. Baisley

PRENTICE-HALL INTERNATIONAL, INC., *London*
PRENTICE-HALL OF AUSTRALIA PTY. LIMITED, *Sydney*
PRENTICE-HALL OF CANADA, LTD., *Toronto*
PRENTICE-HALL OF INDIA PRIVATE LIMITED, *New Delhi*
PRENTICE-HALL OF JAPAN, INC., *Tokyo*
PRENTICE-HALL OF SOUTHEAST ASIA PTE. LTD., *Singapore*
WHITEHALL BOOKS LIMITED, *Wellington, New Zealand*

Contents

2   ORGANIZING TO GET WORK DONE, 21

3   THE MOTIVATION TO WORK, 43

LEADERSHIP AND SUPERVISION, 65

COMMUNICATING EFFECTIVELY, 87

---

section two
Supervising
Human Resources

**6 THE SUPERVISOR AND
THE STAFFING PROCESS, 117**

THE SUPERVISOR AS TRAINER, 137

THE SUPERVISOR AND REWARDS, 160

**THE SUPERVISOR AND
PERFORMANCE APPRAISAL, 179**

**10 THE SUPERVISOR AND
THE PROBLEM EMPLOYEE, 202**

section three
Supervisory Tools
and Techniques

THE PLANNING AND
CONTROLLING PROCESS, 229

PLANNING AND CONTROLLING
TECHNIQUES, 247

13 PROBLEM SOLVING AND DECISION MAKING, 273

14 SUPERVISING CHANGE AND CONFLICT, AND WORKING WITH OTHER SUPERVISORS, 293

15 SUPERVISING YOUR TIME AND DEVELOPMENT, 312

section four
The Supervisor and the Law

16 THE SUPERVISOR AND THE UNION, 337

EQUAL OPPORTUNITY IS THE LAW, 361

THE SUPERVISOR
AND SAFETY, 383

Preface

"No organization can function well if its supervisory force does not function. Supervisors are, so to speak, the ligaments, the tendons, and sinews, of an organization. . . . It's the supervisor's job to be in the middle." *—Peter Drucker

We first became interested in writing a book about supervision when searching for what we felt was an appropriate text to use in supervisory courses and programs. The available books had several features that were not quite right for our purposes. Many considered supervision only in an industrial setting. Others were too academic for what should be an applied course. Still others were too "how to do it" oriented, ignoring the many contributions that the areas of behavioral science and management have given us. Some were simply not up-to-date and didn't deal with some of the current concerns of supervisors such as equal employment opportunity and occupational safety and health laws.

Since we found none of the existing books to be exactly what we

* Peter Drucker, *Management* (New York: Harper & Row, Publishers, Inc., 1974), pp. 280–81.

wanted, we checked with a number of colleagues, found they shared our views, and decided to write a book to fulfill the needs we perceived. We feel strongly that many of the basics of supervision apply whether the supervisor is operating in a large business organization, a small business organization, a hospital, a government agency, or an educational institution. The same basic concepts and tools can be and *are* used in all of these situations.

We have tried to aim this book at two audiences because they have so much in common. Many colleges and universities offer courses in supervision or first-level management. Students in these courses seem to want a firm understanding of what supervision is, what supervisors do, and examples in the form of cases upon which to base this understanding. The second audience is that group of people who have (or are about to have) supervisory responsibilities, and who want to benefit from the experiences of other supervisors as well as from the solid management research that has provided new answers to old supervision questions.

In trying to reach these two groups we have attempted to be very practical in our approach, presenting case examples based on real life supervisory problems. We have included sections on "tools" to be used by supervisors in doing their jobs, and "how-to-do-it" hints.

In addition to providing the helpful, practical hints on how to supervise, we have tried to provide a good strong *understanding* of why these techniques are successful. It is not possible to anticipate every situation in which a supervisor might find himself or herself. By understanding the *reasoning* behind the things one might do, the supervisor will be better prepared to deal with the unique situations each will come across in the performance of his or her job.

The past 15 years have provided us with a number of supervisory tools that the competent supervisor knows how to use. For example, basic tools in the areas of interviewing and counseling, training, planning and controlling work, making decisions and managing time have been well developed and are available for the supervisor's use. In other areas where tools are not as well developed, a good understanding of various things one might do, and the pros and cons of various approaches is important. These areas include such things as motivating employees, communicating with employees, understanding the basics of leadership and approaches to change and conflict in the organization.

Learning objectives are included in each chapter. They help the reader pick out the main points and the main lessons to be learned in each chapter. Each chapter also has several short cases. These cases come from our experiences as supervisors and from the experiences of several hundred supervisors who have been with us in supervisory development courses. We have asked these supervisors to write down short problem situations they have faced; we have accumulated these and they appear throughout the book to add realism to the chapters.

We have tried to combine in each chapter the two elements that are important in training supervisors. First, an *understanding* of the particular topic, and second, details as to how one goes about *using* the understanding that has been gained. Finally, we have included a section in this book that is critical for modern supervisors: The Supervisor and the Law. Supervisors find themselves more and more involved with equal employment opportunity, occupational safety and health and labor-management legislation that places constraints on their activities. To train a person in the basics of supervision and to ignore his or her responsibilities under the law isn't fair to that person.

We have taken a "personal experience approach" to presenting the material. This approach emphasizes the day-to-day problems confronting the supervisor and provides a basis for understanding and evaluating those problems.

We would like to thank Vanita Fowden for the excellent photographs used in this volume. We would also like to thank the individuals whose comments helped shape this volume: Professor Frank Beaton, School of Business Technologies, State University of New York; Professor William M. Berliner, Graduate School of Business Administration, New York University; Professor Stephen C. Branz, Triton College; Professor R. D. Miller, Hillsborough Community College; Dr. George L. Frunzi, Wesley College; Professor Edward Nicholson, Wright State University; Professor Carl Reed, Monroe Community College.

The book was designed and written to provide a practical, usable, but most of all *accurate* training tool for developing high-quality supervisors in organizations of all kinds. We sincerely hope we have succeeded in doing so.

Successful Supervision

GETTING WORK DONE WITH PEOPLE

section one

Section one introduces the supervisor's job in terms of his or her position in the work organization. In order to help you understand human behavior in a work context, we also discuss some of the most important issues about human beings and their behaviors in work organizations.

1

The Supervisor's Job

SUPERVISORY PROBLEM

What do effective supervisors do?

When you have finished this chapter, you should be able to

1. Describe some problems associated with being the "person in the middle"
2. Indicate how a supervisor spends his or her time
3. Describe the supervisory management process and tell why it is important
4. List some reasons why people accept supervisory positions

THE NEW SUPERVISOR

Tom Wilson put his feet on the desk that Friday afternoon and stared at the wall. His thoughts centered on his first week's experiences as a supervisor of the loading dock at AMIX Corporation. It had been an unbelievably busy week, and Tom was only now beginning to realize how many things were involved in his new supervisory role.

The week seemed to have been marked by a series of crises. First, Tom found out that next week's schedules were due on Monday afternoon, but while he was trying to get these in order, he was confronted with the more immediate problem of three absentees. Then, later in the day, equipment trouble had prevented him from completing the schedules on time.

On Tuesday one of the workers who had been absent called in to resign, and Tom had to concern himself with replacing that person. On Wednesday afternoon he was asked for an immediate decision as to whether his work group would participate in a flexible work hours schedule that upper management had devised. On Thursday he had to attend a meeting with other supervisors in the organization to try and solve a work coordination problem that had been a major problem for a long time. Finally, on Friday morning, he had to fire an employee who had been tardy for the tenth time in a month.

It had been a busy week indeed and Tom was rapidly discovering that more was involved in successful supervision than he had envisioned. He sincerely wished he'd had a little more guidance in handling some of these problems before he was forced to deal with them.

Tom Wilson's case illustrates a few of the very common problems that all supervisors face. Tom was supervising a loading dock, but the same problems face nursing supervisors, accounting supervisors, supervisors in education, police and fire departments, and so forth. Perhaps a good place to begin our study of supervision is to examine our answers to the question, Who is a supervisor?

WHO IS A SUPERVISOR?

The supervisors have often been referred to as "people in the middle." Between employees on one side and upper management on the other, supervisors have typically come up through the ranks and have been chosen because they demonstrated above-average work performance. In his or her new role, the supervisor has not only a responsibility to maintain technical competence but also the duty to learn new skills as a supervisor. Technical expertise and competence in human relations require the supervisor's attention as well.

As a person in the middle, the supervisor must put up with the complaints and work problems of subordinates and must also meet the expectations of upper management. These expectations include production quotas and company rules and regulations. The supervisor is one of the most important positions in any organization for two reasons. First, employees deal with management mostly through their supervisors, and, second, upper management deals with the employees primarily through its chosen supervisors.

The case in Block 1–1 illustrates just one of the many problems that that can be caused by being the person in the middle.

BLOCK 1–1   The Boss's Friends

A supervisor at a state highway department reports the following problem:

Bob and Jim are summer hourly help who are working painting highway guard rails. Neither of them seems to need the money very badly, and neither plans to stay with the organization after the summer is over. Consequently, both try to do as little as possible, and repeated comments I have made about improving their work seem to have had little effect.

I would have fired them both, but they are off-the-job friends of my boss. His son goes to school with them. He told me at the start of the summer to put them on the painting job until August. I've thought about separating them, but the job takes two people and there's no one else to help out. I can't fire them or the boss will be unhappy; meanwhile, however, the job isn't getting done.

Here the supervisor's tough position at the first level of management is quite obvious. Because of the dual nature of the position, the supervisor may have to act as a member of the management group and at another time as leader of the employee group. The supervisor may have to represent unpopular employee views in management meetings or pass on unpleasant management directives to employees.

The supervisor is usually identified as part of the management team and his or her agreement with management decisions may often be taken for granted. On the other hand, the new supervisor may find it difficult to establish the necessary "distance" from employees he or she has worked with.

Differences Between Supervisors and Upper Management

Figure 1–1 illustrates the supervisor's position in the work organization. The figure suggests that supervisors and upper managers have dif-

FIGURE 1–1

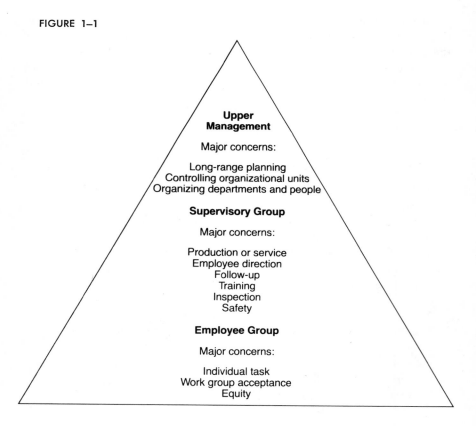

Upper Management

Major concerns:

Long-range planning
Controlling organizational units
Organizing departments and people

Supervisory Group

Major concerns:

Production or service
Employee direction
Follow-up
Training
Inspection
Safety

Employee Group

Major concerns:

Individual task
Work group acceptance
Equity

ferent major concerns in their jobs. Upper management is shown as being mostly concerned with planning, controlling, and organizing the work of the organization, while the supervisory group is primarily concerned with production, employee direction, follow-up, implementing training, inspection, safety, and so forth. However, these differences are really only a matter of degree. For example, to suggest that upper management is not concerned with production would be totally incorrect, and to suggest that supervisors do no planning, controlling, or organizing would also be incorrect. However, upper managers do spend *more of their time* planning, controlling, and organizing than do supervisors. And day-to-day production problems are clearly more a pressing problem to the supervisory group than to upper management. Since supervisors work directly with employees on a day-to-day basis, they naturally are more concerned with employee direction, training, and so forth.

Decisions

There is a difference, too, in the kind of decisions that are made at the supervisory level. The supervisor's decisions tend to be more repetitive and involve issues spanning a shorter time than do those at higher levels in the organization. For example, a supervisor must take action immediately if a machine goes down, while upper management decisions tend to be less immediate in nature such as planning the location of a new plant or determining the advantages of alternative production methods.

Control

Another distinction between upper management and supervisory management is the amount of control that upper managers and supervisors have in their own jobs. Upper managers usually have more control over the specific activities that they will tackle on any given day. Supervisors, on the other hand, have somewhat less control over specific activities because so many things have to be taken care of as they occur.

Since supervisory problems tend to demand immediate solutions, supervisors are often in the position of *reacting* to a given situation. There is some evidence, however, indicating that certain people, regardless of their level within an organization, are able to control their jobs better than other people. Thus the supervisor *need not* be a slave to the immediate situation. The materials in this book are designed to help supervisory candidates increase the level of control they have over the job. Better control over the job allows a supervisor to concentrate on the overall functioning of the work unit and leads to successful supervisory performance.

WHAT DO SUPERVISORS DO?

The supervisory job involves two major areas of responsibility—*things* and *people*. Things include the equipment, machinery, materials, and schedules that get the job done. A nursing supervisor, for example, is not only in charge of a group of nurses but is also responsible for a number of *things,* such as medical supplies used in the treatment of patients, certain medical test equipment, syringes, and X-ray equipment (in certain hospitals).

Supervising "Things"

This portion of a supervisor's job varies widely depending upon the organization, industry, and technology involved. Someone supervising grocery store stockers will be doing different specific activities than someone supervising a military work detail or someone supervising scientific report editors. However, there are several techniques for managing the production part of the job that can be used by all supervisors.

Planning the work to be done, scheduling jobs, maintaining control over needed items of material or equipment, managing a supervisor's personal time so that the job can get done, and making decisions are job concerns that all supervisors share. These techniques will be covered in a separate chapter each in this book.

Supervising People

Supervisors must also be concerned with people and interpersonal relations, since the job they must do can only be done through the cooperation of the employees. For this reason, persons in managerial positions who have no employees reporting directly to them are not really supervisors in the sense we are using the term here.

It is the unique mix of time spent on things and people that really makes the supervisor's job different from many other management jobs. Figure 1–2 shows the results of a study that indicates how certain supervisors spend their time in an eight-hour day. Several similar studies have arrived at similar figures. The figure shows a mix of concern with both things and people. About 25 percent of the supervisor's time is concerned with directly supervising the job; this may include concern with both people and things. Another 28 percent is concerned with such interper-

FIGURE 1-2   How Supervisors Spend Their Time

Activities	Percent of Time Spent
Directly supervising the job	25%
Other interpersonal matters	28%
Things (equipment, materials)	22%
Planning and scheduling work	5%
Meetings and other	20%
	100%

Source: Adapted from Chester E. Evans, *Supervisory Responsibility and Authority,* Research Report No. 30 (New York: American Management Association, 1957).

sonal relationships as handling grievances, appraising performance, and other personnel matters; 22 percent is spent solely on things, including equipment, materials, and so forth; 5 percent is spent on planning and scheduling the work; and a final 20 percent is spent in meetings and other time expenditures. Other studies have shown that poorer supervisors tend to spend more time actually doing individual employee jobs rather than coordinating the efforts of workers.[1]

Thinking about Figure 1–2 suggests that a supervisor who is good at handling people but is technically incompetent will probably not succeed. By the same token, a supervisor whose technical knowledge is extremely good but whose interpersonal skills are not is not likely to be very successful either. Another recent study concluded that upper management *expects* people it promotes to supervisory positions to have a good technical background, from which they can then build the people-oriented skills that become crucial to successful supervision.[2] We should note that different supervisory jobs will have somewhat different mixes of time spent on things and people. The percentages given in Figure 1–2 represent averages, but all supervisory jobs will include responsibility to some degree for both.

Getting Work Done Through Your Employees

We suggested earlier that the supervisor must do a major portion of his or her job through other people. It is the nature of many jobs to require the efforts of a number of persons. In Chapter 2 we will discuss in greater detail the process known as *division of labor* that occurs when a job gets too big for one person to handle and requires a coordination of diverse efforts through supervision.

As a result of having to get the job done through others, the supervisor is *dependent* on other people for seeing that the job is done properly. This dependency can result in some very unfortunate situations if the supervisor doesn't do a good job of delegating, communicating, motivating, and leading. Fortunately, there are a number of skills the supervisor can use to minimize people problems. Many of these skills are based on developing good interpersonal relationships—the ability to get along with others—while others rest on more specific techniques such as leadership, working with other supervisors, dealing with conflict, and disciplining effectively.

THE SUPERVISORY MANAGEMENT PROCESS

Management is the process of taking many diverse elements (people, money, materials, equipment, and ideas) and turning them into a product or service that people need. Since supervisors are the first level of management in an organization, they must utilize some of the same skills and abilities as other managers.

Supervisory management can be viewed as an ongoing process. There are certain behaviors that successful managers/supervisors must learn to get the job done. Many studies have shown that successful supervisors demonstrate these behaviors *more often* than less successful supervisors. Figure 1–3 shows the cyclical nature of the management process.

Planning

Planning is the beginning point of the supervisory management process. The logic behind the need to plan surfaces in the old saying, "In the long run you hit *only what you aim at.*" If a supervisor hasn't planned, he or she probably has no set goals, and whatever success is achieved may just as well be attributed to chance or luck.

FIGURE 1–3   The Supervisory Management Process

Yet planning is probably one of the most difficult things to force yourself to do. Many supervisors seem to resist the mental exercise required in trying to estimate where their unit should be in six months or a year or two from now and the steps that will get them there.

Planning will be discussed in greater detail in Chapters 11 and 12. Basically, however, it involves making an estimate of what goal is to be reached and deciding what steps are necessary to accomplish that goal. Planning serves as both the beginning and ending point for the supervisory management process. Plans made during the first step become benchmarks or criteria against which *actual* performance is measured in the control step. Comparing planned and actual results provides the supervisor with a sound basis upon which to make necessary adjustments in the work.

Organizing

Organizing is the grouping together of activities to make individual jobs, as well as the process of dividing up labor to get things done. Organizing at the upper levels of an organization usually includes designing the overall framework for the organization. At the supervisory level, however, organizing is usually more specific and may involve the following activities:

1. Developing methods to help people understand what portion of the job is their responsibility
2. Coordinating individual efforts through work schedules to avoid unnecessary delay in task accomplishment
3. Designing a good system for making day-to-day work assignments should these be necessary
4. Cross-training employees to avoid disruptions in the job caused by absenteeism

Organization will be covered in greater detail in Chapter 2.

Staffing

Staffing is that part of the supervisory management process which deals with getting the proper match between the jobs available and applicants for those positions. In larger organizations, supervisors usually have only minimum responsibility for finding and hiring new employees. Those activities are done by the personnel department, although many organizations allow supervisors to veto a job applicant the supervisor feels will not measure up to work expectations.

By contrast, supervisors in smaller organizations are commonly involved in recruiting, interviewing, and hiring new employees, issues we shall deal with in Chapter 6.

The entire staffing process consists of

1. Recruiting
2. Hiring
3. Inducting (orienting)
4. Training
5. Appraising

Clearly, *all* organizations should involve their supervisors in inducting, training, and appraising employees. These activities are fundamental to the concept of supervision and will be dealt with in Chapters 7 (inducting and training) and 9 (performance appraisal).

Directing

Directing people sounds simple—in fact, it is often equated with "giving orders." However, giving orders is only a very small part of directing people's work.

Before one can successfully "give orders," he or she must understand how the people to whom the orders are being given are likely to react. Understanding people in work situations includes understanding motivation and human behavior, topics we will discuss in Chapter 3.

Next, the "order giver" must have some idea of how to approach the giving of orders: Should he or she simply *tell* subordinates what is to be done, or is it better to *ask* for their opinions? An understanding of leadership and communication is important for answering these questions; so we will present some guidelines for developing these skills in Chapters 4 and 5.

Supervisors often consider directing the most difficult and frustrating part of their job because people are so "unpredictable" and "hard to understand." Given a basic understanding of human behavior in the work place, much of the mystery disappears and the supervisor's job, while not any easier, is at least less frustrating.

Controlling

As shown in Figure 1–3, controlling completes the cycle of supervisory management activities. Supervisors who do a poor job of controlling the work in their unit are easily identified—they are the ones who are continually surprised when trouble occurs. Such supervisors never seem to be able to pinpoint what went wrong or to say exactly what their employees are doing.

Control is the responsibility of *every* supervisor. It may simply consist of walking around the work area to see how things are going, or it may involve designing sophisticated checks on the quality of the work, but it *must* be done if a supervisor is to be successful.

In any form, control consists of checking the *actual* performance of a person or unit against the *planned or expected* performance and making adjustments when the two are out of line. Such adjustments might call for disciplining an employee who consistently fails to meet acceptable standards or even applying self-analysis to the supervisor's own work habits and use of time. These topics are covered in Chapters 10 and 15, respectively. General guidelines to good control are presented with information on planning in Chapters 11 and 12.

Employees and the Supervisory Management Process

The supervisory management process of *plan, organize, staff, direct,* and *control* is more than just a convenient summary of the things a supervisor should be doing. It is also a good summary of what employees *expect* their supervisor to do. Figure 1–4 is a sample of quotes taken from nursing employees who were asked to describe their best and worst boss. After reading the comments, try to determine which elements of plan, organize, staff, direct, and control were present in the successful supervisors and which were lacking in those considered failures. Notice that among these descriptions of nursing supervisors there is no "one best" set of characteristics for a good supervisor, but that certain elements are present in each picture.

The "blueprint" for learning about supervision that follows is a summary of the issues raised so far. By referring to this outline at any point in your studies, you will be able to regain perspective on how a particular issue fits into the supervisory process.

A BLUEPRINT FOR LEARNING ABOUT SUPERVISION

This book is divided into four sections that are designed to provide the supervisor with the information and the tools necessary to function effectively. The first of the four sections is "Getting Work Done with People."

FIGURE 1–4   Find the Elements of the Supervisory Management Process

Best Boss

Worst Boss

The best boss I ever had was a shift supervisor. She knew what was happening in the hospital and what the staff was doing. You had her support and knowledge in decision making, but the people involved were allowed to make the decisions. Problems were handled in private with only the people involved there. She praised staff when warranted.

My best boss was an intelligent, compassionate, strong woman. Knew her nursing. Knew the staff. She would stand behind the staff against anybody. Her main concern was patient care and getting the job done, and she enforced it.

My best boss never seemed to get upset no matter what went wrong or who may have been shouting at him. He would try to calm the agitated party or would get with the group involved and try to find what went wrong and then made a decision to rectify the situation. If I was snowed under with work, he would help out or get help for me. He listened to your problems and gave the time necessary to complete the task. You never actually thought of him as a boss and were never intimidated by him, you did tasks he gave you because you wanted to, it gave you satisfaction working for him. He also stood up for what he thought was right, including sticking up for his workers.

The worst boss I ever had was a shift supervisor. She berated personnel in front of patients, visitors, and other staff. Her planning was crisis oriented. She was always quick to criticize, but slow to praise. She couldn't handle constructive criticism.

My worst boss got her job as assistant manager by reason of experience. She loved the people she'd worked with before, but didn't like anyone else. She criticized in front of others, got unnerved when busy, did not help train new personnel, just shouted at them when they did something wrong. I quit within three months.

The worst boss I've ever had when put in a crisis situation couldn't handle it; she would begin shaking, shouting, screaming at employees over very minor things. She wouldn't allow you to finish a task. She would come and tell you to do something and wouldn't allow you to finish your present task and then when both tasks were half done, she would scream, actually scream at the workers. Totally out of control.

Getting Work Done with People

To be successful, supervisors have to understand (1) exactly how their job fits in with the jobs of others and (2) basic principles of human behavior in a work situation. Figure 1–5 outlines how information relating to these two categories will be presented. To really understand some of the limitations supervisors face in their jobs, students of supervision must be aware of several factors. Among these are why authority relationships are important, what motivates employees to work, how good leadership complements good supervision, and what kind of communication problems are likely to arise.

Each chapter in this section deals with one or more general super-

FIGURE 1–5   Getting Work Done with People

Supervisory Problems	*Chapter*	
What do effective supervisors do?	The Supervisor's Job	Ch. 1
How does the supervisor fit into the organization? Why do organizations look the way they do?	Organizing to Get Work Done	Ch. 2
What explains the effort that people put into their work? What can a supervisor do to improve the motivation of subordinates?	The Motivation to Work	Ch. 3
In what different ways can a supervisor lead employees? How does a supervisor decide which leadership approach to use?	Leadership and Supervision	Ch. 4
What can I do to minimize "communication breakdowns" and failure to communicate?	Communicating Effectively	Ch. 5

visory problems that are identified at the beginning of the chapter as outlined in Figure 1–5.

Supervising Human Resources

The second major section of the book will deal with the specific knowledge and tools that the supervisor should have to handle people—the organization's most important resource. Figure 1–6 summarizes the

FIGURE 1–6   Supervising Human Resources

Supervisory Problems	*Chapter*	
How does the organization go about getting people, and how does the supervisor fit into this process?	The Supervisor and the Staffing Process	Ch. 6
What does the supervisor need to know about training to be effective? How can this knowledge be applied to the job?	The Supervisor as Trainer	Ch. 7
How can the supervisor keep employees satisfied with their compensation?	The Supervisor and Rewards	Ch. 8
What are common errors made in evaluating employee performance? How should the supervisor conduct an appraisal interview?	The Supervisor and Performance Appraisal	Ch. 9
How can a supervisor bring about a change in an employee's behavior? What methods constitute effective discipline?	The Supervisor and the Problem Employee	Ch. 10

general supervisory problems in section two associated with effective supervision of human resources.

Supervisory Tools and Techniques

The third major section of the book provides tools and techniques that help get the job done. The competent supervisor will have a tool kit of supervisory methods that allows him or her to do the job well. Included in this section are a look at the planning and controlling process and management by objectives, as well as specific techniques associated with planning and controlling. Problem-solving and decision-making methods, supervising change, conflict and working with other supervisors, and supervising one's own time and development are all discussed in this section. Figure 1–7 shows the general supervisory problems associated with each chapter in section three.

FIGURE 1–7   Supervisory Tools and Techniques

Supervisory Problems	Chapter	
Are planning and control really necessary? What exactly is involved?	The Planning and Controlling Process	Ch. 11
What techniques are available to see that the work gets done on time?	Planning and Controlling Techniques	Ch. 12
When should I make the decision myself and when should others have a say?	Problem Solving and Decision Making	Ch. 13
How can I handle conflict among my employees and make changes smoothly? How can I best work with other supervisors?	Supervising Change and Conflict, and Working with Other Supervisors	Ch. 14
How can I get the most out of the hours of the day so I can get my work done? How can I identify areas in which I need to develop as a supervisor?	Supervising Your Time and Development	Ch. 15

The Supervisor and the Law

Finally, we deal with three legal areas that the competent modern supervisor simply *must* understand. The union is an institution that puts constraints on supervisors whether or not their subordinates are union members. There are things that a supervisor can do to make living with the union easier, and also steps he or she can take to prevent unionization. The constraints that state and federal law have placed on hiring, promotion, performance appraisal, and job evaluation have changed the

FIGURE 1–8   The Supervisor and the Law

Supervisory Problems	Chapter	
What role does the supervisor have in effective labor-management relations?	The Supervisor and the Union?	Ch. 16
What are the equal employment laws and regulations which a supervisor must understand? How do they affect the supervisor's job?	Equal Opportunity Is the Law	Ch. 17
What can I do to keep the work place safe? What are my responsibilities under the Occupational Health and Safety Act?	The Supervisor and Safety	Ch. 18

ground rules for a great many supervisors in the last ten years. We attempt to provide you with an exposure to the issues of equal opportunity as they affect the supervisor. The law has also impacted the supervisor's job in the area of health and safety, specifically through the Occupational Safety and Health Administration (OSHA). The final chapter in the book will look at OSHA and safety programs. The general supervisory problems that go along with these three areas are presented in Figure 1–8.

THE SUPERVISOR'S JOB
FROM A DIFFERENT PERSPECTIVE

Now that you have a fairly good idea of what is expected of a supervisor, you may well ask, What do supervisors find in their jobs that keeps them in these demanding positions?

Salary

It is often rumored that supervisors receive less take-home pay than the people they supervise. This occurs, it is contended, because hourly employees have the opportunity to earn overtime while salaried employees do not. A recent study of the top 100 manufacturing firms in the United States found that the typical first-level supervisor's after-tax salary exceeds his or her highest paid subordinates after-tax wages by 25 percent. Even when overtime is factored in, there is still a 20 percent differential.[3] So even though there may be some instances of supervisors receiving inadequate pay, it appears that on the average the extra responsibility is rewarded.

17

Job Rewards

Salary may be the first thing we associate with greater job responsibility, but a recent survey found that salary ranked a poor second to interesting work as a motivator of supervisory performance.[4] Figure 1–9 shows the top five job characteristics in order of their importance to first-level supervisors. In fact, salary trailed interesting work by quite a margin as a first-priority item—40 percent to 11 percent. It should be noted that these figures represent United States national averages and that some variation in rankings were discovered from one geographical region to another. Where jobs are scarce or salary low, job security and salary items undoubtedly take on more importance.

Supervisors as a group evidently value interesting work. Certainly the vast majority of supervisory jobs are not lacking in either challenge or demand for innovative thinking. As we have just seen and as will be reemphasized throughout the book, the problems of managing both people and things to get a job done are many and varied.

SUMMARY AND CONCLUSIONS

The supervisor holds an intermediate position between upper management and an organization's rank and file employees. Although supervisory personnel are members of management, their jobs weigh heavily on the directing and controlling functions rather than the planning and organizing functions of upper management.

Supervisors manage both people and things. A supervisor who cannot handle the management of both will be held in low esteem and will not succeed in supervision.

The supervisory management process of planning, organizing, staffing, directing, and controlling can be used to pinpoint not only what upper management expects of supervisors but also what employees expect of

FIGURE 1–9 Percentage of Supervisors Indicating Job Characteristics as First, Second, or Third Priority

Percent who rated item:	1st	2nd	3rd	Totals
Interesting work	40%	16%	11%	67%
Salary	11%	30%	14%	55%
Chance for promotion	8%	13%	27%	48%
Job security	18%	8%	17%	43%
Appreciation	13%	11%	7%	31%

Source: "What Do Supervisors Want from Their Jobs?" by Michael J. Abboud and Homer L. Richardson. Adapted with permission *Personnel Journal* copyright June 1978.

their supervisors. Supervisors who perform the process well and are considerate of their employees receive high ratings, while those who do not are candidates for "worst boss" status.

The text presents supervisory information in four major sections: Getting Work Done with People, Supervising Human Resources, Supervisory Tools and Techniques, and The Supervisor and the Law.

Finally, supervisors seem to value the challenge and variety of work that can be found in most supervisory jobs. This, plus a substantial salary differential, greater opportunity for promotion and job security, and a sense of being appreciated, explains why people choose to become supervisors even though the work is highly demanding.

QUESTIONS

1. "The person in the middle represents sometimes management and sometimes the rank and file. This is a difficult situation." Discuss.
2. Why might someone be quite good at handling technical problems but feel inadequate about handling "people" problems?
3. Draw a diagram representing your own conception of upper management's and supervisors' share of the planning, organizing, staffing, directing, and controlling functions in your organization or one with which you are familiar. Show a percentage of the time you estimate the two management groups spend in each activity.
4. Weigh the pros and cons of being a supervisor. List the positive aspects in one column and the negative in another. Write a short paragraph in which you defend one or the other viewpoint. (Since we did not deal with this question *exactly in this fashion*, you will have to pull together information from many places in the chapter and also from your own experience.)

CHANGING BEHAVIORS

I have several supervisors who report to me. One of them has just been promoted from the regular crew. He is still friendly with all of the crew and still likes to work on the problems that require the special skills of a repairman, his former job. However, during the time he spends trouble shooting, the rest of the crew are not completing their work, and their accomplishments are not what top management would like to see. I know this man has potential as a supervisor, but he apparently doesn't have a good idea of the supervisor's function, or else has not yet been able to bridge the gap between worker and foreman. What can I do to get him to manage rather than actually do the work for his subordinates?

1. Does being a supervisor require different behaviors from those of an employee?

2. Do you suppose this is a common problem with new supervisors?

NOTES

1 Robert H. Guest, "Of Time and the Foreman," *Personnel,* 1956, p. 32.

2 Thomas DeLong, "What Do Middle Managers Really Want from First-Line Supervisors?" *Supervisory Management,* September 1977, pp. 8–12.

3 G. S. Crystal, "Paying for Performance," *Wall Street Journal,* July 11, 1978, p. 14.

4 M. J. Abboud and H. L. Richardson, "What Do Supervisors Want from Their Jobs?" *Personnel Journal,* June 1978, p. 311.

Organizing to Get Work Done

 SUPERVISORY PROBLEMS

How does the supervisor fit into the organization?
Why do organizations look the way they do?

Courtesy Sybil Shelton

LEARNING OBJECTIVES

When you have read this chapter, you should be able to

1. Explain why organizations take the form they typically do
2. Identify problems associated with having more than one boss
3. Describe why supervisors must have both authority from above *and* acceptance from below
4. List the basics of good delegation

A CLASSIC ORGANIZATION PROBLEM

Bill Morgan was quite happy when he found out that he had been put in charge of the group that was to design and oversee the building of the new work center.

Bill's boss, Tom Johnson, had made it quite clear that he was to have sole responsibility for the success (or failure) of the project. It was important that the needs of all the groups using the work center be accommodated in the design. Bill had been given what he felt was a first-rate group of people to work with, but that is where the problems began.

Frank Samuels was an engineer by training and would be a key man in much of the design. But Frank was being "loaned" to another project for the next six weeks and would be available only on a part-time basis until that was over. Bill was uncomfortable about that; it really put a strain on his schedule, but it appeared there was little he could do about it.

Then there was the money problem. He had been told that there would be enough money available to incorporate most of the equipment needed to meet the needs of the building's users. But now that seems to be in doubt. Again, there isn't much Bill can do about it.

But the most frustrating problem of all has turned out to be the boss. Tom is gone a lot but nevertheless wants to be informed about what is going on before any final decisions are made. This is putting Bill in the position of having to hold back decisions on matters that really need to be settled quickly until Tom has enough time to review the situation.

Bill now wonders if he made a mistake in accepting the assignment. He is responsible for seeing that things work well and there's no doubt he will be blamed if they don't. But he is beginning to doubt that he has the authority necessary to fulfill that responsibility.

Most supervision takes place within an organization of some kind. The accounting supervisor at the state highway department, the nursing supervisor at the Memorial Hospital, the line supervisor at the assembly plant, or the owner of a small business with four employees all practice supervision in *organizations.*

Organizations certainly are not new things. They have been with us since the dawn of civilization when primitive humans banded together to accomplish a task of some sort. Even early hunting and farming societies were faced with tasks that required "organization" of some kind to minimize injuries or simply to produce enough foodstuffs to survive.

Even though organization predates recorded history, most people, including supervisors, probably have never really understood why modern organizations are the way they are. Most of us work within an existing organizational framework without ever examining the basic functions or structure of organizations, or realizing what they *could* be. The remainder of this chapter will thus attempt to explain a bit about the nature of organizations and tackle some typical organizational problems.

HOW DO ORGANIZATIONS GET THAT WAY?

Modern organizations do not always appear to have the most logical arrangements for accomplishing their various tasks. For example, an organization may have a number of people engaged in actually "doing the work" but also a sizable number of jobholders whose relationship to the final product is hard to determine. Then, too, the student of supervision may be confused about the differences among such terms as *authority, responsibility,* and *accountability.* Another reason to examine the organizational process is for clues that can help a supervisor succeed and survive in an organization. For example, the supervisory candidate should be aware of such things as management by exception, understanding the concept of a limited span of control, and knowing how to delegate effectively.

There is a difference between understanding the basics of organizing work and merely surviving within an organization. The difference is between being able to *use* the organizational arrangements to get work done, and not being able to do so. To aid our understanding of how the various features of a modern organization have developed, let's consider how a hypothetical small organization grew into a large organization.

Artco, Inc.: An Example

Fred Bell had worked for a number of years for Williams Manufacturing Inc., as a production supervisor. Fred had always wanted to be his own boss, and having come up with a better way to make picture frames in his spare time he worked perfecting his new process. He proved to himself again and again that he could make high-quality picture frames quickly and inexpensively.

Before long, word got out that Fred could make very nice frames, and a number of people at work ordered frames from him. As Fred's reputation for quality workmanship spread, he found himself spending a great deal of time at this second job.

Eventually the demand for the frames exceeded Fred's ability to meet it. He hired a college student to work part time on the weekends to help him build frames. But as the reputation of Fred's picture frames spread throughout the region, even this proved to be not enough. Fred and his new helper were overwhelmed by orders, so he hired two other employees full time. Unfortunately, this made the garage where they were working very crowded. However, because the money was coming in so rapidly, Fred was able to move the operation out of the garage and into a small metal building downtown.

Still, keeping up with the expanding business was taking more of Fred's time than he could give to it. After working eight hours at the plant, he would have to come home and work until 11 o'clock at night trying to keep up with the paperwork and the back orders for frames, and his entire weekends were devoted to the demands of the new business. Fred felt he had to make a decision whether to try and continue with his job *and* the business, or give one up. He decided the business was doing well enough that he could give up the job he had held for so many years and finally go into business on his own. Artco, Inc., was created.

The picture frame business continued to expand and get better. Fred hired five more employees and promoted his first helper, who had now moved to a supervisory job overseeing the work of the other employees. Yet Fred *still* lacked time to effectively manage the business. For instance, now that it was his full-time job, Fred realized the importance of advertising the frames and of contacting owners and managers of art supply stores to build up a greater clientele. But he didn't really enjoy the traveling that this entailed. Besides, it was taking a good deal of his time away from the other things that needed to be done in the organization.

Fred decided to hire a salesperson. It was the salesperson's job to scout the entire sales territory and inform potential buyers of the advantages of Artco's frames. Even this, although it helped for a while, didn't solve Fred's basic problem of lack of time. For example, one of his pet peeves was keeping the books. A tremendous number of records, forms, and financial statements had to be filled out to satisfy the requirements of local, state, and federal governments (including the Internal Revenue Service). Fred found that there simply wasn't enough time to do everything he felt he should be doing, such as planning next year's production and trying to determine whether his supplies could be gotten elsewhere at a cheaper price. So Fred hired an accountant and gave her the title of corporate treasurer. It was her job to fill out all the reports and to maintain the financial statements that Fred needed to determine how well the business was running.

Also, by now, the actual production force had grown to over 100 employees, and it was clear that the one supervisor could no longer keep up personal contact with so many people. So Fred decided once again to change the structure of the organization by promoting his first employee to a second-level management job and promoting five of the best workers to supervisory positions beneath him. (See Figure 2–1 for a visual summary of how Artco, Inc., developed its functions.)

Fred Bell's successful frame company is a good illustration of how organizations grow to meet the needs of expanded production. The key to understanding why this work organization came to look as it did is the very simple fact that *one person could no longer do a given task.*

Lessons from Artco

The implications for the organizations in which we work are tremendous. When Fred could no longer do everything himself, he had to entrust some of the tasks of supervising the work to other individuals. When he did this, he ran into the problems of *controlling* the work performance of other individuals. How could he be sure when he assigned a job to someone that it would get done? As the organization got bigger, it became harder to know everyone personally and much harder to communicate intentions and expectations accurately to everyone. This problem certainly isn't unique to Fred Bell's enterprise. The same problems have been faced by all supervisors and managers over the years. In dealing with these problems, managers have tried a number of different organizational arrangements and techniques. Some worked, and some did not. Some work in certain situations and not in others. By the process of elimination over centuries of organizational activity, a certain body of generally effective organizational "principles" has come into being.

Our purpose here is not to discuss all possible organizational arrangements for getting work done, but rather to deal with some of the *major* concepts that explain why organizations are the way they are and how these concepts affect the supervisor's job.

WHAT IS A WORK ORGANIZATION?

We have talked about organizations in general, and Fred Bell's organization in particular, but we have purposely not defined a "work organization" to this point. We wanted you to think about organizations

FIGURE 2–1   Artco, Inc.

(1) Original organization

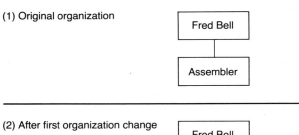

(2) After first organization change

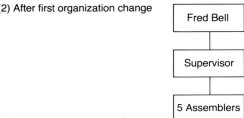

(3) After third and fourth
organization changes

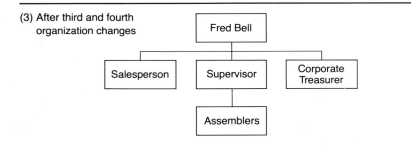

(4) After fifth organization change

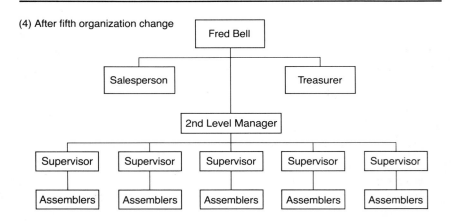

as you always have, while reading about how they grow and develop. But now consider a definition of an organization as *a grouping of activities necessary to achieve work objectives. This grouping of activities includes structuring of duties, responsibilities, and authority.* This definition provides a good basis for talking about well designed and poorly designed organizations.

The grouping together of *activities* and *duties* and the provision for orderly *responsibility* and *authority* relationships makes up the organization as we usually see it.

The way in which organizations are designed depends on many variables. Four of the important variables are

1. The external environment in which the organization operates
2. The tasks or technology involved
3. The size of the organization
4. The strategy of the top management group

How Does the External Environment Influence Organization?

The kind of environment in which an organization operates helps determine how it will be organized. To illustrate, an organization that operates in a rapidly changing environment will probably have to spend a greater amount of time staying in tune with that environment than one which exists in an essentially stable environment. This means more emphasis will be placed on activities such as sales, public relations, and developing new products. The organization in the stable environment will place more emphasis on such things as production, seniority, and human relationships.[1]

How Does the Task Influence Organization?

The work to be done (task) and the technology used to get it done are important influences. Job shops are organized differently from assembly line operations. Refineries are organized differently from universities. In each case, the nature of the task requires a certain technology. Job shops handle a series of *different* jobs while mass production operations process the *same* items over and over again. Refineries, too, process the *same* product(s) but in a continuous operation, while universities handle very *diverse* problems and interests in their research and teaching duties. The organization that works well for one set of tasks will not necessarily work for the others.

How Does Size Influence Organization?

You saw in the Artco case that as the organization got bigger, Fred Bell had to change authority relationships and add functions (sales and accounting). Size tends to *complicate* organizations. There are more things that have to be coordinated, and they are harder to control. For an example, see Block 2–1. Size also leads to more impersonal working conditions. It's hard to know all your employees well when you have 200 of them. The way the organization is put together to get work done is, therefore, influenced by its size.

How Does Strategy Influence Organization?

The long-range plans upper management has for an organization are reflected in the way it is designed. If long-run plans include expanding the business across the country, very likely some sort of geographical division will be necessary. If upper management feels organizational growth depends largely on sales, sales importance may be increased in the organization. After all, upper management designs the organization, and the design should reflect logical strategies for accomplishing goals.

Are There "Principles" to Guide Organizing?

The most difficult task in any area is to lay down a set of guiding principles for that body of knowledge. This is particularly true for organization, because what is a good design in one situation may fail miserably in another. In considering the following "principles" of organizing work, you should keep in mind two limitations.

1. While these principles form the basis for most organizational relationships, it is easy to find situations in which flagrant violations seem to have no effect on organizational functioning. In other situations, some of these principles might not work at all.

2. The effective use of these principles of organization requires the application of a good bit of common sense that takes into account differences in both technology and human behavior.

Perhaps it might be best to think of these "principles" as *concepts for organizing work*. Even though some academics have charged that these concepts are "out-of-date," a study conducted by the American Management Association found that over two-thirds of the companies surveyed named one or more of these "principles" as useful management concepts.[2] Keep in mind, however, that not all of the principles are applicable in *every* situation.

The reason for organizing in the first place is because one individual *can't* do all of the work alone, so that delegation becomes a necessity. Over the years, supervisors have found that some ways of delegating assignments have worked better than others. Yet the concept of delegation has remained fundamental to getting work done, and successful supervisors delegate.

Delegation

The nature of delegation suggests that when you assign or delegate a job or duty to someone else, you have done two things:

1. You have given that person *authority* (permission) to make commitments and to use resources necessary to get the job done; and

2. You have created in that individual the *responsibility* (obligation) to do the job, to do it well, and, hopefully, to use good sense in doing it.

For example, when Margaret Boltz, a nursing supervisor, asks one of her employees, Randy Daniels, to see that the storeroom is cleaned and the stock inventoried, Margaret has *delegated* the job to Randy. In so doing, he will assume that she has granted him the authority necessary to get the job done. If he has to get cleaning supplies or tools to do the job, he has the authority to do so. Further, if no system currently exists for inventorying the supplies, it is his responsibility to come up with such a system. At the same time, a responsibility (obligation) was created for satisfactory performance. When Margaret told Randy to do the job, she assumed that he would do it and he would do it well. It would clearly be unacceptable for him to come back to his supervisor the next day and tell her that he had forgotten to do the job. The responsibility for doing the work would not have been met.

Authority Should Equal Responsibility

Delegation involves both authority and responsibility. Ideally, an individual should be given as much authority as responsibility. If a supervisor makes an employee responsible for the quality of work turned out, then that employee should have the authority necessary to do a high-quality job. The chapter opening case is a good example. Bill Morgan did *not* have the authority he needed.

Too little authority results in the subordinate's having to consult a superior about minor details of the work. If employees must constantly run to their supervisor for permission to do their jobs, then proper delegation of authority has not taken place. Authority is obviously kept in check by organizational policies, budgets, and the nature of the organization.

Clear Lines of Authority

One mark of a well-designed organization is the existence of clear lines of authority from the top to the bottom of the organization. In Figure 2–1, for example, we can trace the lines of authority from Fred Bell through his second-level manager to the supervisors and finally the individual workers. In most organizations, ultimate authority is at the top of the organization. Through delegation of authority from superior to subordinate, each individual has received his or her responsibility and authority from above.

The military calls this the "right to command." Authority *does* have this "command" aspect to it, even in nonmilitary organizations, but in most organizations authority given from above does not automatically ensure a supervisor's success. If there is no *acceptance* of this authority from people in the work group, the supervisor's efforts will be unsuccessful.

The relative importance for a supervisor of authority from the top and acceptance from below differs from organization to organization. In military organizations, for example, authority from the top is enforced by strong mechanisms. In voluntary organizations, on the other hand—perhaps the local Boy Scout troop, a hospital auxiliary group, or the district PTA—the acceptance of authority by the membership is much more important, since people do not have to participate.

Most work organizations fall somewhere between these two extremes, so that it is necessary for supervisors to have not only formal authority granted by higher levels of the organization but also informal authority coming from the consent of their subordinates. If employees do not recognize a supervisor's authority to "be the boss," he or she must resort to giving formal orders and threatening disciplinary action. This normally occurs from time to time in most organizations, but it is simply not an effective supervisory technique over the long run. Block 2–2 illustrates what happened in one company when first-level supervisors relied too much on "command" and ignored acceptance.

Only One Boss

A second general principle of organizing to get a job done is to see that no one has more than one immediate superior. This concept has been referred to as *unity* of command, and there are some very good reasons for it.

Let's consider, for example, a steno pool in a large office. The steno pool consists of ten typists who take typing from anyone in the organization. Since there is no steno supervisor, each typist is responsible to every "boss" in the organization. Rhonda Johnson is an efficient, hardworking, extremely accurate typist. When Rhonda receives a typing job from someone, she starts it as soon as possible, finishes it well ahead of schedule, and hands in an excellent job. As a result, everyone in the organization wants Rhonda to do their typing. She has more typing than she can do and generally has to work much harder than some of the other employees in the organization, but she's a conscientious person and does it. Bert Willis, on the other hand, is a bit lazy. Bert is very good at looking busy when somebody comes around with typing work to do and he's been fairly successful at avoiding work.

One Friday afternoon at 3 o'clock, two of her "bosses" came to Rhonda's desk. Each had a two-hour typing job that needed to be done, and each of them needed it by 5 o'clock. They both put the work on

Rhonda's desk and said, "I've got to have this by 5 o'clock," and then turned and left. Rhonda doesn't know which of her "bosses" to obey in this situation.

This example shows some of the problems associated with having more than one boss. *First,* the most effective employee gets the most work. *Second,* the lazy employee can get away with doing hardly any work because he or she is too "busy" to take on anything else. *Third,* employees are put in the difficult position of having to judge which of several superiors they should obey. This is not only unfair, but also a poor management practice, because employees are not being paid to make those decisions. A *fourth* problem centers around performance appraisal. If the organization has a performance appraisal system, who is going to appraise Rhonda's or Bert's performance? Which individual is in a position to do so?

Control and Follow-up

Another organizational concept that supervisors especially need to understand is that responsibility cannot be completely delegated. In other words, supervisors cannot disassociate themselves from the acts of their subordinates, or from what employees fail to do. This is one reason why supervisors are, or at least should be, paid more than the people they supervise. They are responsible for *all* the actions of their subordinates. Block 2–3 illustrates.

Block 2–3 shows why control and follow-up are crucial to supervising. Simply to assign someone a job is no guarantee that it is going to be done. Since you as supervisor retain the responsibility for seeing that it gets done, you have to be very careful about checking on the operations to see that it *is* being done correctly.

BLOCK 2–3   The Supervisor's Dilemma

Julie Peoples is a lunchroom supervisor at a large cafeteria. Her boss, the owner, has delegated to Julie the responsibility for seeing that the lunchroom is cleaned and meets public health standards. If one of Julie's employees fails to carry out his or her assigned cleaning responsibilities and the health inspector pronounces the cafeteria unfit and closes it down, Julie can't really argue "it wasn't my fault that one of my subordinates failed to do his job." She cannot rid herself of that responsibility. She can assign responsibility to the subordinate, but she can never free herself of ultimate responsibility for accomplishment of the task.

Specialization

Another organizational concept that helps explain why organizations look as they do, and that supervisors can put to good use, is specialization. This concept applies to individual employees as well as to entire departments within organizations. If used properly, specialization can be a source of great efficiency in your work group.

When an individual specializes in one small part of an overall operation, he or she can become more skilled at that job than anyone else. For example, in many large organizations, personnel administration is becoming a specialized department because a knowledge of many federal rules and regulations on hiring, testing, and promotion is now required. It isn't feasible for everyone in the organization to become an expert on these rules and regulations. Instead, the duties are assigned to a limited number of people and they become specialists in the area. This results in freeing up other people in the organization to perform *their* special duties.

Line and Staff

An offshoot of specialization that is often seen in many organizations is the distinction between line and staff. The *line organization* is that part of the organization which is directly responsible for turning out the end product. In an automobile assembly plant, for example, it would be that portion of the organization which turns out finished automobiles. In a hospital, it would be those employees who deal directly with patients, and in a hotel, those who service the guests and prepare the rooms.

By contrast, the staff organization does not directly deal with the final product, but gives *advice* to line personnel on how best to accomplish their goals. For example, in Artco, Fred Bell, the second-level manager, the five supervisors, and their employees constitute the *line* organization. They are directly involved in making picture frames. The salesperson and the accountant are *staff* personnel. Their job is to provide advice and services to the line, not to produce picture frames.

Unfortunately, in many organizations line and staff often find themselves at loggerheads. Perhaps a line supervisor feels at a psychological disadvantage when dealing with staff people, because he or she knows that these people are experts and have upper management's ear. Staff personnel, on the other hand, may be acutely aware of their lack of knowledge of "the business." Because each group has only a limited knowledge of what the other does, misunderstandings can lead to minor (or major) conflicts. Line and staff conflict can be avoided if attempts at cooperation are sincerely carried out. Staff may provide advice at any time but line need not necessarily follow that advice, and both can certainly appeal to a higher authority.

Supervisors may be either line or staff depending on the nature of the job their work unit does. The line-staff distinction is muddied somewhat by the fact that in some organizations, staff personnel in one department may report to upper-level line managers, while staff and line may exist separately in another department. In some cases, line people may report to staff people, division lines between the two may overlap, or a specific manager may do both jobs. The line-staff distinction in Artco is fairly clear (see Figure 2–2), but as organizations grow, the distinctions may blur.

Span of Control

Another organizational concept of importance to the supervisor is *span of control,* which is simply the number of subordinates for which a given supervisor is responsible. The most important thing to remember about span of control is that *there is a limit* to the number of people any one supervisor can control.

This limit depends on a number of factors. For example, supervising subordinates who are all doing *essentially the same job* is easier and re-

FIGURE 2–2   Staff Positions in Artco

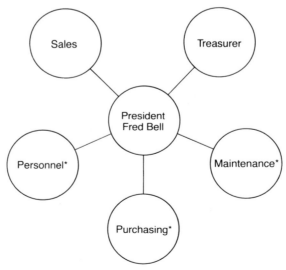

*Possible future staff positions

quires fewer different behaviors and less knowledge on the part of the supervisor. So a supervisor can have a larger span of control (successfully supervise more people) if subordinates' jobs are essentially similar. Further, the *geographic location* of the subordinates makes a difference. If subordinates are assigned to several different areas of a work organization or are scattered among several cities, a supervisor can successfully handle fewer than if they are all located in one area.

The *complexity of the duties* the subordinates perform makes a difference. More complex duties require more supervisory time, so that a supervisor can successfully oversee fewer subordinates. The *stability of the organization* can also exert a powerful influence. An atmosphere of certainty with few surprises will allow supervisors to successfully supervise more subordinates. The *frequency with which new and different problems appear* is another important consideration. If the supervisor and the work group are constantly facing new and different problems, it stands to reason that the supervisor can handle fewer subordinates.

We have mentioned several factors that are of great importance in organizing to get work done. How each issue is met helps decide the way an organization is put together and defines the kind of place it is to work. The benefits of a well-designed organization are many, including

1. Fewer conflicts between departments
2. A minimum of duplication since the responsibilities of each work group are made explicit
3. Better communication up and down the hierarchy and between line and staff
4. A good basis for appraising the work of its employees based on predetermined standards made known to all

THE INFORMAL ORGANIZATION

Formal organization structure can easily be shown on an organization chart, much as the skeleton appears on an X-ray. But informal contacts, friendships, and power positions of individuals in the organization, like the body's soft organs, do not show up on the chart. However, this "informal organization" provides a good bit of the communication and social satisfaction in the organization.

Many supervisors wish they could abolish these informal networks and work only within the formal organization framework. This simply is not possible. As long as there are people, there will be informal groups. For this reason, the supervisor must learn to use these groups to accomplish the task more easily and efficiently.

Advantages
of the Informal Organization

Official policies, rules, and plans can never be so exact as to apply to every situation. The informal organization can help get work done despite bad rules or policies by sharing knowledge and knowing where to cut corners.

The informal organization can also serve to fill in gaps in a supervisor's abilities. If, for example, a supervisor is not a good "detail" person, an employee may informally handle some of the detail work that is essential.

The informal organization can also act as a release for employee frustrations. The discussions that take place in the informal organization may help prevent some problems from becoming major.

Disadvantages
of the Informal Organization

Probably the most often discussed disadvantage of the informal work organization is *work restriction*. Informal groups at work may band together and decide to work just so hard. These decisions are sanctioned by group disapproval or punishment if one of the members chooses to be a "rate buster." This presents a supervisor with a difficult problem. Possible options for dealing with it are reassignment, discipline, talking with the group leader, or readjusting the reward system to accommodate increased group effort.

Another problem associated with the informal organization is *resistance to change*. People are by nature hesitant to change ways of doing things that are familiar and comfortable. The fact that others within the informal group share the same opinion may reinforce their feelings.

Then, too, the informal organization is often the source of rumors. The term *grapevine* is usually used to describe the mechanism that transmits informal information in the organization. The grapevine, like the informal organization itself, cannot be abolished. In fact, studies have shown that about three-fourths of the information carried over the grapevine is accurate, although the accuracy is probably not so great for personal or highly emotional information.[3] Grapevine information, however, is usually incomplete and, therefore, can lead to misunderstandings.

Rumor is *incorrect* grapevine information. The best way for a supervisor to deal with it is to get to the source of the rumor. This usually means releasing the facts that show the rumor is wrong.

One of the former members of my work unit was promoted to a new job. She still comes back to our area occasionally and has coffee with former colleagues. I have had quite a time getting my unit to do what I want them to do instead of what she thinks they should be doing. I think her influence will go away with time, but right now it's both distracting and annoying. I'm planning on simply being a little more forceful with my people and explaining clearly why I want to do things a certain way.

Living with Informal Organizations

Supervisors have to learn to live with informal organizations. The following suggestions can help.

1. Try to show employees that the interests of the formal organization often coincide with the interests of their particular informal organization.
2. Calculate the effects on the informal organization of supervisory actions *before* taking them.
3. Try to minimize *threats* to the informal organization *when this can be done.*

Certainly this is not to say that concern for the informal organization gets in the way of getting the job done. It does suggest that a supervisor needs to be aware of the informal organization and to avoid *unnecessary* conflicts with it. The informal organization can often serve as a supervisory support, but not if it hinders task accomplishment. See Block 2–4 for an example of an informal organization that is presenting a problem.

USING WHAT YOU KNOW
ABOUT WORK ORGANIZATIONS

As we saw earlier, delegation is a basic building block of a good organization. It is also the *only* way a supervisor can find enough time to do his or her own job. Delegation involves nothing more than assigning work to your subordinates, yet, if this isn't done properly, it won't work.

How Can I Delegate Successfully?

Six basic steps will help you delegate effectively:

Step 1. Carefully decide what the job is that has to be done and how and when you will check on progress. Before assigning the job *think it through* carefully in your own mind. This includes deciding on where to put "checkpoints" (to see whether or not it is going well). You can't explain such things to your subordinate unless you have first thought it through yourself.

Step 2. Decide in your own mind what a good job will look like. What is important here is how you will *measure* the success or failure of a job. You usually know when you assign the job what excellent, average, or poor performance will look like, but make this explicit. Then, when these standards are clear in your own mind, you can go on to assign the job to your subordinate.

Step 3. Decide on the *date* by which it should be completed.

After you have determined three things—job specifications, performance standards, and deadline—it is time to call the subordinate in to delegate the work.

Step 4. Explain the work, your criteria for success and failure, the completion date, and the checkpoints to the subordinate. Then ask for *his or her ideas* as to whether these are realistic and whether there are any specific problems the person foresees.

Step 5. Use your *checkpoints* as you said you would to keep tabs on the ongoing work.

Step 6. If the work is well done, *praise* should be given the subordinate. If the work is *not* done well, you should determine why, again getting feedback from the subordinate.

What Problems May I Encounter in Delegating?

We have said delegation is critical. In fact, we would go so far as to say supervisors who cannot delegate are very often not successful. However, not everyone *can* delegate. Why? There are a number of reasons: First is *training.* Certain individuals have been trained to pay great attention to details. Perhaps they were somewhat oriented toward being good "detail persons" in the first place and their training emphasized precision. Engineers and accountants are two groups among whom training has fostered a great deal of attention to detail. This is not to say that people with this kind of training *can't* learn to delegate, certainly many can. But it may be more difficult for those who have learned to do a job by themselves to delegate it to someone else.

Second, some people have a tendency to want to *avoid major issues.* They can't cope with central important points so they bury themselves in minor details. If a supervisor can't see the major issues—the "big picture," he or she certainly will have some difficulty delegating portions of the big picture in a meaningful way to subordinates.

Third, some people have a very great *fear of failing.* Delegation requires that you take a gamble on another person's doing the job right. As the supervisor, you are risking possible failure if the subordinate doesn't carry out the responsibilities properly. You can minimize the probability of failure by checking on the subordinate from time to time. Yet even such reduced risk frightens some people to such a degree that they simply cannot delegate.

Finally, some people do not delegate because of a *basic insecurity.* They feel that delegating creates a competitor for their job, someone else who can do the job as well as they can. Perhaps that makes them expendable in the organization. We could go on. There are other possible reasons why not everybody can delegate, but successful supervisors *must* learn to delegate. It's a key to getting work done. If a supervisor is having difficulty delegating work to others, he or she might consider the points we have raised and see if any of them fit.

LIVING IN AN ORGANIZATION AS A SUPERVISOR

Now that you have a feel for some of the basics of work organization design, we turn to how to cope with two of the most common frustrations that supervisors express about their relationships with work organizations.

Person in the Middle

It has been said again and again that the supervisor is in an intermediate position between management and the labor force, a position that creates some unique problems. Technically, most organizations recognize the supervisor as part of the management team, but upper management prefers to retain a distinction between the supervisor's role and theirs. And there *is.* As noted in Chapter 1, supervisors spend the greater proportion of their time *directing* and *controlling* and relatively less time *planning* and *organizing* than does upper management.

But the employees cannot fully accept the supervisor as a member of their group either, even if he or she has recently been promoted from employee ranks. After all, the supervisor has the power to discipline, re-

ward, and punish, and the presence of that power changes former relationships.

Such role conflict is never pleasant or comfortable, but supervisors
must learn to live with it. Someone must direct the work on a day-to-day
basis, and good organization design suggests that a *specialist*—that is, a
person skilled in supervision—is best suited to the job. There are no
specific rules for surviving in this difficult position. But simply knowing
why the role conflict in the supervisor's job is there sometimes makes it
easier to live with the pressures from above and below.

Going Through Channels

Because most organizations have more than one level, communication
between the supervisory level and top management is rarely direct.
Commonly, supervisors are frustrated by having to go up several levels
before having their question answered or by having to go through their
superior to deal with another department. Block 2–5 illustrates the problem.

Going through channels is both time-consuming and frustrating. However, there are some sound reasons for following such a procedure. In
Block 2–5, if John Jones "went around" Mr. Drake directly to the superintendent with the dispute, Mr. Drake would have no knowledge of what
had been done. He would have been "bypassed" and unable to help or
respond, and he would probably be angry at having been passed over.

If John Jones had gone directly to Mr. Downes to resolve the problem, a similar situation would exist. Mr. Drake again would have been
bypassed. Although such moves to "cut through red tape" are tempt-
ing, the nature of work organizations demands that each member follow
protocol if the organization is to avoid problems associated with more
than one boss and unclear lines of authority.

SUMMARY AND CONCLUSIONS

Over the years, managers and leaders have tried different ways of organizing to get work done. Some have proved effective most of the time
or in certain situations and others have proved less applicable and were
discarded. In this way a body of basic concepts for organizing work has
come into being. Such concepts as delegating assignments, matching
authority to responsibility, unity of command, specialization, span of
control, and distinctions between line and staff positions are widely used
in organizing work.

In addition to formal organization structure, there exists an informal
organization of which the supervisor must be aware. Such groups can-

At the highway department, a repair crew and a road striping crew report to different supervisors who report to different second-level managers. (See organization chart.) The repair and striping supervisors cannot agree on the schedule of work to be done on State Highway 490. Since John Jones and Wilson Woods can't agree, they must go up the organizational hierarchy until the problem is resolved, a process known as "going through channels." If Mr. Drake and Mr. Downes can't resolve the problem between them, it will have to be done by the superintendent.

Organization Chart: Highway Department

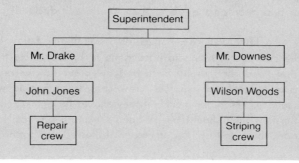

not be labeled "good" or "bad"; they simply arise from the fact that workers bring their whole selves into the organization. For this reason, the supervisor is wise to learn how to use such groups to facilitate achieving organizational goals.

Effective delegation is a real key to being a good supervisor. It is important because the supervisor cannot possibly do all the work alone. Understanding *why* the supervisor is frequently caught in the middle may help new and potential supervisors anticipate, and thus avoid, some of the problems that position entails. Finally, the pros and cons of going through organizational channels suggest that for the most part such procedures must be adhered to even though they are frustrating.

In the next chapter, we try to understand one of the most important concepts in supervising people—motivation.

QUESTIONS

1. If organizations take shape based upon division of labor (one person can no longer do all the work), what is the effect on that shape of increased size?

2. Unity of command is an outmoded concept that no longer applies to modern organizations. Discuss.

3. What will happen in the long run to a supervisor who has constantly to rely on "orders" to get things done?

4. Why do you suppose a successful supervisor will have thought out the ramifications of a task, performance standard, checkpoints, and deadline *before* asking employees for their ideas?

THE NEW MAN

Roger Moon was new on the job. He had somewhat more education than the other members of the crew and seemed a hard worker. Wil Lamat, his supervisor, felt he could use some extra help with the book work, and after Roger had been on the job for two weeks, Wil decided to assign him this job.

A short time later, Wil commented, "I assigned this fellow to the book work on the crew but it seems to have gone to his head. He thinks he has authority that he doesn't really have and the other fellows resent this."

There is a related problem. The crew consists of people with varying lengths of service. The older men feel they should have their choice of jobs and that the new men should be assigned the more physically demanding jobs and work their way up. Roger has not followed the pattern.

---

1. How would you predict the informal organization will act out its resentment toward Roger if he stays in his present job?

2. If you were Wil, how would you handle this situation?

NOTES

1 See, for example, J. H. Jackson and C. P. Morgan, *Organization Theory: A Macro Perspective for Management* (Englewood Cliffs, N.J.: Prentice-Hall, Inc., 1978), chap. 8.

2 Ernest Dale, *Organization* (New York: American Management Association, 1967), p. 41.

3 Keith Davis, *Human Behavior at Work,* 5th ed. (New York: McGraw-Hill, 1977), p. 290, footnote 9.

The Motivation to Work

SUPERVISORY PROBLEMS

What explains the effort that people put into their work?
What can a supervisor do to improve the motivation of subordinates?

When you finish this chapter you should be able to

1. List important needs that can be satisfied in a work context
2. Explain the two-factor approach to motivation
3. Discuss how a person decides how much effort to expend based on equity and expectancy evaluations of the work situation
4. Identify the problems caused by assuming that if an employee is satisfied or happy, then that person will work hard
5. Understand why it is important to make rewards and job satisfaction dependent on level of job performance
6. Indicate several ways in which knowledge of motivation can be used by a supervisor

---

THINGS HAVE CHANGED

"I just don't understand people anymore. It used to be that you hired someone, told them what to do, paid them a fair wage and they did a good job, and everyone was satisfied. Now they not only have a good wage, they have fringe benefits, a clean and safe work area, and job security. Still they are not satisfied. They complain about the boring work and all the orders they have to follow."

The person speaking in the previous paragraph assumes that people work mainly for money, and that providing good wages and job security should be enough. You probably can think of many examples from your own work experience which demonstrate that this is not the case.

Probably since primitive people first organized to survive, those in leadership positions have wondered why individuals behave in so many different ways in work situations. We still don't have all the answers, but psychologists have provided us with some ideas that supervisors can use to deal with various employee behaviors. If we can understand *why* people behave the way they do at work, certain steps can be taken to encourage high levels of job performance and, conversely, to discourage poor job performance.

WHAT IS MOTIVATION?

For our purposes motivation is simply the amount of *job-related effort* a person puts forth. In a more general sense, motivation can also be thought of as a tendency to do things that can result in the satisfaction of personal needs.

Two basic questions will help us understand motivation: (1) What are people's important needs? and (2) How do people decide how much effort they will exert? The answer to the first question guides a supervisor in determining what rewards to offer, since *only* those rewards which satisfy important needs will motivate employees. The answer to the second question will reveal different options that are the basis for an employee's choosing to perform at a marginal, an average, or an outstanding level.

Understanding the answers to these questions will help you as supervisor attain higher levels of performance from subordinates. It can also aid the organization in establishing policies, rules, and procedures to promote high levels of morale and performance.

WHAT ARE PEOPLE'S IMPORTANT NEEDS?

Maslow's Need Hierarchy

One answer to the question of what motivates employees has been provided by psychologist Abraham Maslow.[1] There are three key points to understanding his ideas. First, he proposed a set of categories for human needs. Second, he pointed out that as a need is satisfied it *decreases* in importance to the particular individual. Third, Maslow suggested that as a given need is satisfied the next higher need in the hierarchy will *increase* in importance. Maslow's hierarchy of needs may be briefly outlined as follows:

1. *Physical needs.* These most basic human needs include the need for food, water, rest, and physical activity. If these needs are not met, their satisfaction will be the dominant drive in an individual's behavior. For example, a starving person will be motivated by his or her need for food.
2. *Safety or security needs.* This category of needs refers to avoiding harm or threats to a person's well-being. In a work situation, these needs might surface as the desire for stable and secure employment, supervision that is fair and predictable, and nonhazardous working conditions.
3. *Belongingness or social needs.* This refers to the need for friendship, affection, companionship, or, in general, the need to relate to other

people. In a work organization this might surface as the desire to be accepted by one's co-workers and to have people to talk with at work. It might also be expressed as a desire to avoid working in isolation without feedback from others.

4. *Esteem needs.* These are needs both for *self*-respect and respect from others. People need to feel that they are competent in performing their jobs, and that they are doing a job that is meaningful and worthwhile. It is important not only to feel subjectively that our work counts but also to feel that others share that view. The supervisor who compliments the good work a subordinate has done may be contributing to the satisfaction of the subordinate's need for esteem.

5. *The need for self-actualization, or development.* This designation refers to the need to become what we are capable of becoming. It is the need to develop new skills and to meet even more difficult challenges, a need that is never really satisfied. In a work situation, supervisors would do well to allow individuals to achieve expertise in a given area and to develop their skills and capabilities to the fullest. Another good technique is to give employees opportunity to participate in decisions affecting their work in the organization.

Figure 3–1 shows the Maslow need hierarchy in the form of a ladder. As a person satisfies physical needs, he or she looks for ways to meet security needs, and so forth. (It should be noted that although a given category of needs may be basically satisfied, it still continues to play a background role in the individual's life and may reemerge in certain situations.)

Maslow provides a second key to understanding job-related needs when he says that as a need is satisfied its importance to a particular individual declines. For example, as the need for security is satisfied, its importance as a motivator of behavior declines. This is important because most organizations find that high wages and stable employment

FIGURE 3–1   Maslow's Need Hierarchy

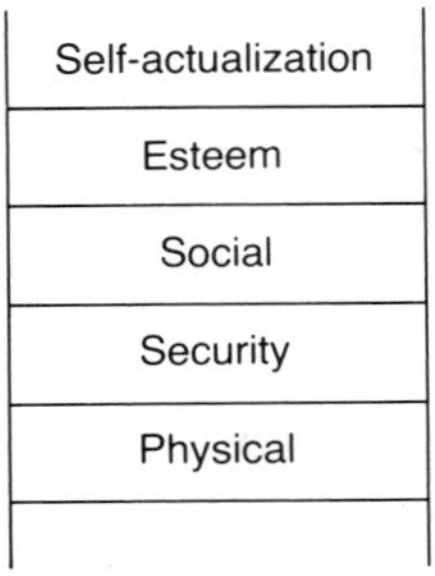

| Self-actualization |
| Esteem |
| Social |
| Security |
| Physical |

(security-related items) cease to be effective in motivating employees to work, beyond some undetermined level. It then becomes necessary to develop other kinds of rewards and other incentives to motivate the work force. A good example of this second principle is provided by the labor relations officer who asks: "Won't the union members ever be satisfied? They used to bargain for better wages and fringe benefits, and now our company is an industry leader in wages and fringes. Yet union officials complain that the work is boring and that union members don't have a say in decisions affecting their work."

The third key to understanding human motivation is that as one need is satisfied, even partly, another immediately moves in. For example, when physical needs are satisfied they decrease in importance and security needs become the dominant force in the individual. After security needs are satisfied, they also decrease in importance and belongingness needs emerge as paramount. And so on down the list until some individuals are motivated chiefly by the need for self-actualization, a drive that is never fully satisfied. Figure 3–2 shows the sequence of satisfaction of a need category, decreased importance of that need category, and increased importance of the next category of needs, that is part of motivation.

FIGURE 3–2   Satisfaction of Needs

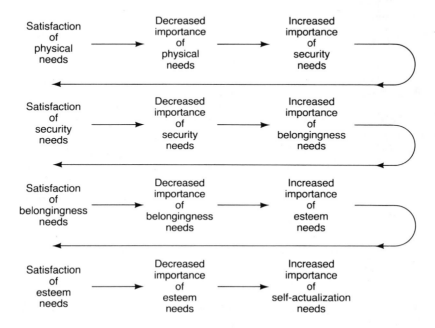

Recent Modifications
to Maslow's Need Hierarchy

Several changes have been suggested that build on Maslow's need hierarchy and expand our knowledge of human needs. One concerns Maslow's classification scheme. Studies focusing on categories of human needs have come up with several different classificatory schemes. Although none can be branded either true or false, a more useful classification device might be simply to distinguish between higher-order and lower-order needs. The lower-order needs would include Maslow's physical, safety or security, and belongingness categories, and the higher order would include the need for esteem and self-respect as well as the need for self-actualization.[2]

Maslow's idea that the more fully a need is satisfied, the less important that need becomes, does have the support of several studies. The implication for supervisory people is that the use of only one kind of reward—for example, praise—will lessen that reward's effectiveness over time. It then becomes necessary for the supervisor to find other kinds of rewards to satisfy employees' unmet needs.

A second implication is that when a certain set of needs has been met, changing a work situation to provide even more satisfaction of this same category of needs will have no effect on motivation. However, changing the situation so as to leave these needs unsatisfied once again will usually cause them to resurface as highly important. Therefore, since highly important needs are not being met, dissatisfaction will be great. Block 3–1 illustrates this problem.

The Two-Factor Approach to Motivation

Frederick Herzberg, an organizational psychologist who developed the two-factor approach to motivation, feels that there are two classes of rewards in a work situation.[3] These he terms *motivator factors* (intrinsic rewards) and *hygiene factors* (extrinsic rewards).

What Are Motivators? The motivators factors that have been identified are

1. *Achievement,* or completing an important task successfully
2. *Recognition,* being singled out for praise
3. The nature of the *work itself,* that is, whether it is interesting or meaningful
4. *Responsibility* for one's own work or for the work of others
5. *Advancement,* changing one's status through promotion

BLOCK 3–1   Change of Supervisor

Marlene thinks that her supervisor, Ed Wheeler, is fair and predictable, and does not worry about unfair treatment by her supervisor. Setting up a grievance procedure in which an employee can appeal what are felt to be unfair or unreasonable actions by supervisors will not create greater satisfaction for Marlene.

Time passes and Ed Wheeler is transferred to another location and is replaced by Mike Paulson. Mike does not treat people consistently. There have been a number of instances, but this week has been too much. On Monday and Tuesday, Marlene and Stella worked together getting out a crash report. Both had worked late Monday night and had come in early Tuesday to get it done. Mike complimented Stella personally and later told his supervisor, in front of other members of the department, what a fine job Stella had done. Not a word was said about Marlene.

This morning, Wednesday, both Stella and Marlene came in two hours late. With Ed Wheeler it had been the practice that if you had to put in some extra time to get your work done, you could take a couple of hours off the next day if there wasn't anything pressing. Marlene arrived a few minutes after Stella. Nothing was said to Stella, but Marlene was called into Mike's office and told, "If you don't have a good reason for being late, I will have to give you a one-day disciplinary layoff."

Regardless of Mike's reaction when Marlene explains why she was late, Marlene would probably like to have some means available for initiating a grievance. This example demonstrates how a change in a work situation can withdraw the satisfaction of a need and thereby cause that need to reemerge.

Motivators are job factors that are thought to lead to high levels of satisfaction with work and the motivation to put forth superior effort. When motivators are absent from a work situation, dissatisfaction does not necessarily occur, but high motivation will not be forthcoming either. Motivator factors are assumed to reflect a need for personal growth. Relating them to Maslow's need hierarchy, motivators seem roughly equivalent to self-actualization and self-esteem.

What Are Hygiene Factors?   Hygiene factors identified by Herzberg are

1. *Pay* or salary level
2. Technical *supervision,* or having a competent supervisor
3. The *human relations quality* of supervision, that is, the interpersonal skills of a supervisor

4. Company *policies* and administration
5. *Working conditions* or physical surroundings
6. *Job security*

When hygiene factors are absent, workers usually have job dissatis-faction. However, their presence does *not* automatically ensure high levels of job satisfaction and motivation to work. Hygiene factors reflect a need for avoiding the unpleasantness in one's job. They relate to the environment in which the job is done.

Figure 3–3 shows the relationship between motivator and hygiene factors, job satisfaction and job dissatisfaction, and the motivation to work. When motivators (achievement, recognition, responsibility, ad-vancement) are present, high levels of job satisfaction will occur and, in turn, a high level of motivation to put forth effort on the job. When such factors are absent, the worst situation will be neutral feelings to-ward one's job. If hygiene factors (pay, supervision, human relations, policies, working conditions, job security) are present and acceptable, *at best* an employee will have neutral feelings toward his or her job. How-ever, when hygiene factors are lacking or unacceptable, job dissatisfaction will occur. According to Herzberg, when job dissatisfaction is present, a person is not inclined to put forth effort on the job.

Problems with the Two-Factor Approach

One of the problems with the two-factor approach is that motivators and hygiene factors may not really be easy to pick out. For example, the

FIGURE 3–3   The Relationship of Motivator and Hygiene Factors to Job Satisfaction and Dissatisfaction

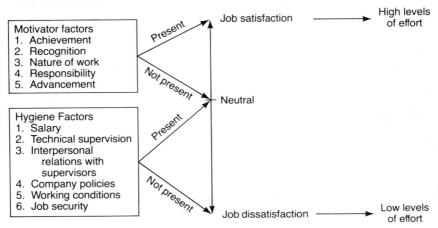

chance for advancement and pay are related. Another problem with this approach to understanding motivation is that some of the factors seem to have an influence on *both* satisfaction and dissatisfaction. Figure 3–4 highlights this problem. Employees were asked to describe incidents at work that made them feel either very good or very bad about themselves—for example, the feeling one has when a challenging task is done well, or the feeling one has upon discovering that a trainee for the same position is being paid more. These descriptions were then classified on the two-factor dimensions.

Notice in Figure 3–4 how often recognition and the nature of work, which are motivator factors, are mentioned in connection with bad feelings toward one's work. On the other hand, notice that salary, a hygiene factor, is mentioned almost as frequently when talking about high levels of job satisfaction as when talking about low levels of job satisfaction.

Achievement Motivation

Other psychologists have also studied human needs.[4] Most such work has focused on three needs: (1) the need for achievement, (2) the need for affiliation, and (3) the need for power. Of these, the achievement need (n-Ach) has been given the most attention, especially in work-oriented situations. Individuals with a high need for achievement

1. Like situations in which they have personal responsibility for finding solutions to problems
2. Tend to set goals which are moderately difficult; that is, high n-Ach

FIGURE 3–4   Percentage of Good and Bad Incidents in Which Each Factor Appeared

	Percentage	
Factor	Good	Bad
Achievement (M)	41	7
Recognition (M)	33	18
Nature of work (M)	26	14
Responsibility (M)	23	6
Advancement (M)	20	11
Salary (H)	15	17
Technical supervision (H)	3	20
Interpersonal relations with supervisor (H)	4	15
Company policies and administration (H)	3	31
Working conditions (H)	1	11
Job security (H)	1	1

Source: Adapted from F. Herzberg, B. Mausner, and B. Snyderman, *The Motivation To Work* (New York: John Wiley, 1959).

individuals avoid both those situations in which success is impossible and those in which the outcome is a foregone conclusion

3. Want to have concrete feedback indicating how well they are doing

In research measuring the presence of n-Ach among different occupational groups, self-employed businessmen were found to have higher need for achievement than any other group—hardly a surprising discovery since they assume the risk of a business.

These findings on achievement motivation have important implications for the supervisor. Employees identified as high n-Ach individuals will respond well to having responsibility delegated to them and to being given projects and tasks that are challenging (difficult but not impossible). However, they will need to have frequent feedback on how they are doing. This suggests that the supervisor should

1. Identify the high n-Ach individuals
2. Structure their job situations so that they can satisfy those needs through responsible, challenging work
3. Let them know if they have succeeded or failed

We have discussed some general categories of needs we all have to varying degrees. But what are typical thoughts a person might have in choosing among different kinds of possible work behavior? Or, stated differently, what process does an individual use in arriving at a decision to work hard—or not?

An understanding of the way choices are made can help us formulate answers to the following questions about the Gillette Coal case:

1. What explains Roger's change in work behavior?
2. Why are others picking up Roger's work habits?
3. What policies or supervisory actions would get rid of Roger's poor performance?

Evaluating this situation in terms of the actors' concepts of *equity* and *expectancy* can help provide answers. These are things that we all do in determining what our level of satisfaction with a situation might be and what we are going to do about it.

Evaluating the Job on Equity

People want to be fairly treated, in rewards and penalties as well as other areas at work.[5] We can visualize the following going on in the minds of employees as they determine whether or not they are being treated fairly or equitably. Comparisons are made between one's own *outcomes* and the *outcomes* of others. The following are examples. Such things as the pay, praise, or recognition one receives from a job, and the degree to which the job is challenging and meaningful, are compared with what co-workers or friends are receiving. Other factors considered are the degree to which the job is dangerous or boring and the degree to which the working environment is uncomfortable.

In making equity or fairness evaluations, individuals consider another category of factors as well—their *inputs,* or what each individual

FIGURE 3–5 Equity Evaluations

Feelings of Equity

$$\frac{\text{Outcomes (own)}}{\text{Inputs (own)}} \quad \text{is equal to} \quad \frac{\text{Outcomes (others)}}{\text{Inputs (others)}}$$

Feelings of Inequity

(A) *Overcompensation*	(B) *Undercompensation*
$\dfrac{\text{Outcomes (own)}}{\text{Inputs (own)}}$ are greater than $\dfrac{\text{Outcomes (others)}}{\text{Inputs (others)}}$	$\dfrac{\text{Outcomes (own)}}{\text{Inputs (own)}}$ are less than $\dfrac{\text{Outcomes (others)}}{\text{Inputs (others)}}$

brings to the job. Inputs include such factors as level of education or training, experience, skill, seniority, and effort expended on a job. In an equity evaluation, when the ratio of outcomes to inputs is in line with the ratio of outcomes to inputs for other people, a person feels fairly treated. This is the situation or feeling that people want.

Figure 3–5 shows the three possible situations or feelings that can result from an equity evaluation. Feelings of fairness or equity mean that our own situation and the situations of others are viewed as equal.

Two kinds of feelings of inequity or unfairness are possible. One is a feeling that we are being overcompensated. This means that when comparing our own inputs and outcomes with the outcomes and inputs of others, we decide that our own situation is more favorable that that of others. An equity evaluation where one feels overcompensated may result in feelings of uneasiness or possibly guilt.

The other possibility is undercompensation—when we compare our own outcomes and inputs with those of others and conclude that others are in a more favorable situation. When individuals are plagued by feelings of inequity, they will usually try to *remove* or *diminish* those feelings.

What Happens if People Feel Over- or Undercompensated?

Possible reactions to feelings of *overcompensation* might be for an individual to increase his or her efforts on the job. For example, if others are perceived as working harder, the individual might put forth greater effort to equalize the situation. On the other hand, he or she may try to persuade others to reduce their inputs or efforts. For example, the "rate buster" label that is sometimes applied to the hard worker is an attempt to get these people to slow down. By means of group pressure such individuals can usually be made to conform to group standards, which in turn removes the source of guilt for the rest of the members of the work group.

The easiest, and therefore, most likely result is that the person will *change* his or her view of things so that the feeling of overcompensation is removed. For example, one can change the evaluation of inputs as well as change the evaluation of outcomes. See Block 3-3 for an example.

Research in the field of equity finds that feelings of overpayment or overcompensation are relatively uncommon. In one way or another people who might have these feelings seem to be able to get rid of them—probably by rationalizing them away as Tim did in Block 3-3.

On the other hand, feelings of undercompensation are relatively common and a potential source of trouble to supervisors. If an employee feels underpaid, he or she may react by reducing inputs, that is, the level of effort going into one's job. This may take the form of absenteeism or reduced levels of effort while at work. Recall in the Gillette Coal case presented in Block 3-2 how co-workers reacted to Roger's slipshod performance. By slackening their own standards of performance, members of this work unit were simply ridding themselves of feelings of inequity. Of course, such a reaction is more likely when an individual is *not* working with an incentive pay system in which what you produce determines the level of your pay. Under an incentive system, for example, a piece rate system, feelings of undercompensation are usually balanced by a reduction in the *quality* of work and an attempt to increase the number of units of production. This reaction will increase take-home pay.

BLOCK 3-3 It's Only Fair

Tim feels uneasy because he earns 50 cents an hour more than Fred. Tim thinks about their backgrounds. He remembers that Fred learned the trade through on-the-job training, while he (Tim) attended a vocational school, and Tim decides that vocational school training is a lot better than on-the-job training. Another thing Tim remembers is that Fred has newer equipment, so Fred's job is less demanding because he doesn't have to contend with so many breakdowns and so much maintenance. After thinking it over, Tim concludes that it is only fair that he is paid 50 cents an hour more than Fred.

Evaluating the Job on Expectancy

Equity evaluation plays a major role in determining a person's motivation to work. But another evaluation occurs as well: an evaluation of what rewards and outcomes the individual *expects* will be associated with work effort.

Outcomes or rewards can be thought of as being in two classes. One class is the rewards that are directly associated with personal feelings about the work itself, such as feeling good about having done a job well. These are referred to as *intrinsic* outcomes. *Extrinsic* outcomes are indirectly related to the job done. Examples are level of salary, promotions, raises, and recognition from co-workers or superiors.

When a person makes an expectancy evaluation, he or she estimates the chances that a certain outcome will occur. Expectancy evaluations may be personal or organizational. Personal expectancy evaluation is the chance you think you have of performing at a particular level given your efforts. For example, if I put forth my best effort, can I perform at an *outstanding* level or will my performance be merely average or even *marginal?* Each individual estimates his or her chances of performing at a given level in a given situation.

Organizational expectancy evaluations involve estimating the chances of getting rewards for a particular level of performance. For example, one might ask, If I perform at an outstanding level, what are the chances of getting an above-average raise? What are the chances of receiving recognition from my supervisor? What are the chances of receiving a promotion?

The intrinsic outcomes are such things as achievement, growth, and accomplishment. The supervisor and the organization cannot directly control these rewards. The only thing the supervisor can do is try to match a person with a job for which he or she is properly trained or one which involves doing things the person views as interesting and important. If a person considers a job worthwhile and has a need for achievement and growth, then that person will *try* to perform the job well.

Figure 3–6 illustrates the points at which personal and organizational expectancies enter the work performance situation. Different levels of performance are possible between the extremes of outstanding and marginal performance. To motivate high levels of performance for a given employee, the employee must associate important extrinsic outcomes with high levels of performance. In addition, supervisors must see to it that valued outcomes cannot be had through poor job performance and that negative outcomes *do* follow unsatisfactory performance. In other words, those who perform at outstanding levels should receive higher levels of

FIGURE 3–6   Expectancy Evaluation

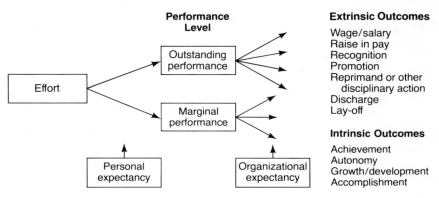

compensation, larger raises, more recognition from peers and supervisors, and have better chances for promotion. They should have *no* chance of disciplinary action, discharge, or layoff (assuming the company stays in business). But poor or unsatisfactory performers should not receive recognition, raises, or advancement, and after the proper warnings, should be subject to disciplinary action and possibly discharge.

Does Satisfaction Positively Affect Performance?

To rephrase the question in simpler terms, Is a happy employee a more productive employee? Many people think that the answer to both questions is yes. According to this reasoning, if a supervisor does everything he or she can to make employees happy or satisfied, they will react by doing good work. This is not necessarily true. Rather, we suggest that expectancy evaluations explain how *performance can lead to satisfaction.* Consider the two individuals described in the top half of Figure 3–7.

Figure 3–7 shows us the performance ratings of four workers at the end of the year and all four are motivated by a high need for extrinsic rewards. Jane is a high performer and gets a big increase. The things that money can buy are important to her and she is satisfied. Expectancy evaluations by Jane should lead her to conclude that high performance leads to high rewards and therefore to need satisfaction. We expect Jane to continue doing those things she was rewarded for, that is, we expect no change in Jane's effort.

Now consider Jim. His performance was marginal and he received a small wage/salary increase. The things money can buy are also important to Jim, but since his raise is small he is dissatisfied. Jim knows that Jane

FIGURE 3–7   Performance Ratings of Four Workers

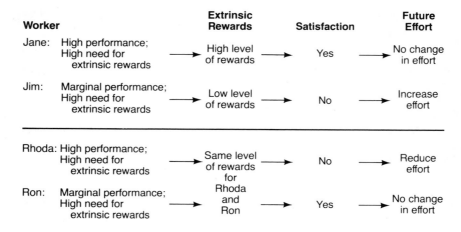

Worker		Extrinsic Rewards	Satisfaction	Future Effort
Jane:	High performance; High need for extrinsic rewards	⟶ High level of rewards	⟶ Yes	⟶ No change in effort
Jim:	Marginal performance; High need for extrinsic rewards	⟶ Low level of rewards	⟶ No	⟶ Increase effort
Rhoda:	High performance; High need for extrinsic rewards	⟶ Same level of rewards for Rhoda and Ron	⟶ No	⟶ Reduce effort
Ron:	Marginal performance; High need for extrinsic rewards	⟶	⟶ Yes	⟶ No change in effort

was a high performer and also knows that Jane got a big raise. Therefore, expectancy evaluations by Jim should lead him to conclude that high performance leads to high rewards and to need satisfaction. We expect Jim to increase his effort and presumably his performance during the coming year. (We are assuming that Jim has the ability to do his job better and all that is required is increased effort.)

Now consider another situation, that shown in the lower half of Figure 3–7. Both Rhoda and Ron have high needs for extrinsic rewards. Rhoda was a high performer and Ron was a marginal performer. The organization gives an across-the-board wage/salary increase, so both Rhoda and Ron get the same raise. To explain their reactions to this situation we rely on equity evaluations. Rhoda knows that her performance has been superior to Ron's, but that Ron received the same raise. Because Rhoda's effort and performance (inputs) exceeded Ron's, and because their raises (an outcome) were the same, Rhoda feels undercompensated. We predict that she will restore feelings of equity by reducing the effort she puts into her job and, therefore, her job performance will suffer.

Ron, on the other hand, may for a short time feel overcompensated, but we have confidence that he will be able to justify things somehow. For example, he may notice that Rhoda has newer equipment so her performance *should* be better. One way or another, Ron will be able to justify his continued marginal performance.

The point of this is that a supervisor *can* help motivate good performance by ensuring that good performance leads to job satisfaction and that poor performance leads to job dissatisfaction. While there are many things we do not know about human behavior in work organizations, there is one thing we can be pretty sure of: *People do those things*

58

FIGURE 3–8   Reward Objectives

FIGURE 3–8   Reward Objectives

Good performance ⟶ Rewards ⟶ Satisfaction

Poor performance ⟶ Absence of rewards ⟶ Dissatisfaction

they think will lead to satisfaction and avoid those things they think will lead to dissatisfaction. Figure 3–8 summarizes the process in graphic terms.

USING WHAT YOU KNOW
ABOUT HUMAN MOTIVATION TO WORK

This part of our discussion of human motivation in work organizations provides a number of guides and suggestions to which supervisors can refer when an employee's performance is in question. Figure 3–9

FIGURE 3–9   Summary of Motivation

What motivates? ⟶

Need Hierarchy

A. Types of needs
   1. Higher-order needs (esteem and self-actualization)
   2. Lower-order needs (physiological, security, and acceptance)
B. Gratification or satisfaction of a need tends to reduce its importance.

Two-Factor Approach

A. Motivator factors (achievement, recognition, nature of work, responsibility, advancement)
B. Hygiene factors (salary, technical supervision, interpersonal relations with supervisor, company policy, working conditions, job security)

Achievement Motivation

A. Responsibility
B. Moderately difficult goals
C. Feedback on performance

How are people motivated? ⟶

Equity Evaluation

A. People compare themselves with others to judge if they are being fairly treated
B. People will try to reinstate feelings of equity if they do not feel fairly treated

Expectancy Evaluation

The motivation to work, or put forth effort on the job depends on:
A. The value placed on available outcomes (rewards)
B. The perceived connection between effort and performance
C. The perceived connection between performance and rewards

highlights the ideas associated with our explanation of the motivation to work.

One of the major duties of the first-level manager is to explain top management's decisions to workers, particularly those decisions involving extrinsic rewards. A worker may ask, for example, Why did Mary get promoted instead of me? Why did Jack get a 75 cents per hour raise while I got only 50 cents? To explain such actions so that the less-rewarded employee can accept them, the supervisor must generally cite objective evidence. Since such evidence usually centers around merit of performance, we cannot overemphasize the importance of a good performance evaluation system for the supervisor.

A System for Dealing with Motivation Problems

Expectancy evaluations have three basic ideas:

1. The motivation to put forth effort on the job depends on employees' evaluation of the rewards/outcomes provided in the organization
2. If the employee tries, he or she can perform the job successfully
3. Successful performance will lead to highly valued outcomes, for example, a big raise, and the avoidance of negatively valued outcomes such as layoff or discharge

To take advantage of expectancy evaluations, supervisors do the following.

1. *The organization must have available those rewards that are highly valued by its employees.* This means that supervisors must be aware of the needs of their subordinates. Only after judging the current importance of a subordinate's needs, can a supervisor consider what actions to take to promote need satisfaction.
2. Each employee must believe that he or she is capable of performing the job satisfactorily. Therefore, *in staffing an organization* (that is, matching employees and jobs) *the supervisor must make sure that people are placed in jobs they are able to perform.* Training also influences people's perceptions of their ability to perform. A supervisor who is an effective trainer will see to it that employees know how to do their jobs. Of course, if a subordinate does not have the aptitude to learn a job, training will not be effective. In such a case the problem results from poor staffing, and the employee should be assigned to a different job. Regardless of the phase, staffing or training, the first-level supervisor plays the key role in ensuring that employees' jobs are suited to their abilities.
3. The final lesson for the supervisor is basically one of *demonstrating that the connection between performance and outcome is fair, visible to all*

concerned, and consistent. Those who consistently perform well should be rewarded according to a predetermined company policy. Consistency in both praise and discipline is one mark of a good supervisor.

How Can I Relate Outcomes to Lower-Order Needs?

Leadership.   The way a supervisor deals with his or her work group can have a major impact on the motivation to work. A supervisor should be perceived as supportive, demonstrating an attitude that helps foster a sense of security among members of the work group.

Performance Appraisal and Compensation.   The satisfaction of lower-order needs depends more on an organization's compensation program than any other single program. The objective should be to ensure that the going wage rate, size of raises, and stability of employment (who gets laid off in a business downturn and who runs the risk of discharge) are all related to level of performance. The administration of these programs is typically outside the control of first-level supervision. *However, the critical information for the successful implementation of such programs is provided by the immediate superior.* That is, the supervisor as performance evaluator must see to it that appraisals are accurate and objective so that individuals can be appropriately rewarded.

Employee Discipline.   So far, our discussion of expectancy evaluations has focused on providing valued outcomes for good performers and withholding valued outcomes from poor performers. However, an organization can also associate the presence of negative outcomes (discipline) with poor performance and the absence of negative outcomes with good performance. While you can generally rely on rewards or positive factors to influence the motivation to work, this approach is not always effective. In those few instances, it may be necessary to use punishment or discipline to influence the motivation to work.

How Can I Relate Outcomes to Higher-Order Needs?

Staffing.   The satisfaction of higher-order needs depends largely on placing individuals in jobs best suited for them. The key here is to assign people to jobs they perceive as meaningful, interesting, and challenging.

Training.   Maslow argued that self-actualization and development is a need that continues throughout one's work life. This implies that the supervisor who is a good coach may be able to help people experience higher levels of self-actualization by showing them how to take advantage of opportunities they might have let slip.

Work Design.   A job which is found to be interesting and challenging provides intrinsic rewards when performed successfully. We have already seen that staffing is one approach to the employee-job match. Another approach is to change the nature of the job or to redesign jobs to make them more intrinsically rewarding.

Leadership and Decision Making.   The supervisor who recognizes and openly rewards good performance is contributing to the satisfaction of esteem needs. It is important for people to know that others recognize good work. The way in which decisions are made in a work group will also help determine the motivation to work. When employees are given an opportunity to participate in decisions affecting them and their place of work, they usually find that it satisfies higher-order needs such as the desire for autonomy, responsibility, and self-development.

When a supervisor can classify subordinates into two broad categories, those whose lower-order needs dominate and those whose higher-order needs dominate, he or she can devise a course of action to increase the motivation to work. For the first group, one can focus on manipulating wages, job security, and disciplinary action to motivate job performance. Motivating the second group is not as simple, however. Initially, the supervisor should try to ensure that these employees are properly matched to positions. This can be achieved through staffing, work design, and through leadership and decision-making patterns. However, such rewards, since they are intrinsic, are controlled by the individual. Thus, the supervisor can provide feedback by telling the person, "Well done. You can take pride in your work," but the individual need not concur in this opinion.

The key step, from the supervisor's view, is correct identification of those people with unsatisfied higher-order needs. This can be accomplished by experimenting with subordinates. Try having them participate in a decision. Who responds to it? Who sits back and appears disinterested? Who seems befuddled and threatened?

SUMMARY AND CONCLUSIONS

This chapter has highlighted the basic principles of motivation to work. Human needs and the kinds of need satisfaction available on the job are important. So are the mental processes of equity evaluation and expectancy evaluation. We have briefly pointed out how an organization's personnel policies (staffing, training, and compensation) and the way in which a supervisor approaches the job (leadership, designing work, making decisions, and disciplining employees) can influence the motivation to work.

Supervisors have many opportunities to use their knowledge about motivation because they are involved to some degree in every phase of organizational life. Our objective in this chapter has been to point out how the motivation to work can be useful to a first-level supervisor in various phases of the job. A fuller understanding of how to use leadership style, work design, discipline, and so forth to motivate is provided by the respective chapters of the book dealing with those topics.

QUESTIONS

1. What do high *n*-Ach individuals want from their jobs? In what way, if any, do they differ from those whose dominant needs are for esteem and self-actualization?
2. Given the objective of trying to motivate a person to work,
   a. Explain why it is so important to know what an employee's dominant needs are.
   b. Explain why a person's perceptions of the connection between effort and performance are important.
   c. Explain why a person's perceptions of the connection between performance and rewards are important.
3. Outline what a supervisor could do to motivate a person whose lower-order needs dominate.
4. Outline what a supervisor could do to motivate a person whose higher-order needs dominate.

NANCY WILLIAMS, SUPERVISOR

Nancy Williams has been supervisor of the 11 women in the typing pool at Equity Insurance for a year now. Basically her job is to receive work requests from Equity Insurance agents in the region, northern California, review the requests for completeness, and assign them to personnel within the pool. If the requests are not complete or accurate, Nancy must first contact the agent submitting the request.

After the typing job has been completed, Nancy reviews the work to see that it has been done properly. If there are errors, she sometimes returns it to the person assigned the work but often tries to correct minor errors herself.

Members of the typing pool are on salary. Differences in compensation in the typing pool stem from differences in seniority.

As Nancy reviews the operation of the typing pool over the past year, she makes note of the following two personnel problems:

a. Sue Doyle has been in the typing pool at Equity for two years. Sue was initially the best worker in the pool, but lately her work seems to be falling off. Nancy has talked to her about this, and Sue has countered that the work just doesn't seem as interesting or challenging as when she first came to Equity.

b. Fran White is the first person Nancy hired. She has been with Equity about 11 months and is probably the poorest performer in the pool. She is rough with the equipment, takes long breaks, and is frequently late. Also, she doesn't complete as much work as others in the pool. Nancy has spoken to her a few times, but she always has some excuse.

1. What additional problems do you foresee in the near future if Nancy does not handle these problems?

2. What alternative approaches can be taken to solve these problems? Consider both those things that could be done if Nancy were free to change personnel programs and actions she might undertake in her day-to-day dealings with these individuals.

NOTES

[1] A. H. Maslow, "A Theory of Human Motivation," *Psychological Review, 50* (1943), 370–96.

[2] M. A. Wahba and L. G. Bridwell, "Maslow Reconsidered: A Review of Research on the Need Hierarchy Theory," *Organizational Behavior of Human Performance, 15* (1976), 212–40.

[3] F. Herzberg, B. Mausner, and B. Snyderman, *The Motivation to Work* (New York: John Wiley, 1959).

[4] J. W. Atkinson, "Motivational Determinants of Risk Taking Behavior," *Psychological Review, 64* (1957), 359–72; and D. C. McClelland, "Business Drive and National Achievement," *Harvard Business Review, 40* (July-August 1962), 104–5.

[5] J. Stacy Adams, "Inequity in Social Exchange," in *Advances in Experimental Psychology,* ed. L. Berkowitz (New York: Academic Press, 1965).

Leadership
and
Supervision

In what different ways can a supervisor lead employees?
How does a supervisor decide which leadership approach to use?

LEARNING OBJECTIVES

When you have finished this chapter, you should be able to

1. Define leadership
2. Explain the connection between power and leadership
3. Identify the contribution of the behavioral approach to the study of leadership
4. Describe the contingency approach to leadership
5. List and describe alternative leadership approaches
6. Identify the key factors in a situation by means of which a supervisor selects the appropriate leadership approach

THE PLIGHT OF THE SUPERVISOR

Jim McKinsey was reflecting on his 30-year career as a supervisor and foreman in construction. He had worked for several companies in the Midwest. After having been employed in various construction jobs for five years, Jim was offered a promotion to supervisor.

The early years were easier than today. Back then it seemed that when a person took a job he expected to work. The supervisor told the person what to do and he did it. Of course, if someone didn't pull their weight, all the supervisor had to do was say, "Pick up your check at payroll. You don't work here anymore." The next day the supervisor would hire someone else.

Another thing, the work was simpler then, too. Nowadays, there seems to be no end to new tools, equipment, and processes. It's tough to keep up with this advancing technology.

Yes, Jim reflected, it's a lot tougher now. With some employees you just tell them what to do and they go ahead and do it, no questions and no problems. Do the same thing with other employees and they start asking questions and telling me what to do: "Well, did you think of doing it this way, Jim?"; "I think this way would save time, Jim."

It seems that a supervisor is supposed to be all things to all people. When something comes up that the employees don't know how to handle, old Jim is supposed to jump in and lay it out for them. When things aren't going well and work is falling behind, old Jim is supposed to tell them to hang in there, we will get the job done on time. Then, too, when someone is having problems—it doesn't matter what kind, family, co-workers, or the

66

job itself—the person comes to Jim for his suggestions and help in working it out. It has been a good 30 years, Jim concludes, but today's supervisor needs better leadership training than he had when he started as a supervisor.

WHAT IS LEADERSHIP?

For anyone who has been a supervisor for some time, many parts of Jim McKinsey's reminiscing will be familiar. Jim is describing some leadership aspects of a supervisor's job and some of the changes that have made leadership more difficult.

A leader is the individual in a group who is given the responsibility of directing and coordinating group activities so that goals are achieved. Leadership is influencing the members of the group to behave in the desired way. The study of supervision is basically the study of effective leadership. To grow and prosper, work organizations need supervisors who can lead subordinates to get the job done.

Power and Leadership

Power results in the ability to get things done—somehow. In any social relationship one person (A) has power over another (B) if A is able to influence the behavior of B. From these descriptions of power and leadership, it is clear that the two concepts are closely related.

What Are the Sources of Power?

Power can come from many sources. One study lists the following sources of power: [1]

1. *Legitimate power* stems from a person's position in an organization. Having legitimate power in an organization is usually indicated by such titles as manager, supervisor, or director. The effectiveness of this form of power depends on people recognizing the organization's right to appoint leaders.
2. *Reward power* is based on an individual's ability to control the rewards of others. Examples include salary increases, bonuses, promotions, or praise. A leader who controls these rewards is able to influence the job behavior of subordinates more than is a leader who has little or no control over such rewards.
3. *Coercive power* is one's ability to control or administer punishment. Forms of punishment which might be under the control of a supervisor

are discharge, demotions, layoffs, and reprimands. As with rewards, control over the different forms of punishment increases a supervisor's ability to influence the behaviors of subordinates.

4. *Expert power* stems from the knowledge, skill, or expertise that an individual possesses. A supervisor who is expert and knowledgeable in the performance of the jobs under his or her supervision has more influence or power over those supervised than a supervisor who is unfamiliar with those jobs.

5. *Referent power* is power resulting from being well liked or from having charisma. Leaders who are well liked are better able to influence others than unpopular leaders. This source of power depends on being likeable, trustworthy, or inspiring.

Formal and Informal Leaders

A formal leader is one that is appointed as leader by an organization, such as a supervisor. An informal leader is an individual who is looked upon as the group leader by the group members. The formal leader's *potential* sources of power are legitimate, reward, and coercive power. However, all of these sources of power may not be available to the supervisor. Informal leadership can be based on either referent power or expert power.

Implications for Supervision

A supervisor should have as many sources of power as possible to influence the job performance of those under his or her direction. This means that the members of the work group should feel the organization appoints good supervisors, and also that supervisors should have a great deal of control over rewards and punishment. Finally, it suggests that individuals promoted into supervisory positions should be knowledgeable about the jobs they oversee and that they should be likeable individuals.

If we look again at our opening case, in the old days Jim McKinsey had control of hiring and firing, and, with fewer technological changes, he probably knew the jobs he supervised a lot better, too. No wonder people did what they were told.

Trends Affecting These Sources of Power

Block 4–1 describes actions taken by one organization which affected the power of first-line supervisors.

The situation described in Block 4–1 is not an isolated case. In recent

BLOCK 4–1   Increased Control by the Home Office

The organization in question has branch offices throughout the state. Formerly, decisions concerning hiring, promotion, salary increases, and disciplinary action were delegated to the branch offices. In other words, supervisors at the branch locations had a great deal of reward and coercive power.

Many complaints of favoritism were received by the home office under this system. To deal with these problems it was decided to centralize decision making about personnel at the home office. The supervisor's role under the centralized system is only to make recommendations that someone be hired, discharged, promoted, or receive a raise. The final decision is made at the home office.

The centralized system has reduced the number of complaints of favoritism. On the other hand, it has led to complaints by supervisors. They say that they no longer have the tools necessary to be effective leaders.

years, supervisors' control over rewards and punishment has tended to decrease. The days when the supervisor had complete control over hiring and keeping personnel in the unit or department have long since gone. Partly this is a result of unions. Union contracts have led to the right to appeal supervisors' decisions. Another factor that has tended to reduce the reward and coercive power of supervisors is civil rights legislation. One side effect of this legislation is that personnel departments review supervisors' decisions concerning selection, promotion, and discipline. And personnel can reverse those decisions they feel are biased. Finally, today's supervisors have less power because of the knowledge explosion. In many situations, supervisors are not as knowledgeable about specialized jobs as are the employees in these positions, and this results in a loss of expert power.

Why Are Some Leaders More Effective than Others?

Our overview of the sources of power provides some tentative answers to this question. In addition, a number of studies have addressed this question. Basically, this research can be placed in two categories: (1) that concerning the behaviors of leaders and (2) that concerning the contingency or situational approach to leadership.

BEHAVIORAL STUDIES OF LEADERSHIP

Autocratic-Participative Leadership

The autocratic approach to leadership means that a supervisor retains personal control over planning and decision making. Other labels for this approach are *authoritarian* leadership and *directive* leadership. Early writings on leadership focused primarily on the leader's responsibility to get the job done (goal accomplishment) and almost completely ignored interpersonal relations and need satisfaction.

By contrast, participative leadership involves providing an opportunity for subordinates to have a say in decisions affecting their work. This approach to leadership thus implies a great deal of concern for the satisfaction of subordinate needs and welfare. Other labels for this approach are *democratic* and *employee-centered* leadership.

McGregor's Theory X and Theory Y

Management psychologist Douglas McGregor investigated the assumptions and beliefs held by managers concerning the nature of human motivation.[2] Traditional beliefs, which resulted in the then current theory of direction and control, Theory X, were basically that

1. The average human being dislikes work and will avoid it if possible.
2. Because of this dislike of work, most people must be coerced, controlled, directed, or threatened with punishment to get them to put forth adequate effort to achieve organizational objectives.
3. The average human being prefers to be directed, wishes to avoid responsibility, has relatively little ambition, and above all desires security.

By contrast, Theory Y beliefs, based on an updated psychology of motivation, include the following:

1. Putting forth physical and mental effort in work is a natural thing for people to do. The average human being does not inherently dislike work. Work can be a source of satisfaction.
2. External control and threat of punishment are not the only means to bring about effort toward organizational objectives. People will use self-direction and self-control to accomplish objectives to which they are committed.
3. Commitment to objectives depends on the rewards associated with their achievement.
4. In the right circumstances, the average human being can learn to seek responsibility. Avoidance of responsibility, lack of ambition, and emphasis on security, according to McGregor, generally result from one's

experience in an organization. Such attitudes and behavior are not inherent characteristics of human beings.

5. The capacity to exercise imagination and creativity in the solution of organization problems is widely distributed in the general population.

6. Most modern industrial organizations only partially tap the potentials of the average human being.

A supervisor who adopts an authoritarian style of leadership behavior probably does so because of Theory X assumptions about people. Use of the participative approach indicates that a supervisor generally agrees with Theory Y assumptions.

Block 4–2 shows some results of an exercise we regularly use when conducting supervisory development programs. The participants are asked to write a paragraph describing the best supervisor and poorest supervisor they have ever had.

Notice that in the eyes of conference participants, the best supervisors give employees an opportunity to decide how the work is to be done, and the poorest supervisors discourage suggestions from subordinates.

The Ohio State Leadership Studies

During the late 1940s and early 1950s, a large-scale effort to understand leadership behavior took place at Ohio State University.[3] Two dimensions of leadership behavior were identified. One dimension was

---

BLOCK 4–2 Open to Suggestions?

Common descriptions of the best supervisor include:

Had an open mind and was always willing to listen to ideas about how to improve things.

Was interested in my suggestions and always had time to listen to what I had to say. If the idea was a good one she would do what was necessary to implement it. If there was a problem with it, she explained why it would not work.

Common descriptions of the poorest supervisor include:

Was determined to do things the way they have always been done. Regardless of the suggestion, he had tried it in the past and it did not work.

Any suggestion to change things was viewed as a direct attack on his ability to supervise. He would never listen to new ideas of subordinates.

called *initiating structure* or simply *structure*. This refers to the extent to which a leader organizes and defines activities for subordinates. Structure involves assigning tasks and planning and establishing methods for completing the work. A supervisor who rates high in structure plays a very active role in directing a group through planning, communicating information, scheduling work, criticizing subordinates, and trying out new ideas.

The other dimension of leadership behavior was called *consideration*. It includes behavior indicating a mutual trust, respect, and rapport between a superior and his or her work group. In other words, a leader high in consideration supports the employees in his or her work group and is concerned for their welfare.

The Ohio State leadership studies found that a leader could be

1. High in concern for employee welfare and low in concern for accomplishing work goals
2. Low in concern for both employee welfare and goal accomplishment
3. Low in concern for employee well-being but high in structuring behavior
4. High in both concern for employee welfare and achievement of work objectives

Prior to the Ohio State leadership studies, leadership behavior was thought of as a single continuum. (See Figure 4–1a.) At one extreme, the

FIGURE 4–1   a. Earlier View of Leadership Behavior

Task-centered,   Employee-centered.
Autocratic   Democratic

b. Leadership Behavior. Ohio State Leadership Studies

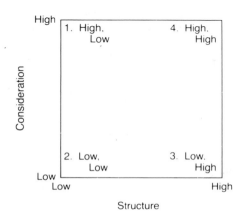

job- or task-centered leader was assumed to adopt an autocratic or authoritarian approach to dealing with subordinates. At the other extreme, a democratic or participative approach in dealing with subordinates was characteristic of the employee-oriented leader. In the Ohio State leadership study, there were not two but *four* combinations possible with the two dimensions. As is shown in Figure 4–1b, it is possible for a leader to be high in both consideration and structure, to be low on both dimensions, or to be high in one and low in the other.

The Managerial Grid

Management consultants Blake and Mouton build on these ideas in their managerial grid.[4] On the basis of two dimensions, concern for people and concern for production, Blake and Mouton arrive at a model of leadership behavior. These approaches are described as follows:

1. *9–1 management* means a high concern for production and a low concern for people. This approach assumes there is necessarily an inconsistency between the production goals of an organization and the needs of its employees. This supervisor can be characterized as a task master. Production is all-important and satisfaction of employee needs will not stand in the way of attainment of objectives.

2. *1–9 management* indicates a low concern for production and a high concern for people. As with the 9–1 approach, it assumes a contradiction between employee needs and goal accomplishment. To this supervisor, employee needs dominate and production will suffer in the event of a conflict between the two priorities.

3. *1–1 management* implies a low concern for both production and employee welfare. This supervisor does not see a conflict between production and people and more or less allows problems to resolve themselves.

4. *9–9 management* implies a high concern for both production and people. The 9–9 style assumes that there need not be a conflict between production goals and personal need satisfaction. The basic aim of 9–9 management is to promote the conditions that combine creativity, high productivity, and high morale through team action. According to Blake and Mouton, the effective integration of people with production is possible by involving them and their ideas in determining how the job will get done. They argue that the 9–9 managerial style is the best leadership approach.

SITUATIONAL APPROACH TO LEADERSHIP

So far, we have looked at leadership style as a constant trait that a leader can show in any given situation. Now we will look at some ideas about leadership that suggest leader behavior depends on the particular situation a leader is faced with. The situational approach suggests that while a particular approach to leadership may be effective in one situation, another set of circumstances may require a totally different approach.

A Continuum of Leadership Behavior

Leadership behavior can be viewed as a continuum (Figure 4–2) from boss-centered or directive leadership to subordinate-centered or participative leadership.[5] Along this continuum, Figure 4–2 shows a number of variations in the leadership behavior available to a supervisor.

If we move from left to right across Figure 4–2, we notice that the use of authority by the supervisor decreases and the amount of participation by subordinates increases at each of the seven leadership styles. At one extreme the supervisor makes the decision and simply announces it to his or her subordinates. No opportunity for subordinates to participate in the decision-making process is provided. When the supervisor sells a decision, he or she makes the decision but takes the additional step of explaining or persuading subordinates to accept the decision. The supervisor thinks there may be resistance to the decision and assumes that with additional information, he or she can remove some or all of this resistance. With the next variation, subordinates are given an opportunity to ask questions. Presumably during this give-and-take session the su-

FIGURE 4–2　Continuum of Leadership Behavior

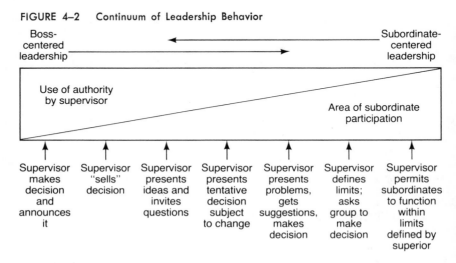

Source: Adapted from Robert Tannenbaum and Warren H. Schmidt, "How To Choose A Leadership Pattern," *Harvard Business Review, 36,* 2 (March–April 1958), 96.

perior and subordinates are better able to explore the implications of the decision.

The midpoint on the continuum assumes that the supervisor presents a tentative decision to subordinates subject to change after their input is received. Note that this is the first point on the scale at which subordinates have an opportunity to influence the decision. Before finalizing the decision, subordinates are given the opportunity to react to the tentative decision. Perhaps they will furnish information or point out considerations which you as supervisor overlooked. The next more participative approach has the supervisor presenting the problem to the group and getting their suggestions and recommendations *before* arriving at even a tentative decision. The supervisor thus attempts to remain more open-minded but nonetheless reserves the right to make the final decision. In the next variation, you define the limits of the problem and then turn the final decision over to your subordinates. The last variation is one in which the group is permitted to define or diagnose the nature of the problem, develop alternate solutions, and finally arrive at a decision to be implemented.

How to Decide on a Leadership Style

The continuum can be carried one step further by asking the question, How should the individual decide on a leadership style? Each situation is determined by forces at play within the supervisor, the subordinates, and the situation itself. We will present a series of ideas under each heading for the supervisor to keep in mind when determining which leadership style to use.

Forces in the Supervisor

A supervisor's behavior is influenced by longstanding beliefs and attitudes that must somehow be reconciled to a personal approach to leadership.

1. One factor to consider is your attitude toward responsibility. Do you feel that the title of supervisor requires you to make all the decisions yourself?
2. Another factor is the amount of confidence you can muster in your subordinates. Can the people under your supervision be trusted to handle the problems?
3. Your own leadership inclinations are also important. Some people are quite comfortable supervising in a highly directive manner. Others want to share their functions with subordinates.
4. A final factor is the amount of risk you are willing to shoulder. When a decision has been turned over to subordinates, the outcome is no longer

under your control, and the way things will turn out is more uncertain or ambiguous than if decision making is retained by the supervisor.

Forces in the Subordinate

Subordinates should also be evaluated on a number of dimensions:

1. Do subordinates have high needs for independence? In other words, do they want to have the opportunity to control their own job situation or do they prefer to have things laid out for them?
2. Are subordinates ready to assume the responsibility for decision making? Some individuals will view participation as an opportunity to develop their own initiative; others will feel threatened and unjustly put upon by a superior who delegates to them responsibilities he or she should assume.
3. Do subordinates have a high tolerance for ambiguity—that is, can they handle uncertain situations? This trait or characteristic will be related to an individual's need for independence.
4. Do subordinates have an interest in the problem and feel that it is important? If employees view the problem as essentially irrelevant, they will not be highly motivated to resolve it.
5. Do employees identify with the goals of the organization? An organization faced with an excess number of employees on the payroll because of a decline in sales would not be wise to let the employees decide if the company should lay people off or operate at a loss. The interests of the work group will in this instance be in opposition to the goals of the organization.
6. Also, of crucial importance, do subordinates have the necessary knowledge and experience to deal with the problem? If they do not have the skill or knowledge to deal with the issue, the problem should not be turned over to them.
7. Finally, do employees *expect* to share in decision making? People who expect to participate in decision making and are not given this opportunity will be resentful. On the other hand, the reverse situation can also be quite disruptive. Abrupt changes in leadership style should be avoided.

Forces in the Situation

1. What approach to leadership has been traditional in the organization? Is the climate of the organization one in which supervisors are expected to provide maximum direction for their subordinates? If this is the case, the participative style is not appropriate.
2. What is the nature of the problem being considered? Obviously, if the problem involves a new technology that is only familiar to the supervisor and higher-level managers, subordinates cannot be involved to any great extent in decision making.

3. Finally, how much time can be allotted to making the decision? Participative decision making is time-consuming. When decisions must be made quickly, a supervisor has no choice but to use a directive approach.

This approach makes several contributions to an understanding of effective leadership. First, a successful leader is one who is aware of the relevant forces operating in a situation. Second, a successful leader is able to use different leadership approaches. Third, a successful leader is able to diagnose which approach is appropriate in a given set of circumstances. Rather than trying to make all situations amenable to a single leadership style, analyze the situation and select the leadership style or approach which is most appropriate to that situation.

Many of the ideas pointed out above can be seen operating in the following incident described in Block 4–3.

Captain Jones was a member of an organization that is virtually equated with directive leadership. It is not so strange, then, that Specialist Andrews preferred directive leadership. While Captain Jones was more comfortable with a participative leadership style, forces in the subordinates, coupled with forces in the situation, made it necessary for him to use a different leadership style in supervising three of the four members of this work group.

Research tends to confirm this aspect of leadership effectiveness. One researcher, for example, found that the effectiveness or productivity of a work group depends on a match between the supervisor's leadership style and the degree to which a situation is structured.[6] In either highly structured or completely unstructured situations, the directive leadership style was more effective. When a situation permitted a wide range of rational choices, the democratic approach led to more effective work groups.

Intuitively, when everything is functioning smoothly, employees have no reason to oppose directive leadership. Also, when the situation is chaotic, a strong-willed supervisor is the only one likely to accomplish anything. However, when there are a number of equally viable alternatives, it is a good idea to include subordinates in decision making and thus elicit more information and greater commitment in the process.

The Path-Goal View of Leadership

This final view of leadership helps tie together the two concepts of leadership and motivation, and also unifies the various ideas about leadership that we have already encountered in this chapter.

The path-goal approach has its foundations in expectancy evaluations

Captain Jones supervised a group that made available to Army Headquarters certain statistical information concerning Army personnel in Europe. There were four enlisted personnel assigned to the group. The group's work could best be described as project work. Upon receiving a request for information, the best way, or a practical way, to obtain the information would be decided on. The information would be gathered, presented in report form, and sent to the office that requested it.

Since all of the enlisted personnel were college graduates, Captain Jones thought they would all like to participate in decisions on how to gather the information. He reasoned this would increase their satisfaction with the work. Therefore, when a request was received, he would call a meeting of the group to consider alternative ways to answer the request and to decide on the approach that would be used.

Captain Jones used this approach for some time. However, he noticed that Specialist Andrews never said anything during these meetings. After one meeting, when the others had left, Jones asked Andrews if anything was wrong. After exchanging a few comments, Specialist Andrews said he didn't like these meetings and didn't think it was part of his job. He said he preferred to be told when and what to do. According to him, decisions on methodology were part of Captain Jones' job.

Captain Jones was surprised. He believed that everybody liked to participate in decisions affecting their work. Besides, he preferred to use a participative rather than a directive style.

After talking to the other members of the group, it turned out that only one person liked to take part in these planning sessions—the others shared Andrews' feelings. After that, when a request for information was received, Jones got together with this subordinate for a planning session, and after agreeing on a course of action, Jones would tell the others what needed to be done and when it was due.

which were discussed in Chapter 3. Recall that an individual's work behavior can be predicted from

1. The degree to which the job or job performance is seen as leading to various rewards or outcomes
2. The value placed on these rewards and outcomes

In other words, job satisfaction depends on whether certain rewards are forthcoming to satisfy employees' felt needs. People must believe that by working hard they will receive rewards and that by failing to put forth effort, and thus performing poorly, they will be denied those rewards.

The path-goal view of leadership says that leaders will be effective in motivating subordinates when they are able to make rewards potentially available to subordinates, depending on the accomplishment of certain agreed-upon objectives.

The supervisor's duties as leader under the path-goal view consist of

1. Recognizing or awakening subordinates' needs for outcomes *over which the leader has control*
2. Increasing rewards or payoffs to subordinates for accomplishing work goals
3. Making the path or route to these payoffs easier to travel by coaching and direction
4. Helping subordinates clarify expectancies (expectations)
5. Reducing and removing frustrating barriers or roadblocks
6. Increasing employee opportunities for need satisfaction, assuming these opportunities depend on effective performance.[7]

Alternative Leader Behaviors

According to the path-goal idea, there are four kinds of leadership behavior: directive leadership, supportive leadership, participative leadership, and achievement-oriented leadership. *Directive leadership* is essentially the structured approach described by the Ohio State leadership studies. A directive supervisor gives specific guidance to subordinates concerning what is to be done, how it is to be done, and when it is to be completed. In other words, he or she makes clear to subordinates what is expected of them.

The *supportive leadership* style emphasizes a concern for employee needs and welfare. A supportive leader demonstrates to subordinates that he or she is friendly and approachable and strives to create a pleasant atmosphere in the work place.

Participative leadership maintains an open attitude toward suggestions from subordinates about decisions affecting the group. A participative leader will actively solicit suggestions from subordinates and consider their input in making decisions.

Achievement-oriented leadership is characterized by goal setting that challenges subordinates to perform at high levels and encourages them to improve their performance. This leader is confident that subordinates are capable of meeting these high expectations.

Subordinate Characteristics

Characteristics of the subordinate and the work have an effect on the usefulness of a particular leadership style. The following subordinate characteristics are relevant:

1. *Ability.* The greater the employee's ability on the tasks involved, the less the subordinate will view leader directiveness and coaching behavior as acceptable. In such circumstances, directive leadership is likely to be viewed as excessively close supervision.
2. *Location of control.* People who have a high degree of self-confidence, or who believe that they have a great deal of control over what happens to them, are likely to be satisfied with a participative leader. On the other hand, those who are low in self-confidence or who believe that their own behavior has little impact on what happens to them, are more likely to be satisfied with a directive leader.
3. *Employee needs.* An individual with high needs for security is more likely to accept a directive leader. An individual with high needs for esteem and social interaction is more likely to prefer supportive leadership behavior. Yet another possibility are those individuals whose dominant needs are self-control and growth or development. Such people respond well to a participative style.

The Nature of Work and Organizational Controls

Regarding the environment, the important characteristics according to the path-goal approach are (1) the degree to which work tasks are routine and (2) whether or not the controls of the organization and work group norms are clear and understood. When both of these conditions are met, attempts by the leader to further clarify the situation will be viewed as unnecessary and too much control. On the other hand, the more unstructured and "fuzzy" the requirements of the job and the organization controls, the greater subordinates will accept directive leadership.

As the nature of the work becomes less satisfying, employees will be more resentful of leadership behavior which emphasizes increased productivity or compliance with organizational practices and procedures. What employees prefer in such a situation is supportive behavior. In general, the path-goal approach says that leader behaviors which help subordinates cope with uncertainties, threats from others, or sources of frustration will be viewed by subordinates as preferable and motivating.

Figure 4–3 summarizes the principal points of a review of research on the path-goal leadership approach.[8] Concerning *directive* leader behavior, in situations where both the nature of the work and organizational rules were unclear, directive leader behavior was preferred. However, in situations where the work tasks were routine and repetitive, in order to pre-

FIGURE 4-3   Research Concerning the Path-Goal Approach to Leadership

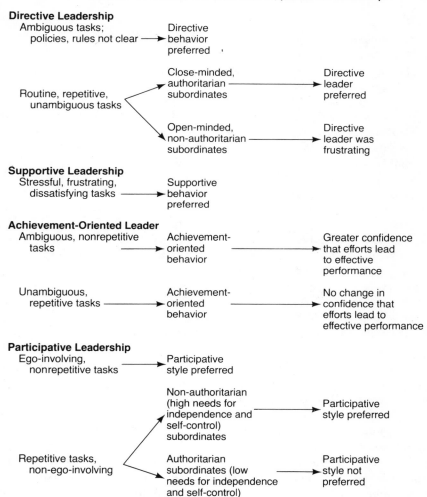

Directive Leadership

Ambiguous tasks; policies, rules not clear ⟶ Directive behavior preferred

Routine, repetitive, unambiguous tasks
- Close-minded, authoritarian subordinates ⟶ Directive leader preferred
- Open-minded, non-authoritarian subordinates ⟶ Directive leader was frustrating

Supportive Leadership

Stressful, frustrating, dissatisfying tasks ⟶ Supportive behavior preferred

Achievement-Oriented Leader

Ambiguous, nonrepetitive tasks ⟶ Achievement-oriented behavior ⟶ Greater confidence that efforts lead to effective performance

Unambiguous, repetitive tasks ⟶ Achievement-oriented behavior ⟶ No change in confidence that efforts lead to effective performance

Participative Leadership

Ego-involving, nonrepetitive tasks ⟶ Participative style preferred

Repetitive tasks, non-ego-involving
- Non-authoritarian (high needs for independence and self-control) subordinates ⟶ Participative style preferred
- Authoritarian subordinates (low needs for independence and self-control) ⟶ Participative style not preferred

dict reactions to directive leader behavior, one had to be familiar with employee thought patterns. When the tasks were routine and employees were not open to different points of view (closed minded) or had low needs for independence and self-control (authoritarian), directive leader behavior was preferred. However, when the work situation was routinized and the subordinates were nonauthoritarian and open-minded, directive leader behavior was viewed as frustrating. Block 4–4 describes a situation which highlights these ideas.

81

BLOCK 4–4   Flexible Leadership

Heather Johnson supervises the bookkeeping section of the Greenville State Bank. This section is responsible for ensuring that customer deposits and cancelled checks are accurately recorded to their accounts. The jobs are generally routine, but occasionally something out of the ordinary comes up.

Heather was just thinking about how different the women in her section are. Because of these differences she has to treat them differently when a problem affecting their jobs occurs. For example, if Alice has a problem, she *expects* to have a say in deciding how to handle it. If Heather took charge and told Alice how to deal with the issue, Alice would be angry for days. As a result, her work would suffer.

On the other hand, when Jane comes across something out of the ordinary, she brings it to Heather and expects her to take care of it. If Heather turns the problem back to Jane and asks her to recommend how to handle it, Jane becomes flustered and makes numerous errors in recording deposits and cancelled checks until Heather takes care of the problem. Jane gets along much better when everything is laid out for her in detail.

Heather tries to modify her leadership style to best fit the situation. She feels the work group is more effective this way.

Block 4–4 points out how a supervisor can be more effective by selecting a leadership style appropriate for the situation. For one employee, Heather uses a participative style and for the other a directive style.

In situations involving stressful, frustrating and dissatisfying work tasks, *supportive* behavior on the part of the leader was preferred by subordinates.

Achievement-oriented leadership led to increased confidence among subordinates that their efforts would be effective *when the work tasks were nonrepetitive and ambiguous.* But, when tasks were repetitive, achievement-oriented behavior on the part of the leader produced no increase in the confidence that efforts would lead to effective performance.

The studies concerning *participative* leadership suggest that reactions to this approach are also complex. When the nature of the task is nonrepetitive and subordinates are highly involved in their work, the participative style is preferred. However, when the work is repetitive and individuals are not truly involved in it, the degree to which subordinates have needs for independence and self-control comes into the picture. When the work is repetitive and employees have high needs for independence and self-control, the participative style is preferred. Alternatively, when the work is repetitive and employees have low needs for independence and self-control, directive leadership is preferred.

Summary of Contingency Models

The continuum of leadership behavior and the path-goal approaches to the study of leadership emphasize the complex nature of the task facing a supervisor. They show that an effective supervisor cannot simply assume once and for all a particular leadership approach. Rather, they point out the need for a supervisor to be able to size up a situation and then assume a leadership approach that is most likely to be appropriate in that situation. The supervisor must be able to analyze the nature of the subordinates. What are their abilities relative to the tasks facing them? What are their needs? The supervisor must also be able to assess the nature of the work and nature of the organizational setting. Is the situation highly structured and routinized? Is the work situation perceived to be stressful, frustrating, and dissatisfying? The answers to these questions will serve as guides to a supervisor in deciding how best to approach these leadership situations. Guidelines for assessing a situation and selecting a leadership approach are listed below. Some supervisors are more effective than others because they are able to match their leadership style to the situation better than others.

Guidelines for Selecting
a Leadership Style

1. If the work is routine and clear-cut and the employees have high needs for independence and self-control, participative leadership is preferred.
2. If the work is routine and clear-cut and the employees have low needs for independence and self-control, directive leadership is preferred.
3. If the work tasks are not clear or company policies and rules are not clear, directive leadership is preferred.
4. If the work tasks are not definite and nonrepetitive, achievement-oriented behavior leads to greater confidence among subordinates that they will be effective.
5. If the work is stressful, frustrating, and dissatisfying, supportive leadership is preferred.
6. If the work is ego involving, participative leadership is preferred.
7. If the work is not ego involving and employees have high needs for independence and self-control, participative leadership is preferred.
8. If the work is not ego involving and employees have low needs for independence and self-control, directive leadership is preferred.

SUMMARY AND CONCLUSIONS

Supervisors have an important stake in understanding leadership. Good leadership ability helps a supervisor get the job done more effectively.

A leader is one who influences the behavior of group members so as to facilitate achievement of the group's goals and objectives. Power is a related idea. A person has power over another if he/she can influence the other person's behavior. The forms of power are legitimate, reward, coercive, expert, and referent. A supervisor's ability to lead depends partly on the amount of power he or she has.

Both organization policies and a supervisor's behavior can affect the power at his or her disposal. Legitimate power can be ensured by screening out applicants who do not accept the notion that organizations have a right to designate supervisors and managers. A supervisor's reward and coercive power depend to a great extent on the organization's compensation system and disciplinary procedures. Expert power can be ensured by promoting only those supervisors who are good at performing the jobs they supervise. Finally, referent power can be affected by the procedures used to select supervisors; for example, insightful managers often promote informal group leaders.

Most important, however, supervisors need to know the "tricks of the trade"—how to select a leadership style, how to make decisions, and how to get things done in the organization. After being selected for promotion, supervisors need to be properly trained. As discussed in the path-goal approach to leadership section, certain styles are preferred in certain situations. Newly promoted supervisors as well as experienced supervisors should be able to identify the situations in which each is appropriate and be able to *use* each.

While all the material covered here contributes to an understanding of leadership, we believe the situational or contingency approach to leadership is most useful. Avoiding the fallacy of a single best leadership style, it focuses on choosing an approach that is appropriate to a given set of circumstances. So far, the path-goal approach has presented the best explanation of leadership in various contexts.

QUESTIONS

1. Describe how each form of power can contribute to the ability to lead.
2. Discuss the similarities and differences among each of the following behavioral approaches to the study of leadership.
   a. Autocratic and participative leadership

b. Theory X and Theory Y

c. The managerial grid

3. Describe the Tannenbaum and Schmidt model of leadership. How did this model broaden our understanding of the leadership phenomenon?

4. How is the path-goal approach to leadership similar to and how is it different from the Tannenbaum and Schmidt model?

5. Discuss the guidelines for selecting a leadership style.

STATE BOARD OF NURSING

A series of situations are described below. Assume you are the supervisor. Select a leadership approach to use in each situation.

1. You are the supervisor of records for the state board of nursing. Each year during June all nurses must renew their licenses. Three members of your staff will be responsible for processing the incoming renewal forms. Involved in this processing will be:

a. Reviewing the forms to see that they have been properly completed

b. Issuing receipts for license renewal fees

c. Mailing the receipts

d. Maintaining records of license fees

e. Forwarding license renewal forms for keypunching

Your analysis of those individuals who will process the renewal forms is as follows:

Molly Tyler:
  Three years experience in this office
  Excellent at detail work
  Very conscientious
  Very independent

Mary Mayes:
  Four years of experience in this office
  Very good to excellent at detail work
  Very dependable
  Also very independent

Meghan Martin:
  Two years with this office
  Average to good at detail work
  Average dependability
  Prefers to have work procedures specified

Decide how you will approach this work group in establishing the assignment of work for license renewals. Among the options in organizing this project are:

> Designate specific phases of the process to a specific individual.
>
> Rotate people among phases of the renewal process.
>
> Let each person process a renewal form from beginning to end.
>
> Use other ways of organizing this project if you prefer.
>
> Remember it is critical that accurate records be maintained.
>
> 2. During the course of processing the license renewals, the following occasionally occurs. At the end of each day the checks for renewal fees are tallied. Also, the license fee entries in the office records are tallied. The two should match but sometimes do not. When this occurs the three ladies become tense, and if the error is not found quickly, tempers flair. This is compounded by the fact that each person finds the work boring!
>
> Be prepared to role play the leadership approach you would select in each of these situations.

NOTES

[1] J. R. French, and B. Raven, "The Bases of Social Power," in *Group Dynamics*, 2nd ed., ed. D. Cartwright and A. F. Zanders (Evanston, Illinois: Row, Peterson and Co., 1960).

[2] Douglas McGregor, *The Human Side of Enterprise* (New York: McGraw-Hill, 1960).

[3] Edwin A. Fleishman, "The Leadership Opinion Questionnaire," in *Leader Behavior and Its Description and Measurement*, ed. R. M. Stogdill and A. E. Coons (Columbus, Ohio: Bureau of Business Research, Ohio State University, 1957).

[4] Robert R. Blake, and Jane S. Mouton, *The Managerial Grid* (Houston, Texas: Gulf Publishing Company, 1964).

[5] R. Tannenbaum, and W. H. Schmidt, "How to Choose A Leadership Pattern," *Harvard Business Review*, 36, 2 (March–April 1958), 95–101.

[6] Fred E. Fiedler, *A Theory of Leadership Effectiveness* (New York: McGraw-Hill, 1967).

[7] Robert J. House, and Terence R. Mitchell, "Path-Goal Theory of Leadership," *Journal of Contemporary Business* (Autumn 1974), pp. 81–97.

[8] House and Mitchell, "Path-Goal Theory of Leadership."

Communicating Effectively

SUPERVISORY PROBLEM

What can I do to minimize "communication breakdowns" and failure to communicate?

Courtesy H. Armstrong Roberts

LEARNING OBJECTIVES

When you have finished this chapter you should be able to

1. Answer the question, Does poor supervision cause poor communication or vice versa?
2. Identify the percentage of information lost at various points in the organization and explain why some of this is inevitable
3. Contrast the various steps a supervisor can take to encourage "upward" communication
4. Construct a chart showing when the supervisor should use face-to-face communication, telephone, and written comments
5. Diagram the human communication process
6. Discuss at least three interpersonal communication problems and ways to solve them
7. Compare counseling and exit interviewing
8. Identify four basics of giving good job instructions

A FAILURE TO COMMUNICATE?

One of my biggest problems as a supervisor centers around one of my subordinates. John Delph is usually a good worker who puts into his job a good deal of effort. However, I must constantly remind him of specific job duties. For example, I can assign him a job, and I can count on it being done. But in the process he'll step over a half a dozen other things that he knows have to be done.

For example, last Tuesday I asked John to go over the report we had just completed for AMPACS Corp. and check all the figures to make sure that the arithmetic was right. He did it, did it well, and was finished by lunchtime. After lunch he came back asking for another assignment. I've told John many times that an important part of his job description is seeing that the accounts receivable ledger is kept current. Tuesday it wasn't current. I had to sit down and review with him the jobs included in his job description and his level of progress on each before we decided that the accounts receivable ledger needed to be updated.

This situation is extremely frustrating because it seems that there is a serious breakdown in communications between John and me. You would think an employee who is obviously not stupid could make some of these decisions himself without my having to tell him what to do all the time.

High on the list of organizational and supervisory effectiveness issues for most people is communication. In fact, communication has achieved the status of a "sacred cow" in many instances. For example, in one recent study, roughly 74 percent of the managers sampled from companies in Japan, the United States, and Great Britain cited communications breakdown as the greatest barrier to organizational effectiveness.[1]

Communication failures can cause a number of different problems: (1) Lower productivity as a result of supervisors' giving unclear directions; (2) increased employee turnover because of frustration associated with lack of communication; (3) mistakes traceable directly to poor communication; (4) good ideas lost because they aren't properly "sold" to top-level management.

However, many times the "communications" dilemmas cited by people are not communications problems at all. They may be symptoms of other problems such as the way rewards are given, organizational design, personality clashes, and so forth. Nonetheless, poor communications is often blamed for these failures. To illustrate, in a recent series of supervisory development seminars, the authors of this book asked participants to list their most pressing problems. Nearly half of all the problems listed were attributed to communication breakdowns, but when the problems were explored a little more carefully a majority turned out to be instead problems of control, organization, discipline, or performance appraisal.

The point is that communications is an easy scapegoat. It's common to assume that *if only we could communicate* perfectly with one another many of the supervisory difficulties and problems would disappear. That simply isn't so. The feelings that people may have about the organization and the people they work with—feelings of distrust, resentment, insecurity, concerns about having been passed over for promotions—help determine the kind of communication that is realistically *possible* in an organization.

It has been noted that when management and supervision are effective, organizations experience few problems with communication. Only when management is poor and members of the organization can't seem to relate to one another, do complaints about communication breakdown occur.[2] This argues that bad management often *causes* communication problems rather than the other way around.

Yet even though improving communication may not be the answer to all supervisory problems, it can contribute significantly to smooth interpersonal relations. Supervisors certainly need a good understanding of the communication process and how they can use interpersonal communication skills to their best advantage.

There *will always be* some "failure to communicate" in organizations. The process of communicating between human beings is such that a certain amount of failure is inevitable. However, this doesn't mean that it cannot be reduced, managed, and kept within bounds. An understanding of the nature of communication in work organizations is the place to start.

THE NATURE OF COMMUNICATION
IN WORK ORGANIZATIONS

A supervisor must realize the information employees receive is not always the same as the information that was sent to them. People cannot absorb most messages in their entirety. To illustrate: a study was conducted to determine the effectiveness of the overall employee communication effort in one organization. The questionnaire contained a 10-item quiz on information that had recently been transmitted to the employees.[3] Employees responded correctly 27 percent of the time and incorrectly 9 percent of the time. Surprisingly, they answered 59 percent of the questions on the questionnaire with "I don't know" responses.

The results of this study and others suggest that most employee communication systems result in the information being accurately received by between 20 and 30 percent of the people involved. The typical work force, therefore, knows something about many subjects on which management informs its employees but not a lot about anything. Even when employees *feel* that they are well informed, they probably have absorbed only a small part of the message.

How Much Communication
Usually Occurs in Organizations?

Supervisors spend a lot of time communicating. One study reported that first-level supervisors spent 74 percent of their time communicating; second-level managers spent 81 percent, and third-level managers, an astounding 87 percent.[4] Employees spend a lot of time communicating, too. The same study showed that nonmanagement employees spent between 57 and 60 percent of their time communicating.

A management consultant who has studied communication among employees notes that when employees are asked to communicate about their work problems, their responses are quite predictable. On the basis of thousands of interviews with both blue- and white-collar workers, he has classified their comments into four categories: [5]

1. *Complaints about the working environment.* Almost one-third of employees' comments deal with work environment deficiencies.
2. *Misunderstandings about company policies and procedures.* About 10 percent of employees' up-the-line communications focus on perceived problems with company policy.

3. *Harsh, abrasive, tyrannical, arbitrary, or inept supervision.* Another 30 percent of the problems communicated involved supervisory problems.
4. *Management sins of omission and commission.* The final 30 percent of the problems are directed at upper management.

Information Overload

A major communication problem in organizations is information overload, that is, too much information. The solution is obviously *less,* not more, communication. The myth that more communication is better has been interpreted to mean that for supervisors to be effective, information must flow freely upward, downward, and across their positions. However, the studies cited above don't indicate that restricted flow is always the problem.

In fact, one of the supervisor's main duties in communicating is to help *decrease* the problems of information overload for employees. The supervisor's job includes interpreting and passing on to employees only those bits of information that are pertinent and important to them. The overloaded individual is not only personally inefficient but, as the overload increases, he is likely to neglect obligations to other work group members, thereby increasing their errors. The supervisor acts as a "gatekeeper" in screening both those messages that go up the line and those that filter down to employees. The crux of the matter for the supervisor is to select the proper information to transmit.

Figure 5–1 shows "normal," "overload," and "breakdown" information processing. For the supervisor facing more information than he or she

FIGURE 5–1   Supervisory Information Processing

Information → Supervisor → Summary of all important communications → Employees or boss

Normal Processing

Information → Supervisor → Summary of most important communications → Employees or boss

Overload Processing

Information → Supervisor → No summary possible

Breakdown

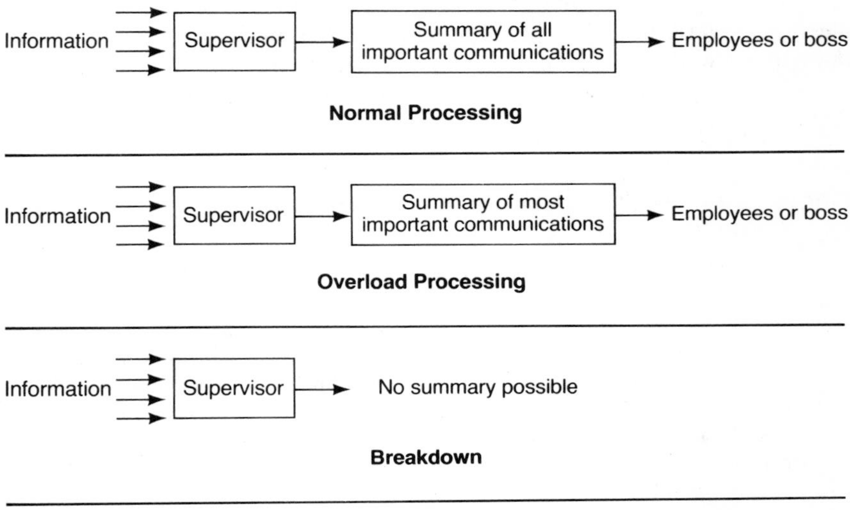

can reasonably process, three choices are available: (1) More communications channels can be made available, for example, by hiring an assistant supervisor to help with some of the work overload; (2) communications can be prioritized and those that are less important can simply be put in a stack for later; (3) information can simply be shelved, which of course results in a communication breakdown.

Human Tendencies
in Organizational Communication

At every level within an organization, people communicate primarily in order to accomplish things they feel are important. And they tend to do it in such a way as to maintain the approval of their superiors. If employees don't have the necessary information to do their jobs or to answer questions of interest to them, they may manufacture it by filling in the gaps in the information with their own opinions or predictions.

Increasing the number of levels in an organizational hierarchy is often seen as "bad" because it affects communication. We often hear it said that as organizations get bigger and more levels of management are necessary, communications fail. There is a certain amount of truth to this; yet, as we saw in Chapter 2, the organizational hierarchy is necessary for the organization to get things done. Figure 5–2 shows the features of the organization that affect communication and their influence on human communication tendencies.

We saw earlier that rules become necessary as organizations become larger. Yet rules limit new solutions to old problems. People are not likely to communicate new solutions or approaches if there are rules that state exactly how that problem must be handled. Further, specialization usually means more effective organizations. But specialization limits the ability of people to communicate with one another. Common points

FIGURE 5–2   The Effect of Organization on Communication

Organizational Feature	*Effect on Human Communication Tendencies*
Rules	Limits originality, communications about new solutions and approaches
Specialization	Limits common perspectives, common vocabulary, understanding of others' problems
Control at each level	Curtails downward flow of information
Formal lines of authority	Curtails upward flow of information

of view, vocabularies, and the understanding of other people's problems are limited by a high level of specialization.

Control at each level in the organization for its own operations is an organizational feature that allows authority and responsibility to remain equal. Yet this control may result in different organizational levels deciding not to pass along information which *should* be passed to lower levels in the organization. That results in a curtailment of the downward flow of information. Finally, formal lines of authority are a feature of good organizations. Yet keeping communication within those formal lines of authority sometimes curtails the upward flow of information. For example, a supervisor may choose not to tell the boss something because it reflects badly on the supervisor.

Downward Communication

Despite these obvious problems, downward communication of certain kinds of information sometimes tends to be better than we might think. Subordinates "read" their bosses better than is usually recognized and tend to react to those matters they judge to be of greatest personal interest to the boss. Among the various commands, policies, practices, and suggestions that come from above, subordinates tend to select those most in keeping with their perception of the boss's character, personal motivation, and style and to give them priority.[6]

However, in spite of (or perhaps because of) this tendency, a tremendous amount of information gets lost between the top of the organization and the bottom. Figure 5–3 shows the results of a study on the communications efficiency of 100 business and industrial organizations.[7] This study reveals that only 20 percent of the information that started down reached the bottom of the organization. Information along

FIGURE 5–3   Downward Information Received

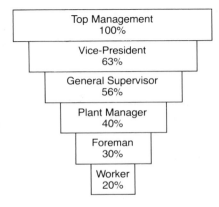

the line was filtered out, distorted, misinterpreted, or ignored. Different bits of information were seen as important by different levels in the organization each acting as "gatekeepers."

However, information flows both ways in the organization and some of the difficulties associated with upward communication should be considered as well.

Upward Communication

Upward communication is poor in most organizations. The reason is that the ability of persons at higher levels to perceive the feelings and concerns of lower-level members of the organization is simply not very well developed. Yet it is important for information at the lower levels of the organization to find its way upward, because top-level decisions are based in part upon management's perceptions of workers' attitudes, abilities, and desires.

Several things can be done by the supervisor to promote more effective upward communication. One is to maintain an "open door policy." This simply means that the supervisor's door is always open for subordinates to come in and talk about anything that is troubling them. Unfortunately, the open door policy doesn't always work. Perhaps the supervisor is busy at a particular moment and the subordinate views this as lack of interest in the problem. Then again, the supervisor may make every effort to be available yet discourage subordinates from bringing their problems by having a closed mind when they do so.

The grievance procedure can help upward communication. Most collective bargaining agreements provide for a formal grievance procedure. But even where there is no union, a good grievance procedure can help the supervisor and upper-level management determine what kinds of things are bothering subordinates.

Participation can help upward communication, too. The process of allowing employees to participate in making decisions *forces* a good deal of communication between supervisor and subordinates. This can greatly aid a supervisor's understanding of the major concerns of subordinates.

Finally, exit interviews can help, but their usefulness is often limited to hindsight. Frequently, employees who resign or are discharged make valid points about things that need to be changed. However, the immediate supervisor is usually not the best person to conduct an exit interview mainly because of a lack of objectivity. This will be expanded upon later in the chapter.

Block 5–1 presents a case that illustrates quite plainly how problems of upward and downward communication show up in a typical work organization.

Rumors and the Grapevine

In Chapter 2 we introduced the informal communication network known as the grapevine. This mechanism, consisting of "friendship group" members, is *inevitable* in all larger organizations. It cannot be outlawed or done away with.

The grapevine becomes especially active when official communication channels fail to provide the information that people want or need. For example, the rumor of an impending layoff is something of great concern to everyone in the organization. If the official communication network fails to provide information about this kind of situation, the grapevine will swing into action and fill in the gaps in the official information.

As rumors are transmitted through the grapevine, three different things tend to occur.

1. There is a *loss of detail* regarding people or events. Things tend to become generalized and specific bits of information fall out.
2. Certain things are *added* to the message or become emphasized. These may or may not be the things that are of major importance in the original communication.
3. A "motivational warping" takes place. The biases and prejudices of those spreading the rumor tend to color the communication.

How active the grapevine is generally depends on how badly people need to know the information that is being transmitted and how much formal information is available. The grapevine may transmit both factual information and rumors (by definition, nonfactual information). The supervisor is well advised to listen to the grapevine and use it as a way of keeping informed about subordinates' concerns. However, he or she should realize that the information being received may not be completely accurate.

On the other hand, a supervisor *should not* use the grapevine to spread information. Since any communication a supervisor has about a work-related topic should be as accurate as possible, "leaking information" to the work group through the grapevine is generally not good practice. Block 5–2 shows one supervisor's reaction to the grapevine in her

BLOCK 5–2   The Supervisor and the Grapevine

First-level supervisor: "Communication by the grapevine always seems to travel more rapidly than through normal channels, but the information is seldom complete or factual so I have to spend a lot of my time correcting misconceptions. Unfortunately, it also tends to pass along a lot of idle gossip and back-biting. When this is the case, it leads to dissension and unfavorable working conditions. This is a hard problem to crack because comments made via the grapevine are seldom out in the open where I can deal with them."

unit. One of the more effective ways to be sure that information is accurately transmitted is through the use of written communication.

Written Communication

When the supervisor is faced with communicating an idea to someone else, there are basically three choices; he or she can (1) call on the telephone, (2) deliver the message face to face, or (3) write a memo or letter. The idea that *everything* has to be put into writing isn't necessarily a good idea. There are usually too many pieces of paper floating around already. A better way is to consider the *purpose* of the message before deciding which of the three ways is most appropriate for the situation.

For example, *persuasion* works best on a face-to-face basis, so that reactions can be observed and positions can be changed if necessary. *Negotiation* and *compromise* obviously are best done face to face.

The telephone call, on the other hand, while not quite as flexible as the face-to-face situation, is generally *faster*. Telephone calls typically don't take as long as face-to-face conversations because a great many of the pleasantries ("How's the weather, how's the family") that are usually required in a face-to-face contact can be done away with. However, the telephone call doesn't allow you to "read" the other person quite as well either.

Sometimes it's best to put things in writing, particularly if *defensive tactics* are called for. If you don't trust the motives of another individual, it may be best to put things in writing, so there is a written record of the agreement. Writing things down also can help if you need *time to think* to avoid being trapped into making careless statements or statements that you might regret later on.

Memos are simply brief written communications that should deal with *why, who, what, where, when,* and *how.* As such they serve as a more accurate factual record of a communication.

Letters may take many forms, and it would be impossible to deal exhaustively with letter writing in this chapter. However, one kind of letter supervisors should be familiar with is the confirming letter. Confirming letters are very useful when you have had a telephone conversation or a face-to-face conversation with someone, and you think you have understood what that person said, but you want to get it in writing to make sure. For example, let's say you talked to a supervisor in another department and agreed that you would get together in three weeks to consider a mutual problem. When you get back to the office after the meeting, you might send a memo or letter confirming the date, the time, and so forth.

FIGURE 5–4   Comparison of the Use of Various Forms of Communication

		Changes in Operations	Changes in Wages or Salary
Verbal	{ Group meeting	44%	29%
	{ Face-to-face	31%	45%
Written	(Memo or letter	21%	31%
	} Article in employee publication	13%	14%
	} Bulletin board	12%	12%
	(Union or union contract	8%	13%

Note: Percentages will not add to 100% because the categories are not mutually exclusive.

Source: Adapted from "Employee Communications," *Personnel Policies Forum* (Washington, D.C.: PPF Survey No. 110, BNA, July 1975), p. 16.

Written versus Verbal Communication

Figure 5–4 compares the extent to which organizations use written and verbal communication for special kinds of information passing. The two different kinds of information in Figure 5–4 are *major changes in operations* and changes in *salary levels for employees*. In the survey of 219 personnel executives from U.S. companies, the group meeting was used more often for informing employees about changes in operations (44 percent), while the face-to-face method was used most often to inform employees about changes in wage or salary levels (45 percent). According to this survey, then, verbal methods are preferred for passing along such fundamental decisions affecting employee work life.

The same survey asked how these organizations kept their first-level supervisors informed. Figure 5–5 shows that information. The question asked was, What methods are used to keep first-level supervisors briefed so they can inform their subordinates of important developments or be prepared to answer employee questions? Although verbal communication once again predominated, written communication was used as much as one-third of the time and, therefore, warrants a supervisor's serious study. This survey shows that written communications, while not as

FIGURE 5–5   How Are Supervisors Kept Informed?

Supervisory meetings	85%
Memos	33%
Face-to-face communication	9%
Training programs	5%

Source: "Employee Communications," *Personnel Policies Forum* (Washington, D.C.: PPF Survey No. 110, BNA, July 1975), p. 16.

widely used as verbal communication, are a very important part of the supervisor's job.

Written communication plays an important role in the day-to-day operation of any business and can be crucial at the supervisory level. Let's look at one instance (Block 5–3) in which written communication seems indispensable.

INTERPERSONAL COMMUNICATION

Given the shortcomings of interpersonal communications, or communication between two people, it's a miracle that human beings communicate with one another at all. The big problem is that the words we use are only symbols, and they mean different things to different people. For example, an employee says, "I'll be glad to get off this job," and was thinking about job #402, a particularly difficult job he's been on for the last week. The supervisor, however, was thinking about the employee's employment with the organization and feels the employee is asking to leave.

Figure 5–6 shows that a whole host of factors affects the human communication process. These include the experiences, verbal ability, and attitudes of both the communicator and the receiver. The processes of encoding and decoding refer to the communicator's putting the message into words and the receiver's extracting meaning from those words, respectively. We turn now to a discussion of some of the factors that affect a communicator's ability to encode and a receiver's ability to decode.

FIGURE 5–6   The Human Communication Process

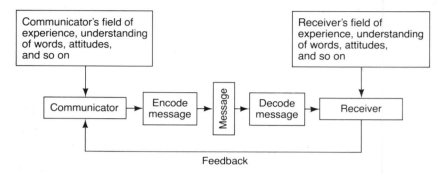

Common Interpersonal Communications Problems

The bases of a "failure to communicate" are quite varied, and in some cases supervisors must resign themselves to the fact that nothing can be done to improve the communication process. One example of such a frustrating situation is presented in Block 5–4. Any listing of problems in the communication process is necessarily going to be incomplete, but in the paragraphs that follow, we attempt to deal with some of the more common ones.

Superior-Subordinate Relationships

Communication may be hindered by the mere fact there is a superior-subordinate relationship. For example, the fact that you are the supervisor and a new employee is your subordinate may keep that individual from asking the kinds of questions he or she needs to know to do the

---

BLOCK 5–4   Joe Is Slow

I have an interesting problem with Joe Shaw. Joe is a reasonably good employee, but we have a real difficulty communicating. Joe will listen very closely to what I ask him to do—in fact he sometimes takes written notes. Yet he apparently still doesn't understand my directions, because he often ends up doing something else altogether. For example, last week I asked him to check the street light at 5th and Grand Ave. He called me from 21st and Main and said he couldn't find a street light. I ask him if he understands when I give him a work assignment, and he says he does, but he just can't seem to get it done the way it was planned.

job. This need to save face, or not to appear stupid, operates just as well at higher levels in the organization and if not countered by good sense, can stifle effective communication.

Status or Power Position

The kind of status or power that an individual has in a particular organization or work group can curtail the free flow of communication with that person. For example, high-status members of the work group may receive slightly different, more respectful messages from the superior than do other members of the work group. Low-status members may even remain outside the chain of communication between work group members. A word of caution is in order for the supervisor: Prejudging an individual's credibility based on status may be detrimental not only to the sender but to the receiver as well.

Selective Hearing

When people hear selectively, they hear only what they want to hear. It may be that there is *too much* to hear, so they record only those portions they can easily fit into their world. Or it may be that they don't agree with some parts of the message and ignore distressful cues. This is a very common problem in communication and a universal human tendency.

Different Words Have Different Meanings

Many jokes and anecdotes are based on this problem of faulty encoding or decoding, as the case may be. However, when a supervisor gives an order that is misunderstood, there may be no inclination to laughter. Perhaps a supervisor asks a worker to clean up the shop "as soon as possible." The subordinate, however, interprets the boss's words as "immediately," and drops everything to tackle the new job. The supervisor will, of course, probably be unhappy when he finds that the more important work has not been done. The same words and phrases do have different meanings for different people.

Emotional Context

The emotional state of both the sender and the recipient of a communication greatly affect the interpretation of the information. When a sender is very angry, it may be difficult to communicate in a rational, well-thought-out way. Many things may be said more for effect than communication value. Similarly, a very angry or otherwise emotional receiver is likely to assign inappropriate motives and meanings to the words sent. In either case, communication tends to be very inaccurate.

"It Can't Be Done" Attitude

When work-oriented communications are received with a negative "it can't be done" attitude by the supervisor, problems can occur. Such negativism will eventually discourage a subordinate from making any suggestions or even cut off communications altogether.

"I Know It All" Attitude

Like the "it can't be done" attitude, the "I know it all" attitude stifles communications. Somebody who knows it all is not very likely to maintain an open mind to divergent points of view. This attitude, and other attitudes that prejudge a suggestion or communication before it's sent, has a chilling effect on the ability of a communication to be open and useful.

Physical Reasons

There are a number of physical reasons why communication may fail. Inability to hear well and inability to speak clearly are two major reasons. Attempting to communicate across long distances or under noisy conditions presents a major stumbling block to communications. Yet there are people who insist on trying to shout across a long distance or speak to someone whose back is turned. The best physical conditions for communicating are face to face from a reasonable distance where both parties can see each other.

Uncommon Use of Words

Some people have a talent for using words in an unusual way or using uncommon words. This doesn't contribute to smoother communication at all. Remember, the essence of communication is that both sender and receiver have the same message. When words are used that other people aren't likely to understand, communication isn't going to be accurate.

Body Language

The gestures a person uses, the position of the body when speaking, facial expressions, all tell the observer a good bit about another person. Body language that emphasizes the message is a powerful convincer, but, interestingly enough, conflicting body language is likely to be believed over the message. For example, suppose a supervisor tells a subordinate that "everything is all right; there is no need for concern about layoffs, regardless of the rumor." However, if the supervisor refuses to make eye contact with the subordinate, sits rigidly in her chair, and drums her fingers on the desk, the subordinate will almost surely come away feeling that a layoff is imminent.

We have presented quite a list of problems associated with communicating. Perhaps now you can understand our earlier expression of amazement that human beings do manage to communicate successfully. There are many factors that work *against* successful communication. However, there are several things a supervisor, or any communicator, can do to minimize the problems associated with communicating.

OVERCOMING PROBLEMS OF COMMUNICATION: LISTENING

There are several techniques that can be used to overcome roadblocks to communication. Possibly one of the most important is *listening*. Listening is a skill at which most people fail miserably. We tend not to hear a great deal of what goes on around us. This can be particularly disastrous for the supervisor, since a great deal of a supervisor's time is spent listening.

Listening isn't as "natural" as it might seem. People tend to listen to the *words* a person is using rather than listening to the *message* he or she is trying to deliver. It is also difficult to concentrate if you aren't interested in the subject, or if it seems as if you have heard the message once before.

Failure to pay attention while actually engaging in "wool gathering" is another common problem. It's very easy to mentally tune out a person who is speaking and pretend you're listening. For the supervisor, concentrating on what is being said is the key to effective listening. The mind is capable of understanding words much faster than they can be spoken. As a result, listeners may let their minds wander, mentally using up the time until the speaker finishes making his or her point. The only way to avoid this problem is to concentrate on not doing it.

Many listeners interrupt the speaker. This is not only annoying for the speaker, but it may distract from the message the speaker is trying to deliver. Asking questions can help clarify what you think you hear. It may help bring out any hidden or latent content in a message. But the questions should be asked when the speaker is finished making the point. This is especially important if emotions are running high.

Failure to Act

Supervisors should realize that one of the biggest roadblocks to effective communication is the *failure to act on previous communications.* If a subordinate has brought information to you in the past, and you have agreed to do something but have then forgotten or failed to do anything about it, you have reduced the chance that that person will choose to communicate with you on important issues again. The supervisor must be willing to act on information brought by subordinates or have the courage to tell the subordinate there will be no action and explain why.

Prejudging

Since there is a great danger that communicators can misinterpret a subject as a result of their *biases and preferences.* Special concentration must be made to avoid this. Try to listen and communicate with an open mind, without prejudging. *Then* judge the communication on the basis of its merit *when* it is received, not *before* you receive it.

Empathy

Try to maintain *sensitivity* to the world of the receiver if you are attempting to communicate a message and sensitivity to the world of the communicator if you are the receiver. You should attempt to predict the impact of a message on the attitudes and feelings of the receiver. The message should be framed to fit the receiver's vocabulary, interests, and values whenever possible. The word *empathy* has been widely used to describe this sensitivity. To empathize is to try to put yourself in the other person's place. You can't really understand a communication from another person unless you have attempted to put yourself in that person's place.

Feedback

Use feedback whenever possible. As a check on the correctness of information exchanged between individuals, feedback is an important key. In face-to-face situations you can get feedback by observing and judging the total behavior of the other person. Carefully paying attention to the nonverbal cues and "reading between the lines" helps to determine what the person is trying to say as well as what he really is saying. You should use the opportunity to ask questions about things you don't understand, or to restate what you think somebody said to see if you really understood the point.

Avoid Defensiveness

Try to avoid being defensive. Communication will be more direct and easier if you can provide a climate in which no one is blamed for making "ridiculous" statements or thinking "illogically." You are more likely to avoid defensive behavior if you phrase your questions in a neutral way—"Is this what you mean?"—rather than immediately jumping on a subordinate with "You're wrong," or "That's all wet."

Maintaining a neutral position also entails helping a communicator focus the problem in his or her own mind rather than immediately trying to take control of the conversation. Generating a climate in which you can avoid defensiveness means you are more likely to get direct, honest answers and to avoid evasiveness.

Location

Another thing that supervisors can do to help communication is to pick a good location to communicate. If you have a personal communication that will probably generate some concern in the individual, pick a private place to communicate. Don't communicate such things in front of a group. The old (and useful) supervisory rule, "Don't discipline someone in front of the group," has its basis in this principle.

Important communications deserve your undivided attention; therefore, pick a place where you are not likely to be rushed, hurried or interrupted.

Repeating

Another useful suggestion when giving instructions is to ask employees to restate the directions in their own words. This feedback not only allows you to check for possible errors and misinterpretations but also helps you to see how you can improve your own communications. Repetition can be a very useful way to make sure that people understand what's going on. In fact, when giving instructions, repeating more than once is generally desirable.

Using these hints to overcome problems in communication won't guarantee that you'll be an effective communicator, but ignoring them will guarantee that you *will not be!* One very specialized kind of communication that supervisors find themselves engaging in from time to time is interviewing. Selection interviewing will be covered in Chapter 6. However, we will take a look at two specialized kinds of interviews here: counseling interviews and exit interviews.

COUNSELING AND EXIT INTERVIEWS

Supervisors' interviews are usually job related, but tend to be a bit more formal than the usual job contacts. Ordinarily arrangements for a time and place will be made in advance, and the interviewee (person to be interviewed) will often be aware of the topic(s) to be discussed.

There are several types of interview, all of which have different purposes. For example, *performance appraisal* interviews conducted on a regular basis are indispensable to personal and organizational progress. (These are discussed in Chapter 9.) *Counseling interviews* are tools the supervisor can use to nip potential problems in the bud, and *exit interviews* may help determine why people are leaving the organization.

A casual conversation between supervisor and subordinate is not an interview, because it typically does not have the *formal purpose* that an interview has. The interview is *most* valuable in determining the interviewee's attitude toward something. Basic skills in interviewing can also help the supervisor get the maximum amount of feedback from employees.

The real basis for any interview is simply good communications between two people. As we have seen, effective communication depends on the accuracy and the completeness of the information that the sender has, his or her ability to transmit it, and the receiver's ability and interest in understanding the intended meanings of the communications.

For communication to work in an interview situation, it is essential that the supervisor be a good listener. He or she should be alert to both the meaning and feeling components of the interviewee's answers and, based on this feedback, modify what he or she says and how it is said.

An honest, forthright approach toward the interview is best. Use of the "tricky" approach usually succeeds only in putting interviewees on the defensive. By contrast, interviewees will be as frank as they can when they feel that (1) their point of view is appreciated and respected,

(2) the interviewer has the right to the information, and (3) the questions are relevant and not out of line.

How Should I Prepare for the Interview?

To prepare for any of the different types of interviews mentioned, one should consider some general principles.

1. Decide what is to be accomplished before the interview. It may be a good idea to write down the objectives of the interview to keep them in mind.
2. Try to know the interviewee. Find out as much as possible or as much as is necessary for the files or reports, company records, and so forth.
3. Make appointments. This saves time and makes certain the interviewee is available.
4. Provide a suitable place for the interview to avoid interruptions. Interruptions can be embarrassing and may even cause the interviewee to withhold information.
5. Practice taking the other person's point of view. Put yourself in his or her place. This can give you a good idea as to how that person will react to certain comments and may provide insights into handling problems.
6. Know yourself. Try to realize that no one is completely free from prejudices and there is probably no such thing as a truly open mind. You are no different. If you recognize your own attitudes, you can keep them from interfering with the interview.

What Should I Do During an Interview?

The typical interview is short, so that you can expect to observe only a small sample of the interviewee's overall behavior. Since it is easy to overgeneralize from this sample, be on guard against concluding that "Jane is a nervous person," or "Tom is highly emotional."

During the interview, it's important to try to establish a point of mutual interest. The atmosphere can make or break an interview. Many interviewers try to establish such an atmosphere with small talk about today's baseball game or some other topic to put the individual at ease. However, if the person does not share this interest, such an approach might only make the person more uncomfortable, especially if he or she is ready to get down to business.

Once you get onto main topics, do all you can to get the interviewee to talk freely with as little prodding from you as possible. Encourage a person to talk about feelings by asking, "How do you feel about that?" This tends to clear the air somewhat. Avoid coloring the interviewee's remarks by what you say. Do not indicate that there are certain things you want to hear, or others that you do not want to hear. Try not to dominate the interview. This is supposed to be a free exchange.

Listen. This is one of the most important single techniques, and one which creates the most trouble. If you talk more than half the time, you're not interviewing, *you're being interviewed!* Your silence may give the other person a chance to reflect or add more to his or her statement. Looking at a person and giving that person your complete attention is one way of increasing the probability that he or she will tell you what you want to know.

Take all the time necessary. A hasty interview, one in which the interviewee feels the pressure of time, is worse than no interview at all. Enough time should be allowed to let things develop naturally and the conversation will go on to its logical conclusion. This usually means you will need to schedule enough uninterrupted time to complete the interview *before* you start.

Keep the objectives in mind during the interview and keep it on track. If the interviewee wanders too far afield, gently but firmly bring him or her back to the topic of concern. One way to do this is to note, "These are interesting points, and I'd like to discuss them with you during our next meeting, but what about . . .?" An interviewee can wander around the topic so much that an interview ends without any useful end product. Remember, an interview is a conversation with a purpose, and getting that purpose accomplished is a prime concern.

At the close of the interview, be especially alert for additional information that may be contained in casual remarks. If the interviewee is off guard or has been waiting for a chance to say something particularly important, it may come out at the end of the interview. You can bring this about by asking, "What else do you feel is important that we haven't talked about?"

Finally, it may be necessary to record the results of the interview. If so, do it as soon as possible after the close of the interview. The time that passes between the finish of the interview and the recording of the interview notes may result in some errors being made, especially if a number of other things intervene.

Figure 5–7 summarizes the basic principles of interviewing in the form of a checklist. Regardless of the type of interview, the supervisor should make sure that these essential conditions are met.

Counseling Interview

Counseling is a form of trouble-shooting in which the supervisor attempts to get at the underlying cause of a problem and lead the *employee* to understand the basis of the problem. The counseling interview contains

FIGURE 5–7   Interview Checklist

Before the Interview

I. Write down the objectives of the interview (what you intend to accomplish).

II. Find out as much as possible from files, reports, memoranda, and so on.

III. Choose a suitable place for the interview.

IV. Put yourself in the other person's place. This may provide ideas on how the interviewee will react and how you can handle the situation.

V. Try to recognize your own attitudes and prejudices (none of us is completely unbiased) and keep them from interfering during the interview.

During the Interview

I. Establish an atmosphere of mutual interest. Since both of you are concerned about some aspect of work life, try to show how these concerns overlap.

II. LISTEN. (If you talk more than half the time, *you are being interviewed!*)

III. Allow plenty of time.

IV. Keep the interview going in the general direction of the objective.

V. At the close, be alert for new information that surfaces in casual remarks.

After the Interview

I. If information must be recorded, do it as soon as possible (immediately is best).

many elements common to all interviews. We include it here to demonstrate the *nondirective* interviewing technique, a method that has proven most effective in dealing with employee problems. In this form of counseling interview the supervisor does not try to make a diagnosis or give advice, or even suggest solutions. The idea is for the employee to eventually see through his or her own problem by talking about it. The following dialogue provides an example.

Employee: I don't like Mary Jane. She's awful.
Supervisor: You don't like Mary Jane?
Employee: No, she goes out of her way to be nasty to me. I can't stand her.
Supervisor: You feel that she's going out of her way to be mean to you.
Employee: Well, maybe not just to me—since she got promoted she's like that with everyone.
Supervisor: Since her promotion, she's been hard to get along with, you think? . . .

Notice that the interviewer doesn't add any observations of his or her own. The employee's statement is merely restated. This may seem awkward or even "silly" at first, but psychologists have found this to be one of the best ways to get a person to open up and talk a problem out. The solutions arrived at by this method are more readily accepted by the interviewee because it seems that they are his or her own, and not the advice of someone else.

It's important to note in counseling interviews (and other types as well) that moments of dead silence will occur. These are uncomfortable for both the employee and the supervisor, because the natural tendency is to keep the conversation going. But you can use these moments of silence to your *advantage*. Observe the interviewee's reactions—hands, facial expressions, and so on. Let the silence drag on. Remember, the employee is more embarrassed and nervous than you are and will usually want to end the silence. It is at times like these that information otherwise unspoken may come to light. Of course it may be that nothing will be said, but give the silence a chance—a good long chance—to work for you.

The Exit Interview

Exit interviewing can be a useful way of determining why people are leaving the organization. The results from a number of such interviews can be compared to see whether organizational procedures themselves are at fault. To preserve impartiality, exit interviewing is best done by someone who is *not the direct superior* of the person leaving. Therefore, if there is no one person designated to handle the task, supervisors often exchange exit interviews.

The purpose of an exit interview is to try to find the *real* cause for leaving. Usually, however, employees give reasons that are *socially acceptable* or *convincing* rather than real reasons. For example, very common reasons given in exit interviews are "a better job," "more money," or "better working conditions." Although there may be some truth to these statements, a little honest probing can often get beyond the superficial reasons to the initiating causes that made the person want to seek other employment.

All information received from exit interviews should be confidential. The supervisor should take every precaution not to implicate specific individuals; in fact, one of the best ways to avoid hasty generalization is to accumulate several interview results before reporting any of them.

In the exit interview, it may be difficult to get past the defensive feelings of a person who is leaving. As in the counseling interview, the key is listening, reflecting feelings, and summarizing.

USING COMMUNICATION
TO FOSTER RESPONSIBILITY

Supervisors can use communication to help subordinates take appropriate responsibility. An excellent approach is to say to the employee who has a problem, "What would you do if I were you?" The truly expert supervisor can create a climate in which subordinates *want* to assume responsibility. Look at the conversations in Block 5–5. In the first conversation, the boss says, in essence, that *I* have been concerned, and *I* will decide how we're going to change things. In the second conversation, the problem of adjusting the inventory rests squarely on the shoulders of the subordinate. By using the pronoun *you* instead of the pronoun *I*, the supervisor has not only done his own job, but has encouraged his subordinate to assume responsibility for the parts inventory and its related cost.

BLOCK 5–5   Encouraging Responsibility in Subordinates

Conversation 1:

Harry: I've been concerned about the inventory we're running in the parts room.
Supervisor: Oh? Dig out the figures and let me see them.
Harry: Why? Are you going to cut the inventory?
Supervisor: Maybe. I'll decide that later.
Harry: Okay. I'll get the figures. Will you let me know what you decide?
Supervisor: Yes, I will.

Conversation 2:

Supervisor: Harry, is your inventory in the parts room within standard?
Harry: Right on the mark!
Supervisor: We are getting too good. Maybe you should be thinking about a new standard level.
Harry: Why? What's wrong with the present one?
Supervisor: Nothing—unless you can find a way of having it make us more money by a quicker turnover. Do you think you can?
Harry: I'll try. Let me think about it.

FIGURE 5–8   Ten Guides to Effective Job Instructions

1. Come straight to the point. This is the best way to get a person's attention.
2. Show how the order is for the employee's own (and the company's) benefit. This will arouse interest and bring about cooperation.
3. Don't order—ask. An employee will be in a better frame of mind if you say, "Could you do it this way," instead of a direct "Do it this way."
4. Know the employee and tailor your instructions to him or her. Have the employee do only what you know he or she can do.
5. Word instructions clearly, briefly, and simply.
6. Include all the essential information he or she will need.
7. Don't say the order comes from above—give the order or instructions as your own.
8. If instructions are rather complex or contain a great many details or figures, put them down in writing.
9. Keep in mind that instructions should be easy to read and easy to remember.
10. After giving the instructions, make sure the employee knows what he or she is supposed to do. One way to do this is ask that the essence of the instructions be repeated. At the same time, ask if he or she has any questions or is unclear as to what is expected.

Source: "Why Management Training Fails and How to Make It Succeed" by Kenneth H. Recknagel. Quoted with permission *Personnel Journal* copyright August 1974.

Giving "Orders" Is a Communication Art

Giving job instructions or "orders" should be done properly to get the most out of the process. Giving instructions properly entails using a great many of the communications principles that we've talked about in this chapter. Figure 5–8 summarizes ten guidelines for issuing job instructions that will get effective performance from your employees.

SUMMARY AND CONCLUSIONS

"Failure to communicate" is high on the list of supervisory problems. However, it seems more likely that poor supervision *causes* poor communication than the other way around. Communication in work organizations is reduced by such organizational features as the hierarchy, rules, specialization, and control. Only 20 to 30 percent of the information transmitted down the organization gets to the bottom. Much of what is lost is screened out as managers and supervisors exercise their "gate-keeping" function. Yet without some screening of the amount of information sent down the line, information overload can result. Supervisors can increase upward communication by following an "open door" policy, using grievance procedures, employee participation in decision making, and exit interviews.

The grapevine is inevitable and hums loudest when information that people want or need isn't being supplied. The supervisor should *not* use the grapevine to send important information to the employees.

Whether face-to-face, telephone, or written communication is most appropriate for a supervisor depends on the situation. Studies have shown that whether written or face-to-face communication is used in a particular situation depends on the information being transmitted.

Interpersonal communication in organizations is riddled with problems, including those caused by the hierarchy itself, by status or power position, the credibility of the sender, selective hearing, different meanings attached to the same words, emotions, attitudes, physical limitations, uncommon word usage, and body language. Listening, empathizing, avoiding prejudging, using feedback, avoiding defensiveness, and repeating things help overcome these problems.

Counseling and exit interviewing skills can be very useful for supervisors. Preparing for and doing an interview requires understanding certain key points. A checklist is provided as a reminder of these considerations. Counseling and exit interviews lend themselves well to use of the nondirective interviewing style. Exit interviews are usually best done by someone *other* than the immediate supervisor.

There are benefits to poor communication for certain people. Realizing this helps dispel the myth that "if only we could communicate with each other all our problems would be solved." Careful communication can be used to encourage responsibility in subordinates. Giving job instructions or "orders" requires some attention to detail and technique for the supervisor.

QUESTIONS

1. Why should a supervisor be concerned about communication? Can good communication solve all supervisory problems?
2. Identify several bits of information that are likely to fall out as new five-year plans for a company are passed down the line.
3. Why does "upward" communication tend to get so filtered as it goes up the line?
4. A fellow supervisor has some big problems and you think she's trying to implicate you as well. How should your communication in this situation be handled?
5. How do your values and attitudes relate to your ability to encode and decode?
6. Which interpersonal communications problems have you seen the most often? Give an example.
7. Practice nondirective interviewing with a friend in casual conversation.

Did the reflective questioning result in that person's doing a lot of talking?

8. Under what conditions are you likely *not* to want to have an employee repeat job instructions?

THE CASE OF THE BOSS
WHO COULD COMMUNICATE

Mary MacMillan is probably the best boss I've ever had. She's very interested in me as a person and in helping me to develop more fully in my job. She shares her knowledge with the staff and she encourages all of us to study and provide good service to our patients. She certainly is willing to criticize, but she does it in a very productive way and she gives praise when praise is due. Before criticizing, she asks us why something was done in a specific manner; if she feels it's wrong, she shares her reasoning with us.

She's very good at communicating our needs to the higher administration and demanding action when it's warranted. She seems to be respected by upper administration, and as a result she usually knows what's going on up the line as well. She isn't perfect—she makes mistakes, too, but she's willing to acknowledge her own errors and attempts to correct the situation. I feel free to talk to her when problems arise and I know she feels free to talk to everyone in the unit.

When she has something for us to do, she doesn't "order," she asks. Yet it's clear that the things have to be done, so no one questions her authority to specify a course of action.

---

1. What communications techniques has this successful supervisor used?

NOTES

[1] R. R. Blake and J. S. Mouton, *Corporate Excellence Through Grid Development* (Houston, Texas: Gulf Publishing Co., 1968), p. 4.

[2] Ibid., pp. 3–5.

[3] E. Walton, "Levels of Information, Misinformation and Uninformation in a Large Organization," *The Personnel Administrator,* October 1975, pp. 24–25.

[4] J. N. Smith, "Operation Speak-Easy, an Experiment in Communication," *Management Review,* March 1973, pp. 46–50.

[5] Reprinted, by permission of the publisher, from "Letting the Employee Speak His Mind," by W. I. Imberman, *Personnel,* November–December 1976, © 1976 by AMACOM, a division of American Management Associations, page 13. All rights reserved.

[6] B. Harriman, "Up and Down the Communications Ladder," *Harvard Business Review,* September–October 1974, p. 144.

[7] R. G. Nicholls, "Listening is Good Business," *Management of Personnel Quarterly,* Winter 1962, p. 4.

SUPERVISING HUMAN RESOURCES

section two

In this section, we treat in detail many of the tools and techniques a supervisor will need in order to supervise subordinates successfully on a day-to-
day basis. From hiring through firing, and all the points in between, we
consider the best techniques for supervising human resources in work organizations.

The Supervisor and the Staffing Process

SUPERVISORY PROBLEMS

How does the organization go about getting people, and how does the supervisor fit into this process?

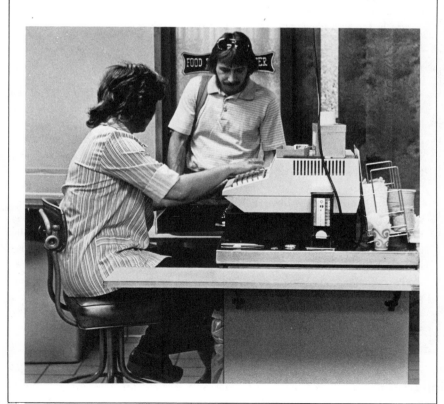

LEARNING OBJECTIVES

When you have finished this chapter, you should be able to

1. Describe the staffing process
2. Indicate the key components of the person-job match
3. Identify the personnel department—supervisor interface
4. List the steps in a comprehensive selection process
5. Describe the rationale behind a good application blank
6. List the types of employment tests and uses of each
7. Discuss the reliability and predictive validity of the typical selection interview
8. Recommend how to (a) plan a selection interview, (b) select questions to use in the interview, and (c) conduct an interview

THE STAFFING PROBLEM

Art Collins supervises a U.S. Fish and Wildlife station. Staffing his three biologist positions is a major problem. These jobs require a college degree in the biological sciences; however, a major portion of the biologist's duties can be performed by a physically strong high-school dropout. In other words, a significant part of the job physically involves manual labor. For this reason, job incumbents typically become dissatisfied in a few months to a year.

Another problem involves a particular biologist, Nancy Carson. Each summer several temporary employees are hired to assist the biologists. They are college students majoring in the biological sciences who are usually interested in a career in the Fish and Wildlife Service or a state game and fish agency. Nancy is unable to supervise these temporary employees effectively. Somehow she manages to make discipline problems out of good employees by the end of the summer. Also, it is typical for those under her supervision to decide against a career in this field after a few months. The same is not true of those working for the other biologists.

Art Collins' problems are not that unusual, particularly for those supervising employees with training and education beyond the high school level. An understanding of the staffing function can help Art and all other supervisors deal with this type of problem.

The success of any organization depends in large part on the nature of its personnel, who must possess the necessary skills, abilities, and motivation to work. It is very common for employee handbooks to preface their rules and regulations section with a sentiment to the effect that "our employees are this organization's most important asset. While our physical resources can be replaced in a relatively short period of time, it takes years and years to develop an effective work force."

THE STAFFING PROCESS

Staffing is the process of matching the skills of an organization's work force with the requirements of the organization's jobs. *External staffing* is recruiting employees from outside the organization, while *internal staffing* draws on current employees for more advanced or specialized positions.

External Staffing

Figure 6–1 describes the parts of a staffing process. Albright discusses the staffing process in detail.[1] The beginning of the process is personnel planning and forecasting. In this phase, the organization forecasts both the supply of current personnel and its needs for people with various skill and knowledge levels. A comparison of these two figures will show how many additional people are needed for each job classification.

Next in the process is recruiting. In this phase the organization attempts to attract job applicants. Activities involved in the recruiting phase are advertising, visits to schools, encouraging employee referrals, and contacting both public and private employment agencies.

The next step is selection from among job applicants. An important part of the selection phase is job analysis. It is by means of job analysis that one identifies the traits, experience, training, and education that are needed to perform a job satisfactorily. The activities involved in the selection process include interviews, analysis of application blanks, testing, checking of references, and physical examinations.

After enough information has been gathered, a decision can be made to hire or not to hire an individual. If the decision is not to hire, the recruitment process continues. If an individual is hired, management must decide where that individual will be placed, how orientation will proceed, and what on-the-job training will involve. Most supervisors

FIGURE 6–1   The Staffing Process

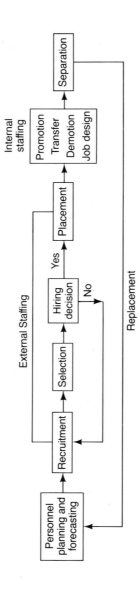

Source: Adapted from L. E. Albright, "Staffing Policies and Strategies," in *ASPA Handbook of Personnel and Industrial Relations: Staffing Policies and Strategies*, Vol. I, ed. D. Yoder and H. G. Heneman, Jr. (Washington, D.C.: Bureau of National Affairs, 1974), p. 4–3.

play a critical role in this phase, because orientation and training for the initial assignment are usually the responsibility of supervisors.

Internal Staffing

What we have described so far is often thought of as the entire staffing process. However, we should recognize that even after someone has been employed with an organization for a number of years, job retraining and interdepartmental transfers are common. Decisions about promotion, demotion, and transfer, as well as redesign of jobs to better fit an employee's abilities and interests, are all part of internal staffing. In each of these decisions, the supervisor plays a key role through performance appraisals and estimates of an employee's promotability. Also, with job changes, the supervisor is in charge of orientation and retraining, just as with new hires.

The final phase of the process is separation from the organization— by retirement, death or disability, or by resignation or dismissal. When an employee separates from an organization, the process begins again.

MATCHING THE PERSON AND THE JOB

Whether we are talking about selecting a new employee or the decision to promote, transfer, or demote a current employee, there is a common concern with finding the right person for the job. The theory of work adjustment describes the key considerations to keep in mind in the person-job match (see Figure 6–2).[2] The left side of the figure indicates that for any individual there is a set of abilities and skills. Every individual also has a particular "need set": things that person wants to obtain or satisfy by having a job.

In addition, each job has a particular set of ability requirements and rewards associated with it. *Job descriptions* not only specify the day-to-day tasks of jobholders, they should also include such things as general responsibilities, supervision received, machines and equipment used, and working conditions. *Job specifications* are an outgrowth of job descriptions. They list the key qualifications necessary to perform the job satisfactorily—education, experience, skill requirements, personal requirements, and mental and physical requirements. While the job description outlines the work to be done, the job specification describes the person necessary to fill the job.

The supervisor usually participates in the preparation of job descriptions for the various jobs in his or her unit. Of course, job descriptions

FIGURE 6–2   The Person-Job Match

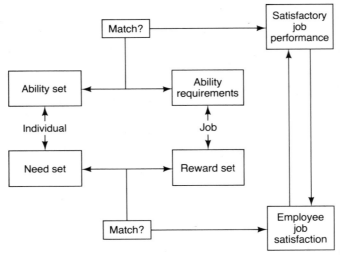

Source: Adapted from R. V. Davis, G. W. England, and L. H. Lofquist, *A Theory of Work Adjustment* (Minneapolis: Industrial Relations Center, University of Minnesota, Bulletin 38, January 1964), p. 6.

and specifications must be kept up to date. This is not always an easy task in industries with a rapidly changing technology.

Matching the person and the job can be easier if good job descriptions and specifications are available. Prospective employees should be made aware of all job duties so that expectations can be met and disappointments avoided. The case presented in Block 6–1 is probably not too uncommon.

Key Questions

For any job there is both a particular set of skills required to perform it and a particular set of rewards that result from it. The key questions are:

1. Does the ability set of the individual match the ability requirements of the job? If this is the case, then we can say that the individual has the potential to perform the job satisfactorily.
2. Does the individual's need set match the rewards available from the job? If this match takes place, then we can reasonably expect that the individual will be satisfied with the job.

Superior Products Company has recently hired a new assistant, Virginia Smith. Virginia just completed a two-year certificate program in mid-management at Jackson County Community College. Frederick Mills, the personnel supervisor, was extremely pleased to find someone who had some familiarity with basic management concepts since he was the entire personnel department except for a clerk-typist. During the interview, Frederick emphasized that he planned to have Virginia function as his assistant and she would be doing some interviewing and be responsible for maintaining employee records. Because Superior has about 300 employees, Frederick had been too busy to prepare anything resembling a job description except for some scrawled notes on the back of an envelope.

Everything went fine during the first week for Virginia. On Monday of the second week, Frederick called her into his office and explained that there was another minor duty that he had not mentioned to her. Frederick said, "In order to get approval to hire you from the president, I had to agree that whoever was hired would be the relief receptionist from 11:30 to 12:30 every day. The switchboard is usually quite busy and we wanted to be sure someone who is capable would be the backup." Virginia was not very happy about this assignment being sprung on her, but she agreed to try it for a while. Within two weeks she was beginning to dread having to work the switchboard an hour every day. Also, she discovered that she was expected to be the relief if the receptionist was sick or unable to work. On Wednesday and Thursday of the third week the regular receptionist was sick and Virginia filled in for her. On that Friday Virginia told Frederick she was quitting in two weeks. When asked why, Virginia replied, "You misrepresented the job to me. You never said anything about my receptionist duties. If you had, I probably would not have taken the job."

In Figure 6–2 there are lines between the "satisfactory job performance" cell and the "employee job satisfaction" cell. These lines reflect the idea that if an individual is satisfied with his or her job it may have an effect on that person's job performance. On the other hand, as was suggested in the chapter on motivation, the organization can attempt to make the receipt of rewards dependent on satisfactory job performance. If this is the case, we would expect a strong relationship between satisfactory job performance and employee job satisfaction.

FIGURE 6–3   The Personnel Department–Supervisor Interface

Personnel Department	*Supervisor*
Provides recruitment and initial screening of both internal and external applicants	Requests employees with certain qualifications and characteristics
Evaluates the staffing process	Provides information for the evaluation of the staffing process
	Makes final hiring/placement decisions

THE PERSONNEL-SUPERVISOR INTERFACE

Figure 6–3 shows a common split of staffing duties between the supervisor and the personnel department. The personnel unit provides the expertise to assist in the staffing process. The supervisor, on the other hand, is the key source of information concerning the qualifications and characteristics necessary for the job. In addition, supervisors' experience with specific employees over the long run enables them to pass judgment on the effectiveness of selection procedures. Finally, the supervisor should have the final say in making the decision to hire a particular individual, or if the person is already an employee of the organization, in making the decision to promote, transfer, or demote a particular individual to a particular position.

EQUAL EMPLOYMENT OPPORTUNITY STAFFING AND THE SUPERVISOR

Recent legislation concerning civil rights and discrimination has had an impact on the role of the supervisor in the staffing process. Generally, the impact has been to *reduce* the control an individual supervisor has over the staffing process. This is because organizations have had to demonstrate fairness in hiring and promotion decisions. To reduce the possibility of bias in such decisions, the supervisor's independence has been reduced and the power of the personnel unit has increased. The implications and effect of civil rights legislation are discussed in Chapter 17. However, the reader should keep in mind during the present discussion that a great deal of what happens in the staffing process is affected by this legislation.

The Hiring Process

The typical sequence of steps in the hiring process may vary somewhat from one organization to another. But the following sequence is common:

Initial
Screening
$\left\{\begin{array}{l}\end{array}\right.$
1. Recruitment of applicants
2. Reception and preliminary interview
3. Completion of application blank
4. Completion of employment tests
5. Interview with employment specialist
6. Reference checks

Final
Screening
$\left\{\begin{array}{l}\end{array}\right.$
7. Preliminary hiring decision by personnel department
8. Interview with supervisor
9. Final hiring decision by supervisor
10. Physical examination
11. Job placement

Recruiting

After receiving a request to fill a particular job (assuming that someone is not available internally), the first step in the selection process is to engage in a recruiting effort. The objective of the recruiting effort is to generate several applicants for the job opening. The form of the recruiting effort will vary depending on the nature of the position. It could be as simple as putting up a sign by the firm's main entrance indicating that applications are being taken for the particular job or placing an ad in local newspapers or trade journals. Other sources of potential employees include the state employment service and various schools and specialized training institutions.

Initial Screening

The first phase in the screening process by the personnel department is a preliminary consideration of the candidates. A judgment is made whether the applicant is obviously unqualified for employment by the organization. Essentially, what goes on in the selection process is a series of decisions which can be viewed as successive hurdles. At each step in the process, the decision maker, either the personnel unit or the supervisor, decides if the applicant should be rejected or if additional information is needed.

After the initial interview, the applicant is asked to complete an application blank. Then there may be various employment tests, followed by an interview with an employment specialist. Assuming satisfactory test scores and a successful second interview, the next step is to investigate the applicant's previous work history. This involves contacting previous employers. They would be asked about the individual's work habits, job performance, and other information which would aid the organization in making the hiring decision. At this point, the personnel department may make a preliminary decision to hire the applicant.

Final Screening

It is often best if the personnel department plays an advisory role in the selection decision. The *final* decision to hire an applicant should be reserved for the supervisor for whom the applicant will be working. Several purposes are served by reserving this decision for the immediate supervisor. The immediate supervisor is more familiar with the job in question and should be better able to judge whether the applicant has the necessary expertise for performing the job. Another factor is that the supervisor is really the only one who can judge whether the applicant and supervisor will be able to work together. Admittedly, one must guard against bias entering into the decision at this point.

Another advantage of allowing the immediate supervisor to make the final decision is that by doing so the supervisor has a stake in the success of the new employee. The supervisor can be expected to put a little more effort into seeing that the new employee is a success.

The typical employment process also involves a physical examination. This is particularly true for jobs involving manual labor and for older applicants. Since most organizations have life insurance and health care programs, they seek to avoid hiring individuals in poor health because of the long-term costs that can result.

Evaluation of the Staffing Process

Predictive Validity

A central idea in the staffing process is the "predictive validity" of the information used in making a decision to hire or promote an individual. In all staffing decisions, whether it is hiring a new individual or promoting someone, the key question is whether or not the individual will be successful in the position.

The reason for completing an application blank and an employment test, and for conducting interviews, is to gather information to help in predicting if a person will be successful in the job. If that information does not separate the good performers from the poor performers, it does not have predictive validity. To state the definition positively, predictive validity is the extent to which a piece of information gathered in the selection process accurately predicts success on the job. Block 6–2 shows the predictive validity of *educational background* for two different jobs.

We would say that *level of education* has predictive validity for Job A but not for Job B. Information such as that presented in Block 6–2 highlights the teamwork necessary between the personnel department and supervisors for an effective staffing system. *Supervisors* judge whether employees are successful in any particular position, and personnel usually centralizes the information and does the analysis.

Job A: Valid		Job B: Not Valid	
Education	Percent Successful	Education	Percent Successful
High school graduates	75%	High school graduates	60%
Less than high school education	45%	Less than high school education	58%

Joe North supervises a day shift of the filler section at the American Cereal Company plant in Midville. Joe recently pulled together some figures on the good performers on his shift. Joe had always thought that more education was better. The figures concerning one of the jobs he supervised (Job A) seemed to show this was true, but for another job (Job B), education didn't seem to make any difference. Joe decided he had better change the way he was making hiring decisions. For Job A, he would continue to require a high school diploma, but for Job B he would eliminate this requirement.

Reliability

In making employment decisions about candidates it is essential to have *reliable* information. For example, in Block 6–2, the background information of the employees was level of education. By contacting the schools each of the applicants attended, you should be able to obtain reliable information on their educational accomplishments. However, some information is not so easily verified—for example, absenteeism in previous jobs. You could ask on an application blank how often the applicant missed work at his or her previous job, but there is no guarantee that the applicant will answer honestly. Another alternative is to contact the applicant's former employers, who may or may not answer your request.

METHODS OF GATHERING INFORMATION
FROM APPLICANTS

Three methods are used to gather information in the typical employment process. They are the application blank, the interview, and employment tests.

Application Blank

The application blank is usually a series of questions in which the applicant is asked to report prior experience and training. Applicants sometimes distort information reported on an application blank. Research focusing on the accuracy of information provided on an application blank has found that the tendency is for applicants to overstate or embellish answers to questions about previous jobs.

For example, it is common to overstate both the wage received at previous jobs and the difficulty or level of responsibility of the position. Also, applicants tend to "modify" the reasons for leaving previous employment. Because of this tendency of candidates to embellish previous work experiences, it is particularly important to take the time to contact former employers to verify the data given on the application blank.

Past Behavior Predicts Future Behavior

The information gathered on an application blank focuses on previous job performance and previous experience. The main reason for getting this information is that past job performance is usually the best predictor of future job performance. For example, in checking an individual's work record, you may find that a particular candidate has never held a job more than three months. While it may be true that the applicant has finally settled down and has seen the importance of steady employment, the odds are that he or she will not hold your job long either.

Employment Tests

There are three basic categories of employment tests that could be used in making hiring and promotion decisions: aptitude tests, achievement or skill tests, and personality or interest tests. Each category attempts to measure a different applicant characteristic. An *aptitude test* attempts to determine if the applicant has the potential to acquire skills and expertise in a particular job. For example, one aptitude test is a test of finger and hand dexterity. Such a test might be particularly valuable in identifying those candidates who will be able to perform an assembly job in a satisfactory manner. Another kind is a number or math aptitude test. Such a test might be useful in identifying those individuals who would work out well in a job involving counting money or keeping books.

The second category of test, *achievement* or *skill tests,* assumes that the applicant already has training or experience in the job. The objective of this test is not to determine trainability but rather an individual's current skill or level of achievement in the job. For example, assume you are interviewing candidates for a job involving the use of electric welders and an applicant claims to be able to use an electric welder. An achievement test appropriate for this situation would be to provide the individual with the welder and the proper safety equipment and have him or her weld two pieces of metal together.

Achievement tests can take two different forms. They can be paper-and-pencil tests in which individuals attempt to demonstrate their knowledge of a particular field of work. Another achievement or skill test is called a *job sample* test. The welder applicant example would be a job sample test. As the label implies, in this kind of achievement test, the applicant is asked to perform a sample of the behaviors required on the job. Typing and shorthand tests are commonly used job sample tests. Job sample tests have the best possibility of high predictive validity.

The third type of test, *personality* and *interest measures,* attempts to identify the nature of an individual's needs and interests. When an organization is aware of potential employees' needs and interests, it can better judge whether those individuals will be satisfied by the set of rewards associated with a particular job.

The Selection Interview

This is the most commonly used technique for gathering information about applicants. Both supervisors and personnel specialists may be involved in selection interviewing. There are many purposes served by the selection interview. One use is to sell the organization to the candidate. Another purpose is a public relations function. Even when an applicant is rejected by an organization, if he or she has spoken to someone face to face about the job and about the organization, the applicant is likely to have a better feeling about the organization than if there were no interview. Also, the interview can be used as a selection tool. It can be a means of gathering information to use in making the hiring decision or, if the individual is already in the organization, the promotion or transfer decision.

Finally, the interview can be used to give applicants a realistic job preview.[3] This means that the negative aspects of the job are pointed out as well as the positive features. Block 6–3 represents this approach to hiring.

While this is only a hypothetical example, studies show that when applicants are given a clear picture of the job, turnover is lower and job satisfaction is higher. Of course, this use of the interview may run

Ann House supervises the Wonder Cosmetics sales force in Clearview. An assertive person with an ability to talk to strangers could do well financially selling Wonder Cosmetics. The job consists of knocking on doors and trying to interest women in buying Wonder Cosmetics. The company sent new hires to a five-day training course. During this period and the first two weeks of working his or her territory, a new hire was on salary. After that it was straight commission.

Voluntary quits during the first two weeks of selling had been high. The main reason was that some people don't like getting the door "slammed" in their face.

To provide a better idea of what an applicant was getting into, Ann added a new step to the screening process. Each applicant was told that part of the process was to role play contacting a customer. Ann's secretary played the customer. Applicants role played two contacts. During the first one, things went smoothly and the "customer" bought something. During the second contact, Ann's secretary told the applicant in very clear terms that she didn't like door-to-door peddlers.

Ann would then explain the purpose of the "customer contacts." Some applicants dropped out of the hiring process at this point. Others would call in one or two days later and say they didn't think they would like this work.

The number of applicants considered went up as a result of adding this step. However, turnover among those hired dropped significantly.

counter to "selling the organization" and can often be replaced by adequate job descriptions.

Studies on the Selection Interview

In this section we will refer to "the interviewer." You should keep in mind that this label is synonymous with "the supervisor" as far as the selection interview is concerned.

The selection interview typically has poor reliability and predictive validity. The following generalizations seem to hold:

1. *Reliability of interviewer judgments.* There is a good deal of evidence to indicate that an individual interviewer will be consistent in a series of evaluations of the same individual. Let's label that type of reliability "intra-interviewer reliability." On the other hand, there is also a great

deal of evidence that when different interviewers evaluate the same individual, they tend to arrive at different evaluations. Label this type of reliability "inter-interviewer reliability."

Since the applicants didn't change significantly over the course of these studies, we are forced to conclude that while an individual interviewer may be consistent within himself or herself, different interviewers will arrive at different evaluations of a single candidate.

2. *Predictive validity of interviewer judgments.* Recall the concepts of reliability and validity. We said that reliability, or consistency in evaluation of candidates, is critical for making successful employment decisions. In view of the findings concerning inter-interviewer reliability, it is not surprising that research typically finds selection interviews to have poor predictive validity. To put this in other terms, generally it has been found that interviewers are not able to predict who will be successful on the job!

It has been shown, however, that a patterned or structured interview will yield satisfactory levels of reliability and predictive validity. This type of interview is characterized by a planned set of questions that each applicant is asked.

The Interviewer Decision Process

The decision-making process of selection interviews has been carefully studied.[4] It seems that most interviewers make a tentative accept or reject decision early in the interview before even asking all of the questions on their list. After this initial decision is made, apparently the remainder of the interview is spent searching for information to reinforce that tentative decision.

Interviewers must be aware of this tendency and guard against it. Supervisors who conduct selection interviews infrequently are probably more guilty of this mistake than are full-time interviewers. A conscious decision to refrain from decision making until all of the information is gathered can help prevent the supervisor from falling into this trap.

Recommendations for Conducting a Selection Interview

We all think of ourselves as good judges of character. It is only natural, then, to assume that we can easily be effective interviewers and can use information gathered in an interview to make good staffing decisions. However, research on the selection interview demonstrates over and over that this is simply *not true*. People are effective interviewers when they work at it. The following are some factors to keep in mind when one is going to be conducting employment interviews.

Plan the Interview

Keep in mind that the whole purpose of the interview is to decide which candidate will be the best match with the job. The employee-job match decision should take into consideration both the candidate's abilities and skills relative to the ability requirements of the job *and* the person's needs relative to the rewards associated with the job.

Before conducting an interview or a series of interviews, you should review both the job description and the specifications a qualified candidate should demonstrate—that is, the kinds of training and job experience that are relevant to the job. Also, identify the rewards that go with the job. Of course, without knowing an individual in depth, it is difficult to judge whether he or she will be satisfied with a particular job. A good technique is to provide the applicant with accurate information about the job and allow the person to make his or her own judgment.

Having completed this step, you should now review the application blanks of those applicants who will be interviewed, being careful to note areas which are not clear or incomplete. These would be topics that a supervisor should explore during the interview. Now you are ready to decide on the questions you will ask. These questions should be written out so that you not only know exactly *what* you are going to say but also *the order* in which you will ask them.

Watch Your Questions

Use open-ended questions. Open-ended questions are those that cannot be answered with a simple yes or no. Compare the following questions:

"Did you quit your last job?"
"Why did you leave your previous job?"

The second question is an open-ended question. In order to answer it, the applicant must give some sort of description. On the other hand, the first question can be answered with a simple yes or no. The open-ended question provides the interviewer with a great deal more information. Note that when the first question is answered, the interviewer still does not know why the applicant left the previous job.

The following is a list of words that would fit in with an open-ended question approach:

"Tell me about . . ."
"Why . . ."
"What . . ."
"When . . ."
"Who . . ."

Avoid leading questions. A leading question is one that suggests the desired answer. For example, if the position you want to fill involves a lot of contact with the public, questions such as the following would be leading questions:

"You do like to talk to people, don't you?"
"You do enjoy meeting people, don't you?"

Such questions make it obvious to the applicant what *should* be said in order to make the best possible impression. These questions might be rephrased as follows:

"Describe how you feel when you are in a situation that involves meeting strangers."
"Describe how you feel when you are in a situation in which you have to talk to people you don't know."

Avoid questions that can rarely be expected to elicit a negative or unfavorable answer. For example, "How did you get along with your supervisor or co-workers on your last job?" or "How often were you absent or tardy?" Asking questions such as these will almost always result in the candidate's presenting a more favorable description than is really justified. If such information is critical to the employment decision, we recommend that you rely on contacts with previous employers to gather this information.

Avoid illegal questions. Questions which discriminate on the basis of race, religion, sex, or national origin are prohibited. The kinds of questions that are prohibited as a result of civil rights legislation go far beyond items that focus directly on these characteristics. A detailed discussion of those questions to avoid in the employment interview is presented in the chapter on equal employment opportunity (Chapter 17).

Avoid questions seeking redundant information. When planning the interview, you typically have access to the application blank. Therefore, you should avoid redundant questioning that will merely make the applicant unfriendly or hostile.

If you do want more information about something that is covered on the application blank, we recommend using a lead-in phrase such as:

"Tell me more about . . ." In other words, make apparent to the applicant that all the information needed is *not* on the application blank and you wish further information or clarification.

Conducting the Interview

Establish a friendly atmosphere. At the beginning of the selection interview, it is important to establish a friendly atmosphere. The first couple of minutes of an interview could be devoted to such small talk items as current sports events, comments on the weather, or an event that happened on your way to the office. You might start off by asking the applicant, "How do you wish to be called?" The key point is to set a friendly tone for the interview or at least to avoid creating a stress interview situation.

Avoid interruptions. For the sake of your own concentration and to demonstrate personal interest in a potential employee, it is particularly important that the interview not be interrupted. This means arranging for a room which is free from noises and other distractions. Do not receive phone calls or other callers during the interview.

Avoid inappropriate listening responses. You should also be careful to avoid the use of improper listening responses. Listening responses such as constant nodding or overuse of such phrases as "Oh yes" and "I understand" serve as cues to the applicant to expand or continue on the line of discussion that immediately preceded the feedback. In this way, extraneous information becomes part of the interview and can easily distort the image presented by the applicant.

Beware of early bias. As outlined earlier, interviewers tend to reach a tentative decision early in the interview. Be aware of this tendency and try to keep an open mind during the interview.

Watch out for halo error. This occurs when one characteristic or piece of information about the applicant affects your judgment or evaluation of other characteristics. For example, studies have demonstrated that when the interviewer is from a small town, applicants from small towns tend to be rated more acceptable than those from cities. Most people are especially susceptible to halo error, but an awareness of this tendency will hopefully help you remain objective in evaluating the fitness of an applicant.

Control the interview. Someone *will* take charge of the interview. If it is not you then it will be the applicant. When you have decided on the questions to be asked and how to phrase them, you will have little trouble in controlling the interview. Here the key is following through on a well-thought-out strategy.

SUMMARY AND CONCLUSIONS

The staffing process can be divided into two components, external staffing and internal staffing. The first concerns recruiting and hiring new employees. The second concerns the promotion, transfer, and demotion of current employees.

Whether one is involved in external or internal staffing, the objective is the same: To try to ensure a job match that

1. Coordinates the individual's abilities and skills with the requirements of the job, and
2. Relates the individual's needs and interests to the reward set associated with the job.

Ideally the personnel department and the supervisor complement each other in the staffing process. Personnel provides the special expertise for staffing, and supervisors provide the detailed knowledge that permits a job description and specifications to be drawn up. In addition, the supervisor provides feedback in the form of employee performance appraisals necessary for an evaluation of the staffing process.

We recommend that the personnel department perform a preliminary screening function in the selection process. The final hiring decision (or, in the case of current employees, transfer decision) should be left to the immediate supervisor.

The supervisor will almost certainly use the interview in screening applicants. Supervisors should recognize that the interview lacks reliability and validity unless used properly. We recommend the structured or patterned selection interview. This approach requires the supervisor to decide in advance what information is to be gathered and how it can best be done. Both the manner of questioning and the site of the interview should be controlled in order to ensure reliable and valid judgments of applicants.

QUESTIONS

1. Contrast the external staffing process and the internal staffing process.
2. Why should the supervisor have the final staffing decision concerning jobs under his or her supervision?
3. What role does the supervisor serve in the evaluation of the staffing process?
4. Define reliability and predictive validity.
5. Discuss why reference checks are useful.
6. Describe how to plan a selection interview.

135

7. List and discuss factors to be kept in mind when deciding how to phrase questions to ask during an interview.
8. List and discuss factors to consider when conducting an interview.

THE ANSWERING SERVICE

You supervise the phone operators at Friendly Answering Service (FAS). The basic task of a phone operator is to take messages for clients of FAS. A pleasant voice and the ability to remember and record readable messages, names, and phone numbers are the key skills.

Turnover among newly hired phone operators is high. The reason is that many calls are from dissatisfied customers of FAS clients. Even when a FAS operator explains that he or she is with an answering service, many callers take out their anger on the operators. This abuse is uncalled for, but it goes with the job.

---

1. How would you go about identifying the key skills necessary for this job?
2. Recommend ways to cut turnover among new phone operators.

NOTES

1 L. E. Albright, "Staffing Policies and Strategies," in *ASPA Handbook of Personnel and Industrial Relations: Staffing Policies and Strategies,* Vol. I, ed. D. Yoder and H. G. Heneman, Jr. (Washington, D.C.: Bureau of National Affairs, 1974), pp. 4-1 through 4-34.

2 R. V. Davis, G. W. England, and L. H. Lofquist, *A Theory of Work Adjustment,* (Minneapolis: Industrial Relations Center, University of Minnesota, Bulletin 38, January 1964).

3 J. P. Wanous, "Tell It Like It Is at Realistic Job Previews," *Personnel, 52* (July–August 1975), pp. 50–60.

4 E. C. Webster, *Decision Making in the Employment Interview* (Montreal, Quebec: Industrial Relations Centre, McGill University, 1964).

The Supervisor as Trainer

SUPERVISORY PROBLEMS

What does the supervisor need to know about training to be effective?

How can this knowledge be applied to the job?

LEARNING OBJECTIVES

When you have finished this chapter, you should be able to

1. Explain what role training plays in the supervisor's job
2. List and identify the three basic steps for successful coaching
3. From a list, discuss each of the "principles" of learning
4. Describe the training process
5. Teach someone about the major issues in orientation
6. Contrast lecture and programmed instruction as training methods

AN ACCOUNTING SUPERVISOR
WITH A TRAINING PROBLEM

To keep up with its steadily expanding business, Acme Freight has had to add many new employees to its accounting department over the last five years. Turnover has not been especially high, but lately a major problem has arisen. New employees are faced with learning large amounts of information about company policy and office procedures, and many mistakes are suddenly being discovered at the administrative level.

Helen Williams, the accounting supervisor, has just come back from a meeting with her boss. At that meeting, her boss made it quite clear that these mistakes are unacceptable. A number of the reports that upper management uses for making decisions have been just plain wrong. Further, a great deal of unnecessary time and money has been spent in correcting the mistakes. Helen has traced a number of these mistakes and finds that almost all of them are attributable to employees with less than one year service.

It seems clear to Helen that a training program of some sort is necessary. The accounting department has traditionally relied almost exclusively on on-the-job training. It doesn't seem to have worked. Helen's problem is threefold: to determine exactly *what* the training program should cover, *how* it should be implemented, and *who* should do it. She is also concerned about evaluating the program once it has been implemented without simply waiting for errors to occur to test its effectiveness.

Probably the most important thing for a supervisor to realize about training is that it is going to happen whether the supervisor takes an active role or not. Employees *are going to* learn. *What* they learn may not be what management wants them to learn and it may even be incorrect, but they will learn ways of doing the job and of getting along in the organization.

Second, every supervisor plays a role in employee training, even though this may be totally unconscious. One of the most effective learning methods is through observation of others' behavior. Therefore, a supervisor is training every day, all day, whether or not the supervisor is aware of it.

ORIENTATION

A special kind of training that is extremely important for supervisors is the orientation, or induction, of new employees. Even though the personnel department may be responsible for transmitting certain information, the supervisor has the major role in inducting a new employee into the work force.

Careful orientation is very important for two reasons. First, a high percentage of turnover and quits comes in the first few weeks that a person is on the job. This is often because new employees encounter situations for which they are unprepared and thus feel inadequate to do the job. Properly done, orientation helps the employee make the transition to the new work environment with greater ease.

The *second* reason that good orientation is essential rests on our earlier statement that, regardless of whether management formally trains its employees or not, they're *going to learn*. They will learn either correctly or incorrectly about the organization and about the job. It's much better to teach people the right way to do things initially than to go back and have them "unlearn" the wrong way. Block 7–1 illustrates the problems one company faced with their induction program. It represents common problems associated with orienting new employees.

Orienting a new employee is very important. Remember the first job you ever had and the adjustments that were necessary. Feelings of fear and anxiety are difficult to overcome even under the best of conditions, so that making the newcomer feel welcome is especially important. Greeting a new employee with "I didn't realize you were coming today" will almost surely create misgivings about the job and about the organization.

Starting Orientation

A good place to start an orientation program is by determining what the new employee needs to know *now*. There is real danger in giving a new employee too much information the first day or even the first week

Several major problem areas were identified when the orientation process at DEICO was studied. Most obvious was the fact that many first-line supervisors were not trained in inducting employees. They didn't understand what should be done and why it was important.

Second, many of the projects new people were assigned were meaningless jobs totally unrelated to the job descriptions they received during their interviews. Third, supervisors' expectations about employee performance were never clarified, and as a result, new employees were confused and frustrated about what they were to be doing. Related to this was a significant lack of feedback on job performance that left them floundering as to acceptable standards.

Finally, very little effort was made to bring the new employee into the existing work group. The person wasn't introduced to the work group, and was given very little information about peers or significant others in the department.

These problems had led to an extremely high turnover rate, especially during the first two weeks of employment. However, once an orientation program was introduced that included a checklist of things to be done and a training curriculum for supervisors, the new hire turnover rate dropped by 50 percent during the first year.

on the job. Informing the employee about the company's retirement plan, for example, may be wasted time and actually give rise to information overload, with the result that the employee forgets most of what has been communicated.

Three general categories of information should be covered by any orientation program, but not necessarily during one session:

1. Information on the normal work day
2. Information on the nature of the organization
3. The organization's policies, rules, and benefits

The Orientation Process

Figure 7–1 outlines a process the supervisor can use in inducting new employees.

Planning

First is proper planning for the new worker. Since first impressions usually have a lasting impact, the supervisor should be present when the new person arrives and have prepared an assignment for the new individual to do after induction. The supervisor should have reviewed

140

FIGURE 7–1   The Orientation Process

I. Planning for the new worker
    1. Ensure that supervisor is there when new person arrives
    2. Have work ready
    3. Look over resume
    4. Line up "sponsor" if needed
II. Short interview
    1. Establish friendly relations
    2. Answer questions
    3. Outline nature of work group
    4. Explain immediately relevant company policies and rules
III. Short tour
    1. Visit work place (and perhaps rest of the organization)
    2. Meet work group members
    3. Locate lunchroom, restrooms, parking areas, and so forth
IV. Introduction to the job
    1. Review the job
    2. Show work station and introduce to "sponsor"
    3. Begin training with cooperation of "sponsor"
V. Follow-up
    1. Check on progress each day for a week
    2. Check twice a week for the next month
    3. Do *not* fail to give performance reviews frequently for first year

the new employee's resume or job application blank, to become familiar with the new employee's strengths and weaknesses. If it is appropriate to have a sponsor or someone who will work closely with the new employee the first few days, that individual should be told about it beforehand and be made aware that the new employee is coming.

Interview

When the new employee arrives, the supervisor should have a short visit with the new employee and attempt to establish friendly relations from the start. The new employee should be given some information about the positive aspects of the work group and should have an opportunity to ask questions about material you may have omitted. Finally, the supervisor should cover those company policies and rules the new person might need immediately, such as no smoking areas, time permitted for lunch breaks, coffee breaks, and so on.

Short Tour

Next, a short tour is usually appropriate, including the immediate work area and, if time permits, a bird's eye view of the other departments. Then the new employee should have an opportunity to meet briefly with the rest of the work group members, on an individual basis if possible. Special emphasis on the location of the lunchroom, restrooms, parking areas, and so forth concludes the tour.

Introduction to the Job

Now it is time to go to work. The supervisor should review the job with the new employee before bringing him or her back to the work station or work area. At this time, the supervisor should introduce the individual to the "sponsor" who will assist in on-the-job training and be available to answer any questions that can be taken care of directly at the work station.

Follow-up

The final step in the orientation program is a systematic follow-up schedule. This entails checking daily on the progress the new employee is making for the first week and checking at least twice a week for the first month after that. The supervisor should remember to give frequent performance reviews to help the new employee understand what the supervisor expects and the way the job should be done. Both good performance and performance that needs improvement should be mentioned.

Checklist

Many organizations use a checklist to aid supervisors in reviewing what has been done, and what remains to be done, with each new employee. The supervisor can devise a checklist appropriate to his or her unit with the aid of current employees. Many times the personnel department will cover certain items, so that the supervisor should check with personnel to avoid any overlap.

Figure 7–2 shows an example of a simple orientation checklist for a supervisor. Although the figure is by no means comprehensive, it does suggest the *kinds* of things a supervisor might want to include in an orientation checklist. By systematizing the information that all employees receive, the supervisor can ensure equal opportunity for all and provide a fair basis for performance appraisal.

Orientation in Perspective

Perhaps the most useful way to think about employee orientation is as an opportunity for the employee to find reasons to stay with the organization. An employee who isn't properly oriented is much less

FIGURE 7–2   Orientation Checklist

Employee _____ Starting Date _____

First Day

Tour of work area	_____
Meet work group	_____
Tour of company	_____
Explain job	_____
Cover safety rules	_____
Working hours	_____
Pay policy	_____

End of First Week

Cover fringe benefits	_____
Cover vacation policy	_____
Emergency situations	_____
Follow-up on performance	_____

End of Second Week

Job posting	_____
Sick leave	_____
Discipline procedures	_____
Grievances	_____
Follow-up on performance	_____

Other Items:

_____
_____
_____
_____

likely to find reasons to stay with the job. Employees who go through their first week with negative feelings, confusion, mistrust of their supervisor and work group, and a high level of fear and anxiety will probably evidence little motivation to come back for the second week. Also, of course, these problems can very clearly affect the rate at which the employees learn their job.

TRAINING AND THE SUPERVISOR'S JOB

The opening case is not meant to suggest that on-the-job training cannot work. It can and does work. In fact, on-the-job training is the most common form of training found in organizations today and one that is used overwhelmingly by supervisors. However, because on-the-job training is so widely used, it is also the most widely *abused* kind of training.

Often a supervisor assumes that introducing a new employee to a worker who is skilled in a particular task and allowing that person to assume the responsibility of training will solve this problem. However, without an understanding of learning principles, there is no guarantee that a person can train another to do something.

For example, some of the most skilled athletes have been very poor coaches. They have been unable to teach those skills easily to other people. This may be because the skills came so easily and so naturally to them. Alternatively, some of the best and most famous coaches have not been particularly skilled athletes themselves. Being able to teach someone to do something and being able to do it yourself are not the same thing. Yet on-the-job training remains a major method of getting people trained. In this chapter, we will focus on the knowledge the supervisor needs to be a successful trainer or coach.

Examples of poor training or a lack of training in a supervisor's unit are relatively easy to spot. Errors, poor quality, large scrap loss, and general inefficiency may all be related to inappropriate or non-existent training.

Workers will often ask, "Since the supervisor has responsibility for training most employees in the work unit, shouldn't he or she be able to do the job better than anyone else?" No, not necessarily. Although the supervisor may have come up through the ranks and may have had experience on many of the jobs in the unit, it doesn't necessarily follow that he or she has expertise on a majority of the tasks. Like a successful athletic coach, however, the supervisor must be able to determine the best way for the new employee to get the training he or she needs. This often involves delegating the training responsibility to those who have both high skill levels and good communication ability. Coaching these people to train others is another aspect of the supervisor's job.

Supervisory Coaching

Coaching is one of the primary methods of on-the-job training. Unfortunately, many people who coach others in the "right way" to do a job aren't aware of the pitfalls of the coaching process. If a salesperson doesn't know the correct way to demonstrate a product, or a machine operator turns out items haphazardly and with numerous mistakes, some coaching may be needed. Coaching is simply well-planned communication.

Coaching Mistakes

There are several things that should be *avoided* when trying to coach a subordinate. For one thing, merely stressing the things that go well and failing to deal with the mistakes every learner makes isn't good coaching. Dealing with failures or inadequacies is not particularly pleasant, and, as supervisor, you may feel that to point out mistakes and negative occurrences on the job may make you less well liked. However, part of your job is to facilitate task accomplishment, so that if things go wrong, you must make people aware of the problems in a mature, rational way without making them feel stupid.

Another common mistake is to threaten people with punishment of some sort for continued mistakes. Since this behavior does not provide a plan or objectives for the subordinate to follow to improve, it is virtually useless. Also, constant criticism can result in the employee disliking the supervisor so much that they cannot work together.

Another common pitfall is for supervisors to assume that once a certain performance level has been reached, employees will be able to work through all the problems themselves. In many instances, even long-term employees will fail to recognize that a problem exists. It's an important part of the supervisor's job as trainer to point out problems and help suggest solutions.

Successful Coaching

Successful coaching consists of three basic steps. Careful attention to this procedure plus a conscious avoidance of the mistakes just mentioned should result in a measurable improvement in on-the-job training.

1. Observation. The supervisor doesn't attempt to guess what problems the subordinate is having. *Evidence* of problem areas, based on work samples, data, and so forth, is gathered during an observation period. This may require the supervisor to observe the subordinate on several occasions, to ask questions of co-workers, or to collect work samples. With inductees, the supervisor must be able to state clearly what the person knows and what he or she still *needs* to know.

2. Formal coaching session. Next, the supervisor meets with the subordinate in a formal coaching session to map out the employee's current position and where he or she ought to be. Begin by eliciting from the employee his or her feelings about the situation. This is very important because some aspects of the problem may surface of which you were unaware. Often you will be able to aid the subordinate by making some minor procedural changes in the situation.

Most supervisors are surprised at how often the subordinate's view of a problem is quite similar to theirs. During this coaching meeting, the supervisor should try to be as specific as possible about what is expected and where he or she sees the problems. The more you, as supervisor, can *quantify* your expectations, the more clearly you can communicate with the subordinate. If a supervisor feels that a salesperson should be able to sell five units a week, or that an operator ought to be able to do a specific job in 30 minutes, that should be made clear to the subordinate. The more you can quantify (or express in numbers) your expectations for the employee, the more accurate job of communicating you have done. When expectations have been made clear, the employee may need a demonstration of certain techniques or a practice and critique session. These and other specific learning techniques will be described later in the chapter.

3. Follow-up.   When you and the subordinate have reached a mutual agreement on what needs to be done, allow a reasonable period of time before following up to see how the employee is doing. It may be that you have still not identified the real problem or that another coaching session is necessary. Then again, perhaps the employee needs training from some other source. In any case, review or follow-up of the employee's development and training is essential for further progress to take place.

Remember, *people generally want to do a good job.* Effective training helps them do that good job. Training and the opportunity for continued personal development can be one of the most important pluses that a job offers. In fact, to ignore this basic human need for continued development, especially for professional people, can cause some problems. See Block 7-2 for a classic example.

The Wilson County Community Hospital situation shows how strongly many employees value the opportunity to learn more about their

---

BLOCK 7–2   Wilson County Community Hospital

As nursing supervisor at Wilson County Community Hospital, I constantly hear complaints about an administration that is viewed as hampering continued professional development. The administration does not advocate programs that help keep nurses up to date or allow them to advance in their field. They won't even allow us time off to attend continuing education programs of a day or two in length *on our own money.* There is a lot of disappointment and dissatisfaction, and many of the nurses are concerned about the level of professional competence they will be able to demonstrate if they stay at Wilson for more than a few years. They view the decrease in their current skill level as an important reason for not staying.

field or gain advanced training that will make them more valuable pro-
fessionally. In this case, the supervisor was hampered by a rigid hospital administrative policy. Puzzled by a high turnover rate among its
nurses, the administration did not even ask the supervisors for input as
to the nature of the problem.

TRAINING: DOING IT RIGHT

For some supervisors, it is difficult to learn the difference between
training others to do a job and doing the job oneself. The best supervisor is one who encourages subordinates to develop their talents fully,
even if that means outshining the supervisor. Supervisors who are fear-
ful of subordinates' progress aren't doing an important part of their
jobs. They have forgotten or perhaps never understood that their job
involves expertise of another kind—that of developing, directing, and
coordinating. Yet there are undoubtedly many supervisors who continue
to feel threatened by employees who want more training and experience.

The supervisor who *is* willing to train his or her people to do the job
properly is likely to reap the following benefits:

1. People will be able to work better *without close supervision*. Better, more
   assured job performance leads to fewer errors and less attention to detail
   on the supervisor's part.
2. Employees will be able to carry out directions without unnecessary repetition. *Delegation* will allow the supervisor more time to do the planning,
   organizing, directing, and controlling he or she is being paid to do.
3. Subordinates will be better able to provide you with information about
   trouble spots because of their familiarity with all aspects of the work.

To simply provide a list of the techniques available to the supervisor
for training would not provide the insight and knowledge necessary to
be an effective trainer. Therefore, before we talk about techniques, let's
discuss *how people learn.*

HOW PEOPLE LEARN
AND HOW TO APPLY LEARNING TECHNIQUES

Although some learning takes place without conscious effort, generally there has to be *motivation* to learn before a noticeable change in
behavior can take place. Simply stated, if people don't want to learn
something, they won't. Since most employees *do* want to learn better

ways of doing the job, they will evidence motivation by paying attention to what is being said and done during training.

How people learn has been the subject of much study by psychologists. We will now examine some of the major discoveries in the psychology of learning and point out how a supervisor can use this information in training subordinates.

Immediate Feedback

It has been found that people learn best when they know *immediately* whether what they did was right or wrong. For example, suppose you were trying to learn to play darts, but your trainer insisted that you be blindfolded during the training session. You select a dart and throw it at the dartboard, then five minutes later the trainer takes the blindfold off so you can see where the dart hit. You see that it was low and to the left of the target.

However, since you have waited five minutes, you can't remember how you held the dart, exactly how you threw it, how hard you threw it, and so forth. This is obviously a very bad way to learn, yet much of our training in organizations is like that. For example, it is not unusual to hear of trainees completing a project and then not hearing for two weeks whether that project was done properly.

Every supervisor should find a way to get immediate feedback to trainees so that they know their mistakes and can correct them as soon as possible. Giving a trainee a chance to see how he or she is doing on a day-to-day basis utilizes this principle of immediate feedback. The best learning builds on a foundation of small steps. If the supervisor is there to assist the learner at every step, there is little chance that important material will be overlooked. Then, too, correcting a mistake during the early part of training is relatively easy, but if you wait until the student is farther along, locating the original error or misconception may be virtually impossible.

Positive Reinforcement

Another important learning principle is that positive reinforcement, or giving a reward for correct behavior, will increase the probability of that behavior occurring again. A raise given at the conclusion of a well-done assignment is a positive reinforcer. However, praise, approval, or pride in achievement are often more powerful reinforcers of behavior. Since people tend to repeat a behavior that has been positively reinforced, supervisors should not be afraid of publicly praising a trainee's progress. This doesn't suggest that the failures, mistakes, and problems be ignored when they occur, but *if you want to see a behavior again, reward it.*

Spaced Practice

Many experiments have shown that for acquiring skills, practice that is *spaced* over a period of time results in greater learning than the same amount of practice that is *massed* in one short period of time. Instead of asking a trainee to practice a complicated procedure until he or she can do it perfectly, the supervisor can explain some portion of it and allow the trainee to practice this segment for a while before going on to another step. For most kinds of jobs and organizations, spaced practice is superior to massed practice. Only when the material or tasks to be learned are simple and can be learned in a few hours is massed practice recommended.

The Big Picture

Studies of how people learn have shown that a trainee learns best if he or she first receives a general impression of a complex task. Then as it is studied, more and more details become apparent.

The supervisor can make use of this principle by first showing how the employee's task fits into the organization's total mission and then working into coverage of more specific details. Psychologists have proven that providing an overall view of a job and how it fits into other jobs is a vastly superior technique to describing the details of a job and then trying to compose a big picture.

Because most supervisors/trainers are close to the job and quite experienced, they often take the overall view for granted. As supervisor, you must remember that the new trainee may know *only* what you have told him or her about the job. If you haven't provided an overall picture, he or she may know how to perform some of the operations but not really understand the reason for the operations.

Active Practice

Actively practicing something—especially for developing such skills as equipment operation or report writing—is superior to just listening or reading about the subject. Active practice demands attention and concentration and helps the learner focus upon self-perceived weaknesses or gaps in the knowledge or skill level. For most jobs, the supervisor should try to mix reading and listening with more active methods. For example, reading a book about bowling will not make you a good bowler if you have never bowled. However, reading tips about how to improve your bowling when done in conjunction with active bowling practice might be useful.

Two-Way Communication

In order to find out if learning is really taking place, the supervisor must establish two-way communication with the new employee. If learners feel intimidated by a supervisor, they will probably not come forward with problems or things they don't understand, and the learning process will be quite painful. A supervisor can best encourage two-way communication by demonstrating an openness toward questioning and then rewarding those who *do* ask questions.

Plateaus

The learning process is marked by several points at which there is no apparent progress. Periods of this sort are very common and are called *plateaus in learning* (see Figure 7–3). Plateaus may be the result of fatigue or other temporary physical limitations, but the point is that they are a natural part of the learning process, particularly where developing skills or speed in completing a task is concerned. Supervisors who expect trainees to evidence learning plateaus and communicate an attitude of patience and perseverance will achieve the best results. *Encouragement* is the key to dealing with plateaus in the learning process.

FIGURE 7–3   Learning Plateaus

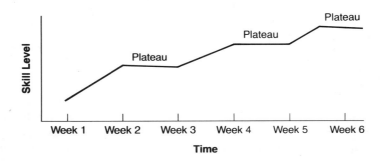

Peaks and Valleys
in Learning Effectiveness

Studies have shown that learning gradually falls off during the late morning and late afternoon. As fatigue sets in, the learner makes more errors and training efforts become ineffective.

One way to delay the onset of this kind of learning ineffectiveness is to schedule frequent short rest periods during the day. Pauses of around five minutes usually lead to a rapid recovery from fatigue. Too long a rest period may be disturbing because a person can lose continuity of thought or "get out of the mood" for doing a task.

The supervisor can take advantage of this knowledge about peaks and valleys in learning effectiveness not only by scheduling frequent rest periods but by scheduling the most difficult part of the training for the early morning or right after lunch when the person is more likely to be alert and receptive to learning.

Modeling

Modeling is one of the most fundamental methods of learning a skill. Small children model or copy the behavior of their parents and learn to speak and act in certain ways. Because it is a method of learning we have had experience with since childhood, modeling is an excellent way to teach certain kinds of on-the-job behaviors.

Modeling need not be limited to an in-person demonstration—films and videotapes, for example, may prove to be good learning devices if carefully selected. As with any of the other techniques, it is important that the supervisor positively reinforce the proper behaviors when they occur so that they will be repeated again.

Learning Transfer

Learning transfer is the ability to apply what you have learned in training to real-life situations. Many training programs suffer from a kind of "ivory tower" syndrome that makes it difficult for trainees to transfer the knowledge directly to the job.

There are two basic ways to deal with this problem. One is to try to make the teaching situation and the on-the-job situation as similar as possible. This may not always be feasible. If it isn't, an alternative is to focus on the "general principles" necessary to learn a task. With this second approach, it is important to stress the *underlying reasons* for doing a task by asking the learner to apply the general principle to a variety of real-life situations. This type of training results in a much more flexible employee, one who is able to handle different situations and emergencies when they occur.

A SPECIAL TECHNIQUE: BEHAVIOR MODIFICATION

Behavior modification is a relatively new tool for the supervisor. Basically, it stems from our second learning principle, also termed the law of effect: People tend to repeat the things that are positively rewarded and *not* to repeat those things that are either negatively rewarded or go unrewarded.

Remember, rewards can be a number of things. They don't have to be simply money, although that is usually an important reward. Rewards can also be praise, favorable job assignments, days off, and so forth.

Behavior modification with its emphasis on positive reward is somewhat different from the attempts supervisors have traditionally made to change unacceptable behaviors. Punishment is still widely regarded as the most effective way of *reducing undesirable behaviors,* but there are negative side effects of punishment that limit its usefulness in training.

A simple approach to behavior modification that has been proven effective involves three steps: (1) make sure a trainee understands your expectations; (2) observe the person at work and immediately appraise his or her performance level as compared to an agreed-upon standard; (3) *praise* (positively reinforce) the employee when the performance meets expectations.

Behavior modification is a technique that successful supervisors have used for years without necessarily knowing a great deal about it or why it works. It is not elaborate but it will work if properly and consistently done.

THE TRAINING PROCESS

Figure 7–4 demonstrates the training process with a five-step procedure that supervisors can follow in training new hires or retraining employees for a different job.

The first step is *assessment.* At this point, the trainer needs to determine exactly what knowledge or skill must be learned. A training program that is "old hat" leaves an employee feeling discouraged, but simply to assume that an individual possesses a certain skill makes the entire learning process very difficult. The supervisor's first job is to

FIGURE 7–4   Supervisor's Training Process

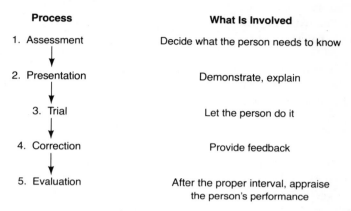

Process	What Is Involved
1. Assessment	Decide what the person needs to know
2. Presentation	Demonstrate, explain
3. Trial	Let the person do it
4. Correction	Provide feedback
5. Evaluation	After the proper interval, appraise the person's performance

thoroughly assess the situation and determine what the trainee knows and what he or she *needs* to know. This is the same for both new hires and long-term employees.

Next is the *presentation.* Many of the learning principles that were discussed earlier in the chapter apply here. New material should be presented in such a way as to make transfer of knowledge to the job as easy as possible. The supervisor should explain the big picture, encourage successful two-way communication, and, where possible, allow the learner to model either the supervisor's behavior or an exemplary worker's behavior.

Third, the trainees should get a chance to *try it* themselves. The learning principles of positive reinforcement, immediate feedback of results, spaced practice, plateaus, and peaks and valleys should be kept in mind here.

Fourth is *correction.* Here the supervisor provides information on how well the trainee did during the trial. Immediate information and positive reinforcement are very important in this step.

The final step is *evaluation.* After a reasonable period of time has elapsed, the supervisor should follow up and see that the training has worked. The trainee should now be able to function as expected, but continued reinforcement will be necessary upon successful completion of difficult tasks.

NEEDS ANALYSIS

We suggested earlier that one of the most important parts of a successful training program is correctly analyzing where employees' knowledge or skills are lacking. *A successful supervisor must be good at diagnosing training needs.* This holds true both for new employees and for long-service employees who are unable to do the job well.

Needs analysis or assessment is nothing more than comparing the individual's performance against each job requirement. Figure 7–5 illustrates needs analysis. The supervisor must determine exactly what skills are required on the job; what time limits apply, if any; and the extent to which independent judgment must be exercised in doing the job. Then the supervisor must look at the jobholder and the person's current level of performance. Is performance satisfactory or are certain weak areas clearly identifiable? If so, exactly what skills are lacking to bring this individual up to the level expected? Finally, is the person motivated to learn new and better ways of doing the job? From this kind of analysis comes an idea of exactly what course of action should be taken.

We suggested earlier that people have to *want* to learn for training to be effective. To train someone who is totally uninterested in improving his or her performance may be a complete waste of everyone's time. If such a person's performance is unsatisfactory, transfer, demotion, or termination might be a better solution.

Spotting Problems in Needs Analysis

Additional problems can enter into the needs analysis that may at first glance appear to be training problems. For example, unsatisfactory performance may result from several causes besides a low knowledge or skill level. Perhaps the person is not aware of company policies, does not understand the reasons behind some of the work procedures, or is unable to manage his or her personal affairs so that sufficient attention is focused on job performance. Some of these problems can be dealt with by providing more information, others cannot.

Another problem that masquerades as a training problem is bad judgment or memory. Despite a high level of skill in their particular assignment, some employees are unable to remember things or exercise such poor judgment that they undo any positive results they may have achieved. These are usually not things that training can help. Placing such people in jobs where judgment isn't required or where memory

FIGURE 7–5   Needs Analysis

isn't a crucial factor may be a better solution. Block 7–3 is a direct quote from a second-level manager, one of whose supervisors was having difficulty training a new employee with such a deficit.

TECHNIQUES OF TRAINING

There are many different kinds of training methods and techniques that are available to the supervisor. Our purpose here is simply to make the supervisor aware of some of the tools at his or her disposal. (For greater detail, see I. Goldstein, *Training: Program Development and Evaluation.*)

The Lecture Method

The lecture method is one of the most commonly used ways of training people. It is good for presenting a lot of information to many people

---

BLOCK 7–3   What if They Cannot Learn?

How do we handle a "new" employee who does not have the mentality to learn the job or execute instructions after they are explained? How long do we tolerate the situation before the employee is dismissed, and what valid grounds for dismissal can be cited under present employment laws? The employee has worked approximately eight months at her present job. She is female and middle-aged.

The supervisor in this case should do a needs analysis and determine *exactly* where the employee is failing. This should allow him to test his hypothesis that the employee lacks the "mentality" to do the job or whether it is simply a matter of inadequate training. This situation has been allowed to go on for eight months, which is entirely too long. These kinds of problems should be picked up within the first month or two of employment. If the problems cannot be solved by training, the supervisor's only recourse is to recommend dismissal or transfer to a job suited to the individual's capabilities.

The "valid grounds" for dismissal that the supervisor cites are simply *inability to do the job.* If the case is well documented, it should be clear to an impartial observer that the employee has had sufficient opportunity to correct her deficient performance but hasn't been able to do so. It should be clear, too, that the organization has dealt with her in a fair manner by trying to help her learn to do the job. If so, the requirements for dismissal have been met.

in a short period of time. Most people are familiar with the lecture technique from past schooling, but study after study has shown that merely listening to information will not usually cause it to be retained, especially for any significant period of time.

Programmed Instruction

Programmed instruction is a process whereby information is broken down into very small pieces and the trainee is reinforced for learning each bit of information. The armed forces and several large organizations have used programmed instruction relatively effectively. This individualized process requires a trainee to pace him or herself by means of a "teaching machine" or programmed instruction book. Although programmed instruction can greatly reduce training time, the materials themselves are very expensive to prepare. Finally, trainees do not usually show enough motivation to use programmed instruction by itself. They seem to prefer programmed instruction mixed with lecture, conference, or discussion with a teacher.

Audiovisual Aids

Television, videotape, and films can be used as we suggested earlier to provide models for imitation. Well-thought-out audiovisual aids are effective because most people are familiar with this form of communication through watching television and movies, and because the addition of the visual element (plus action) to the purely auditory technique of the lecture reinforces the message. However, these devices are essentially one-way communication that provide little or no opportunity for the student to interact and ask questions unless the trainer is present. They are a useful addition to some of the other training methods.

Simulations

A simulation is nothing more than duplicating some part of the job so that it can be practiced in different surroundings. Simulations are particularly useful in those situations where it is impossible or unsafe for an untrained individual to learn something on the job. An example is where it's impractical for an inexperienced person to operate machinery. Because of the cost and risk involved, for example, the airlines use flight simulators in training members of the cockpit crew. Learning to handle emergency situations in an aircraft is more safely done in a simulator than in a real aircraft. Many different kinds of machinery can be simulated. Such training, however, can be expensive.

Apprenticeship

Apprenticeship is widely used in business and the trades. An individual serves as a helper to a journeyman or master craftsman while learning the job. This method is appropriate for many different kinds of training; however, fixed apprenticeship periods may hold back a trainee who is faster than the rest and ready to move on to the job.

Coaching

Coaching was mentioned earlier and is probably one of the most widely used on-the-job training methods available. It is similar to apprenticeship except there isn't a formal time period involved in fulfilling the training responsibilities.

The techniques mentioned here are some of the more commonly used training methods. All have their advantages and disadvantages but, if used in combination, can yield a well-rounded training program.

EVALUATION
OF TRAINING EFFECTIVENESS

An important but often overlooked topic is the evaluation of a training program. For many people, training comes right after motherhood and the flag. There is a general belief that more training of *any* kind somehow makes one a better person. Supervisors should be critical, however, and make sure that training isn't simply just being done for training's sake alone. Training should be done to improve job performance.

In evaluating training, the supervisor would do well to ask the following questions.

After training, has a change in the worker's performance occurred?
Is that change a result of the training?
Will the same training likely produce similar changes in other participants?

If the answer to any of these questions is no, the supervisor might do well to examine the training process critically. It may be that it is not beneficial for his or her work group.

SUMMARY AND CONCLUSIONS

In this chapter we have examined the role of supervisor as trainer. Every supervisor is necessarily a trainer, even if he or she does not consciously assume that role. Supervisors who neglect this portion of their job will probably encounter a good many problems later with unprepared personnel.

Being a good trainer means understanding the do's and don'ts of coaching, the most widely used training technique. There are a number of principles about how people learn that can help a supervisor be a better coach. These include immediate feedback, positive reinforcement, spaced practice, the big picture, active practice, two-way communication, plateaus, peaks and valleys, modeling, and transfer.

The special technique of behavior modification was discussed. This technique is a useful alternative to punishment during training. A training process itself was described with special attention being paid to the importance of orientation and needs analysis.

We also outlined several techniques for training and concluded by noting that every training program should be evaluated in terms of its contribution to on-the-job performance.

QUESTIONS

1. A supervisor who doesn't know the job well enough to do it himself or herself cannot possibly supervise the training of others. Do you agree or disagree?
2. Why is observation the important starting place for coaching?
3. On your last job, which principles of learning were violated during the training period?
4. What problems might occur in the trial phase of the training process?
5. What kinds of things would you have included on an orientation checklist for your last job?
6. What would be a good combination of training techniques for a supervisor who is teaching a nurse to run an X-ray machine?

JOE FRANKLIN, SUPERVISOR

Joe Franklin became supervisor of plant maintenance after about five years as a repairman in the maintenance area. Three years later, the floor space in the plant had tripled and the work force had increased by several hundred.

Joe found that his responsibilities were much greater. Often he had to return to the plant during the night to make necessary repairs. However,

he succeeded in keeping the equipment repaired and was considered a good employee. The next year, it became necessary to add men to his crew and he found himself responsible for the efforts of 16 repairmen.

Joe's problem was that he still preferred to repair the machines personally rather than direct his subordinates to do so. The plant manager had told him that one person couldn't do all of the work alone. He said Joe should be selecting and training capable subordinates to help him with the work.

Joe tried, but it wasn't long until department heads were complaining that the machinery constantly needed repairs, and work schedules were disrupted due to idle machines. They complained that when the physical plant repairmen were summoned, they were often unable to do the job without calling in Joe. One department head griped to the plant manager that Joe was possessive about the machinery and seemed to be deliberately *not* selecting and training qualified repairmen, because he seemed to feel secure only if others regarded him as indispensable.

At this point, the plant manager was compelled to make a decision. Work wasn't being done right. Yet he knew that Joe had been a loyal employee for many years with the company.

1. What should he do?
2. What doesn't Joe understand about being a supervisor?
3. Briefly describe a system of training that Joe could use to bring his subordinates up to standard.

The Supervisor
and Rewards

SUPERVISORY PROBLEM

How can the supervisor keep employees satisfied with their compensation?

When you have finished this chapter, you should be able to

1. Explain why pay is important to employees
2. List factors that influence employees' feelings about how much they should be paid
3. Describe how a wage or salary structure is formulated
4. Indicate the supervisor's role in
   a. Job analysis
   b. Job evaluation
   c. Explaining a compensation plan to employees
5. Describe the difference between a time-based and an incentive compensation plan

---

MODERN DEPARTMENT STORE

You are the supervisor for the home furnishings warehouse section of Modern Department Store. Recently John Anderson raised a problem. John reported to you that a friend of his who works in the clothing and apparel section of the warehouse, is getting more money than he is. John claims that both of them have the same kind of job. They unload trucks and store items in the warehouse. Both use the same kind of machinery in performing their work. According to John, however, his friend in the other section receives two dollars per hour more. Both have been with the company about two years.

After checking with the personnel department, you have found that John's information is accurate—his friend is making two dollars an hour more. You have also checked with the supervisor of the clothing and apparel section of the warehouse and have found that the jobs are essentially the same. John is going to check with you in the morning to see what you have come up with.

AN OVERVIEW OF EMPLOYEE COMPENSATION

How important is pay? In a review of 49 studies on the importance of various factors in the work environment, including interesting work, job security, compensation, and good supervision, the average rank assigned to compensation was three.[1] Among the 49 studies, pay was first in 14 of them, or 27 percent of the time.

This emphasizes how important pay is to employees. One can be misled because many of the recent books on supervision emphasize the importance of interesting and meaningful work and downplay the importance of compensation. We do not dispute the fact that employees have many and various needs, but neither do we wish to oversimplify the motivational effect of money, especially as a symbol of worth, appreciation, power, and so on.

Why Is Compensation Important?

Recall from the chapter on motivation that Maslow lists five categories of needs. Recently, E. E. Lawler, the author of the above-mentioned research on compensation, has proposed a revised list of six needs, which are presented in Figure 8–1. Lawler's analysis of the motivating power of pay asks us to answer two questions: (1) Can pay satisfy a particular need, for example, certain physical needs? and (2) Are these needs important to the individual? When the answers to both questions are yes, then that category of needs contributes to the overall importance of pay. Furthermore, when the answers to several (or all) categories of needs are yes, then the individual attaches more and more importance to pay.

Looking at compensation in this way helps explain why it continues to remain important, even for people who are highly paid. It is obvious that pay is needed to satisfy physical and security needs. If we looked only at physical and security needs, we would conclude that at some level of income, pay ceases to be important. After all, there is only so much food you can eat. However, Figure 8–1 points out that pay may serve as

FIGURE 8–1   Pay and Need Satisfaction

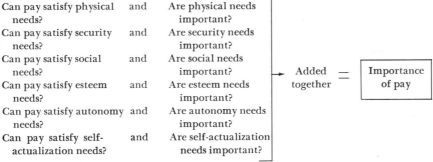

Source: Adapted from E. E. Lawler, *Pay and Organization Effectiveness* (New York: McGraw-Hill, 1971), p. 27.

a means to satisfy esteem needs. For example, the amount of money you have to spend determines the kind of house and car you have and the places you can go for entertainment. For some, these are signs of social status and esteem. Pay and pay raises can affect feelings of esteem in another way, as shown in Block 8–1.

A person's salary level or the size of a raise can be viewed as a sign of the boss's estimate of that individual's worth. If your boss's opinion is valuable to you, this may be an important motivating factor.

Pay can also contribute to the satisfaction of autonomy needs, that is, feelings of self-control and independence. The phrase "independently wealthy" captures the meaning of economic autonomy—not being at the beck and call of others.

Lawler cites evidence that pay can satisfy four needs: physical, security, esteem, and autonomy. The satisfaction of self-actualization and social needs does not seem to depend on money, but the possibility for some individuals can't be ruled out. The key point is that pay *is* a way to satisfy some higher-level needs. Thus, even for high-paying jobs, pay continues to be an important factor.

How Much Should an Employee Be Paid?

Several factors influence employees' views of the amount of pay they should receive. An overview of these factors, presented in Figure 8–2, groups them into three categories. The first is called "personal inputs" and includes the person's perception of: skill in the particular job; experience; training and education in the field; seniority or time with the organization; and merit. Merit is a combined measure of the amount of effort put into the job and the level of job performance. The more of each of these personal inputs a person has, the more that person feels he or she should be paid.

The second category of factors is called "job characteristics." Listed

---

BLOCK 8–1   A Clear Sign

Martha Roberts had just finished her appraisal interview with her supervisor, Ed Allen. She felt great. Ed had made several complimentary comments about her work, but more importantly, he told her she would begin receiving a 10 percent raise next month. According to company pay policy, only employees whose performance is outstanding are eligible for a 10 percent raise. She concluded, "This is a clear sign of Ed's evaluation of my job performance."

FIGURE 8–2   Factors Influencing Employees' Estimates of Amount They Should Be Paid

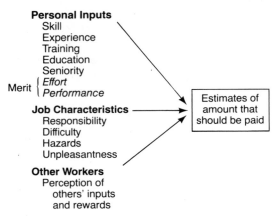

Source: Adapted from E. E. Lawler, *Pay and Organization Effectiveness* (New York: McGraw-Hill, 1971), p. 213.

are level of responsibility, either for equipment or for important decisions, amount of difficulty, the hazards or risks involved in the job, and the pleasantness or unpleasantness of work surroundings. Of course, this list is not comprehensive. In particular work situations there may be other factors that enter into employees' feelings about the amount they should receive.

The third factor that enters into people's estimates of the amount they should receive, "other workers," is related to the discussion of equity estimates in Chapter 3. People compare themselves with others. If an employee sees that other people with similar jobs and similar personal inputs are being paid more, that person will increase his/her estimate of the amount of pay that should be received.

Pay Satisfaction

An organization should strive toward a situation in which employees feel neither overcompensated nor undercompensated. Under such conditions, employees feel satisfied, and the organization has achieved one important objective. Studies have shown that satisfaction with compensation is associated with low absenteeism and low turnover. When absenteeism is low, supervisors can more easily plan individual assignments and better coordinate them to achieve their work unit's goals. Low turnover is important because recruiting, hiring, and training new employees costs a lot of money.

164

It is also important for employees to be productive. Figure 8–2 shows that one of the items under personal inputs is job performance. To motivate performance an organization must build into the compensation system a way to measure job performance, and then reflect performance in the level of compensation that is paid.

There are two issues here: How to develop a pay system that will result in pay satisfaction, and how to ensure that employees see that high performance leads to high pay. We will tackle each of these problems in turn.

THE SUPERVISOR
AND EMPLOYEE COMPENSATION

An alert wage and salary administrator usually delegates as much administration as possible to the first-line supervisor and prepares him or her to perform well. Adequate preparation requires a formal course of at least six or eight group training conferences of two hours each on the fundamentals of compensation. Several follow-up seminars should likewise be conducted every three to six months to clarify questions which have arisen and to brief the supervisor on future activities.[2]

The above quote is from two experts in wage and salary administration. It is intended to impress on the student two key observations: (1) Supervisors are critical to the success of a compensation plan; and (2) a significant amount of work is required if you are to be effective in this part of your job as supervisor.

DEVELOPMENT OF A COMPENSATION SYSTEM

The steps in developing a compensation system are

1. Job analysis
2. Job evaluation
3. Establishment of wages and salaries

What Is Job Analysis?

Job analysis is the study of jobs. The information gathered as a result of job analysis is used to write job descriptions. A job description indicates the tasks and duties performed on a job, the materials and equipment used, interactions with others, and the kind of supervision required. Job descriptions also indicate the physical and social environment in which the job is performed. An example of a job description appears in Figure 8–3. Results of job analysis are also used to formulate job specifications. Job specifications are the personal characteristics necessary for successful performance of a job. Examples of job specifications are amount of work experience, amount of training and education, and personal traits such as ability to work with others.

Job descriptions and job specifications serve a number of important purposes. The information is used in job evaluation to determine the worth of jobs to the organization. It is also used in making hiring and placement decisions and in designing training programs. Both the supervisors and the jobholder are usually involved in analyzing and evaluating jobs.

How Is Job Analysis Done?

Information concerning the nature of jobs can be gathered by observing employees performing the job, by interviewing employees or their supervisors on the job, by asking employees or their supervisors to answer

FIGURE 8–3
Marshall Publishing Company
Job Description and Satisfaction Sheet

Job Title: Bookkeeper

Department: Administrative Services

Job Description

Summary: Keeps records of financial transactions of the organization.

Duties: Verifies and enters in the account journals details of financial transactions as they occur from sales slips, invoices, check stubs, inventory records, and requisitions.

Summarizes these transactions using an adding machine and enters the summary data in the general ledger.

Balances books and compiles reports to show cash receipts and expenditures, accounts payable and receivable, and profits or losses.

Calculates employee wages from time cards. Calculates social security and other withholding taxes. Prepares payroll checks.

Computes monthly statements to be mailed to customers.

Job Specifications

Education: High school education required. Junior college preferred. One year of courses in bookkeeping or accounting required.

Experience: One year of bookkeeping experience required for those without junior college degree.

Special Aptitudes: Must be able to perform arithmetic operations quickly and accurately. Must have the ability to work with details. Must notice errors in arithmetic computations.

Interests and Temperament: Must prefer work of a routine, concrete, and organized nature. Must prefer doing things under specific instructions which allow little or no room for independent action or judgment.

a questionnaire, or by having the supervisor compose job descriptions and specifications for each of the jobs in his or her unit. When jobs are physical in nature and when the duration of the job tasks is short, then observation is a useful approach. However, when work is mostly mental or when the job cycle is long, then an interview or questionnaire approach is typically used.

To ensure that the data on any given jobs are accurate, a widely used approach is to gather information in several different ways. For example, a personnel specialist might first interview employees performing the job or have them complete questionnaires describing their job. Next, the supervisor might be asked to complete a questionnaire or to give an interview about the job.

Figure 8–4 describes job analysis practices reported by a survey of American organizations. The percentages in sections A and B indicate that more than one approach is frequently used by an organization. The reason for showing these percentages is to emphasize the involvement of the supervisor in job analysis.

Section C of Figure 8–4 concerns the methods used to keep job descriptions up to date. This is an important aspect of the supervisor's job,

FIGURE 8–4   Job Description Practices

	Percent
A. Job descriptions written by	
Job analyst	80%
Supervisor	42%
Employee holding job	23%
B. Job descriptions developed from	
Interview with supervisor	57%
Interview with person holding job	47%
Observation of employee doing job	48%
Questionnaire completed by person holding job	36%
Questionnaire completed by supervisor	34%
C. Job description reviewed for possible revision	
Annually	28%
As needed	15%
On request	10%
Every two years	9%
Periodically/no set time	9%
When job changes	7%
Other/no response	20%

Source: Adapted from *Personnel Policies Forum: Job Evaluation Policies and Procedures*, Survey No. 113 (Washington, D.C.: Bureau of National Affairs, June 1976), p. 5.

because as job descriptions change, so do specifications. Consider the ramifications of the incident described in Block 8–2.

In this example, new equipment has been installed that requires additional skills. Jobs can also change because tasks and duties are reallocated. Supervisors are responsible for seeing that these changes are reflected in the job description.

What Is Job Evaluation?

The objective of job evaluation is to determine the relative worth of jobs within an organization. To do this it is necessary to have accurate job descriptions and specifications. In establishing the wage and salary structure of an organization, management must first create a situation in which employees believe they are being fairly compensated and in which they believe that increased productivity will lead to higher levels of compensation.

Look again at Figure 8–2. Most of the factors employees feel should be related to the level of compensation are also factors commonly used to estimate the relative worth of jobs in an organization. The exception is actual performance or merit, because at this point we are concerned not with performance appraisal but with the relative worth of the job itself.

Approaches to Job Evaluation

The basic approaches to job evaluation are job ranking, job classification, factor comparison, and the point method of job evaluation.

Job Ranking Method

The job ranking method is the simplest approach to job evaluation. With this method jobs in the organization are ranked or ordered on the basis of their relative worth. An individual or committee familiar with all of the jobs does the ranking. The advantage of this approach is that it is simple. However, it is limited to organizations which have a small number of jobs.

Job Classification Method

When using the job classification method, categories or classifications of jobs are established. The categories are defined in terms of those factors that determine the relative worth of jobs. Figure 8–5 shows examples of job categories.

The job classification method is essentially a variation of the ranking method that allows it to be utilized by large organizations such as the federal government. Since jobs are still evaluated as entities rather than in terms of the various tasks that comprise them, this approach is not as precise as the factor comparison and point methods of job evaluation.

Factor Comparison Method

The factor comparison method is a more complex approach to job evaluation. It builds on what are called "key jobs," positions common to the local community that vary in difficulty and importance. The method involves judging how much of the current wage rate being paid for each of these key jobs should be allocated among the factors used to evaluate the jobs. Once this determination has been made, the factor comparison method consists of comparing nonkey jobs to key jobs on each of the evaluation factors.

Point Method of Job Evaluation

This is the most commonly used approach to job evaluation. With this approach, the important factors that make up each job are identified. A sample list might include skill, experience, effort, responsibility, and hazard involved in a job. Having identified the evaluation factors, the job analyst next develops a scale of degrees for each factor. Figure 8–6 is an example of a measure for experience.

FIGURE 8–5   Example of Job Classification Method of Job Evaluation

Category	Description
1	Repetitive work under immediate supervision: no unusual effort and no prior training necessary
2	Repetitive work under general supervision: some effort is involved and one to two months of training
3	Relatively little supervision involved; unusual amounts of effort involved and specialized training or experience of three to six months

FIGURE 8–6   Example of Measure for Rating Experience

Degree	Description
1	Up to and including three months
2	More than three months and up to one year
3	More than one year and up to three years
4	Three years and up to five years
5	Over five years

The next step is to assign a point value to each level of a designated evaluation factor. Now the total job can be quantified in terms of job specifications and descriptions. A high degree of accuracy is achieved by analyzing each job factor by factor and then summing the points for each factor to estimate the relative importance of that job in the organization.

The Supervisor's Role in Job Evaluation

In any job evaluation process, the first step should be to form a wage and salary committee. This committee should be made up of individuals familiar with the jobs to be evaluated. Job incumbents and supervisors of the jobs in question are two groups of individuals who are most familiar with any given set of jobs. Some organizations choose to ignore this fact, however, often with disastrous consequences. Block 8–3 indicates what can happen when "outsiders" are hired to do the evaluations.

Situations like these give telling reasons why supervisors need to take part in analyzing and evaluating jobs. In this particular case, several years passed before the inequities were removed, which undoubtedly had consequences not only for the state employees but also for the public whom they served.

Studies have shown that the immediate supervisor is involved in only one-fifth of job evaluation plans. However, two out of three plans do make provisions for the supervisor to lodge an appeal with respect to a particular job.[3] This is acutely important, because it is the supervisor who faces the irate employee demanding why he or she is paid less for the same job.

ESTABLISHING THE WAGE AND SALARY STRUCTURE

After evaluating each job in an organization, the next step is to decide how much compensation each merits. Usually an organization will conduct its own wage and salary survey or participate in an employer

170

A personnel consulting firm had been hired to evaluate the entire range of state government jobs. The job classification approach was used. State government employees were interviewed, and based on this information, job descriptions and specifications were written. Employees were not given a chance to review these descriptions and specifications, however.

Jobs were classified by representatives of the consulting firm and the state government personnel department. Neither supervisors of the jobs being classified nor employees performing these jobs took part in the actual categorization.

Many incidents of inaccurate job descriptions and specifications occurred. Also, many jobs were not properly classified, as far as employees and their supervisors were concerned. As a result, there were widespread feelings of unfair and arbitrary treatment. After the new job classification system was installed turnover increased dramatically, as did the view: "Why should I bust my fanny?" among those who stayed on.

association wage survey. The purpose of the wage and salary survey is to identify the prevailing wages or salaries for jobs in other organizations. For nontechnical jobs, the focus is on the going rates in the immediate geographic area. For more technical jobs it is necessary to consider a larger geographic area because of the greater mobility such individuals usually have.

In describing how to establish the wage structure of an organization, we assume the point job evaluation method is being used because it is the most common approach to job evaluation. The first step is to create pay grades. A pay grade is a category of jobs of approximately the same worth to the organization. A pay grade consists of establishing a point range for the grade. For example, jobs in a 50-point range may constitute one pay grade.

Now the organization must decide how much to pay employees working in jobs in each pay grade. On the basis of its wage survey data, managers are able to see what pay rates are necessary for the organization to be considered a wage leader within the industry. At times, however, it may be necessary for the organization to compensate at an average level or even to be a wage follower. Figure 8–7 shows a sample wage structure. The middle line above each pay grade represents the average wage for each pay grade. The lines above and below the middle line show the maximum and minimum pay for each pay grade. Pay ranges should de-

FIGURE 8-7   Sample Pay Range for Pay Grades (Wage Structure)

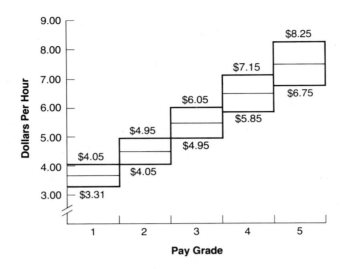

viate at least 10 percent in either direction from the midpoint of each pay grade.[4] This is so that employees have a meaningful incentive to improve their performance and obtain higher levels of compensation. This assumes, of course, that individual employees' wages within the range depend on merit.

USING PAY TO MOTIVATE PERFORMANCE

Recall from our discussion of motivation that expectancy evaluations play a large part in determining effort and performance. Here the key is for employees to see that increased performance results in increased rewards. Employees who are more productive than their co-workers feel they are entitled to higher levels of pay. When high performers do not receive higher levels of pay they believe they are being underpaid. We predicted that when employees feel underpaid, the reaction will be to cut back on their performance. Consequently, the organization should ensure that quality performance results in high levels of pay.

Figure 8–8 is a summary of different methods of compensation. One basic approach is basing pay on time. The options with this approach are hourly wages and a weekly, monthly, or annual salary. Hourly wages are the most common approach among blue-collar workers and are fairly common among office employees. As one moves to higher levels in the organization, the salary method of compensation becomes predominant.

FIGURE 8–8   Basic Methods of Compensation

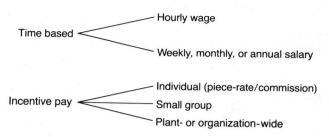

The other basic option is incentive pay. Incentive systems of compensation are those in which pay is directly related to performance and productivity. Variations in this method are based on the number of employees who will receive a given incentive—individual employees, small groups of employees considered as a unit, or all members of a plant or organization.

Individual Incentive Pay

You are probably familiar with individual incentive plans. In a manufacturing situation they take the form of a piece-rate system in which an employee is paid a certain amount per unit of production. In sales work the same principle results in an individual receiving a certain amount or percentage of the dollar value of each item sold.

Studies that have been done over the years indicate that individual incentive plans typically result in 20 percent greater employee productivity than found in a time-based system of compensation. Interestingly, in a supervisory development seminar which one of the authors attended, an experienced supervisor commented on the effects of incentive compensation. He said that in his years as a supervisor of open pit mining he had observed both types of compensation systems. It was his judgment that with an incentive system, he could get 20 percent more work from his subordinates in comparison with an hourly wage system of pay. His off-the-cuff estimate agreed exactly with the studies!

The principal disadvantage of individual incentive plans is the time required to measure and record each employee's productivity. The supervisor must also be in a situation in which it is fairly easy to objectively measure performance. Unfortunately, for most jobs there are few good objective measures of performance.

Another possible problem with individual piece-rate and commission plans is that employees may not trust management. An example of what can happen is provided by Block 8–4.

173

Janice was a new employee of Jackson Fabrics. Sewers were paid a certain amount for each shirt, blouse, skirt, and so on. Since Janice was a good sewing machine operator, she thought she would make good money at this job.

Janice had worked to the best of her ability until yesterday. Mary Jane, a senior seamstress, talked to Janice at lunch. Mary Jane told Janice she should slow down or the company would reduce the piece rates. That would hurt everybody, not only Janice. Mary Jane also said that if everyone worked to the best their ability, people would be laid off much sooner. This was because the company only has so many orders to fill, and when they are completed layoffs follow. Since Janice was new she would be first to go.

Janice was glad that Mary Jane had explained things to her. "Just goes to show you that you can't trust management."

The group bogey indicates what can happen if piece-rate incentives are set too high and it is necessary to reduce them. If this happens, employees will not trust management and will not try to produce as much as they can.

Small Group Incentive Compensation

Small group incentive systems are appropriate where there are small groups of workers who must cooperate with each other to produce a product or to get some work done. This plan is based on measuring the group's performance and compensating everyone in the group accordingly. In addition to motivating performance by rewarding increased levels of productivity, this system promotes group pressure favoring production. When a small group incentive is operative, if an employee holds back and doesn't do his or her share, other members of the work group will probably "encourage" the individual to pull his or her weight. The principal disadvantage of this kind of system, as with the individual incentive system, is that it requires a lot of record keeping and is possible only when there is some means of objectively measuring performance.

Organization-Wide Incentives

The organization-wide incentive system typically includes all employees in the organization. Several organizations have successfully implemented this system of compensation to motivate performance, most notably Lincoln Electric. This company has been using an organization-wide incentive plan since 1934. A recent description of the plan reported that the typical year-end bonus for employees is roughly equal to their annual wage or salary.[5] Regular pay was competitive with that offered by local organizations for employees with similar skills.

The principal advantage of the plant- or organization-wide system is that it gets away from the administrative costs and measurement of production that goes with either the individual or small group incentive plans. Another advantage, when the system is well received by the employees, is that it promotes teamwork throughout the organization. Everyone benefits when the total organization is more effective.

Disadvantages of this setup are that (1) a bonus may not be as closely related to individual performance as with either of the other incentive systems, and (2) since such systems typically pay an annual bonus, positive reinforcement is usually far removed from the time of performance. For example, is an individual's performance on April 13 influenced by the expected bonus which will be received the following January? With any incentive system perhaps the most important factor is employee acceptance. If workers believe that an incentive plan is an attempt by management to rip them off, the system will probably fail.

Compensation Practices

Figure 8–9 shows the results of a survey of American organizations as to the frequency of use of different pay systems. Note that for all employee groups, wage rates for most jobs are determined by job evaluation. This is especially true among office and professional/technical employees. On the other hand, incentive systems are relatively infrequent. This means that most supervisors must depend on merit ratings to relate individual performance to pay.

THE SUPERVISOR:
KEY TO AN EFFECTIVE COMPENSATION PLAN

As in staffing and training, supervisors also play a key role in explaining the compensation plan to employees and gaining their acceptance of the plan. As supervisor you must communicate between employees and staff by

1. Distributing information about the compensation plan
2. Answering employee questions about the plan
3. Promoting or discussing the advantages of the company plan with employees and with job applicants
4. Advising the personnel staff of employee reactions to the existing plan
5. Advising the personnel staff of employee interest in other benefits [6]

FIGURE 8–9   Compensation Practices for Nonmanagement Employees

Practice	Plant	Office	Professional/ Technical	Sales
1. Wage rate determined by job evaluation	54%	80%	71%	55%
2. Incentive plans				
a. Individual incentive	21%	1%	1%	7%
b. Group incentive	12%	1%	2%	4%
c. Productivity or profit-sharing bonus	11%	15%	14%	25%
3. Individual wage adjustments				
a. Automatic length of service increases	24%	17%	21%	10%
b. Pay adjustments based on merit	43%	79%	76%	91%

Source: Adapted from *Personnel Policies Forum: Wage and Salary Administration,* Survey No. 97 (Washington, D.C.: Bureau of National Affairs, July 1972), p. 14.

The first-line supervisor is much closer to rank-and-file employees than is the personnel department. As a result, the supervisor is better able to "take their pulse" about the existing program and any changes they deem necessary. Supervisors can either serve as an effective flow of ideas between employees and compensation specialists in the personnel department or they can filter and block the flow of information. Some organizations have gone so far as to create a committee of supervisors who are responsible for ensuring a free flow of information on compensation policy.

Some students of the subject even feel that the wage and salary administrator should delegate to the first-level supervisor as much of the administration of the plan as is possible.[7] Naturally, this requires proper preparation on the part of the supervisor. Then also, when a new compensation plan is formulated, first-line supervisors should be given an opportunity to participate, otherwise they will not be fully committed to the solutions or modifications that are decided on. Again, the supervisor is the critical link in successful reward systems.

SUMMARY AND CONCLUSIONS

Wages and salaries are important rewards for employees. They are important because pay satisfies needs. Not only can pay be used to satisfy physical and security needs, it can also satisfy needs for esteem and autonomy.

For employees to be satisfied with the pay they receive, it has to equal the amount to which they feel entitled. Employee perceptions about compensation depend on *personal inputs* such as experience and training, *job characteristics* such as responsibility and pleasantness of working conditions, and *what other workers are paid*.

All of these factors should be taken into account in establishing an organization's wage and salary structure. The key phases in establishing a wage and salary structure are job analysis, job evaluation, wage and salary surveys, and pricing the jobs.

You as supervisor play a key role in the success of an organization's compensation plan. The critical functions served by supervisors include

1. Providing information to write job descriptions and job specifications
2. Participating in the development and use of job evaluation plans
3. Identifying inaccuracies in job descriptions and specifications
4. Identifying errors in the evaluation of jobs
5. Keeping job descriptions and specifications current
6. Explaining the compensation plan to employees
7. Communicating employee opinions about the compensation plan to the wage and salary specialists

QUESTIONS

1. How important is pay to employees?
2. Why would pay continue to be important to those with high wages and salaries?
3. When are employees satisfied with their pay or compensation?
4. Describe how pay can be used to motivate job performance.
5. Explain why supervisors are critical to the success of an employee compensation program.

EMPLOYEE DEVELOPMENT AND COMPENSATION

Your secretary, Ann Frost, has come to you with a complaint. She has been working hard on improving her secretarial skills. She recently completed a night school course for secretaries in which she learned to use a dictaphone and to take shorthand.

Until she completed this course, she typed from longhand drafts or from rough-typed drafts. Now you are able to dictate letters and reports either on a tape recorder or directly to her.

Ann feels that since her job has changed as a result of her new skills, she should receive more money. You told her you would think it over and get back to her.

---

1. What should you do in this situation?
2. Be prepared to role play an interview with Ann Frost.

NOTES

1 According to E. E. Lawler in *Pay and Organization Effectiveness* (New York: McGraw-Hill, 1971), p. 39.

2 H. G. Zollitsch and A. Langsner, *Wage and Salary Administration* (Cincinnati, Ohio: South-Western Publishing Co., 1970), p. 751.

3 *Personnel Policies Forum: Job Evaluation Policies and Procedures*, Survey No. 113 (Washington, D.C.: Bureau of National Affairs, June 1976).

4 Zollitsch and Langsner, *Wage and Salary Administration*, p. 349.

5 Zollitsch and Langsner, *Wage and Salary Administration*, p. 588.

6 R. M. McCaffery, *Managing the Employee Benefits Program* (New York: American Management Association, 1972).

7 Zollitsch and Langsner, *Wage and Salary Administration*, p. 751.

The Supervisor
and
Performance Appraisal

SUPERVISORY PROBLEMS

What are common errors made in evaluating employee performance? How should the supervisor conduct an appraisal interview?

LEARNING OBJECTIVES

When you have finished this chapter, you should be able to

1. List how the results of performance appraisal can be used
2. Describe common rater errors and the problems caused by them
3. Discuss the advantages and disadvantages of different appraisal techniques
4. State the advantages of providing employees with clear and definite standards for evaluation
5. Describe how to conduct a performance appraisal interview

TRAVERSE COUNTY HIGHWAY DEPARTMENT

George Andrews, superintendent of the Traverse County Highway Department, has just finished reviewing the annual performance appraisals done by each of the four crew supervisors in the department. Each supervisor rated all of his subordinates on the following dimensions of job performance:

Attendance	Care of equipment
Quality of work	Job knowledge
Quantity of work	Potential for promotion

The following scale was used for evaluating each performance dimension:

1 = Unsatisfactory
2 = Acceptable
3 = Average
4 = Above average
5 = Outstanding

The four crew supervisors' ratings for their units (ten subordinates each) were as follows:

Crew A, Andy Johnson, Supervisor
    All ten personnel were rated outstanding on every dimension.
Crew B, Terry Alberts, Supervisor
    Nine personnel were rated outstanding on every dimension. The remaining person was rated unsatisfactory on every dimension.
Crew C, Frank Olsen, Supervisor
    All ten personnel were rated average on every dimension.

Crew D, Max Kolter, Supervisor
No constant pattern as with the other crews. The average ratings across the six dimensions for each crew member were

Two individuals   = 2.5
Four individuals   = 3.0
Three individuals = 3.9
One individual   = 4.8

A close look at Max's evaluations showed that each member of his crew received a different rating on each job dimension. In other words, Max did not rate an individual the same on every dimension of performance.

George wondered what he was to do with these figures. The county commissioners wanted him to reward performance. He knew perfectly well that Andy's and Terry's crews were not all perfect. He also knew that, as a group, Frank's crew did as good work as any of the other crews.

Also, in this year's budget was $5,000 for training and development. These evaluations did not identify where the highway department needed to concentrate its training efforts. It looks like Max's evaluations might be useful, but not the others.

George had also hoped that these evaluations would help identify "comers," people to keep an eye on when an opportunity for a promotion occurred. Again, only Max's evaluations seem to provide this information.

The problems facing George Andrews are not unusual. The supervisors of crews A, B, and C have fallen into common rater traps. As a result, George is between a rock and a hard place. If he takes the ratings at face value and recommends raises accordingly, crews A and B will be happy but crew C members certainly won't. Another problem: How is he going to identify training needs?

Unfortunately, there is no fast and easy solution to these problems. The solution we recommend is proper training of supervisors in performance appraisal.

WHAT IS PERFORMANCE APPRAISAL?

Performance appraisal is the process of comparing an employee's performance against the standards for the job. In the chapter we just completed, we discussed job evaluation, determining the worth of a job to the organization. Now we will take a look at the people performing these jobs and attempt to establish guidelines for rating performance.

Why Evaluate Performance at All?

The results of a nationwide survey of employers are presented in Figure 9–1. The data indicate the percentage of organizations using performance evaluations for determining raises, making promotion decisions, determining training needs, and validating selection procedures.

All of these uses of performance appraisal are very important. In establishing hiring standards, an organization needs evidence that the standard is necessary for successful job performance. In order to do this, it is necessary to evaluate job performance. If an organization has a requirement that all employees in a particular job must be high-school graduates, for example, there should be evidence that those who have graduated from high school perform the job better than dropouts.

The results of performance appraisal are also needed in training and developing employees. An employee's shortcomings must be identified before it is possible to decide what training and development are needed to improve his or her job performance.

Performance appraisal is also necessary to motivate employees. Recall in the chapter on motivation, one of the conclusions was that to motivate good job performance it is necessary that employees see a connection between good job performance and rewards. One of the more important rewards that an organization has to offer is wages or salaries. Good performers should receive higher levels of pay.

The fourth purpose of performance appraisal is to provide information on which to base promotion, demotion, layoff, and discharge decisions. The reasons for wanting to base such decisions on merit parallel those for basing pay on merit. In addition, equal employment opportunity legislation has increased the importance of relating such decisions to performance appraisal rather than to subjective judgments.

FIGURE 9–1   Uses of Performance Appraisal Data

	Percentage of Organizations with Appraisal Programs	
Use	Office Employees	Production Employees
Determining wage/salary increases	85	67
Promotion decisions	83	83
Determining training needs	62	61
Validating selection procedures	24	30

Source: *Employee Performance: Evaluation and Control,* Personnel Policies Forum (PPF) Survey No. 108 (Washington, D.C.: Bureau of National Affairs, February 1975), p. 9.

Traits, Behavior, or Results: What Should Be Evaluated?

Evaluation of traits means that employees are rated on such personal characteristics as honesty, integrity, cooperativeness, and sociability. Evaluation based on behaviors refers to performance of on-the-job duties. For example, a salesperson might arrange displays of goods to be sold, demonstrate the operation of these goods to customers, and prepare records of sales completed. Evaluation of behaviors implies that employees are rated on how well they do these things. Evaluation based on results focuses on the outcomes or results of an employee's job behaviors. For example, in evaluating a salesperson, results might include dollars worth of goods sold, number of new customers, number of customer complaints, or number of sales records without error.

It has been our experience that organizations should not base employee evaluation on personal traits. Our reasoning here is that focusing on personal traits is more likely to lead to hard feelings between a supervisor and subordinate when the subordinate is informed of the appraisal results. Further, evaluation based on traits is more subjective than evaluation based on either job behaviors or results. The choice between basing evaluations on behaviors or results will be discussed later in this chapter.

What do employers consider in performance evaluation? Survey results concerning this question are presented in Figure 9–2. You can see from these figures that employers do not usually evaluate personal traits.

FIGURE 9–2   Factors Considered in Performance Evaluation

	Percentage of Organizations with Appraisal Programs	
Factor	Office Employees	Production Employees
Quality of work	93	91
Quantity of work	90	91
Initiative	87	83
Cooperation with others	87	83
Dependability	86	86
Job knowledge	85	85
Attendance	79	86
Need for supervision	67	77
Other factors	33	29

Source: *Employee Performance: Evaluation and Control,* Personnel Policies Forum (PPF) Survey No. 108 (Washington, D.C.: Bureau of National Affairs, February 1975), p. 4.

However, some personal traits were found in the "other factors" category. Included were judgment, maturity, and loyalty.

COMMON RATER ERRORS

There are a number of tendencies to which supervisors are prone in making performance appraisals. Since these tendencies introduce inaccuracies into ratings, you should be aware of and try to avoid them when appraising employees.

Halo Error

Halo error occurs when one dimension of performance causes a bias in evaluations of other dimensions of that individual's performance. For example, in Block 9–1 Mrs. Olson places a great deal of importance on good attendance. The halo error occurs when Mrs. Olson rates Marty higher on other dimensions of performance than she should. Halo also occurs when Mrs. Olson rates Donna lower on other dimensions of performance than is justified because Donna does not have good attendance.

To avoid halo error, try to focus on a single dimension of performance at a time, and avoid allowing evaluations of different dimensions of performance to influence each other. One approach that can be used

---

BLOCK 9–1   A Comparison of Observed and True Ratings

At Xerotra Corporation we know what the "true" or accurate rating should be for a group of employees. These ratings are on the right side of the following chart. On the left are the ratings reported by the supervisors of these employees. Mrs. Olson is the supervisor of Donna and Marty. Mrs. Robinson is the supervisor of Alice and Joe.

Factor	Supervisor Ratings for				Actual or True Ratings for			
	Donna	Marty	Alice	Joe	Donna	Marty	Alice	Joe
Quality of work	3	4	5	5	4	3	4	3
Quantity of work	3	4	5	5	4	3	4	3
Cooperation	3	4	5	4	5	2	3	2
Attendance	2	5	4	5	2	5	2	4

Scale: 1 = Unsatisfactory;   2 = Acceptable;   3 = Average;
          4 = Above Average; 5 = Outstanding

to reduce halo error is to evaluate all individuals on a single dimension of performance at one time.

Halo error creates many problems. All uses of performance appraisal results can be affected by employee evaluations containing halo error. For example, think about the identification of a person's training and development needs. If a supervisor evaluates certain dimensions of an individual's performance higher than is justified, areas in which the person needs improvement are overlooked. On the other hand, if a supervisor evaluates some aspect of a person's performance lower than is appropriate, unneeded training efforts may be expended.

Refer back to Block 9–1 and look at the ratings on cooperation. Marty's need for improvement is overlooked while the supervisor's rating of Donna indicates she could improve quite a bit.

Constancy Error

Constancy error occurs when a supervisor's ratings do not reflect real differences in the performance of different individuals. There are several types of constancy error: leniency, central tendency, and toughness.

With leniency error the supervisor evaluates the performance of employees uniformly better than is justified. For example, assume that among the subordinates are some outstanding performers, some average performers, and some below-average performers. When the supervisor evaluates the performance of the average performers as outstanding and the performance of below-average workers as above average, he or she is committing the error of leniency. This is demonstrated in Block 9–1 by Mrs. Robinson's ratings of Alice and Joe.

Central tendency error occurs when a supervisor evaluates the performance of subordinates as average, when really there are some individuals who are below average or above average. As with leniency, the error is failing to reflect accurately differences in performance across individuals. Toughness error is when the supervisor rates the performance of individuals *lower* than is justified. For example, rating outstanding employees as average or average employees as below average.

Of these three forms of constancy error, the most common is leniency error. Many problems occur when raters are lenient. If the supervisor does not identify differences in level of performance among employees, the organization does not have the information needed to decide on the size raise each one should receive. Similarly, performance appraisals should provide valuable information to help decide who should be promoted or who should be discharged or reassigned. Leniency error conceals the information needed to make these decisions.

If employees do not see that above-average performance results in above-average raises, their motivation will be reduced. Those who are actually average or below average, but are rated above average and receive the rewards that go with such performance, will see little reason to improve. On the other hand, those who are actually above average and who see others receiving the same rewards for inferior performance will probably react by reducing their performance so that equity will be restored.

In the authors' experience, leniency in performance ratings is the main reason so many merit compensation plans fail. Regardless of what is stated in the organization's personnel policy handbook, if employees do not see performance rewarded, they will not be motivated to do their best. *When performance appraisals are inflated or lenient, the organization cannot identify who deserves above-average, average, or below-average raises, and consequently, cannot appropriately reward performance.*

Time Dimension Errors

In evaluating the performance of a subordinate, the supervisor usually reviews the individual's performance during a certain block of time, for example, the past six months or the past year. Time dimension errors occur when the rater places too much emphasis on performance during a certain part of the period being evaluated.

Recency error means that a supervisor attaches too much weight to performance during the last month or so. *Primacy error* involves too much emphasis on performance during early parts of the time period being evaluated. The phrases, "What's happened lately" and "First impressions count," exemplify these two kinds of rater errors.

To counteract these errors, supervisors must consciously try to evaluate performance over the entire time period involved. One technique which helps reduce the effects of recency and primacy errors is to make periodic notes describing the performance of your subordinates. For example, once every two weeks or every month a supervisor could make notes concerning the performance of subordinates. When the time comes for the semiannual or annual performance review, the supervisor can review these notes and arrive at an evaluation of performance over the entire period. Because the notes were gathered during the entire year or six months, one period—for example, the first month or the last month—is less likely to dominate the evaluations.

APPRAISAL TECHNIQUES

There are several commonly used approaches to employee evaluation. Rater error is more a problem with some of these approaches than others.

Essay Method

The essay method of appraisal involves writing a story or essay about the performance of each individual being evaluated. The main problem with this approach is that it is hard to compare the evaluations of different raters. Further, a person's chances of being promoted or transferred may hinge on the writing ability of the immediate supervisor.

Ranking

Ranking of subordinates is another approach to employee appraisal. It is easier to use than some of the techniques discussed below. Since it merely involves determining the rank order of the employees being evaluated (who is best, who is second best, and so on), it is easier to use than many of the other techniques that follow. The main advantage of the ranking method is that it forces the supervisor to make distinctions among those being evaluated. However, it can be time-consuming when supervisors must evaluate the performance of many individuals on several dimensions of performance.

Another problem with the ranking method is that people being evaluated are competing with each other, rather than competing with some external standard. In other words, when the ranking approach is being used, somebody is always going to be the poorest performer in the group. This is actually unnecessary because when compared to an external performance standard, the person's performance might be quite satisfactory.

The third implication of the ranking approach is that the only way a person can improve his or her standing in the group is at the expense of someone else. Such a win-lose approach to performance evaluation fosters competition among the members of a work group rather than encouraging cooperation.

A final problem with rankings is that there is no way to compare the performance of individuals in different work groups. The situation described in Block 9–2 illustrates this problem vividly.

As you can see from Block 9–2, the ranking technique is virtually impossible to use on an organization-wide basis. Its only real advantage is prohibiting constancy rater error.

Graphic Rating Scales

Figure 9–3 presents an example of a graphic rating scale, more commonly known as a "rating scale." About 40 percent of organizations with appraisal programs use this technique.[1] It can be used when evaluating personal traits or when evaluating performance factors. To construct

a rating scale you must identify a list of traits or factors to be evaluated
and decide on a scale to be used in evaluating subordinates. The scale
can have any number of places to check, but five-point and seven-point
scales are common. The task facing the supervisor is to mark that point
on the scale for each factor which represents his or her evaluation of
the subordinate's performance on that dimension.

This approach to performance appraisal is susceptible to all of the
errors discussed earlier, especially to halo error and leniency error. Since
it is one of the most commonly used techniques of performance appraisal, we can conclude that users feel that the advantages of this
technique offset its disadvantages. One main advantage is its use of an
external standard against which employees are compared. Consequently,
the motivational problems present when using the ranking technique
are eliminated. Another advantage is its ease of use when a large number
of ratings must be made. Rating scales require much less time than
ranking.

Behaviorally Anchored Rating Scales

Behaviorally anchored rating scales (BARS), or behavioral expectation
scales (BES), are an approach to performance appraisal that has received a great deal of attention in recent years. Figure 9–4 presents an
example of such a scale.

Unlike the graphic rating scale, this technique can be used only in
evaluating *job behaviors,* not personal traits. The advantage of BARS

188

FIGURE 9–3   Example of a Graphic Rating Scale

3. *Rating Form*
(Small central manufacturing company)

Name and Clock No.	**EMPLOYEES RATING RECORD**				
	Department _____ Shift _____ Date _____				
	Job Classification _____ Rated by _____				
	Excellent or Superior	Above average	Average	Below average	Poor
Quality of work					
Quantity of work					
Job knowledge					
Co-operation					
Dependability					
Adaptability					
Mental attitude					
Attendance					
Safety					
Initiative					

Rater's comments: _____

Recommended for next wage level   ☐ Yes   ☐ No

CAUTION: This is a confidential report; let's keep it that way. Be fair to the employee, yourself, and the company by using extreme care in marking this chart. A good supervisor uses good judgment; this personnel evaluation is considered a test of your judgment. A careless, insincere report will be a reflection on your judgment. All decisions should be based upon your personal observation of this employee as he works directly under you.
1. Do not confer with others; use your independent judgment.
2. Avoid personal prejudice.
3. Evaluate this employee according to his job classification.
4. Judgment should cover usual performance over the entire rating period.
5. Please read all descriptions for each factor.
6. Add at the bottom any comment which you think will help in making a fair appraisal.

Source: *Employee Performance: Evaluation and Control,* Personnel Policies Forum (PPF) No. 108 (Washington, D.C.: Bureau of National Affairs, February 1975), p. 24.

FIGURE 9–4   Example of a Behaviorally Anchored Rating Scale

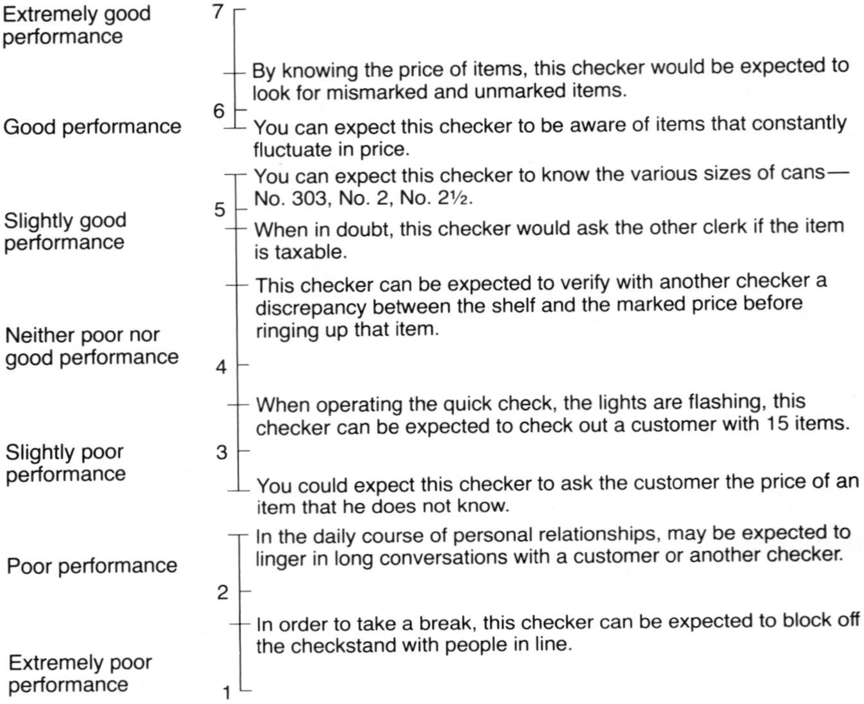

An example scale for the knowledge and judgment dimension.

Source: L. Fogli, C. L. Hulin, and M. R. Blood, "Development of First-Level Behavioral Job Criteria," *Journal of Applied Psychology,* 1971, *55,* 3–8. Copyright 1971 by the American Psychological Association. Reprinted by permission.

is that the behavioral examples given alongside the number ratings clarify the meaning or definition of the dimension of performance being evaluated in the mind of the supervisor. By citing concrete examples of job behavior, BARS helps the supervisor rate much more accurately than with such terms as "outstanding," "average," and so on, used with the graphic rating scales.[2]

Although the evidence is not clear-cut, some studies purport to show that BARS is less prone to rater error than graphic rating scales. Halo error and leniency error appear to be less with BARS than with graphic rating scales. An additional advantage of BARS is that it provides more information for the supervisor to use in counseling and coaching subordinates.

Evaluation of Results

For the pragmatic supervisor, what really counts is results. To re-phrase the old sports saying, "It's not how you play the game, it's whether you win or lose." The modified saying points out the difference between evaluation based on behaviors and evaluation based on results. Evalua-tion of results focuses on the win-loss record. Evaluation based on job behaviors focuses on how you play the game. Coaches and supervisors are usually judged on results.

Management by objectives (MBO) is the best-known method of eval-uation based on results. MBO was originally devised as a performance appraisal program that would overcome most of the problems associ-ated with traditional approaches to performance appraisal. Douglas McGregor, in his widely read book, *The Human Side of Enterprise*, argued that in the typical performance appraisal system the superior was put in the role of "playing God" because he or she had to judge the personal worth of subordinates.[3] In the traditional system that McGregor referred to, the focus of evaluation was personal traits such as dependability, integrity, and loyalty. McGregor felt that traditional per-formance appraisal programs failed precisely because of resistance to this practice by both superiors and subordinates.

As described by McGregor, MBO involves the following steps:

1. Each employee establishes short-term performance goals, which are then approved by his or her supervisor.
2. Each employee arrives at an individual set of plans for attaining these goals.
3. Each employee assesses his or her own achievement of these goals at the end of the planning period.
4. Self-appraisals are discussed with one's superior, along with means to improve future performance and goal attainment.

MBO has many advantages. First, it shifts the emphasis of appraisal from personality strengths and weaknesses to the attainment of work goals and objectives. Another strength stems from the feature of self-evaluation. If employees can be assisted in making objective and accurate performance ratings, then problems caused by a reluctance to accept the results of performance evaluation are nonexistent. This is particularly important when using the results of appraisal for identifying training and development needs. Ideally, self-evaluation should result in the identification of both strengths and weaknesses, and the individual will be motivated to overcome weaknesses in performance. Finally, by shift-ing the role of the superior from judge or evaluator to trainer and coach, MBO helps establish a more realistic supervisor-subordinate relationship.

191

MBO is usually used by two levels of managers, for example, first-level supervisors would be the subordinates and second-level supervisors would be the superiors. However, we have found that this approach or modifications of it can be used with good results by first-level supervisors in the evaluation of subordinates. For example, employees may have to be guided in selecting goals and deciding on the best method of implementing them. However, some measure of participation is probably feasible in almost every case.

The important thing is that when clear goals are established, even by superiors, employees are much more likely to achieve above-average results.

Which Appraisal Technique Is Best?

It is obvious from our foregoing discussion that each of the appraisal techniques has its advantages and disadvantages. Therefore, it is probably not advisable to select a single performance appraisal technique and to ignore all the other approaches. Evaluation of results does offer the advantages of relative objectivity and of focusing on the attainment of goals and objectives. Both public and private sector organizations must be concerned with these factors. Another advantage is that with evaluation of results employees have clear, definite objectives to accomplish. Studies have shown that people perform better when they have definite goals, compared to situations in which they are told to "do their best." [4]

On the other hand, BARS focuses on behaviors, or what people do on the job. BARS also provides a great deal of useful information to assist in training and development of employees. One author has suggested that the most effective approach to performance appraisal might be a combination of a modified MBO approach and BARS. [5]

Figure 9–5 describes alternative combinations of evaluations that could be obtained from the use of this approach. Cell A represents a situa-

FIGURE 9–5   Evaluating Performance Using Both Behaviorally Anchored Rating Scales (BARS) and Evaluation of Results

BARS Appraisal of Job Behaviors

		Inappropriate behaviors	Appropriate behaviors
Evaluation of results	Good results	B	A
	Poor results	C	D

tion in which a subordinate's job behaviors are satisfactory and the attainment of objectives is also satisfactory. This would be a highly desirable situation and the subordinate could be told to "charge on."

Cell B represents a situation in which the objectives are attained but an evaluation of job behaviors indicates a need for improvement. Another way to describe this situation is to say that the employee is attaining the desired objectives *in spite of* what he or she is doing on the job. For example, on a very hot day a person selling beer at a baseball game probably does not have to be very good at getting customers' attention. Any behaviors on such an individual's part, short of failing to show up for work, would probably result in selling large quantities of liquid refreshments. However, would that individual be effective under less desirable conditions? This approach to performance appraisal enables a supervisor to identify problem areas and hopefully to bring about a change in job behaviors before the subordinate's performance deficiencies lead to a failure to obtain objectives.

If only evaluation of results were being used to evaluate employees, employees represented by Cell B would appear to be doing fine. Presumably they would be rewarded for their efforts, and poor or undesired ways of doing the job would be disregarded. This is a poor learning situation, however, for if at some later point they fail to achieve objectives, the task of learning how to do the job properly will be immeasurably more difficult.

Cell C represents the situation in which there is a failure to attain objectives and the subordinate's job behaviors are unsatisfactory. Compare this with Cell D in which there is also a failure to attain objectives, but the person's job behaviors are judged satisfactory. The implications for action by a supervisor who is trying to help a subordinate are very different in these two situations. In Cell D there are probably factors outside the control of the subordinate which are prohibiting the attainment of objectives. For example, contrast the ease of selling residential outdoor swimming pools in Phoenix, Arizona, and Laramie, Wyoming. A supervisor might help a subordinate in the situation represented by Cell D to look at the situational factors holding back goal achievement and see what can be done about them.

In Cell C the cause of failure to achieve objectives is with the employee. The subordinate's behaviors are judged to be unsatisfactory, and what is needed is for the individual to change these behaviors so that goals and objectives will be accomplished.

As we have described it here, a combination of BARS and evaluation of results is probably the best approach to performance appraisal. However, supervisors are usually not in a position to decide what appraisal techniques will be used. Judging from the survey results reported earlier, a majority of work organizations will provide their supervisors with rating scales or checklists. These techniques usually parallel BARS because they typically evaluate job behaviors.

In such cases, we recommend that supervisors keep in mind the subordinate's job goals and objectives. This can be done informally. When a subordinate is in a situation described by Cell B, a supervisor can suggest that even better goal attainment is possible by changing job behavior. On the other hand, when faced by situations characterized by Cells C and D, the supervisor knows where to concentrate efforts to improve goal achievement. The key question: Is the problem with the subordinate's job behavior or with situational factors outside the subordinate's control?

Who Should Evaluate Performance?

By far the most common practice is for the immediate supervisor to evaluate performance. In a recent survey, 98 percent of the organizations reported that immediate superiors evaluate performance.[6] This is because the immediate superior has the greatest opportunity to observe an individual's performance. The next most common approach is to have a panel or committee composed of the immediate superior and the department head perform the evaluations. About one-fifth of the organizations surveyed used this approach. Comparing these two figures means that in about 78 percent of the cases, the immediate superior alone evaluates performance. The main argument for using a panel is that the immediate superior may be biased for or against certain subordinates. Yet even the panel approach has its difficulties; unless regulations are drawn up, the most senior individual on the panel may dominate the evaluations.

Several nontraditional alternatives exist. One possibility is to use peer evaluations. Another is to rely on evaluations by subordinates, and a third is to use self-evaluation. The military uses peer evaluations in its officer and noncommissioned officer training schools. Research conducted in this setting suggests that peers are effective in predicting future promotions in the military. Evaluation by peers might be particularly useful when workers are in close contact with each other or when the behavior being evaluated is not observed by superiors, but is observed by peers. For example, if one were evaluating cooperativeness with co-workers, the people best able to judge this factor would be co-workers and not superiors. If superiors evaluated this dimension of performance, a halo error would probably enter the ratings.[7] Of course, peer evaluations have their shortcomings, too. Factors such as popularity or charisma may bias the evaluations.

Another approach is to use subordinates as evaluators. As with peer evaluations, subordinate evaluations might be particularly useful for certain situations—for example, in rating a supervisor's leadership or effectiveness in communicating with subordinates. One disadvantage of this approach is that subordinates may use it to "get even" with superiors.

A comparable situation is evaluation of college faculty by students. Research on teacher evaluations indicates that those faculty members who are easy graders tend to get better student ratings. When student-teacher ratings are used for making decisions about size of salary increases, faculty members feel pressure to become easy graders. Similarly, if subordinate evaluations were used for making decisions about salary increases and promotions, the pressure would be on the superior to ease up on the demands being made of subordinates in trade for good evaluations. Clearly this would be an undesirable position for the supervisor.

It is our recommendation that subordinate evaluations be considered purely for development and training purposes. Subordinate evaluations can be used as a way to provide superiors with feedback from their subordinates. For example, at Esso Research and Engineering, the results of subordinate evaluations are summarized and made available only to the immediate superior, not to administrative staff.[8] Follow-up studies indicated that subordinates saw changes in the leadership behaviors of their superiors after they had received the feedback.

A final possibility is to use self-evaluation. The arguments in favor of this were discussed in connection with MBO. The principal disadvantage is that self-appraisals tend to be lenient. However, if objective standards are adhered to, self-appraisals can work.

Should Employees Be Informed of the Results of Evaluation?

Some supervisors agree with Martin's statement (see Block 9–3). They feel it isn't necessary to sit down and explain the results of their performance evaluation to subordinates. Actually, this is a very limited view for supervisors to hold. A basic principle from psychology as applied to the work setting is that people need feedback. They need to be told where they stand and how they are doing. Consequently, it is essential that the results of employee evaluations be communicated to subor-

Martin Jenkins and Ray Barney were having lunch. They were talking about the company policy requiring them to sit down with each subordinate and discuss his or her performance evaluation. Ray said that it seems like a good idea to let people know where they stand. Martin replied, "That's a bunch of bunk. Employees know when they are doing a good job and when they aren't. I don't see any need to sit down and tell them, 'You're doing fine in this part of your job, but you need to improve in that part of your job.' Besides, as often as not, the person being evaluated will start making excuses for weaknesses you point out. Then voices get louder and louder, and you're lucky if the two of you are on speaking terms when the interview is over."

dinates. In practice, discussion of appraisals with employees is almost universal among American organizations; 97 percent report doing so.[9]

How Often Should Employees Be Evaluated?

Another principle from applied psychology is that regular feedback improves performance. In practice, however, most organizations evaluate employees only once a year. After the completion of a probationary period during which appraisals may be more frequent, one survey found that 74 percent evaluate office employees annually and 58 percent evaluate production workers annually.[10] Semiannual evaluations accounted for most of the remainder.

Based on the assumption that an organization uses evaluations for both identifying training and development needs *and* determining wage and salary increases, we recommend that employees be evaluated at least twice a year. The supervisor who must serve as both coach concerning development needs and decision maker about raises in pay at the same point in time is in an impossible situation.

By using multiple appraisals annually, the supervisor can direct the efforts of the first interview on the training and development needs of subordinates. Then, after the subordinate has had a chance to overcome deficiencies identified in the development appraisal interview, performance can be re-evaluated. The results of the second appraisal can be used in making decisions about size of raises.

How Do I Conduct
a Performance Appraisal Interview?

There are three basic approaches to conducting performance appraisal interviews:

1. The tell-and-sell approach
2. The tell-and-listen approach
3. The problem-solving approach [11]

Tell-and-Sell Approach

The tell-and-sell approach is the most common way of conducting performance appraisal interviews. In a tell-and-sell interview the supervisor assumes the role of judge of subordinates' performance. He or she approaches the interview as a one-way communication process in which the superior points out what is right or wrong with the subordinate's performance and specifies solutions to any perceived deficiencies. Because the superior does not give the subordinate an opportunity to explain his or her point of view, this approach can lead to arguments, rejection of the supervisor's recommendations for improvement, and outright rejection of the superior's performance appraisal.

Tell-and-Listen Approach

The supervisor also assumes the role of judge in the tell-and-listen approach by enumerating the good aspects and the poor aspects of the subordinate's performance and by recommending a course of action to overcome deficiencies. In contrast to the tell-and-sell approach, however, the subordinate is encouraged to express his or her point of view and, hopefully, to release any aggressive feelings. The subordinate may, therefore, be more receptive to the results of the evaluation and the suggestions for improvement. Also, the superior may discover additional information that could affect both the evaluation and plans for individual development.

Problem-Solving Approach

In the problem-solving interview, the superior is in the role of coach or helper, and the objective is to use a subordinate's self-evaluation to help overcome perceived deficiencies in the subordinate's performance. The principal advantage of such a joint effort is that subordinates will

197

be more committed to implementing the decisions arrived at during the interview.

A suggested series of questions which a supervisor could ask during a problem-solving interview is presented in Block 9–4.

The problem-solving approach to appraisal interviews requires that subordinates be objective in their self-evaluations and that supervisors be both insightful and good psychologists. Additionally, subordinates should be active participants in suggesting ways to improve performance.

This approach to a performance evaluation interview is particularly useful when combined with evaluation by results. With this evaluation technique, measurable goals and results must have been decided on in advance. Consequently, one can rely on self-evaluations to be fairly accurate and objective.

Refer again to Block 9–3. Martin argued that employees are aware of their weaknesses. He also said that appraisal interviews often end up with arguments and hard feelings. With respect to his first statement, research on the topic shows that for the most part employees cannot pinpoint the weaknesses in their performance. Perhaps they sense areas in which they need improvement, but these vague feelings must be clarified.

Second, regarding the claim that appraisal interviews often result in hard feelings, we agree that this is a likely result of the tell-and-sell approach. However, the other two approaches do give subordinates an opportunity to have their say. We strongly encourage the use of either the tell-and-listen or the problem-solving approach to performance appraisal interviews.

BLOCK 9–4   The Problem-Solving Interview

1. Warm-up period: "How have things been going on the job lately?"
2. Explore good points: "What things do you feel have been going especially well on the job?"
3. Explore weak points: "What aspects of your job performance do you feel could be improved or aren't being done as well as you would like?"
4. Discuss causes and solutions: After the subordinate has suggested areas needing improvement, explore causes and possible courses of action. "Why do you feel you are having problems in performing this part of your job?" "What do you feel can be done to improve this aspect of your job performance?"

PERFORMANCE APPRAISAL BY SUPERVISORS: PULLING IT TOGETHER

1. Focus on job behaviors, job results, or both. Do not focus on personality or character traits. Evaluating character traits threatens a person's ego. People naturally become defensive when their ego is attacked. The more an employee is on the defensive, the less he or she is likely to accept the results of the evaluation, and the less likely that person is to try to overcome performance deficiencies.

2. Ensure right from the beginning of the performance period that subordinates understand the standards by which they will be evaluated. Research on goal setting shows that performance is better when individuals have clear and definite objectives. Also, by setting measurable goals, a supervisor avoids having to quibble with subordinates over performance appraisal results.

3. In conducting a performance appraisal interview, discuss the duties and responsibilities of the individual. Be sure that you and the person being evaluated have the same ideas about the nature of his or her responsibilities. For example, you might ask:

"Which of your duties and responsibilities do you feel is most important?"
"Which take most of your time?"
"What are the standards by which your performance should be appraised?"

4. When you are ready to review a person's strengths and weaknesses, ask the person to tell you what he or she has done particularly well and what he or she would like to do better. Remember, an individual is more likely to accept the results of self-evaluation than the results of an evaluation by a superior. Questions which might be used are:

"What do you think are your greatest strengths?"
"What do you think you have done particularly well?"
"Where do you feel less confident?"

A supervisor should also explore what a subordinate feels can be done to make his or her job performance better.

5. Effective listening is crucial to achieving the purpose of an interview. If a supervisor interrupts when the employee clearly wants to make some point, he or she is missing one of the best opportunities to gain

some insight into the other person. Remember, listening is more than just keeping silent while the other person talks. One should try to understand not only how the other person views the facts, but also the values and attitudes which shape that person's perception.

6. If the subordinate appraises himself or herself more favorably than you do, restate the self-appraisal to be sure you understand. If you still disagree, you could review the points on which you do agree with the subordinate's self-evaluation. Then review the points on which you differ and invite the individual to explain the reasoning behind his or her ratings.

7. Be aware of common rater errors, especially halo and leniency. In other words, try to be objective. Try not to be influenced by things that do not affect the individual's contribution to the organization such as appearance or personal habits. Also, in evaluating different dimensions of an individual's contributions to the organization, try to keep each aspect separate in your own mind.

When the results of an appraisal are going to be discussed with the subordinate, it is particularly easy to fall into the trap of leniency. However, overlooking deficiencies in performance solves nothing in the long run. Before a person can overcome a shortcoming in his or her performance, it must be acknowledged. Making people aware of areas needing improvement is the necessary first step.

8. Don't try to do too much at once. Rome wasn't built in a day and you cannot overcome every deficiency in a subordinate's performance in one appraisal period. Select two or three important aspects of performance which are deficient and focus on correcting them. When improvements are made in these areas, other deficiencies can be addressed in future appraisal interviews.

QUESTIONS

1. Explain why accurate performance appraisals are so important for motivating an organization's employees.
2. What should be the basis of employee evaluation and what should be avoided?
3. Why do BARS reduce common rater errors?
4. Describe the advantages and disadvantages of different performance appraisal techniques.
5. Explain why a combination of BARS and evaluation of results might be the most effective approach to performance evaluation.
6. Who should evaluate performance and how often? Why?
7. Describe the basic approaches to conducting appraisal interviews. Discuss their advantages and disadvantages.

THE COUNTY ASSESSOR'S RECEPTIONIST

Martha Schmidt is receptionist at the Grant County assessor's office. In addition to her duties involved with meeting the public, she types and files correspondence for the county assessor. You are the county assessor. Martha is an excellent typist and file clerk. She is also very dependable; she is never absent without good reason and never tardy.

However, at times Martha has difficulty dealing with the public. Many times county residents come in to ask questions or to complain about the assessed value of their property. Often their aggravation will spill over to Martha, and she will reply in a sharper, more impolite manner. Usually things just get worse from then on. Almost without exception you must take charge by calling the person into your office and settling the problem yourself.

1. How should you approach this problem with Martha?
2. Plan a performance appraisal interview. Be prepared to role play the interview with another member of class.

NOTES

[1] *Employee Performance: Evaluations and Control,* Personnel Policies Forum (PPF) Survey No. 108 (Washington, D.C.: Bureau of National Affairs, February 1975).

[2] P. C. Smith and L. M. Kendall, "Retranslation of Expectations: An Approach to the Construction of Unambiguous Anchors for Rating Scales," *Journal of Applied Psychology, 47* (1963), 149–55.

[3] D. McGregor, *The Human Side of Enterprise* (New York: McGraw-Hill, 1960).

[4] G. P. Lathan and J. J. Baldes, "The 'Practical Significance' of Locke's Theory of Goal Setting," *Journal of Applied Psychology, 60* (1975), 122–24; and E. A. Locke "Toward A Theory of Task Motivation and Incentives," *Organizational Behavior and Human Performance, 3* (1968), 157–89.

[5] R. W. Beatty, "A Comparison of the Operationalization of Behavior-Based Versus Effectiveness-Based Performance Appraisals." Preliminary Draft. Mimeographed Paper, Graduate School of Business, University of Colorado, Boulder, Colo., September 1977.

[6] *Employee Performance: Evaluations and Control,* p. 5.

[7] Walter C. Borman, "The Rating of Individuals in Organizations: An Alternative Approach," *Organizational Behavior and Human Performance, 12* (1974), 105–24.

[8] P. Maloney and J. Hinricks, "A New Tool for Supervisory Self-Development," *Personnel, 36* (July 1959), 46–53.

[9] *Employee Performance: Evaluations and Control,* p. 6.

[10] *Employee Performance: Evaluations and Control,* p. 3.

[11] N. R. F. Maier, *Psychology in Industrial Organizations,* 4th ed. (Boston: Houghton Mifflin, 1973).

The Supervisor
and
the Problem Employee

 SUPERVISORY PROBLEMS

How can a supervisor bring about a change in an employee's behavior?
What methods constitute effective discipline?

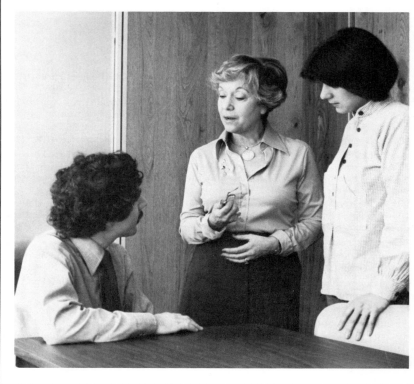

Courtesy Irene Springer

LEARNING OBJECTIVES

When you have finished this chapter you should be able to

1. Describe how to use positive reinforcement to change behavior
2. Discuss the disadvantages of using punishment to change employee behavior
3. Identify corrective discipline
4. List and describe the components of an effective discipline system
5. Describe the "hot stove" rule
6. Discuss factors to consider in deciding on the appropriate discipline for a given rule violation
7. Identify the do's and don'ts of implementing a disciplinary action
8. Recommend how to approach the employee who has a drinking problem or faces a family or mid-career crisis

THE ABSENTEEISM PROBLEM

Jane Adams is the supervisor of the medical records section at the County General Hospital. She has a discipline problem facing her. Under her supervision are 25 individuals who are responsible for maintaining records on patients at the hospital. Three of these individuals were absent yesterday. In each case it was the third absence in less than six months. According to hospital personnel policy, if an individual has three absences within a six-month period, he or she will be subject to a disciplinary layoff of three days. The background and situation of each individual is as follows:

Martha Baker has been with the hospital for over 20 years. She has an excellent record of performance and is typically a highly reliable individual. The reason for her absence was that while on her way to work she was involved in an automobile accident. The time involved in filling out police reports and arranging to have her car towed to a garage had taken almost half a day. Also, she was so shaken by the accident, that she felt unable to resume her usual duties. She did phone in about the accident as soon as she could.

Kathy Larson has been with the hospital for two years and has been a reliable individual. She can be described as a good, solid, average performer. Kathy had also been on her way to work. She lives quite a distance

203

from work. She ran out of gasoline on the freeway. She said that it took a couple of hours to get gasoline. After getting the gasoline, the car wouldn't start so she ended up having the car towed to a station. By this time it was noon so she just didn't think there was any real reason to go to work. Kathy did not call in about her car trouble. Kathy is divorced and is supporting two children. You have heard informally that Kathy's former husband has not been making child-support payments lately. As a result, a three-day suspension will put Kathy in a financial bind.

The third case involved Helen Olson. Helen has been with the hospital for about seven years. She is an average performer and is an informal group leader. As a matter of fact, she is the union steward for the hospital employees union. Helen had called in yesterday that she would be unable to come to work because her husband was out of town on a business trip and her child had come down with a very severe case of the flu. Since the child was sick, he could not be left at the day care center, and it was too late for Helen to make other arrangements.

Our chapter opening case gives us some idea of the day-to-day problems every supervisor must face in disciplining employees. Every organization has a set of policies concerning performance and attendance standards as well as a set of penalties for failure to meet these standards. No one denies that the three individuals in the illustration violated company policy by being absent three times during the past six months. However, should the supervisor apply the same penalty when there are varying degrees of justification for failure to meet the standards? When there are differences in seniority and past work performance? When there are factors beyond an employee's control contributing to the rule violation and varying degrees of hardship resulting from disciplinary action.

What do you do about problem employees? There are a number of possible approaches.[1] One approach, probably the worst, is to do nothing—simply permit the employee who hands in substandard work or breaks the rules to continue with that behavior. Other alternatives are to reprimand the person or to give him or her a disciplinary layoff. The ultimate penalty is to discharge the individual.

HOW CAN I HANDLE PROBLEM EMPLOYEES?

As a supervisor, you will often be faced with the task of bringing about a change in a problem employee's behavior. The law of effect (Chapter 7) suggests that behavior or performance which results in need satisfaction tends to be repeated. Behavior which results in no need satisfaction or the withdrawal of something satisfying—for example, the removal of the superior's esteem through reprimand—tends not to be repeated.

Positive Reinforcement

As supervisor, you must begin by identifying those behaviors which are inconsistent with the attainment of organizational goals. Then, before punishing those individuals who exhibit that behavior, try positively reinforcing those who exhibit the desired behavior. For example, if absenteeism is a problem, you might provide some form of extra reward for those individuals who are *not* absent. Some organizations have rewarded those employees who have perfect attendance for a week or a month with a bonus.

Figure 10–1 describes how to identify positive reinforcers. In keeping with the law of effect, a positive reinforcer is one that increases the frequency of a behavior. The top part of Figure 10–1 represents a reward that increases the frequency of being at work on time. The supervisor provides a reward (praise) which is contingent or depends on the desired behavior (being on time). If the effect of this reward (praise) is to increase the frequency of the desired behavior (being at work on time) we say that the reward (praise) is a positive reinforcer.

On the other hand, when the individual is at work on time and the supervisor praises him or her, but the employee's frequency of being at work on time in the future does not change, then we conclude that praise

FIGURE 10–1   Identifying Positive Reinforcers

Positive Reinforcer

Not a Positive Reinforcer

is not a positive reinforcer for that employee. This is represented by the lower part of Figure 10–1. In such a case, the supervisor would do well to look for a different reward which might be effective. The chapter on motivation discusses the categories of needs, and suggests different kinds of rewards that might be effective.

Block 10–1 briefly describes several examples of how organizations have used positive reinforcement to reduce the frequency of unwanted behavior. The central theme of these examples is the use of money or time off as a reward. One should remember that recognition and praise can be positive reinforcers too.

Punishment

Punishment is the other basic alternative to positive reinforcement for changing behavior. Punishment is widely used in our society to control behavior. In work organizations it can take many forms. It can be a frown, a chewing out, an embarrassing remark, a letter of reprimand, a demotion, a suspension from work, or discharge. A key consideration in the use of punishment or negative control is the side effects it may unwittingly cause. Figure 10–2 outlines the alternative forms of punishment and the potential effects of punishment. As with our previous

---

BLOCK 10–1 Examples of the Use of Positive Reinforcement

Several organizations have tried to use a more positive approach to deal with problem employees.[2] An approach used at one company is to have a lottery at the end of each day. When an individual comes to work, he or she is given a ticket and at the end of each day, a number is drawn from a bowl. The winner receives a cash prize. This has cut down on absenteeism. Other organizations have used leisure time as a reward. Standards of output for superior performance are established. When an employee reaches that level, he or she receives the rest of the day off.

Paid sick leave causes problems in some organizations. While it is a desirable benefit, it can be thought of as a reward for being absent from work. Some organizations allow an individual to build up a bank of unused sick days so that in the event of a major illness the person is able to receive full pay for an extended period of time. Another approach along the same lines is for an employee to go into an extended sick leave period just prior to official retirement, or to take the accumulated sick leave in the form of pay—a nice little bonus received at retirement time.

FIGURE 10–2   The Effects of Punishment

		Short Run		Long Run
Behavior ⟶	Punishment ---→	Future ---→ behavior		1. Temporary behavior change
				2. Undesirable emotional effect
"Late for work"	"Reprimand" or "three-day suspension"	"Decrease in frequency of being late"		3. Permanent damage to desirable behavior
				4. Fear/dislike of supervisor

Source: Adapted from *Organizational Behavior Modification*, by Fred Luthans and Robert Kreitner. Copyright © 1975 by Scott, Foresman and Company. Reprinted by permission.

example, we have selected tardiness as the behavior problem. Punishment can take two forms: (1) A reprimand (a chewing out) is the presentation of something the person would rather avoid whenever the troublesome behavior occurs; (2) the three-day suspension, by contrast, is the *removal of positive reward* when the person engages in the undesired behavior.

Effects of Punishment

The objective of behavior change through punishment is decreasing the frequency of the undesired behavior—in this case, being late. Figure 10–2 indicates that this may indeed be a short-run effect of punishment. However, there are also several possible long-term effects, most of them undesirable. It is these factors that reduce the efficiency of using punishment as a way of controlling behavior in a work setting.

Temporary Behavior Change

What is meant by a *temporary behavior change* is well expressed by the old saying, "When the cat's away, the mice will play." This means that when a supervisor uses punishment to obtain the desired behavior, he or she falls into the trap of having to use it continually in order to gain compliance. When the source of punishment (the supervisor) is not present, the punished behavior is likely to return. In the example presented in Figure 10–2, if the supervisor isn't going to be present, you can expect the subordinates to come in late. Alternatively, if there is some way for employees to get away with coming in late without being caught, they'll probably find it.

207

Undesirable Emotional Effects

Here we are referring to such reactions as anger, aggression, fear, or withdrawal from the situation. Examples might be yelling back or striking a supervisor, sabotaging a piece of equipment or some material, or taking it out on customers when reprimanded. Such a reaction is undesirable because it creates additional problems both for the supervisor and for the employee. Put very simply, it is likely that this kind of behavior will follow disciplinary action.

Permanent Damage to Desirable Behavior

We have pointed out that punishment will probably result in only a temporary change of behavior and that the undesirable behavior may return when the source of punishment is not present. Another possible side effect is permanently removing desirable behaviors. Block 10–2 describes a situation that is common to participants in supervisory development programs.

What might explain Mary's situation is that early in the subordinates' working relationship with Mary, they did try to handle problems without going to her, and she criticized them severely for doing so. As a result, the subordinates never take the initiative. Because of punishment, we see the permanent removal of desirable behavior.

Perhaps early in the working relationship, Mary felt that the subordinates didn't have enough background information or weren't familiar enough with the organization to take the initiative on some problems. Probably what she was trying to do was get the employee to hold off until he or she had more experience in a particular area. However, because of the punishing tones of Mary's "lessons," the employee becomes unwilling to take the initiative *anytime*.

Another example involves absenteeism. One organization has a policy which severely punishes absenteeism, yet in some cases the organization

---

BLOCK 10–2   Why Won't They Take the Initiative?

Mary Fredricks supervises the bookkeeping section for the Central Motel. Something which occurs again and again, which she cannot understand, is the lack of initiative among employees in her section. Whenever anything out of the ordinary happens, her subordinates will not try to solve the problem. Instead they bring the problem to her. Mary knows that they have the experience and ability to handle most of the problems. Why won't they take the initiative?

would prefer to have people absent. Suppose an individual is coming down with the flu. When this person comes to work, the flu is spread to the rest of the work force. In this example company policy results in employees trying not to be absent so long as they are able to come to work but defeats itself in the long run.

Fear/Dislike of Supervisor

Another unwanted effect of punishment is the breakdown of good relations between a superior and a subordinate, or the guarantee that good relationships will not develop. Chapter 4 suggested that a good approach to leadership is for the supervisor to develop a cooperative relationship with subordinates. This assumes participative management in which the leader gets subordinates to make a meaningful contribution to the solution of problems facing the work group. It is difficult for a supervisor to establish this kind of working relationship with subordinates when the supervisor is seen as the source of punishment and discipline.

Overview of Long-Run Effects

Many students of behavior change have argued that the long-run effects of punishment for securing compliance are very costly.[3] Recall that the Theory X supervisor assumes that employees are lazy, that they must be watched closely to get them to work, and that they are immature and passive. We believe that frequent use of punishment and close control to obtain compliance causes employees to behave as the Theory X supervisor says they behave. In other words, punishment leads to dependent, passive, and immature behavior from workers.

Effective Use of Negative Control

Sometimes it is necessary to get rid of some undesired job behavior as quickly as possible. As a result, punishment may be required. Whenever punishment is used, there should be an attempt to couple it with positive reinforcement if possible. The reason for doing this is to minimize the possible negative effects of punishment. For example, if you have a problem with an employee regularly coming in late, it might be necessary to reprimand that individual. This is punishment. Suppose the next morning the individual does come in on time. You could then use positive reinforcement, such as pointing out that you are glad he or she was on time and that you hope he or she will keep it up in the future. Another variation, when the person is on time, would be to acknowledge this fact and point out that it makes it easier for everyone else in the work group when everyone is prompt.

EFFECTIVE DISCIPLINE

There are basically two approaches to discipline: authoritarian and corrective.[4] In the authoritarian approach, disciplinary action is intended to be punishment for breaking a rule and the purpose is to discourage others from doing the same thing. Corrective discipline, on the other hand, emphasizes correction or reform of the delinquent behavior in accordance with the organization's standards. Effective discipline generally falls into the corrective rather than the authoritarian category. This means that the objective should be to improve or bring about the desired behavior change in the employee. Discharge, which is not corrective, should be used only when corrective measures have failed to bring about the desired change or when the offense is so serious that corrective measures are not appropriate.

Corrective Discipline

The following five items represent the basic components of an effective employee discipline plan:

1. Clear statements of discipline policies and procedures
2. Uniform application of discipline rules
3. Supervisors trained in the organization's discipline program
4. A training program to ensure that all employees are familiar with the organization's performance standards
5. A continuous effort by the organization to communicate to employees all changes and modifications in personnel policies and discipline procedures *before* the changes are put into effect [5]

What Are the Basics
of Good Discipline Policy?

The field of labor arbitration provides us with some guidelines about infractions of company rules and regulations and levels of punishment.[6] Offenses fall into two general categories:

1. Major violations, which include such serious offenses as stealing, striking a supervisor, and refusal to obey directions from a supervisor, justify discharge without prior warnings or attempts at corrective discipline.
2. Minor offenses, or less serious infractions of plant rules such as absence

without permission, tardiness, or poor workmanship, do not call for discharge for the first offense, and perhaps not even for a second or third offense. In such cases, it is expected that the organization will engage in a process of corrective discipline.

Labor arbitrators also recommend that the company post a listing of common infractions and the disciplinary action which will be·taken for each infraction. Both supervisors and employees should be aware of these policies at the start of employment.

Uniform Application

The results of one study indicate that effective discipline is closely correlated with the consistency with which disciplinary action is taken when a rule is broken.[7] Figure 10–3 highlights the importance of consistency. With an ineffective disciplinary system, in almost two out of three cases, discipline problems are frequently "overlooked" by supervisors. On the other hand, in effective discipline systems, infractions are overlooked only about one-third of the time.

Why don't supervisors discipline problem employees? A number of reasons have been suggested. One of the problems is lack of training—some supervisors just don't know how to handle discipline problems. Another factor is fear. A supervisor might be concerned about whether or not he or she will be backed up by higher levels of management. Other factors are expressed by the questions presented in Block 10–3.

The prospect of having to discipline a friend is especially touchy. Therefore, we recommend that when an individual is promoted to a supervisory position that person be moved to another part of the organization. By and large, however, these objections to enforcing the rules are what we call excuses or rationalizations to enable one to get out of doing an unpleasant task. There is no question that it is unpleasant to discipline someone. However, if rules are overlooked for some individuals and in some situations, there will be charges of in-

FIGURE 10–3 Overlooking Disciplinary Problems and Effectiveness of Disciplinary Systems

Effectiveness of System	Overlook Frequently	Discipline Sometimes	Seldom Overlook Problems
Effective	35.3%	52.9%	11.8%
Ineffective	62.5%	37.5%	00.0%

Source: Adapted from James A. Belohlav and Paul O. Popp, "Making Employee Discipline Work," *Personnel Administrator*, 23 (March 1978), 24.

equity, and eventually both order and organizational goals will get lost in the shuffle.

Supervisory Training and Orientation of Employees

What does it take to achieve uniform application of the rules? One answer is provided by the "hot stove" rule of discipline. A person who has worked around a hot stove will recognize these consequences of disrespect for the rules (touching the stove):

1. Immediate or prompt reaction to touching the stove
2. Consistent for everyone touching the stove
3. Impersonal or nonpunitive
4. Advance warning

Immediate or Prompt Action

Disciplinary action, when necessary, should come as soon after breaking the rule as possible. As supervisor, you should not delay disciplinary action. The major exception to this principle is when either or both subordinate and supervisor have lost their tempers. In this case, it is best to delay the disciplinary action until things cool off.

Consistency

There are two dimensions to the issue of consistency. One is consistency across units within the organization. An organization cannot have one department taking more severe disciplinary action for a given infraction than other departments. The word will get around and those receiving the more severe punishment will feel unfairly treated. To overcome this problem, a set of uniform disciplinary actions should be specified, and these actions be followed throughout the organization.

The other dimension to the issue of consistency is that the penalties should be impartial. There should be no personal bias or favoritism entering into decisions. This aspect of consistency is difficult to implement. For example, when a disciplinary action goes to arbitration, it is common for the arbitrator to review the disciplinary action in view of the employee's past performance and record with the organization. If inconsistencies are found in the way the employee was disciplined and the way others have been disciplined, the case will be decided in the employee's favor. How to determine whether a proposed disciplinary action is consistent with past actions taken across the organization will be discussed in detail in the section on progressive discipline.

Advance Warning

When an individual has been around a hot stove for a while, he or she knows what happens when the stove is touched. Similarly, in an effective discipline system, employees are informed of the rules and the action which will be taken when the rules are broken. Making available to employees a set of policies and rules of the organization and disciplinary action to be taken with respect to the rules is important. We recommend that when an employee joins the organization, this be included as part of the orientation program. Of course, employees must also be informed of any changes that are made in the rules. This communication must precede the enforcement of the rules. It would be unfair to punish an individual for an infraction that was never made known to all employees.

CORRECTIVE OR PROGRESSIVE DISCIPLINE

The objective of progressive discipline is to change some undesired employee behavior. It involves progressively more severe levels of punishment. The typical sequence of progressive discipline is as follows:

1. Oral or verbal warning
2. Written warning
3. Suspension
4. Discharge

What Is Appropriate Discipline?

Figure 10–4 reports the results of a survey of American organizations concerning various offenses and the disciplinary action taken with regard to each. The typical reaction to the first infraction of most rules is a warning. This is followed with a suspension for the second or third offense. Finally, discharge is common for the third or fourth offense. Violations involving dishonesty are an exception in that discharge is typical for the first offense.

A word of explanation is needed concerning the meaning of the warning category in Figure 10–4. Typically, a warning is a written notice that also appears as an official entry in the employee's personnel record. The report that accompanied this survey indicated that in many cases the warning "is preceded by an oral or verbal discussion with the individual concerning a particular offense." [8]

Legalistic Approach

How much weight should you give to "extenuating circumstances" in deciding what disciplinary action to take? The more legalistic your approach, the less consideration you will give to extenuating circumstances. According to the "hot stove" rule, regardless of extenuating circumstances, if an individual breaks a rule, the specified disciplinary action should follow.

As a practical matter, however, you should be aware that if a disciplinary action is brought before a grievance committee and goes to arbitration, the arbitrator *is* probably going to consider extenuating circumstances. [9] The only infractions in which arbitrators typically take a completely legalistic approach are refusal to obey orders, fighting with a supervisor, and dishonesty.

Factors To Consider

1. Seriousness of the offense. If the violation involves dishonesty or refusal to obey a lawful order, the appropriate action is probably an automatic application of the rules without considering extenuating circumstances. Assuming one is dealing with other kinds of problems, then the following considerations should be kept in mind.

2. Time period. How frequently have you as supervisor had problems with this particular employee? If it is a frequent problem then more serious discipline action is appropriate. However, if it's something that has come up for the first time in two or three years, then a different level of discipline is appropriate.

FIGURE 10–4 Patterns of Disciplinary Action for Various Offenses

Type of Offense	First Offense			Second Offense			Third Offense			Fourth Offense		
	W	S	D	W	S	D	W	S	D	W	S	D
Attendance Problems												
Unexcused absence	84	21	3	60	28	3	13	47	26	2	11	52
Unexcused/excessive lateness	92	1	0	68	24	1	20	53	21	4	12	55
Leaving without permission	78	10	7	33	37	20	6	30	34	0	3	30
On-the-Job Behavior Problems												
Intoxication at work	28	33	36	8	22	32	2	5	22	1	0	7
Insubordination	36	28	34	9	22	35	1	8	22	0	1	7
Smoking in unauthorized places	65	10	5	28	32	15	4	23	28	16	3	18
Fighting	16	25	54	4	9	30	1	1	11	0	0	2
Gambling	39	21	27	11	19	30	4	8	17	1	1	10
Failure to use safety devices	81	2	2	46	31	6	12	30	32	4	8	27
Carelessness	89	3	0	55	31	4	12	44	30	2	5	50
Sleeping on the job	40	34	24	8	23	42	1	5	26	0	1	9
Abusive or threatening language to supervision	34	33	30	8	24	37	1	6	23	0	0	7
Possession of narcotics	10	11	70	3	3	13	1	1	3	1	0	1
Possession of firearms or other weapons	9	10	63	2	4	12	0	1	4	0	0	1
Dishonesty and Related Problems												
Theft	2	6	90	1	0	9	0	0	1	0	0	0
Falsifying employment application	6	0	88	1	1	2	0	0	1	0	0	0
Willful damage to company property	17	17	64	4	11	21	0	2	13	0	0	4
Punching another employee's time card	19	21	40	4	10	38	2	4	8	0	0	5
Falsifying work records	15	18	58	3	4	28	1	2	5	0	0	2

Codes: W = warning   S = suspension   D = discharge

Percentages may not add to 100 because some companies did not respond to all types of offenses.

Source: Adapted from Personnel Policies Forum: *Employee Conduct and Discipline*, Survey No. 102 (Washington, D.C.: Bureau of National Affairs, August 1973), p. 6.

3. Work history. There are two dimensions to this factor. One is the length of time an individual has been with the organization and the other is the nature of his or her performance. Arbitrators take both seniority and level of performance into consideration.

4. Extenuating factors. This deals with the extent to which the employee was at fault or had control of the situation in which the rule infraction occurred. If the individual was in a fight provoked by *another person,* this should be taken into consideration. Another example could involve tardiness. Being late for work because one overslept is different from being late because of an automobile accident and having to stay at the scene of the accident to complete police forms.

5. History of disciplinary practices in the organization. This consideration parallels the issue of consistency discussed in the "hot stove" rule. What disciplinary action was taken when other employees violated this same rule? The organization has to be consistent over time and it has to be consistent across departments within the organization.

6. Awareness of rules. As noted previously, employees must be aware of the rules and the penalties associated with rule infractions. If the organization has failed to communicate this information to employees, then it is unfair for the supervisor to take disciplinary action.

7. Nature of the evidence. How sure or how confident are you that the individual did break the rule? The supervisor should distinguish between fact and allegation. Facts are those pieces of information that are not in dispute, but allegations can be in dispute. This implies that the supervisor should reassess the situation and the charges being made before taking disciplinary action.

The Slide Rule Approach

The previous section shows that common sense is often involved in selecting the appropriate discipline. Some organizations have attempted to minimize discretion on the part of the supervisor in administering discipline. This is referred to as "slide rule" discipline.[10] Basically, it involves establishing a certain time frame associated with offenses. For example, the second time an employee is found smoking in a "no smoking" area within any 60-day period, the employee will be suspended for three days. The slide rule approach sets very specific rules both with respect to the frequency of offense within a certain time period and to the penalty to be imposed. The objective of the slide rule approach is to achieve consistent application of discipline. The disadvantage is that the supervisor has no discretion left in applying the rule. Block 10–4 describes an organization using the slide rule approach to discipline and the problem it can create for a supervisor.

The National Manufacturing Company has a rule that any employee tardy more than three times in any 90-day period will receive a one-day disciplinary layoff. Martin Biggs was late this morning. It was the third time in the last two weeks. The reason he was late is that his wife had a baby. He took her to the hospital. After the baby was delivered and the physician assured him that everything was all right, he came to work.

The other absences in the past two weeks have been connected with his wife's pregnancy. She had false labor pains and Martin had taken her to the physician. In both cases, after being assured that his wife was all right and returning her home, Martin had come to work.

Martin has been with National for six years. He is an above-average performer. Apart from these past two weeks, he has been very reliable.

Martin's supervisor is faced with a number of factors an arbitrator would probably consider extenuating circumstances. However, Martin's supervisor does not have a way to consider these factors and still abide by the rules of the organization. The only choice the supervisor has is either to enforce the rule or to ignore the violation. Unfortunately, ignoring the offense contributes to a breakdown in the effectiveness of the discipline system. For this reason, we feel that the slide rule approach runs counter to a more effective approach to discipline, which is proper training of supervisors in the application of disciplinary procedures and in the weight to be given to extenuating circumstances.

ADMINISTERING DISCIPLINE

The way in which discipline is administered does make a difference. In this section, we will consider warnings, suspension, and discharge and give some do's and don'ts for each category.

Oral Warning

When a rule has been broken and the supervisor must give an oral warning, try the following approach. First, speak with the employee in private. State your view of the situation and then give the employee an opportunity to tell his or her side of the story. Don't interrupt the subordinate once he or she has been given the go-ahead to reply.

Perhaps some new information will come to light during this exchange that will alter your opinion. If you feel, however, that your view of the situation is justified, you should proceed with the oral warning. The tone of the interview should be as positive and cooperative as possible. Focus on the problem or the rule violation and do not criticize the personal characteristics of the employee. Do not let your tone of voice become sarcastic. Instead, try to focus on what can be done to improve the situation or ensure that the problem will not recur. Do not confuse this approach with being "soft"; your goal as supervisor is to ensure that future working relationships will be as positive as possible.

The supervisor should keep a record of the oral warning. If the oral reprimand is the first stage in the disciplinary procedure, a record of the disciplinary interview should be entered in the employee's personnel file.

Written Warning

Assuming the oral reprimand was not effective in changing behavior, the next step in progressive discipline is typically a written warning. Block 10–5 shows the right and wrong ways to compose written warnings. The first example is deficient because it doesn't point out to the employee exactly what is wrong with his or her performance. It indicates neither what rule has been broken nor what should be done to improve. The second fails because of its apologetic tone. It conveys to the employee that, "Gee whiz, it's too bad that I have to write this warning but there are people breathing down my neck so I have to do it." Another problem with the second notice is that it does not make clear to the employee what is likely to happen if the rule is broken again.

Warning 3 is the recommended approach. It notes that an oral reprimand has already been issued and clearly states what behavior is expected from the employee. It also spells out the next step in the disciplinary procedure if a change does not occur. Finally, by asking the employee to sign the memo, the supervisor has a permanent record that the individual has received the written warning. This is critical if it becomes necessary to terminate the individual and the action is grieved. As with the oral warning, we recommend that the written warning be given to the employee in person and in a private setting.

Suspension

The next level of disciplinary action is suspension or disciplinary layoff. For minor infractions, disciplinary layoff usually follows the written warning and the oral reprimand. For more serious rule infractions, it might be the first step in the disciplinary chain. As with the written warning, it is important that an interview take place and a memo be

BLOCK 10–5   Alternative Written Warnings

1. MEMO TO: J. Jones   DATE: July 1, 19_____
   FROM: J. Smith   SUBJECT: Written Warning
   Your performance is unsatisfactory. If you don't straighten out, you will be terminated.

2. MEMO TO: J. Jones   DATE: July 1, 19_____
   FROM: J. Smith   SUBJECT: First Written Warning
   Although you were late to work again today, please do not worry about it. I realize it is hard for you to get out of bed in the morning, and so I am not concerned about your lateness. I am sorry to have to do this, but I am forced to give you this written warning because the personnel office requires that I do so. They also require that I tell you the consequences of continued violations of their rules. Therefore, further tardiness may result in another written warning or possibly discharge.

3. MEMO TO: J. Jones   DATE: July 1, 19_____
   FROM: J. Smith   SUBJECT: Written Warning
   Today, you were 30 minutes late to work with no justification for your tardiness. A similar offense occurred last Friday. At that time you were told that failure to report to work on schedule would not be condoned. I now find it necessary to tell you in writing that you must report to work on time. Failure to do so will result in the termination of your employment. Please sign below that you have read and that you understand this written warning.

_____

Employee Signature

_____

Date

Source: "Administering Disciplinary Actions" by Rodney L. Oberle. Adapted with permission *Personnel Journal* copyright January 1978.

prepared so that it is clear to the employee just exactly what rule infraction was involved and that a change in performance is necessary. The next step in the disciplinary process should also be identified.

Discharge

The final step in the disciplinary sequence is discharge. This is the ultimate penalty and should be used only after all corrective measures

FIGURE 10–5   Discharge Procedures

Authority to Make Discharge Decisions

Department head	56%
Personnel Executive	52%
Supervisor	41%
Division/plant manager	35%
Chief executive	25%

Employees Permitted to Resign Rather Than Be Discharged

Yes	38%
Under some circumstances	38%
No	24%

Discharge Decision Can Be Formally Appealed	69%

Source: Adapted from *Personnel Policies Forum: Employee Conduct and Discipline*, Survey No. 102 (Washington, D.C.: Bureau of National Affairs, August 1973), p. 9.

have failed. Figure 10–5 indicates the results of a survey concerning discharge procedures. Typically, high-level officials in an organization are involved in discharge cases. The figures exceed 100 percent because the discharge decision is typically reviewed by more than one level in the organization. Quite often as many as three or four levels will review a recommendation for discharge before the decision is finalized.

In some circumstances, it is appropriate to give an employee the opportunity to resign rather than be discharged. Figure 10–5 indicates that this is a widespread practice. Some organizations permit resignation only in certain circumstances. For example, some firms give only supervisors and managers this option. Other special circumstances are length of service and character of prior performance. Finally, Figure 10–5 indicates that about seven out of ten companies have a formal appeal system should a discharged employee wish to appeal the decision.

Once the decision is made to discharge an employee, the supervisor should keep the following pointers in mind. First, the supervisor should never be apologetic. The decision should be presented as irrevocable, and the date of discharge clearly stated. We also recommend that termination interviews take place at the end of the day. In this way, other employees will have left the work area when the interview is completed and there will be a minimum amount of embarrassment associated with cleaning up one's work area and leaving the work place.

Another good practice is to notify the employee as soon as possible after the decision is final. One expert recommends that the supervisor maintain a "hands off" policy.[11] That is, during the interview the supervisor should not make any physical gestures or movements of his or her hands that could be used as an excuse to turn the interview into a fight.

The employee is likely to feel angry and any excuse along these lines could lead to physical violence.

As with suspension, a written document should be prepared, informing the individual of the dismissal action. In situations in which an appeals procedure is applicable, we recommend that documentation be prepared and maintained which records the progressive nature of the disciplinary action concerning the individual. This is doubly important when a third-party neutral or arbitrator could be called upon to review the disciplinary action.

SPECIAL EMPLOYEE PROBLEMS: ALCOHOLISM

Alcoholism and problem drinking are widespread and costly problems in the American business community. Alcoholism interferes with production and is associated with problems of labor turnover, lost production time, and increased medical costs. It is estimated that there are between four and six million alcoholics employed in American industry, comprising 3 to 8 percent of the work force. In addition, it is estimated that another 10 percent of the work force has serious drinking problems.

Another significant dimension of this problem is that problem drinking and alcoholism are concentrated in the most productive years, between ages 35 and 55. Because alcoholism is most prevalent among long-service employees—those with 15 to 20 years service—its impact on industry is particularly damaging.

As is indicated in Figure 10–4, discharge has been the usual method of dealing with intoxication at work. However, now it is becoming more common for an organization to try to rehabilitate the alcoholic employee.

Programs for Alcoholics

There are several variations among rehabilitation programs. For a complete discussion see Follmann.[12] However, in most situations the following guidelines are part of the program:

1. The employee acknowledges that alcoholism is an illness he or she is unable to cure without help.
2. Supervisors play the key role in early identification of the problem.
3. When an individual is identified as having a drinking problem, that person is referred to trained counselors or medical units.
4. If an individual is identified as an alcoholic, he or she is provided ample opportunity to receive treatment, but if the employee refuses to participate in the program, the individual is discharged.

5. Employees receive medical benefits and sick leave during a treatment period.
6. Medical records and the nature of the problem are kept confidential insofar as is possible.

As in most other areas of interpersonal relationships at work, the key person in an effective program for the treatment of alcoholism is the supervisor. The success of the program depends on correctly identifying those individuals with drinking problems, preferably as early as possible. It is critical, therefore, that supervisors receive training in the identification of those with drinking problems. Signs or signals of possible drinking problems are absenteeism, tardiness, friction and problems in dealing with co-workers, deterioration in level of performance, inconsistent job performance, lapses of memory, and customer complaints. Supervisors should recognize that alcoholic employees typically have difficulty in recognizing their own problem and are reluctant to admit that they have a problem.

Once a supervisor has good evidence that an employee probably has a drinking problem, that employee should be referred to the medical department or the personnel department. It is at this point that the individual will receive professional aid in the treatment of his or her problem.

Confrontation

When confronting the problem drinker, the focus should be on job performance and behavior rather than personal habits. The tone of the interview should be positive, with an emphasis on trying to improve the employee's performance, and continue his or her employment with the organization.

The importance of focusing on the job cannot be overemphasized. Research on the problem drinker shows that one of an alcoholic's last traces of self-respect is the ability to perform his or her job. Here lies the importance of offering the alcoholic employee a choice between undergoing treatment and overcoming the problem or being discharged. *To repeat, the job is likely to be the last respectable thing left in an alcoholic's life.* When this is threatened then you have the chance of providing the motivation for the individual to overcome the problem and participate in a rehabilitation program.

You should realize that you are not doing an alcoholic employee a favor by covering up for him or her. Confrontation with a clear-cut choice, followed by an all-out organizational effort to help the individual has proven the best solution.

In addition to internal rehabilitation efforts, Alcoholics Anonymous programs can usually be found in the community to assist in the rehabilitation program. Such combined efforts do appear to work. Surveys of companies with programs show that the rehabilitation rate is typically about two out of three alcoholic employees. This suggests that when a full-scale effort is put into a program, it can be quite successful in recovering the formerly productive employee.

SPECIAL EMPLOYEE PROBLEMS: FAMILY CRISES

Another common problem that you will encounter as a supervisor is employees whose on-the-job behavior is affected by such family crises as separation, divorce, or a death in the family. It is natural in these circumstances for employees to have difficulty in concentrating on their work. As a result, their performance deteriorates.

If a supervisor has a good working relationship with an employee undergoing a family crisis, the employee will probably depend on the supervisor for some kind of help. One of the authors heard of an especially hair-raising incident when teaching at a research development seminar. A participant said that one of his employees told him that his wife was seeing another man. The employee said he knew the other man and was going to kill him. Fortunately, the supervisor was able to talk the individual into taking another course of action—getting a divorce from his wife.

Dealing with problems of this kind is particularly difficult because the source of the problem is outside your control as supervisor. As a result, there is often little you can do to bring about a change. The most important thing for a supervisor to remember is to avoid any harsh or severe treatment at such times. By demonstrating a supportive leadership style, you are more likely to be effective in helping the individual to cope with the problem and improve performance.

If the individual is a particularly religious individual, the supervisor might recommend that he or she get in touch with a minister, priest, or rabbi. One expert emphasizes that above all else, the employee must be given time to allow these problems to work themselves out.[13] If it appears to the supervisor that the emotional reaction is too severe, it may be appropriate to recommend to the individual that he or she seek some professional help. In larger organizations, it is common for the personnel department to have available counseling assistance. If this kind of a service is not available within the company, the employee might be referred to a public agency or to a private doctor.

SPECIAL EMPLOYEE PROBLEMS: MID-CAREER CRISIS

A problem that is receiving increased attention in the management journals and one that we frequently come across in supervisory development seminars is called the mid-career crisis. This refers to the individual who, in the middle of his or her career, seems to have lost all motivation and interest in the job. A typical case is described as follows: The employee *used* to be reliable, not cream of the crop, but above average. Now, for some reason or other, the employee does the minimum amount of work, enough to just get by. Attitudes that seem to be behind this reaction are "Life is half over," "I've gotten as far as I'm going to get in this organization," "It's all downhill from here."

What can a supervisor do to deal with such a situation? To the extent that the problem stems from the job, a supervisor's basic options involve some form of retraining to revitalize the skills of the individual and prepare him or her for a different position within the organization. Another alternative is a transfer within the organization to another job that the individual is capable of performing—one which is interesting and provides a much-needed challenge.

SUMMARY AND CONCLUSIONS

This chapter recommends the use of positive reinforcement to bring about changes in job behavior and to eliminate undesired behavior whenever possible. Many organizations have been successful in reducing tardiness and absenteeism, for example, with positive reinforcement programs. We have also emphasized the disadvantages associated with punishment as a means of bringing about change in behavior.

Despite the serious drawbacks of disciplinary action, supervisors will come across situations in which positive reinforcement is simply not successful. Then it is necessary to use discipline to change an employee's performance. Except in cases of major offenses, such as dishonesty, we recommend that discipline be corrective or progressive in nature. This means that the objective of disciplinary action is to correct the employee's behavior. Employees should receive ample opportunity to change their behavior before the organization resorts to discharge.

The typical sequence of steps in progressive discipline is:

1. Verbal warning
2. Written warning

3. Suspension or disciplinary layoff
4. Discharge

Components of effective discipline systems include

1. Clear statements of disciplinary policies and procedures
2. Consistent application of discipline
3. Training in application of the program for all supervisors

In deciding on the appropriate discipline for an offense, a supervisor must consider several factors, including the seriousness of the offense, the employee's work history, any extenuating factors, history of discipline in the organization, and the evidence concerning the rule violation by the employee.

Three types of problem employee a supervisor is almost certain to encounter are the problem drinker, the employee with a family crisis, and the person in a mid-career crisis. For problem drinking, we suggest that the employee be presented with evidence of deteriorating performance and be given the choice of receiving treatment or separation from the organization. When an employee has a family crisis, the supervisor is limited to providing emotional support and referral to counseling. Finally, for the employee going through a mid-career crisis, we recommend transfer to an interesting and challenging position.

QUESTIONS

1. How can a positive reinforcer be identified?
2. Describe positive reinforcement programs which have been successful in reducing absenteeism and tardiness.
3. How can a supervisor reduce the undesired effects of punishment?
4. What should be the objective of discipline?
5. What are the steps in corrective discipline?
6. What factors should be kept in mind when disciplinary action is being considered?
7. List things that should be done and things that should be avoided when conducting an oral reprimand; preparing a written reprimand; administering a suspension; discharging an employee.

THE PROBLEM DRINKER

Ed Mann has been with Campbell Construction Supply for 18 years. For the last two years Ed has been responsible for the lumber section of the warehouse. Lately, however, his performance has fallen off. Examples of problems include failure to deliver orders to construction projects on the specified date; failure to reorder when inventories run low; and storing materials in the wrong areas.

You are pretty certain his problems result from drinking. Hardly a day goes by when you can't smell whiskey on his breath.

He has been having family problems lately. His youngest daughter, Jane, ran away from home a few months before the drinking began. As far as you know, Jane has not been heard of since. Also, you have heard rumors that Ed and his wife haven't been getting along either.

1. You have made an appointment with Ed. Plan what you will say to Ed during the interview.
2. Be prepared to role play the interview with another member of the class.

NOTES

1 For a good overview, see L. L. Steinmetz, *Managing the Marginal and Unsatisfactory Performer* (Reading, Mass.: Addison-Wesley, 1969).

2 See W. C. Hamner and E. P. Hamner, "Behavior Modification on the Bottom Line," *Organizational Dynamics,* Spring 1976.

3 See, for example, F. Luthans and R. Kreitner, *Organizational Behavior Modification* (Glenview, Ill.: Scott, Foresman, 1975).

4 See H. N. Wheeler, "Punishment Theory in Industrial Discipline," *Industrial Relations, 15,* No. 2 (May 1976), 235–43.

5 W. Wohlking, "Effective Discipline in Employee Relations," *Personnel Journal, 54,* No. 9 (September 1975), 489–93 and 500.

6 F. Elkouri and E. A. Elkouri, *How Arbitration Works,* 3rd ed. (Washington, D.C.: Bureau of National Affairs, 1973).

7 J. A. Belohlav and P. O. Popp, "Making Employee Discipline Work," *Personnel Administrator, 23* (March 1978), 22–24.

8 *Personnel Policies Forum: Employee Conduct and Discipline,* Survey No. 102 (Washington, D.C.: Bureau of National Affairs, August 1973), p. 10.

9 Wheeler, "Punishment Theory," p. 230.

10 Wohlking, "Effective Disciplines," p. 491.

11 Steinmetz, *Managing the Marginal and Unsatisfactory Performer.*

12 J. F. Follmann, Jr., *Alcoholics in Business: Problems, Costs, Solutions* (New York: AMACOM, 1976).

13 J. B. Miner, *The Challenge of Managing* (Philadelphia, Pa.: Saunders, 1975).

SUPERVISORY TOOLS AND TECHNIQUES

section three

We feel each supervisor should have a "tool kit" of approaches he or she can apply to solve the problems of supervision. In this section, we have devoted five chapters to providing you with techniques we feel will make you a more effective supervisor in each of the following areas:

227

The Planning
and
Controlling Process

 SUPERVISORY PROBLEMS

Are planning and control really necessary?
What exactly is involved?

When you have finished this chapter you should be able to

1. Describe the planning and control sequence
2. Identify the areas supervisors typically should plan and control
3. Explain the term *supervision by exception*
4. List three major qualities of good planning objectives
5. Discuss a supervisor's role in MBO as a planning and control device

---

PLANNING NEEDS CONTROL TO WORK!

The situation, as first-level Supervisor Sam Henson learned from his boss, was this: The company had been experiencing some real problems with the lawnmowers they produced, resulting in serious accidents to some of the customers using them. Investigation showed that the problem was not in product design but in the quality of the workmanship that had gone into some of the products. The company president had indicated that this had to be changed *immediately*, and had assigned the project to Sam's boss, who then enlisted Sam's help.

A little investigation indicated that the big problem was a safety part that was often left out of the lawnmowers. Sam and his boss found that the assembly shop had no procedure for assuring that all of the parts had been put in before a mower left the shop. Sam's boss suggested that the place to start was by *planning* a method for assuring that the lawnmowers were all properly assembled before they left the shop, and then setting up *controls* to make sure that the plan was followed.

Sam and the boss sat down and planned an inspection procedure that would eliminate the possibility of incomplete lawnmowers leaving the factory. The plan included a full-time inspector, thorough inspection procedures, and planned goals to reduce the number of unacceptable lawnmowers reaching the inspection point. Prior to this time, there had been no planned quality control procedure at all. Now quality control reports were issued weekly. They summarized the number of rejections and the cause for each rejection, as well as the recommended corrective action. These reports, as well as some spot checks after the inspection had taken place, were designed to maintain a careful control on the quality of the product.

Sam's boss had made quite an issue of the fact that the plans were useless unless they were combined with an effective control procedure. His statement had been, "Simply because you plan to do something is no guarantee that it's going to get done. It's the first step, but it isn't enough by itself." The new system worked well after all the bugs were out. Going through the process of planning the control system with his boss, Sam realized how much had been left unplanned and uncontrolled in his own unit. Planning wasn't difficult, he concluded, it just took time and common sense.

WHAT IS "PLANNING AND CONTROL"?

In this chapter, we are considering two topics that are probably among the most critical for the supervisory success: planning and control. A supervisor who fails to plan and control the work for which he or she is responsible will probably not remain in that position for too long a time.

Planning is a process that considers available resources and determines the course of action to be pursued. A plan is simply a written or mental schedule of what *should* happen, *where* it should happen, and *when* it should happen. Control can be thought of as the mirror image of planning. It determines if what was planned is indeed going to happen.

Figure 11–1 shows a typical planning and control sequence. First, plans are made, then they are implemented, which results in some action being taken. This action can be performance by a subordinate or by a particular organizational unit. Then, as a first step in control, the action that has been taken should be measured and recorded. Then the action is compared with the original plans to see if what happened was what was supposed to happen. Plans can be simple or they can be complex. They may be written or simply stored away in someone's mind.

It has been said that in the long run, you hit only what you aim at.

FIGURE 11–1   Planning and Control Sequence

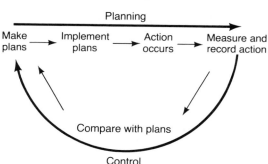

Planning is simply the process of aiming at something. If a supervisor has no idea what he or she *would like* to see happen, it isn't likely that much will. Supervisory wishing and hoping rarely accomplish much. It takes a careful plan made up of step-by-step procedures to accomplish goals.

THE BENEFITS OF GOOD PLANNING

There are many benefits associated with proper planning. For example, employees usually have more confidence in a supervisor who is willing to spend some time properly planning the work. Good planning shows. Poor planning, on the other hand, gives the impression of disorganization and not being on top of the job. Where good planning exists, waste can be minimized; work is coordinated and is more likely to be completed on time; there is less duplication of effort by employees; materials and equipment are available when they are needed; and people's talents are better utilized, all of which results in a feeling of satisfaction shared by all involved.

Yet even with all these benefits, planning is one activity that most of us, supervisors included, seem to avoid. Perhaps we have given up trying to forecast the future because some earlier efforts have gone awry. Or perhaps we conclude that the time and effort involved will not yield enough of a payoff. In any event, planning is one of the supervisory activities that is often very poorly done.

Yet it is clearly a key to successful supervision. Figure 11–2 is a planning checklist. Supervisors who check "no" for any of the items should read on carefully.

Poor planning, or a complete lack of planning, in a supervisory unit is readily observable. Work seldom gets done on time. "Management by crisis" prevails, with crash programs and overtime work often required. The work schedule may be characterized by peaks and valleys that lull employees into idleness and then tax their ability to withstand pressure. Equipment breakdowns are another evidence of poor planning, as is duplication of effort.

HOW CAN I PLAN?

Supervisors seldom do a great deal of long-range planning. This wider perspective of organizational goals—five-year plans and the like—is usually reserved for higher-level management. But if an organization's supervisory personnel cannot seem to solve short-run problems, and

FIGURE 11-2 Planning Checklist

	Yes	No
Do your plans provide that each worker has a relatively steady stream of work?	___	___
Have you planned work so that everyone has useful things to do in odd periods between jobs or at the end of a shift?	___	___
Do you have a system for determining material requirements far enough ahead to prevent shortages?	___	___
Do you plan repairs and maintenance of equipment so that it causes the least interference with regular work?	___	___
Do you plan your labor requirements far enough in advance so that trained personnel are available for assignments as needed?	___	___
Have you made a systematic study of each job you are responsible for to see if job methods can be improved?	___	___
Do your workers understand your objectives in the areas that directly affect them? Are you sure?	___	___
Are you following up on your planning to see that things are going as planned and making corrections?	___	___

higher-level managers find themselves preoccupied with these concerns, some sort of training for planning is necessary. When planning is properly done, it allows *supervision by exception.*

Under the exception principle, a supervisor determines check points and sets up a schedule so that day-to-day routine is handled as a matter of course without becoming the supervisor's concern at all. The supervisor is brought into the picture *only* when there are exceptions to the routine. For example, a manufacturing supervisor has determined that to meet the necessary output goals for the month, 25 units a day must be produced. The supervisor now sets up a reporting system that provides for daily reports of work progress. Unless the reports begin to reflect an output of less than 25 units per day, the supervisor doesn't need to get involved with that particular issue. If the supervisor feels that production of 20 units a day is sufficiently low to cause concern, he or she would note that as an exception and find out what is needed to resume normal production.

The Planning Process

Planning can be a big job, but the process itself is relatively simple. First, determine what the *objectives* are going to be. What is it you are trying to get done? Second, determine the path or *sequence* that the task must follow to completion. Third, determine when each task must *start* and *finish.* Fourth, determine *who* is going to do the work. Fifth, determine when and where you will *check* on the process to see that it's

233

going according to plan. Sixth, *correct* any deviations from the plan as they occur. This relatively simple process provides the basis for your planning work as a supervisor.

Objectives Are the Place to Start Planning

Before you begin planning, you have to have some idea of where you're going. As one proverb has it, "If you don't know where you're going, any road will get you there." The key to knowing where you're going is to pick realistic and attainable *objectives*.

Good objectives have three major characteristics. First, *they are predetermined*—that is, the objectives are set in advance. It's all too easy for us as human beings to complete a project and then change our objectives to match what has been done. For example, a baseball player who compiled a .233 batting average and did not first set an objective for his batting average may be able to convince himself that a .233 batting average was his objective all along. Unless we predetermine objectives, they cannot serve as standards of performance.

Second, *good objectives must be written*. Again, this is a hedge against human nature that allows us conveniently to "forget" our original target. For example, consider the individual who sets an objective on Janu-

---

BLOCK 11–1   Government Agency Objectives

Objective 1: I will use modern personnel methods to get high-quality personnel in the organization. Problems: What is a "modern personnel" method? What is meant by "high-quality personnel?" Both these terms are very nonspecific and not measurable and are, therefore, essentially useless. We won't know whether the supervisor met his or her objective, because we *really* don't know what the objective was.

Objective 2: I will organize the staff in such a way as to accomplish our goals. Problem: Again, this statement is nonspecific and therefore essentially useless as an objective.

Objective 3: I will eliminate all possible wasted time. Problem: This objective is certainly laudable—it makes sense to try to eliminate all possible wasted time. But again the objective isn't measurable. A better way to state the objective would be, "I will have cut direct labor time by 2 percent by the end of next month." That objective is measurable. When the end of next month comes, the supervisor, his or her boss, and everyone else can tell whether or not the objective was accomplished.

Objective 4: I will coordinate the work with other units. Problem: How can you verify whether coordination is increasing, decreasing, or going on at all? Unless it's *measurable*, it's useless as an objective.

ary 1 to quit smoking by April. The plan was to taper off a little bit at a time. But April came, and the individual hadn't quit smoking, and further, couldn't really remember his objective date, but he thought it "might have been" June. Thus, unless objectives are *written down*, we may repress them in order to avoid having failed.

The third characteristic of good objectives is that *they can be measured*. Suppose we set as an objective "good performance." How will we know when that goal has been reached? Unless "good performance" is specified by an increase in production of 10 percent, for example, there will be no consensus on when it has been achieved. One government agency thought it had provided its supervisors with a number of good objectives. Block 11–1 lists several and the problems associated with them.

Objectives should be set at a high, but attainable level. If objectives are set too high, individuals will feel defeated from the start and productivity will be lower than ever. On the other hand, if objectives are set at too low a level, motivation will be lacking and productivity will again suffer.

To be useful, objectives should be communicated to all concerned. People will usually work to achieve a reasonable set of objectives if they understand the objectives and how they fit into the organization's larger purpose. Block 11–2 illustrates one problem with noncommunicated objectives in a government organization.

BLOCK 11–2   Noncommunicated Objectives

At the heart of most of our big problems is a failure to communicate goals and plans. This isn't just a simple communications failure, however. There is a distinct lack of information transfer regarding the *objectives* that other departments in the agency have.

Department supervisors don't relay their programs, goals, and objectives to each other. Within departments, information about objectives often trickles down from supervisors to employees in a distorted fashion. Many individuals remain uninformed about major new policies, especially when these replace familiar ways of doing things.

There is a widespread questioning as to why policies have been changed and what management is trying to accomplish. Supervisors who have problems in common don't share these problems. In fact, it has often occurred that two supervisors have devised completely different objectives and plans for solving the same problems. This results in a great deal of confusion, overlapping of efforts, and general inefficiency. Isn't there some way to improve on this situation? (Author's note: Yes! Communicate objectives to all concerned!!)

What Do Objectives Do
for Supervisors?

By setting objectives a supervisor accomplishes three things. *First, objectives provide direction.* Each unit and each individual in the unit needs objectives. If the individual has no idea what it is he or she is supposed to be doing, the chances are pretty low that efforts will be coordinated. Of course, employees need some guidance in setting objectives, otherwise they are not likely to move in the desired direction.

Second, objectives serve as motivators. We know from behavioral science studies that most behavior is "goal-directed" behavior; that is, people don't behave in a random fashion—they behave to try to attain some goal or objective. At work, if we don't develop personal objectives for employees within the goal structure of the organization, the objectives that develop may be counterproductive. For example, people may choose to develop a goal of minimizing work rather than a goal of maximizing efficiency.

Third, objectives serve as a basis for control and measurement of results. Unless you have some benchmark, some idea of what you are trying to attain, how do you know if you have attained it? How do you know if you're making progress toward attaining it? Without some kind of explicit goal or objective, control and measurement of results is very difficult. Objectives, therefore, are a vital part of planning and controlling a supervisor's work.

A Supervisor's Objectives

It has been suggested that every organization should have *more* than one objective, and supervisory units are no different. For example, to assume that a corporation has the *sole* objective of maximizing profit is naive. That certainly may be *an* objective, but if the firm ignores objectives in the areas of market standing, innovation, productive use of resources, manager development, and public responsibility, it may find that before long its ability to produce a profit has been seriously diminished.

Managing a work unit is in many respects quite similar. The items illustrated in Figure 11–3, "Things a Supervisor Should Plan and Control," represent a partial list of areas in which supervisors should set objectives. Depending upon the specific position, there may be additional areas of concern, or some of those listed may not be applicable. Having objectives in these and other relevant areas allows the supervisor to show upper management that he or she has considered all the facets of the job and is planning on making progress in each.

FIGURE 11–3   Things a Supervisor Should Plan and Control

Tools and equipment
Materials and supplies
Maintenance
Quality of work
Quantity of work
Work scheduling
Work space layout
Work methods
Cost
Personnel development

What Kinds of Things Should a Supervisor Plan and Control?

Many of the areas listed in Figure 11–3 permit the supervisor to set solid objectives for performance. These expected or planned levels of performance should be expressed in quantifiable terms. Let us consider each of the areas separately.

Tools and Equipment

Major issues for the supervisor to consider regarding tools and equipment are (1) whether the tools and equipment are appropriate for the jobs being done; (2) whether they are safe; and (3) whether they are being used properly. As supervisor, you are probably more familiar with the tools and equipment than other members of the management group. It is, therefore, your responsibility to help provide plans to replace outmoded or unsafe tools and equipment.

Another planning issue is how much the equipment is used. Idle equipment is expensive equipment. If machinery isn't being fully utilized, plans can be made either to use it more fully, or to trade it in for newer equipment.

Materials and Supplies

One important consideration regarding materials and supplies is that the quality is adequate to meet the needs of the job. Another major problem is the security of materials and supplies, which includes action to discourage employees from "misappropriating" valuable items. Plans for security also involve keeping accurate inventories, both with respect to shipments received and the amount of materials actually used in the final product. Scrap materials and items ruined during production must also be accounted for.

237

Another important supervisory duty is to make sure that materials are available *on time*. Back-ordered inventory is of no use to a production crew.

Maintenance

Maintenance of the equipment and work area is another supervisory responsibility. Safety hazards may be presented by a cluttered, dirty, or unsafe work area. Machine or equipment breakdowns can cause severe difficulty with work schedules and can be prevented only by a carefully planned, ongoing maintenance system. Preventative maintenance, the idea of replacing parts on a regular schedule *before* they break down, can be a useful supervisory planning tool.

Quality of Work

For each product or service for which a supervisor is responsible, the expected level of quality should be carefully thought out and expressed in terms of measurable standards. Then, as in the chapter opening case, frequent performance checks must be arranged to determine whether the standards are being met; finally, appropriate action must be taken to correct any deficiences. Setting quality control standards can be a frustrating problem, especially in industries where product quality is not easily definable and testing is difficult to devise. Yet for most products, quality *can* be expressed in a meaningful form.

Quantity of Work

Quantity planning and control concerns delivering the amount of output needed within the expected delivery time. This function differs greatly from one work unit to another. In "continuous production" operations such as oil refining or assembly-line operations, for example, there is generally very little flexibility in the manufacturing process. Inputs, equipment, and work assignments are standardized, and this allows controls to be standardized also. The main concern in this kind of industry is maintaining an *ample supply of materials.*

By contrast, in a "job shop" industry such as a machine shop, hospital, or custom cabinet business, where many different end products are produced, *scheduling* the product through each of the production stages is a major concern. Bottlenecks at various stages have to be avoided if the work is to proceed on time.

There is a third category of work we will label "special projects." These include large one-time construction projects, buildings, bridges, dams, and so on. Supervisors and foremen of these projects generally work on site so as to monitor employees' progress and begin corrective actions as soon as work falls behind schedule. *Control* is the most direct concern in these cases.

Work Scheduling

As supervisor, you must *plan* work scheduling to be successful—not only individual employees' efforts but your own efforts as well. Scheduling vacation time and overtime is typically your responsibility. A key consideration in scheduling is treating all employees fairly.

Scheduling a supervisor's personal time may be facilitated through the use of a daily calendar, an appointment book, or a note pad of daily reminders such as those shown in Figure 11–4.

Work Space Layout

Work layout is a task that is obviously limited by the physical capacity of the area and the basically immobile nature of much machinery. The size of the work space obviously limits what can be done to change things. If a desk is too small to spread papers out on, many kinds of activities requiring large papers can't be performed at that desk.

But many things *are* within your control as supervisor. The plant or office can be laid out to facilitate or discourage communication among employees. Work spaces that are located in the path of heavy traffic may be moved to reduce interference factors which distract employees and reduce their effectiveness. Some machinery *can* be moved. Partitions can

FIGURE 11–4   Example of a Supervisor's Daily Work Schedule

Monday	*Tuesday*
8:00 Check with Roy on Friday's delays in shipping	8:00 Schedule work for next week
9:00 Finish scrap report	9:00 Weekly grievance meeting
10:00	10:00
11:00 Scrap report due at noon	11:00
12:00	12:00 Lunch with Mr. Samuels
1:00 Review absenteeism rates for month	1:00 Check up on Charles' progress on changeover
2:00 Meet with engineering on turbine operation	2:00
3:00	3:00 Bill's project due today at 5:00
4:00 Start on next year's budget	4:00 Review cost estimates for tomorrow's meeting

be constructed or removed, and so on. There are no hard-and-fast rules as to what constitutes good use of work space. In general, you should attempt to maximize the amount of usable space available, minimize the distractions, and, if appropriate, design the work space to facilitate employee communication.

Work Methods

The work methods that are used to get the job done should be constantly analyzed and controlled by the supervisor. Methods improvement, which will be discussed in Chapter 12, is any change in the way the work is done to improve effectiveness or efficiency. Methods improvement can result in better use of time, reduction of cost, and greater efficiency.

In planning work methods, a supervisor should realize that management doesn't have a corner on the market for good ideas. Many times, employees can provide suggestions for work methods improvement that can save the organization a great deal of money. Once effective work methods have been established, the supervisor must follow through by enforcing these decisions.

Costs

Planning and controlling for costs should be one of the supervisor's main objectives. As supervisor, you are in an ideal position to review records and identify major cost problems. If adequate records are not available, you should determine what data will be needed to carry out an analysis of current and past costs. This will allow you to pinpoint areas where cost cutting may be useful. Good record keeping of all expenditures within a supervisor's unit provides the basis for controlling costs. This is a primary responsibility of any supervisor, whether that individual be in a profit-making, nonprofit, or governmental organization. The supervisor is the first defense against high and rising organizational costs.

Personnel Development

Personnel development includes planning and controlling the career development of your employees as well as your own development. Supervisors should review subordinates' personnel files and appraisals to identify their strong and weak points and plan such personnel actions as raises, training, or disciplinary measures, to correct weak points and capitalize on strong points. Such planning by a supervisor can go a long way toward ensuring a competent, capable work force.

As supervisor, remember that you will develop in your career only as rapidly as you learn to master the responsibilities of your position. Personal development includes learning the requirements of your job and writing out a personal development plan for improving the areas of weakness. Many supervisors list their personal achievement goals and set a schedule for completion of those goals. Such a plan should be reviewed frequently, and progress toward the goals measured.

WHAT IS MANAGEMENT BY OBJECTIVES?

Management by objectives (MBO) is a technique that allows supervisors to systematically include employees in the objective-setting process. It also provides an opportunity for coordinating those objectives with the objectives of higher levels of management. Management by objectives is a planning technique as well as a coordination and control technique. It builds on a number of excellent scientific studies of human reactions to goal setting. We introduced the idea of MBO under evaluation of results in the performance appraisal chapter. Here we will consider MBO as a planning and control process.

The Scientific Basis of MBO

The basis for management by objectives in scientific fact hinges on four areas: goal setting, feedback, expectations, and participation.

Goal Setting.   Research on goal setting has shown that people tend to set goals at levels somewhat higher than their previous performance levels. For example, if somebody was able to produce 20 items a day and you asked that person to set a production goal for the next day, most often you would find goals in the range of perhaps 21 to 25 units.

Forcing people to set goals increases the level of performance, especially on difficult tasks. If people have set goals to reach a certain level of performance, they will work harder to achieve those goals and the result will be a higher level of performance. Again, identifying goals is important. Agreeing on a specific, measurable goal with a subordinate will result in better performance than merely telling that individual to "try to do your best."

Feedback Research.   It has been found that people who receive feedback on their performance tend to be more accurate and motivated, and to perform better than people who don't. Management by objectives should provide *feedback people can use to measure their performance.* Feedback has been found to be most useful if it can be used as a means of comparing performance with a goal or standard. Simply knowing that you produced 25 units in a given day doesn't tell you very much unless you know what is the standard. For example, if the average rate is 20 units a day, you will feel rather satisfied with your performance. However, if you find out instead that the average rate is 30 units a day, and you produced only 25, you will probably try to improve your performance.

The Expectations of the Supervisor.   A supervisor's expectations affect the level of performance a subordinate delivers. This proven psychological phenomenon has been labeled the "Pygmalion effect." By communicating your expectations for a person, you also convey your confidence in his or her ability. A supervisor who is held in high esteem by workers will, therefore, easily be able to influence their level of productivity by conveying this message of confidence.

Participation.   Another behavioral science finding is that people who help determine work group objectives tend to make *higher demands* on themselves than if the objectives had been set externally. A number of personal needs such as creativity, accomplishment, and satisfaction are fulfilled when people are allowed to participate in the decision-making process. Perhaps the most important issue here is that the *acceptance* of the objective is likely to be much higher if people have had an opportunity to participate in making that decision.

Management by objectives is a technique that can incorporate all of the advantages mentioned in this brief summary of scientific research. In its most simple form, a supervisor and an employee identify major areas of responsibility, set objectives for good and bad performance together, and measure the results achieved against those objectives. For most situations, MBO consists of a conversation with the supervisor and a memo summarizing the objectives that were agreed upon.

MBO may be an organization-wide effort. Goals and objectives and supporting plans may be formulated at the top of the organization and then "cascaded" down the organization so that all of the goals and objectives of the lower units mesh into the goals and objectives of the higher units. Figure 11–5 demonstrates this cascade effect. The cascade of objectives typically begins higher in the organization than the supervisor's level. Yet even if the organization isn't using a formal organization-wide MBO effort, the supervisor can use management by objectives on a more limited basis quite effectively with his or her subordinates. Using management by objectives effectively requires understanding what we have covered here about good objectives and about using MBO for planning and control.

FIGURE 11-5 "Cascade" of Goals and Objectives in an Organization

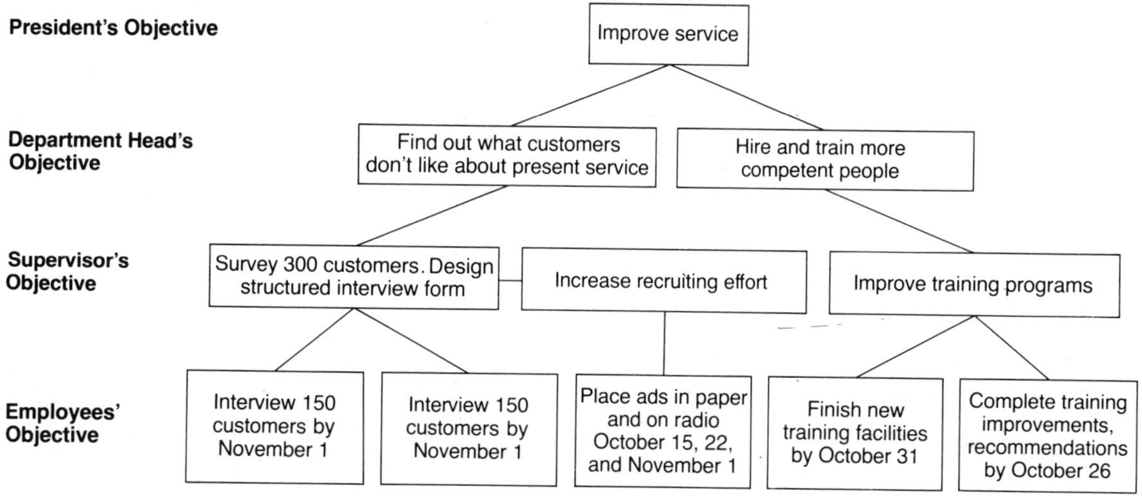

President's Objective

Improve service

Department Head's Objective

Find out what customers don't like about present service

Hire and train more competent people

Supervisor's Objective

Survey 300 customers. Design structured interview form

Increase recruiting effort

Improve training programs

Employees' Objective

Interview 150 customers by November 1

Interview 150 customers by November 1

Place ads in paper and on radio October 15, 22, and November 1

Finish new training facilities by October 31

Complete training improvements, recommendations by October 26

How Can I Use MBO
for Planning and Control?

Objectives can be developed to measure four of the most important things that a supervisor has to deal with—quantity, quality, timeliness, and cost. Good objectives are expressed in such a way that they are *measurable* and thus can be verified in terms of beginning figures and end results. Again, an objective that cannot be stated in operational terms is as good as useless. For example, if a quality objective is stated as "high-quality production," one observer may feel the goal has been met as a result of her definition of the term, but another may view performance as far from the mark. A better way to state the same objective would be "the dollar cost of reworking mistakes will be less than 3 percent of the total labor cost for this unit."

Again, one of your objectives might be to "make things safe in the work area." Again this isn't a measurable objective. A better way to state that objective would be "time missed because of accidents will be less than 2 percent of the total man hours worked for the year." That objective is measurable. At the end of the year, anyone can calculate the percentage and see if that objective was attained.

Expressing Objectives

Objectives can be expressed in terms of *raw numbers* such as, the "number of rejects produced per shift," "total units produced per day," "number of paid subscribers" or "number of complaints or grievances filed." They can also be expressed in terms of *ratios* or *percentages,* for example, "less than 10 percent absentee rate," "3 percent scrap lost," "plus or minus 5 percent of the budgeted figure."

Raw numbers or percentages are the best way to express objectives; if it is impossible to express objectives in these terms, survey scales might be used. For example, if a supervisor wanted to determine whether or not an objective concerning working conditions was being met, he or she might survey the employees and find out on a scale from 1 to 5 how they rated the lighting, cleanliness, noise level, maintenance of the equipment, and so forth.

How Can I Implement MBO
on a Daily Basis?

In its simplest form, management by objectives is nothing more than a meeting between a supervisor and a subordinate and a note or memo confirming the results of that meeting. The "contract" that is arrived at between these two persons should make clear what is expected of each.

It is the *subordinate's* job to determine standards that he or she feels are appropriate for the job. It is the *supervisor's* responsibility to make sure that the subordinate has chosen realistic standards and standards that are challenging. It is the *subordinate*'s responsibility to tell the superior how he or she intends to measure the progress toward those standards. It is the *supervisor's* job to ask how the measurement is going to take place and to suggest possible measurements where appropriate. It is the *subordinate's* job to tell the supervisor exactly how he or she is going to go about accomplishing the objectives. It is the *supervisor's* job to insure that the subordinate makes a recommendation.

Block 11–3 illustrates a case where MBO was successfully used as a planning and control tool.

Management by objectives can be very simple or very complex. It's a planning process that can work on an organization-wide basis or simply in one supervisory unit. But it can be a very helpful planning tool, because by sitting down and comparing objectives, you and your subordinates achieve a better understanding of each other's problems and concerns. It also provides you an opportunity to pass along plans that you have for the unit to subordinates.

SUMMARY AND CONCLUSIONS

Supervision by exception involves planning and designing controls so as to avoid spending the greater part of one's time on routine matters.

BLOCK 11–3   MBO by Any Name Is Still MBO

Marsha Waterman had just taken over as supervisor of the report editing division of Scientific Reports Ltd. When she took the job, her boss told her that the unit was not performing very well in terms of quantity of reports edited and turnaround time on the editing of individual reports.

Marsha's first week on the job convinced her that people were *not* working as hard as they could. She decided to talk with each of the five editors and come to some agreement with each about how long it should take to edit the "average" report. In her conversation, she found a lot of agreement among the employees—an average report should be done in two days. She got commitment from each employee to average 11 reports per month. It was clear to Marsha that no one had ever sat down with the employees and negotiated specific objectives for output before. The editors really had no idea what management expected. They also seemed to appreciate the opportunity to have a say in establishing those objectives.

Marsha did not recognize it as such, but what she had implemented was the basis of a simple MBO system. She now has a basis for planning the work load and controlling the output that falls below 11 reports per month.

The planning process is relatively simple: setting objectives, sequencing tasks, determining start and finish times for each task, deciding who will do the work, setting checkpoints, and correcting deviations as they occur.

Setting objectives is an important but difficult step in the planning process. Objectives should be predetermined, written, and measurable. Management by objectives is a technique in which a supervisor and a subordinate sit down and jointly develop objectives for the subordinate's job. It can be used by a supervisor even if it isn't implemented on an organization-wide basis.

QUESTIONS

1. Where does planning end and control begin? Is it meaningful to consider the two processes separately?
2. Of the ten areas of planning and control listed, which would be most critical for a police supervisor? A hotel manager?
3. Where would you use supervision by exception to make your job easier?
4. Objective: 100 percent occupancy in all hotel units by June 1. Is this a good objective? Why or why not?
5. Write a dialogue of an MBO meeting illustrating the supervisor's role and the subordinate's role in MBO.

"IT DIDN'T WORK—"

Management by objectives was an idea whose time had come in Pam Christianson's mind. Pam supervised a group of men and women hired to inspect county restaurants for cleanliness and compliance with the health code.

Pam carefully developed objectives and devised standards and ways of measuring output. Then she wrote these down for each person in her unit and called them all together. After handing each person his or her "objectives" for the next six months, Pam explained that all future merit appraisals would be based on such semiannual sets of objectives.

After a moment's silence, there was such an explosion of emotion in the room that Pam felt she was suffocating. To a person, the employees were all resentful. Some felt their objectives had been set way too high. Others felt the special problems they had in their territories had not been considered. Still others felt it was unfair to tie the objectives to merit money. Pam stood fast, but afterward wondered if she had made a mistake in the way she handled the whole thing.

---

1. Discuss Pam's handling of this situation.

Planning
and Controlling
Techniques

SUPERVISORY PROBLEM

What techniques are available to see that the work gets done on time?

LEARNING OBJECTIVES

When you have finished this chapter you should be able to

1. Discuss two methods of forecasting
2. Construct a methods improvement program
3. Identify at least five motion economy principles
4. Plan a job using either PERT or GANTT charts
5. Explain the tradeoff involved in preventative maintenance
6. Pinpoint the keys to quality control
7. Analyze a job for cost/waste control

"WHAT WE NEED IS A PLAN . . ."

It was overwhelming. There was so much to be done Jan did not even know where to begin. But she really didn't have time to ponder the situation too long either.

Jan Longworth was office supervisor for Delko, Inc. Last week her boss told her that the company was moving to new facilities. Jan knew, of course, that the present facilities were inadequate and that upper management had been looking around for new facilities, but the suddenness of it all took her breath away.

Jan found out the move was to begin next Monday morning, and had to be completed by Thursday evening because the big Wilson job was due a week from Thursday and would take every minute of a week to complete. The boss had put Jan in charge of seeing that the move was complete and that her unit would be operational by Friday morning to start on the Wilson job.

Jan's problem was one of sequencing all the things that had to be done and making sure they were done on time. For example, the new office was filthy and had to be cleaned and painted *before* moving of furniture could begin. Then if the employees were to continue working on the current job, certain things could not be moved until Tuesday, others not until Wednesday. Certain machines had to be moved before others because they had to be wired in before they could be used, and others had to come later because wooden bases had to be constructed before they could be put in place.

> Jan wished she had a handy planning technique at her disposal to help her manage all this confusion.

The problem presented in the chapter opening case is one of many that can be dealt with by being aware of appropriate planning or control techniques. In this chapter we will examine some of the technical aspects of planning and control. We will explain and give relevant examples of such techniques as forecasting, methods improvement, and PERT. Do not let the terminology used by practitioners of these methods intimidate you. In fact, most are relatively easy to use once the basics have been understood.

FORECASTING

In order to plan adequately, a supervisor must first have some idea of what the future is likely to be. This requires a *forecast* on which to base a plan. A forecast is nothing more than an estimate of future activity or future states. Forecasting is a relatively inexact science, although there are some very sophisticated techniques available.

The more accurate a forecast, the better it is. However, very precise forecasts are usually impossible with currently available techniques, and a supervisor making forecasts should recognize that his or her efforts provide an *indication* rather than the final word on future conditions.

There are two approaches that are commonly used to forecast. The first is to assume that *past history* is going to be a good predictor of the future. Then forecasts are made by simply projecting the past into the future. The second method uses such things as the opinions of other people, recent developments in technology, economic or consumer trends, and information contained in the appropriate literature. Forecasts are then based on these items. In practice, both methods are often used together. A forecast can be derived using past history and then adjusted based upon opinions and technological changes, for example.

The most common method for forecasting from past data is to take a simple moving average such as that shown in Figure 12–1. A moving average is one that adds new information as it is available and drops some of the oldest information, thereby giving weight to both older and newer information. Figure 12–1 shows weekly production figures for six weeks. If the problem is to estimate the production figure for the seventh week using a moving average, one would estimate 1,433 units.

A second easy way to estimate future activity is to visually fit a line to the past data or information. There are two ways to do this. One is

FIGURE 12-1   Simple Moving Average

Weekly Production Figures

Week			*Forecast for Next Week (Three-week Moving Average)*
1	800		
1	1400		
3	1000	(800 + 1400 + 1000 ÷ 3)	1,067
4	1500	(1400 + 1000 + 1500 ÷ 3)	1,300
5	1500	(1000 + 1500 + 1500 ÷ 3)	1,333
6	1300	(1500 + 1500 + 1300 ÷ 3)	1,433

To calculate a three-week moving average, take production figures for the last three weeks and calculate an average. Then *next* week drop the first week's figure and add last week's figure. Calculate another average and so on.

to fit a line through the actual data as shown by the *dotted* line in Figure 12-2. This is easy and gives a "ball park" estimate of where the next data point is likely to fall.

Another way is to draw a straight line through the data points trying to *minimize* the distance between each data point and the line. The solid line in Figure 12-2 is such a line. This gives a more precise estimate of where the next (or forecast) point is likely to fall. Predictions of future amounts of production can then be estimated right from the graph using either method. For those readers who would like to use this method more precisely, it is discussed under "least squares regression" in most statistics books.

FIGURE 12-2   Fitting a Line to Past Data

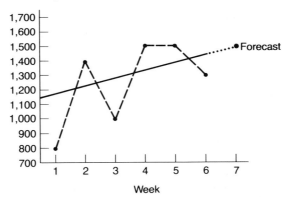

Using the straight line method, the seventh week would be forecast at about 1,500. The line would be *redrawn* every week.

Scheduling

Scheduling is a special kind of forecasting: the detailed planning of work. As such, it is obviously based on a forecast of the work to be done.

How does a supervisor know if he or she is doing a good job of scheduling? Ways of measuring scheduling success or failure include such things as (1) average number of days a job is finished ahead or behind schedule; (2) the percentage of time both people and machines are used (obviously the larger the percentage the better); and (3) the extent to which work waiting to be done is delayed.

It is important for the supervisor to remember that overscheduling can be just as bad as underscheduling. To schedule more than you can deliver may earn you the reputation of being inaccurate and undependable. It is a good idea never to schedule at 100 percent capacity, because doing so leaves no leeway for handling such emergencies as unexpected absences, strikes, lack of understanding of an assignment, mistakes, rush orders, and so forth.

Short Interval Scheduling

One useful scheduling device is short interval scheduling. This is an industrial engineering term that means a supervisor will schedule only a small portion of an employee's work day at a time. It is based on the idea that people work more effectively on shorter projects. A task that takes 100 hours to complete might be assigned to an individual as 50 two-hour tasks. Since presumably a feeling of satisfaction results from the successful completion of a task, this feeling will be multiplied by 50 for the shorter tasks.

Further, some people are overwhelmed by a long-term assignment and spend the first half of the time doing one-third of the work. Thus, rather than lining up a whole day's or week's work at one time, a supervisor might give a secretary one project to do and tell the person it should be done in one hour (or whatever is appropriate). When this job has been completed, the supervisor assigns another short duration job.

Another advantage of short interval scheduling is that the supervisor receives feedback sooner and more regularly than with longer assignments. It also provides greater flexibility in scheduling the workload during the day. However, its success depends on how accurately the supervisor can estimate reasonable workloads. It is obviously more time-consuming for the supervisor, who must now plan in much greater detail. Short interval scheduling has been found to be especially useful in office situations and in breaking down larger tasks into more manageable units.

Why Is Scheduling Important?

Scheduling is important, as Block 12–1 shows, because without planned time usage it is unlikely that things will get done on time. For scheduling to work the supervisor must impress upon employees the importance of meeting deadlines. A good way to do this is by periodic checkups to see that the schedules are followed and by reviewing the preparatory process with employees. Block 12–1 describes the effects on employees when the supervisor fails to see that schedules are followed.

METHODS IMPROVEMENT

The actual work employees are doing is one area where planning is especially useful. Reducing wasted time to a minimum can pay big dividends. Methods improvement is a technique for improving the work employees are doing. Four steps were developed during World War II by the Training Within Industry Service to improve job methods. These four steps are

1. Break down the job by listing every detail performed by the present method
2. Question every detail
3. Develop an improved method
4. Apply the improved method and use it until an even better method is discovered

These four steps have been used by hundreds of thousands of supervisors during the ensuing 40 years to make improvements in many thousands of jobs in American industry. Changing work methods requires a good deal of planning. If you don't have a plan for methods improvement there is a danger you will never get started on a serious job methods improvement campaign in your department. Making a plan for improving work efficiency helps to ensure consideration of each and every job.

A number of questions can be asked that help to expose the details of a job. A supervisor might ask, "Why is this task or action necessary? What is its purpose? Where should it be done? When should it be done? Who is best qualified to do it? How is the best way to do it?"

Methods improvement has been called by many names and encompasses a number of different things including methods engineering, time and motion study, operations analysis, and work simplification. But the essence of work simplification or methods improvement is the motto: "Work smarter, not harder."

Methods for changing a job may take a *team* approach. This can be an advantage since more heads may indeed be better than one in simplifying a job. Further, allowing employees to participate in simplifying a job may increase their acceptance of the changed method. Block 12–2 describes a case in which this was done successfully.

A word of caution is in order on job simplification. Oversimplifying a job may take some of the meaningful components away from the job. It may be that simplifying a job too much results in boredom. Fatigue can result from boredom for the person doing the job. An intelligent tradeoff must be maintained between making the job easier and oversimplifying to the point that the job is no longer worth doing. In the case in Block 12–2 there is clearly no danger in this kind of simplification. But if responsibility, opportunity for achievement, or opportunity to finish a complete unit of work are removed from the job, the problems of oversimplification must be considered.

If a methods improvement result must be "sold" to upper management, it is a good idea to put it in a proposal (in writing) along with the cost or time savings involved. This forces you as supervisor to think through the ideas clearly and completely. A good proposal should carefully consider each detail and possible objections to the idea. Such a proposal should be brief and to the point, containing nothing but essential ideas. Be sure to date the report and keep a copy of it for your own records. When your proposal is written down and signed it has become a matter of record. Clearly presented, there can be no mistaking your ideas. When the new method is installed, it is possible to compare the final results with the actual proposal as you originally submitted it. The

Bill Johnson noticed that one of his operators was spending considerable time sorting parts from a tote box into which the parts had been dropped as he finished his operation on them. He thought to himself, "Why is it necessary for this employee to spend so much time sorting parts?"

He knew he could have figured out an easier way to do the job himself. Instead he said to the operator, "I think that we could figure out some way to handle this job so you could be saved the trouble of sorting all these parts everytime you filled up a tote box. Why don't you give the thing a little thought and try to figure out whether it is absolutely necessary to sort these parts the way you do or if you can't find a better way to do it."

The next day the operator suggested that a tote box be fitted with three compartments so he could drop each of the three different kinds of parts into a separate compartment as he took them from his machine. Then he suggested having three regular tote boxes along the machine so that the three different kinds of parts could be dumped directly into these tote boxes as the compartments of the specially rigged tote box were filled. The time saved amounted to about one hour per day.

source of the suggestion may be easily forgotten unless proposals are put in writing.

Keys to improving methods include eliminating unnecessary or wasteful operations, simplifying operations that perhaps are unnecessarily complex, changing the sequence in which operations are done, and combining two or more things that can be done at one time. Using these techniques and input from employees, a supervisor can make his or her operation much more efficient.

Time and Motion Study

Studying the time and motions involved in doing an operation has been recognized as a useful supervisory tool since just around the turn of the century. The purpose of *motion study* is to make work performance easier and more productive by coordinating the motions an employee uses in doing a job. Motion studies are keyed to an individual's body movements. The proof of improved motion economy is a time reduction.

The objective of *time study* is to determine the "standard time" for an operation—that is, the time required by a qualified and fully trained operator to perform the operation. A job is evaluated and timed. These timings are normalized by applying a rating factor to account for the operator's speed, then allowances are put in to adjust for interruptions in production. The end product should be a realistic evaluation of what length of time is required to do the job. Time and motion studies are typically done by industrial engineers.

Several principles of motion economy have been developed over the years, some of which can be useful for the supervisor:

1. Minimize the number of movements, eliminate unnecessary movements, and try to combine movements.
2. Minimize the length of movements.
3. Symmetrical motion should be used in opposite directions to avoid sharp changes in direction.
4. The hands should be moved simultaneously.
5. Slide objects where possible instead of lifting them.
6. Minimize the effort involved. Use mechanical aids where possible.
7. Relieve hands of simple repetitive jobs by using foot controls where appropriate.
8. Provide holding devices to free hands for more useful motions.
9. Take advantage of gravity. Use gravity feed for materials and dispose of objects by drop delivery.

There are many other motion economy principles as well but these are some of the major ones. Time and motion study can be an important part of methods improvement. By effectively designing the job to minimize the motions and time involved, a job can be greatly improved.

GRAPHIC PLANNING AIDS

From among the many graphical planning tools available to the supervisor today, we will consider three representative types: First, PERT, which stands for Performance Evaluation Review Technique; then GANTT charts; and finally, Objective Charts.

PERT Charts

As we noted earlier, one of the big planning problems supervisors can face is having the resources ready at the right place when they are needed. As projects get more complex they become very difficult to sequence mentally or "carry around in your head." PERT is one kind of "critical path method" that can be used to help visualize a sequence of activities. The PERT chart is a diagram that shows the sequence of activities necessary to complete a project. PERT is also useful as a scheduling tool. First used in 1958 by the U.S. Navy, PERT was applied to the Polaris Ballistic Missile Program with great success.

The steps involved in identifying the *critical path* in a project are as follows:

1. Establish a list of activities
2. Establish a restrictions list
3. Combine the two lists in a diagram showing the graphic network

The activities list includes all the major steps or jobs that must be completed in order to have a finished product. The restrictions list shows what things must be preceded by what other things.

Let's take as an example, building a service station. We will use the PERT technique to help plan the project. We will simplify our list of activities involved in building the gasoline station to those shown in Figure 12–3. Let's assume that today is January 1 and the project must be completed by February 5. The amount of time necessary to complete each of the activities is estimated and shown under the "Time to Finish" column. From the list of activities restrictions and the estimated time to finish each activity a chart is now drawn up.

Three things must be considered when drawing a PERT chart: (1) What jobs have to be done before this job can take place? (2) What jobs can't be done until this job takes place? and (3) What other jobs can be done at the same time?

Now look at Figure 12–4. Each job is indicated by an arrow. The lengths of the arrows aren't important, but their direction indicates the sequencing of jobs. The first item that obviously must be done is to frame the building. We will assume that the gasoline tanks are not go-

FIGURE 12–3   A List of Activities Necessary to Build a Gas Station

Activities	Time to Finish	Restrictions
1. Order tanks	4 weeks	None
2. Frame building	3 weeks	None
3. Put in windows	1 week	Must frame building first
4. Plumbing	1 week	Must frame building first
5. Electrically wire building	1 week	Must frame building first
6. Install and check pumps	1 week	Must have electricity and tanks installed
7. Dig pit for tanks	2 days	None
8. Install tanks	2 days	Must dig pit first
9. Pour cement driveways	2 days	Must have installed tanks first
10. Paint	1 week	Must have everything else finished

FIGURE 12–4   PERT Chart

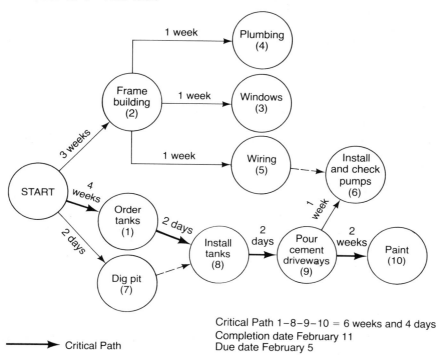

Critical Path 1–8–9–10 = 6 weeks and 4 days
Completion date February 11
Due date February 5

————▶ Critical Path

ing to be placed under the building so they don't have to be installed first. At the same time the framing is going on, the tanks can be ordered and the pit that the tanks are going to be placed in can be dug. The plumbing, windows and wiring cannot be done until the building is framed and the tanks cannot be installed until they have been ordered and the pit has been dug. The dotted line from "dig pit" to "install tanks" is called a *dummy line*. This requires zero time. It simply shows that one activity cannot begin until another activity has been completed. In this case, the tanks can't be installed until the pit is dug.

Once the tanks are in, the cement driveway can be poured. And once the driveway has been poured the pumps can be installed and checked. Note the dummy line from "wiring" to "install and check pumps." The pumps are electrically controlled and cannot be checked until they have electric wiring to them. Finally, the painters have asked that the painting not begin until all the driveway work is done so the dust and dirt from the driveway pouring process doesn't affect the exterior painting. Therefore, painting must *follow* the pouring of the driveway.

Now simply add up the time of all the jobs along each possible path. The *longest* one is called the critical path. If the project time is to be shortened, time must be saved along this path. Saving time on the other paths won't help. The critical path in this instance goes from activity 1 to activity 8, then to 9 and finally to 10—a total time of 6 weeks and 4 days. If the supervisor of this project wanted to speed the project up, efforts would have to be made to shorten either the ordering time of the tanks, the installation of the tanks, the pouring of the cement driveway, or the painting process.

Most PERT charts are not as simple as the one we have constructed here. But for many supervisory tasks the sophisticated additions aren't necessary. Simply recognizing that a critical path exists forces management to estimate the time needed for each step within a project. Adding those estimated times together allows for much more orderly scheduling and planning. In our example, since the due date comes before the scheduled date of completion by six days, this amount of time will have to be knocked out of the schedule somewhere. The usefulness of the critical path is that it pinpoints the activities that must be shortened to meet the deadline.

GANTT Charts

A GANTT chart is a simple visual device that can help a supervisor with planning. Unlike PERT Charts, a GANTT chart assumes that a second job will not start until the first one is completed. For example, in Figure 12–5a a piece of machine work must go through operation A, then B, C, and finally D. The GANTT chart in Figure 12–5a shows that operation A begins on Monday of week 1. It will be completed by Monday of week 2, at which point operation B begins and runs to Tuesday of week 3. Then operation C begins and is finished by Thursday of week 3. The piece of machining is then ready to go to operation D, which will be completed on Thursday of week 4, signaling the end of operations. Deviations from the anticipated schedule can be recorded to show current conditions. By doing this, machine operators can be given their assignments, the patterns of delays that may be occurring is shown, and backlogs, bottlenecks and problems on machines can be shown quite clearly.

Figure 12–5b shows a GANTT chart for sequencing the movements of several products through the same operations. Looking at Figure 12–5b, we can see if products are on time, ahead, or behind schedule. The dotted line shows today's date and the vertical arrow shows the time status for each product. Product 1 is a day ahead of schedule, Product 2 is one day behind, and Product 3 has not yet been started.

FIGURE 12–5   a. GANTT Chart for One Product—Four Operations

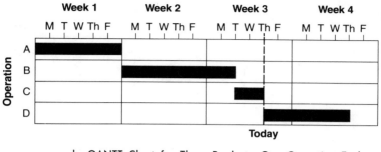

b. GANTT Chart for Three Products—One Operation Each

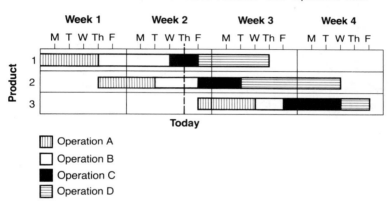

[ ] Operation A
[ ] Operation B
[ ] Operation C
[ ] Operation D

These "deviations" from what had been planned allow the supervisor to control the operations in his or her unit more closely. GANTT charts are useful for planning long-run projects of a less complex nature. They clearly show to people working on the various operations the importance of meeting their schedules.

Objective Charts

Figure 12–6 shows an "objective chart." An objective chart is a graph that compares the planned goals or objectives with actual performance to that point. It shows at a glance where the actual production stands in relationship to the planned production. It does not, however, show where or why trouble exists. The primary advantage of the objective chart is to serve as a quick visual reminder for everyone involved in a project of the status of an activity relative to its proposed status. It also serves as a starting place for an analysis of problem areas.

FIGURE 12–6   Objective Chart

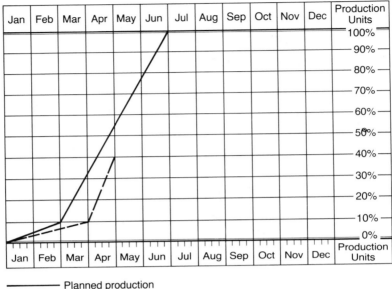

———————— Planned production
— — — — Actual production

PREVENTATIVE MAINTENANCE

Another item that should be planned for and scheduled where appropriate is preventative maintenance. Whether in the factory, office, hospital, or in the construction industry, equipment requires maintenance. Unexpected breakdowns are a major concern of maintenance. The total cost of maintaining the equipment in your supervisory unit can be significantly reduced by determining if it is more economical to service the equipment while it's still working or let it run until it breaks down. Cost figures can be determined for both conditions, and if it is cheaper to repair the machinery before it breaks down, then preventative maintenance is warranted. With some things it is possible to predict approximately how often they will break down. For example, spark plugs in an automobile without electronic ignition will typically be worn out after about ten thousand miles. It may be wise to replace those spark plugs every ten thousand miles even though they haven't quit working yet.

Preventative maintenance can save surprises and unnecessary costs where it is warranted. It is the sort of thing that can be scheduled regularly or used for short interval scheduling between major work projects.

Figure 12–7 shows the increases in cost of preventative maintenance

260

FIGURE 12–7   Preventative Maintenance Considerations

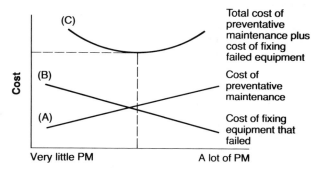

Amount of Preventative Maintenance

(PM) as the amount of PM increases (line A). As PM costs increase, the cost of fixing machines or equipment that has broken down decreases, because repaired machines are less likely to break down (line B). When the costs of the two are added together (line C), it provides an idea of the best *mix* of preventative maintenance and letting machines break down. The lowest point on the total cost curve represents the best mix.

PLANS AS CONTROLS

Control was presented in Chapter 11 as an integral part of the planning process. We will now consider control, and control techniques, in greater detail. Supervisory control is obtained primarily through *reporting* and *observation*. The basis for reporting and observing should be the standards that were developed when the planning for a particular operation was first done.

Good reports make it possible for the supervisor to *pinpoint* the individual operation that is causing trouble. Lumping a number of operations together in one report may prevent this kind of analysis from taking place. Good reports must be available *frequently* enough to pinpoint the problems quickly. If things aren't going the way they were planned, quick adjustment is important.

Reports must be *worth the cost* involved. It is conceivable for a supervisor to spend so much of his or her time—and the employees' time—working with reports that control costs exceed their benefits. Good reports alone don't ensure that control will be accomplished, but they are an important part of the control system. The supervisor will typically use reports and/or direct observation to get the information he or she needs to compare present activity with planned activity.

Analyzing and Simplifying
Control Reports

Reports are an important aspect of control, yet they are often a source of frustration and resentment among supervisors and others who have to fill them out. Report writing often becomes a habit that is hard to justify. As a result, the number of reports a supervisor has to deal with never seems to become less, only more.

The usefulness of various reports should be analyzed periodically. Look for reports that duplicate information, and for reports that are being sent to persons who really don't need them. Often a number of reports can be combined (if they contain overlapping information) into a comprehensive survey of some aspect of the business.

Some organizations calculate the total cost of each report (salaries of those involved in preparing the report, space, and supplies) and periodically ask those receiving them if they are getting enough good out of them to offset the cost. The elimination of unnecessary reports can save the supervisor a great deal of time and the organization a considerable amount of money.

One supervisor of the authors' acquaintance had a report analysis technique that is interesting. When she thought a particular report was no longer important or being used, she simply did not fill it out and waited to see who "squawked." She often found that no one did and was able to eliminate that report from those she filled out regularly. We don't recommend this method in every case, but offer it to show you what can be done to eliminate unnecessary reports in certain situations.

The Importance of Control
and Reports

Control, or follow-up, is the only way of making sure the work you assign is being done properly, and reports are an important part of that process. When a supervisor fails to follow up, he or she fails to do the supervisory job properly.

Good supervision is in no way the same as close supervision, which can unnerve many employees. However, there are instances in which close supervision is necessary, such as on a rush job or on a new job. By expressing a genuine interest in the progress of the job and a readiness to help if difficulties arise, the supervisor can demonstrate that these follow-up efforts are not meant to reflect on the employee.

Reports and other forms of follow-up are also the only way of making the exception principle work. In checking reports, a supervisor will find that many activities are being done the way they should be. The supervisor can then concentrate on the exceptions—those instances in which performance deviates from the standard.

Budgets as Controls

Supervisors have to learn to live with budgets. Basically, a budget is a forecast or plan of costs and income for the next time period. They are usually made on a monthly, quarterly, or annual basis. Some departmental budgets focus only on costs while others include income items as well.

A budget is nothing more than a plan with numbers attached. Budgets provide management with planning information and must therefore be accurate. However, managers at all levels have to realize that a budget is an *aid* to effective management, not a *sacred document*. A budget should be flexible and not so rigid that the supervisors working with it have no flexibility to handle unplanned events.

To make budgets work, we have to realize that budgets are only tools. They can't *replace* good management. In fact, an overly restrictive budget may preclude good management. Subordinate managers and supervisors should have a hand in preparing the budget that they are going to have to live with.

To make budgets work, the supervisor must have ready information on the *actual* expenditures and the *budgeted* or forecast expenditures. Many organizations fail to provide this information for supervisors, with the result that the budget fails to live up to its potential as a management control tool.

A budget is probably the *one* control device with which a supervisor will have the most contact. It is the supervisor's job to take the major parts of the budget and spell out in nonfinancial terms for the employees the expectations or constraints it presents. While dollars serve as a convenient language in a budget, such figures may have no meaning at all for the employees actually doing the work. It means more to explain, for example, that a certain function will be emphasized or deemphasized in the coming budget period or that plans are for things to remain the same.

QUALITY CONTROL

Supervision is most effective when the supervisor sets up clear standards of what he or she expects from the workers in the way of quantity, quality, and cost. These standards should be very clearly defined. An organization's customers are the *final* judges of employees' quality efforts.

However, the supervisor is the *first* judge of quality. Poor quality can very quickly result in lost sales or poor service and eventually show up in layoff and discharge figures.

Common causes of poor quality are poor instruction, unclear standards, lack of appreciation of the importance of quality, unsatisfactory material or equipment, poor working conditions, or bad employee morale. Quality doesn't just happen—it has to be built into a product or service all the way from the original design to the final operation.

A supervisor can do something about practically every cause of poor quality workmanship. Either the supervisor can control the causes directly or exert a great deal of pressure on subordinates and/or superiors to influence the kind of quality that goes into a job. Even if the original design or plan is incorrect, the supervisor can at least call this to the attention of those who *can* do something about that problem.

A supervisor can emphasize quality the minute a new worker comes on the job. He or she can praise quality work when it occurs and see that pay raises are attached to quality work.

Poor quality work reflects on you as supervisor. One of the most important indicators of supervisory success is the quality of your subordinates' work. Mere quantity without quality is not a good recommendation for any supervisor.

A major problem in planning quality control is how to determine the proper standards of quality and then to develop a follow-up plan which allows the supervisor to keep tabs on conformance to standards. Somewhere between the two extremes of no checking and checking every item that comes out of a supervisor's department is a point where control over the errors produces a minimum total cost. A supervisor can sample randomly rather than check on every item of output to reduce inspection costs. The use of the sample, rather than quality control of all items, is especially appropriate for machine output, where the units are not so likely to vary as are units that are produced by hand.

Checking or inspection is a key to high-quality production. Block 12–3 presents a quality control problem and the way one supervisor handled it.

COST AND WASTE CONTROL

Cost and waste control is an area that rests squarely on the supervisor's shoulders, and an area in which planning is indispensable. Perhaps the key for successful cost and waste control is an unflagging *cost consciousness.* Crash programs designed to fight waste and control costs can be successful in the short run, but only through *continual emphasis* can costs be effectively controlled.

An appropriate attitude for approaching this area is that there *is always a better way* to perform most jobs at a lower cost. The supervisor's *personal example* on cost control and waste reduction is one of the most important facets of a good cost reduction program.

The first step in controlling costs and reducing wastes in your department is to identify the most expensive item of waste and then try to find out why. You can usually spot the causes of waste by asking the right questions. Here is a series of questions that can help:

1. Is the right material being used?
2. Is the right equipment being used?
3. Is the equipment in proper adjustment?
4. Is the work around the job to blame?

5. Are you certain that your instructions to the worker were thorough and complete?
6. Are you supervising the job closely enough?
7. Is the method wrong?
8. Is all the planning being done as it should be?
9. Is your departmental housekeeping good?
10. Are the workers properly suited to the jobs they are doing?
11. Are working conditions to blame?

Unless responsibility for waste and cost control is fixed on an individual, the problem becomes a hazy one—waste becomes "nobody's fault."

Giving the right kind of job instruction is next in importance to developing cost consciousness. Be sure that the employee knows *exactly* what causes waste on a particular job and *exactly* how it can be avoided or eliminated. There are several steps to giving proper instructions: (1) Check the employees' knowledge of the cost of waste; (2) present full information regarding what that individual can and should do to prevent waste and cut costs; (3) let the individual try out the method you have suggested; and (4) follow up to see that your instructions are being followed. Block 12–4 illustrates how this simple approach was used to control waste in a packing department.

Analyzing Costs

In analyzing costs, four major areas are particularly fruitful. Those are *materials, direct labor, indirect labor,* and *facilities.* The left-hand portion of Figure 12–8 shows the component costs that are likely to contribute to excessive costs or waste in these four areas. The right-hand portion of Figure 12–8 shows the major problems associated with high direct labor costs, a major concern for many supervisors.

Perhaps one of the most useful things a supervisor can do is to report cost *by area.* The categories used in Figure 12–8 can be quite useful. These may, of course, be further broken down as appropriate. Such a system of cost reporting can provide valuable information for supervisors in pinpointing problem areas.

Zero Defects Programs

Zero defects (ZD) programs have been quite successful in the aerospace defense industries in reducing errors and improving the quality of work. ZD means *no* defects, *no* errors. It is a program that emphasizes *prevention* of mistakes instead of curing mistakes. The idea is to get a job done correctly the first time.

Foreman Bill Jones of the packing department is worried. The waste record in his department is getting worse. He has warned his workers about waste. He has bawled them out and threatened them time and again, but nothing has worked.

Jones is particularly concerned about the waste in packing materials, of which wrapping paper is the biggest item. This item of waste is causing him even greater concern because of the increasing cost of paper. No matter how much he "jumps on" his workers, they soon slip right back into wasteful work habits. Jones has frequently been on the carpet because his superintendent isn't satisfied with his performance in reducing packing paper waste.

A study of the situation indicated the following five causes of excessive waste of paper: (1) Packers don't appreciate the value of the paper they are using; (2) they are rough in handling the paper; (3) they are careless in cutting off sheets for packing; (4) they don't keep their paper supply on the bench but let it get underfoot, where it is frequently damaged and can't be used; and (5) the packers draw an oversupply of wrapping paper for stock.

Jones decided to let the packers know the cost of the paper they were using and the total cost of the waste resulting from the poor usage. He put the roller holders in the center of the packing bench to keep the paper supply in good condition and undamaged. Then he marked off a scale on the wrapping bench specifying the dimensions of the paper to be used for each of the parts to be packed and he spent a day and a half instructing the workers in the proper method of handling paper to conserve it. The actual time saved and the dollars saved in waste reduction from these changes were considerable.

A zero defects program is basically a motivational program that capitalizes on feedback of results. It realizes that those who are best prepared to eliminate errors are the individuals who made the errors in the first place. The program suggests that errors may be caused from lack of knowledge or lack of attention. Special training in job skills and in developing their attention span can convince workers that they are capable of nearly perfect production. The attitude that people are going to make mistakes can be replaced by a belief that mistakes are *not* normal and that we don't *have* to have them.

Zero defects programs are previewed and introduced by an employee committee, and usually involve a good deal of publicity throughout the organization. In many industries, zero defects has been extremely success-

FIGURE 12–8   Major Cost Control Items with an Emphasis on Direct Labor Costs

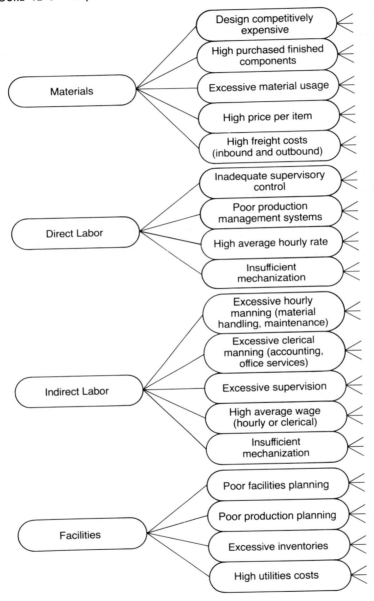

FIGURE 12-8 (cont.)

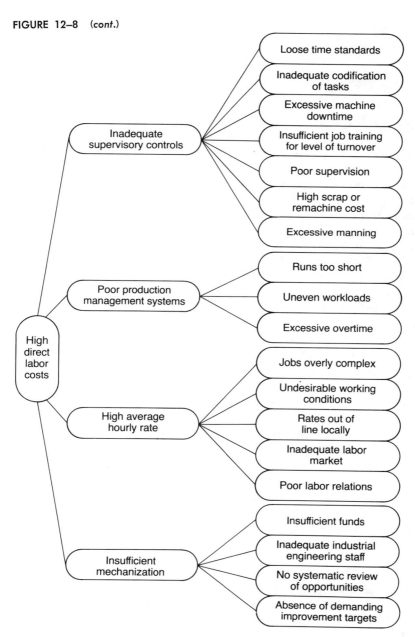

Source: H. E. Geissler and P. C. Buhler, "Zeroing in on Cost Savings," *Modern Manufacturing*, November 1970, p. 84. Reprinted by special permission of *Factory*, November 1970. Copyright, Morgan-Grampian, Inc., November 1970.

ful. Whether or not it is successful in your department depends on a number of situational factors.

People Problems with Control

Controls often are thought of as causing a lack of freedom for many people, but the *kind* of control someone in authority exercises can either minimize or maximize resistance to a course of action. To minimize people problems, controls should be *made meaningful* to those involved by specifying them in operational terms. In order to make clear how each person is expected to perform on his or her job, a supervisor must speak with employees face to face and assess their understanding.

Second, controls are meaningful only if the person can *affect the outcome*. To try to control something that the person can't really change only leads to frustration for that individual. Next, controls should be *accepted*. This means that they should be relevant to the particular job, and where appropriate, people should be allowed to participate in developing the controls that will affect them. Management is often surprised at the kind of successful controls employees can design if given the chance.

Control standards should be tough but attainable. If standards are set too high, the common reaction is, "What the heck—I can't do it anyway; I won't even try." If standards are set too low such that people don't have to stretch to reach them, they become a joke. If you expect low quality or effort, that's what you get.

Finally, it is wise for a supervisor to *keep an eye on the total "control load"* that each person has. People differ in their psychological tolerance for controls. Some people can tolerate a great many controls with no problem at all, while others feel hemmed in and uncomfortable very quickly if a very few aspects of their performance is controlled. Thus, the supervisor is well advised to consider the total psychological control load before adding an additional factor. You will find some people *want* more control and others less. Again, you can determine this in individual cases only by talking with individual employees.

SUMMARY AND CONCLUSIONS

Forecasting is simply a method for trying to estimate what the future holds. For the supervisor this is usually the more immediate future rather than any long-range plans. Moving averages and graphing a line to past data points are two useful techniques.

Scheduling is an important part of supervisory planning. Short interval planning can be quite useful. It is based upon the psychological tendency of people to perform more efficiently on short duration jobs. Methods improvement requires a constant search for a better way to do the various jobs in a supervisor's unit. "Work smarter, not harder" should be the motto. Time and motion studies are actually a part of the methods improvement effort.

PERT is a useful graphical planning aid. It consists of listing activities, restrictions, and estimated completion times then graphing these factors in a network diagram. GANTT charts, another device that can be used for planning and scheduling, is especially appropriate for simpler operations. A third type of diagram, objective charts, can be used to compare current operational output with the standards or objectives that have been set.

Preventative maintenance involves calculating the cost of replacing parts *before* they break down and comparing that with the cost of having them break down. Supervisors usually have to live with budgets and for that reason they should have a hand in their preparation and administration.

Two other important parts of the supervisor's job are quality control and cost and waste control. Clear standards, an ongoing emphasis on the specific objectives, and participation of the employees in the process help make these supervisory jobs easier. Finally, employee objections to control can be minimized with some attention to the problem by the supervisor.

QUESTIONS

1. Using a five-week moving average, what would you predict for weeks 7, 8, and 9 given these figures?

    Week 1   95
    Week 2   100
    Week 3   98
    Week 4   85
    Week 5   105
    Week 6   101

2. What would the prediction be if you fitted a line to the data in question 1?
3. What questions can a supervisor ask to help improve work methods?
4. Use motion economy principles to help improve a butcher's job.
5. Use a PERT chart to plan the writing of a term paper.
6. If radiator hoses on an automobile normally wear out at 40,000 miles, what are the costs of not replacing them before 40,000 miles?
7. Poor quality reflects on the supervisor. Discuss.
8. Analyze the job of post officer letter carrier for direct labor costs.

MARGARET WARD'S PROBLEM

Margaret learned the job assigned to her in less than a year. As substitute for practically any of the operators in the department, she quickly became familiar with all the jobs in the unit, so it was not surprising that she was promoted to supervisor when the vacancy occurred.

Since assuming the position, however, she has learned that supervision is not as simple as it looks. She has had reasonably good results, because she is well liked by all the people in the department and they felt she was a logical person to be selected for the supervisor's job. One problem, however, is giving her great cause for concern. The number of rejects has been steadily climbing since she has taken charge.

Recently she talked her problem over with the supervisor of another department whose work was similar to Margaret's. The other supervisor, Lottie Spencer, has maintained an unusually good record for quality in her department. "I had much the same kind of experience some time back," Lottie explained to Margaret, "but I solved it using a fairly simple plan. After listing all the operations in my department, I checked off the ones that seemed to be causing difficulty in meeting quality control standards. Then I called in the workers on those particular operations one at a time. On a table I put samples of good quality work and samples of poor work. I asked each of the workers for suggestions on how we could cut rejects in the operation. I was really surprised at the number of suggestions I got and the various reasons for difficulty that were pointed out to me.

"I came to the conclusion that planning and controlling the quality of work in my unit was a matter of teamwork. When we hit a problem on a certain operation that the operators were unable to work out themselves, I got assistance from the department inspector or from the general foreman. I also got help by calling in employees who were turning out high-quality work regularly and explained to them that some of the people were having difficulty meeting quality standards. I found that by getting everyone in the department to share in helping solve the problem, employees began to feel it was their responsibility as much as mine. It was a case of many heads being better than one. I'm sure if I'd merely bawled them out for poor work, my inspection record would have gotten worse instead of better." Margaret felt there were many aspects to Lottie's quality control technique that might work well in her own situation.

1. Will Lottie's approach work for Margaret?
2. Why or why not?

Problem Solving
and
Decision Making

---

13 SUPERVISORY PROBLEM

When should I make the decision myself and when should others have a say?

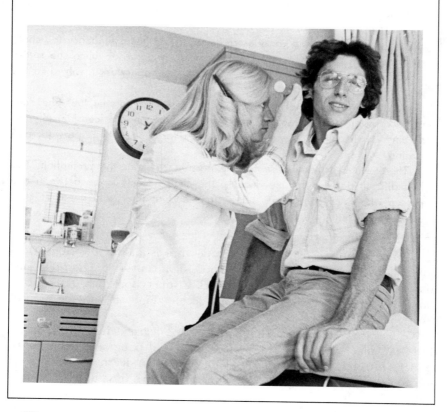

LEARNING OBJECTIVES

When you finish this chapter you should be able to

1. Identify the steps in the decision-making process
2. Classify the types of decisions supervisors may face
3. Discuss what is necessary for a decision to be effective
4. Choose the appropriate decision-making style for a given problem
5. Describe how to conduct a group decision-making meeting

THE DECISION

There is an opening coming up for assistant supervisor. As supervisor, I have to make a recommendation. The final decision is my boss's, but I know that my recommendation will be the deciding factor.

Two people are being considered. Barbara Pier has a tendency to "chat" with everyone who comes around but can do a good job once she settles down. She would do a really good job on the paperwork involved in the job.

Mary Kent is the second person being considered for the job. She does an acceptable job but could improve her performance considerably by slowing down a little. However, Mary has a problem with paperwork and writing.

There will be a pay raise for the person who gets the promotion. This is a difficult decision for me because the choice seems to be between one person who does good work but is slow, and another who needs to slow down to do better work.

An important part of your job as supervisor is making decisions. Decision making is simply the process of choosing a course of action designed to solve a particular problem. The work a supervisor must oversee constantly presents things he or she must decide alone or with the help of others, perhaps subordinates.

We feel that decision-making skills can be learned just as any other skill—playing golf, operating a machine, or driving a vehicle. With proper instruction, practice, and effort, one can learn to be a good decision maker. Not only must the supervisor learn how to use decision-making skills, he or she must be able to pass along this skill to subordinates. A major point we will stress in this chapter is that in some situations it is *best* to involve subordinates in decision making. But for employee participation to work, the supervisor must be sure that subordinates can also use appropriate decision-making skills.

THE DECISION-MAKING PROCESS

The basic decision-making process is as follows: First, the basic problem must be identified and properly defined. Second, the alternative courses of action must be laid out. Third, the advantages and disadvantages associated with each course of action must be analyzed and weighed. Fourth, the best solution or the best alternative should be identified. Finally, it is necessary to follow up and appraise the effectiveness of the decision.

Identify the Problem

The first step in identifying any problem is to identify the main objectives you are trying to achieve. Some questions you can ask yourself to aid in the identification of primary objectives are, What are the particular objectives that I and those under my supervision are expected to attain? What are the criteria on which the unit I supervise will be evaluated? A smart supervisor focuses resources on the attainment of these primary objectives.

Keep in mind that there is an important difference between *wants* and *needs*. An employee under your supervision may *want* a new piece of equipment, but is that new piece of equipment *needed* to get the job done? For example, a typist may *want* a new electric typewriter, but is it really necessary to meet the typing requirements of your work group? As the typing load increases perhaps a "yes" answer can be justified. Thus *time* is an important factor in distinguishing between wants and needs.

Attempts to identify a problem may at first lead only to *symptoms* of the problem. For example, two employees may be constantly bickering. On the surface this may seem to be a problem of interpersonal relations or styles of interaction. However, gathering more information about the situation may lead you to discover that the real problem is lack of understanding about each other's responsibilities. Neither clearly understands where the duties of one leave off and the duties of the other pick up. What appeared to be a problem of interpersonal relations turns out to be an organizational problem or a problem of job descriptions. Only after the true nature of a problem has been identified can you, as supervisor, deal with it effectively.

Identifying a problem is a crucial step in decision making. Typically, it involves gathering information and that takes time. But it is useless to proceed until the real problem has been identified.

Identifying Alternative Courses of Action

Figure 13–1 is a graphic illustration of the decision-making process. Beginning on the left, we assume that the problem has been properly defined. The next stage is to identify alternative courses of action that could be used to solve the problem. As a general rule, it is best for a supervisor to consider as *many courses of action* as possible in order to arrive at the best decision.

Alternative 3 is a course of action outside the control of the decision maker. One example of such an alternative is the situation in which a supervisor has little to say about the amount of pay increases subordinates receive. This presents real problems in rewarding good performance, since one method of rewarding performance is pay increases. Pay raises are an alternative course of action which is outside the control of the decision maker under those conditions.

Alternative 5 represents a possible solution to the problem of which

FIGURE 13–1   The Decision-Making Process

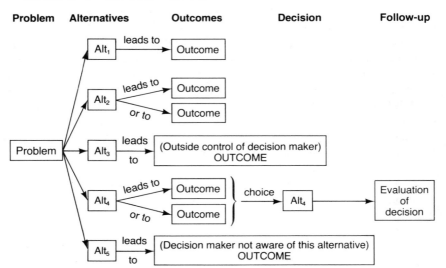

the supervisor is not aware. Often there may be several approaches to resolving a problem that do not come to light because important participants have not been involved in the decision-making process. Careful thought about those who will be affected by a decision will help the decision maker involve all concerned parties and thus reduce the probability of overlooking important alternatives.

Evaluation and Comparison of Alternative Courses of Action

Once the alternative courses of action for resolving the problem have been identified, it is necessary to examine each of these courses of action. What can you expect to follow from each alternative? Of course, you cannot know every outcome with complete certainty, but you can ask some key questions to evaluate the various alternatives: (1) Will the alternative solve the problem? (2) Are there any desirable or undesirable side effects of the alternative? (3) What is the cost of the alternative? (4) Is the alternative feasible?

Selecting An Alternative

After developing the alternatives and identifying the outcomes which can be expected to follow from each, the decision maker must now select that alternative which offers the *greatest advantage* at the *least cost*. This will be a relatively straightforward matter if one alternative course of action is clearly superior. In other cases, the decision maker must learn to rely on judgment and intuition.

Follow-Up

After a decision has been reached and sufficient time has been allowed for its implementation, the supervisor is ready to follow up and appraise the results. Follow-up is important for two reasons. First, failure to follow up may result in nothing being done, as the supervisor in Block 13–1 discovered on his first attempt to assign a project.

A second purpose served by the follow-up stage is to evaluate the effectiveness of the decision. Did the chosen alternative actually solve the problem? Did expected side effects in fact occur, or were there side effects that were not anticipated? If the decision has turned out well, then the supervisor can be confident that it was a good one. But if the follow-up stage reveals some unexpected side effects or failure to resolve the main issue, then the decision-making process must begin all over again. Many upper-level managers say they are satisfied if 51 percent of their decisions have good results. However, for the supervisor, that figure is probably too low to set as a goal.

TYPES OF DECISIONS

It is useful to distinguish between two basic types of decisions, programmed (or structured) decisions and nonprogrammed (or unstructured) decisions. We suggest that you think of any decision as some mix of each, with highly programmed decisions at one extreme of the continuum and nonprogrammed decisions at the other. In Figure 13–2, the horizontal part of the figure represents the programmed dimensions of decisions.

Decisions are programmed or structured if they are repetitive or a definite procedure has been worked out for handling them. Problems for which programmed decisions will work do not have to be reconsidered each time they occur. The decisions have been made routine. Examples

FIGURE 13–2   Types of Decisions

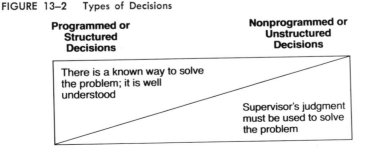

278

of programmed decisions are reorder points for inventory items and pre-determined policies on absenteeism and tardiness. Many modern quantitative decision-making techniques can be used in these situations. Such approaches to decision making as operations research, linear programming, simulation, and queuing are useful when problems of a particular type occur on a fairly regular basis.

Decisions are nonprogrammed or unstructured when the problem is unique or unusual. In such cases, there can be no predetermined rule or standard procedure for handling the problem. It is necessary to treat such problems on an individual basis. The role of judgment or "intuition" in these cases is greatly expanded, as one can see in moving from left to right across Figure 13–2.

The term *intuition* can be somewhat misleading here. Intuition suggests that the supervisor is basing decisions on hunches or "gut feelings." In some cases this may be an appropriate description of the basis for decision making. But more often judgment comes into play, that is, the prior experience and training of the decision maker. Those individuals who have participated in similar situations can also contribute their judgment to the decision-making process.

EFFECTIVE DECISIONS

Effective decisions are based on the facts in a situation and contribute to the achievement of organizational goals. Decisions made by capable supervisors can usually be expected to make proper use of facts and contribute to the accomplishment of organizational goals. But a high-quality decision can be made a bad decision if those who must implement the decision *do not accept it.*

This tells us that there are two components to effective decisions: decision *quality* and *acceptance* of the decision. Quality is concerned with facts and organizational objectives, while acceptance is concerned with the behaviors and opinions of the people who execute the decision.

Figure 13–3 presents an approach to viewing problems based on these two dimensions, acceptance and quality. It also shows who should be involved in the decision-making process based on the classification of problems.

Look at the upper left-hand corner of Figure 13–3. *Acceptance* is a crucial factor of decisions that fall into this category, but decision quality is a relatively minor concern. Decisions of this type are primarily concerned with "fairness." Block 13–2 describes such a problem.

When a supervisor is facing problems of this sort, we recommend that the decision be turned over to the group. Let the group discuss it and

FIGURE 13–3   Classification of Problems

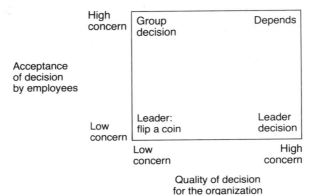

decide. Other examples of decisions of this type are: Who should receive a new piece of equipment and whose old equipment will be traded in? Who will get the corner office recently vacated by an individual who retired? The main issue in this kind of problem is *fairness*, and the individuals best able to decide *what is fair* are those who are affected by the decision.

The lower left-hand corner of Figure 13–3 represents problem situations that are of low priority both to the employees and to reaching the

---

BLOCK 13–2   Scheduling Vacations

John Sullivan supervises the Orange Soda distributorship in Jersey City. Summer is the company's season of peak demand. As a result the distributorship policy is that no more than one-fourth of the drivers can be on vacation at any one time during the summer. All drivers are entitled to two weeks vacation between June 1 and August 31, although they can take their vacation at other times of the year if they choose to do so.

Almost all the drivers are married and have children. Naturally, these drivers want to vacation during the summer. Some drivers' spouses are also employed. They want to schedule their vacations to coincide with their children's vacations. Some drivers have other special reasons for scheduling their vacations at a particular time.

John dislikes deciding who goes on vacation at what time. Regardless of what he decides, some feel they are unfairly treated. As far as the organization is concerned, it doesn't make any difference who goes. Any combination of drivers can meet the distribution needs of the company.

organization's objectives. An example might be the choice of an office supplies or maintenance service firm. If the alternatives are equally good in quality and the decision makes little difference to those who execute it, there is really no problem at all. The supervisor can simply flip a coin.

The lower right-hand corner represents a decision situation in which the quality of the decision is very important to the organization but the choice does not materially affect the employees. An example might be deciding among several suppliers of raw materials if there are significant differences in quality or cost. Since employees usually are not concerned with *who* supplies raw materials so long as they are available when needed, we recommend that the supervisor make such decisions alone.

The remaining corner of the chart represents a category of problems in which both quality and acceptance are important. Such problems might include improving the safety record of a work group, improving work methods, increasing labor productivity, deciding which employees are entitled to large raises in wages, or deciding which employees must be laid off in a business downturn.

If the goals of the individuals and the organization are the same—for example, as reducing accidents—group decision making may prove effectual. But if the goals of the group and organization are different, we recommend that the supervisor make the decision himself or herself. An example might be deciding on the size of raises for members of a work group.

In this fourth corner where both the quality of the decision you make and its acceptance are important, ground rules have yet to be clearly spelled out. However, with conflict situations of this sort, it has been found that a supervisor's *decision-making style* is the crucial factor. For this reason, we will now consider a decision-making aid to help you choose the appropriate style when facing decisions in that fourth corner area.

CHOOSING A DECISION-MAKING STYLE

How does the supervisor decide who should take part in making a decision? Two management writers have proposed a set of categories that can help supervisors analyze a given situation.[1] Their classification scheme is presented in Figure 13–4. The styles are automatic, consultive, and group decision making, respectively. There are two variations each of the autocratic and consultive decision styles.

In the first autocratic approach the supervisor makes the decision alone without consulting subordinates at all. The supervisor acts on the basis of information available at the time he or she was presented with the problem. In the second autocratic approach, the supervisor relies on

FIGURE 13–4   Types of Management Decision Styles

Autocratic (I) Decision Style

You solve the problem or make the decision yourself, using information available to you at that time.

Autocratic (II) Decision Style

You obtain the necessary information from your subordinate(s), then decide on the solution to the problem yourself. You may or may not tell your subordinates what the problem is in getting the information from them. The role played by your subordinates in making the decision is clearly one of providing the necessary information to you, rather than generating or evaluating alternative solutions.

Consultive (I) Decision Style

You share the problem with relevant subordinates individually, getting their ideas and suggestions without bringing them together as a group. Then you make the decision, which may or may not reflect your subordinates' influence.

Consultive (II) Decision Style

You share the the problem with your subordinates as a group, collectively obtaining their ideas and suggestions. Then you make the decision, which may or may not reflect your subordinates' influence.

Group Decision Style

You share a problem with your subordinates as a group. Together you generate and evaluate alternatives and attempt to reach agreement (consensus) on a solution. Your role is much like that of chairperson. You do not try to influence the group to adopt "your" solution, and you are willing to accept and implement any solution which has the support of the entire group.

Source: Adapted, from "A New Look at Managerial Decision Making," Victor H. Vroom, *Organizational Dynamics,* Spring 1973 (New York: AMACOM, a division of American Management Associations, 1973).

subordinates as a source of information but is the sole determiner of the weight to be given to the information.

In both of the consultive decision styles, the supervisor again keeps the final decision-making powers but lays greater weight on subordinates' input. In the first consultive style, the supervisor contacts subordinates individually, getting their ideas and suggestions about the problem *without calling them together as a group.* In the second approach, subordinates *do* come together as a group to make suggestions for the supervisor's consideration, but again the final decision is up to the boss.

Group decision making involves giving the problem to the subordinates as a group. The supervisor's role is merely to chair the meeting, and he or she consciously tries to *avoid* influencing the group's decision process. The supervisor is willing to accept and implement any solution which the group recommends.

Understanding the Decision Situation

The nature of the decision to be made determines which of the five decision styles will work best in a given situation. Figure 13–5 shows seven features of a decision-making situation and seven diagnostic questions corresponding to each feature which can be used by the supervisor in selecting the proper decision-making style for a situation. Let's consider each of the features

Quality of Decision (A). This feature, as mentioned earlier in connection with Figure 13–3, is the extent to which one solution or another will result in a better level of goal attainment for the organization. If a number of solutions to a problem would be equally effective for attaining organizational goals, we can answer the diagnostic question "no." On the other hand, if the nature of the problem is such that one solution is likely to be more effective than another, then the problem *does* have a quality dimension.

Consider an example of a problem which *lacks* such a quality

FIGURE 13–5   Identifying Features of the Decision Situation

The Decision Features	*Questions To Ask Yourself*
A. The quality of the decision.	Is there a quality requirement such that one solution is likely to be more rational than another?
B. The extent to which the supervisor has enough information to make a high-quality decision alone.	Do I have sufficient information to make a high-quality decision?
C. The extent to which the problems is structured.	Is the problem structured?
D. The extent to which acceptance on the part of subordinates is critical to the effective implementation of the decision.	Is acceptance of decision by subordinates critical to effective implementation?
E. The probability that a decision made autocratically will be accepted by subordinates.	If I were to make the deceision by myself, is it reasonably certain that it will be accepted by my subordinates?
F. The extent to which the subordinates want to attain the organizational goals in this situation.	Do subordinates share my goals in solving this problem?
G. The extent to which subordinates are likely to disagree over solutions.	Is conflict among subordinates likely in preferred solutions?

Source: Adapted, from "A New Look at Managerial Decision Making," Victor H. Vroom, *Organizational Dynamics*, Spring 1973 (New York: AMACOM, a division of American Management Associations, 1973).

dimension. Your organization has built a new building and is moving to the new site. There are four parking spots for supervisors in front of the building, but there are six supervisors. Two supervisors will have to park in an area somewhat removed from the front row of parking spots. Is there a quality requirement such that one alternative is best for the organization? There is clearly *no* quality dimension for the organization, all that is necessary is to arrive at a decision that will be satisfactory for the six supervisors.

Contrast this problem with the following problems which do have a quality dimension. What is the most effective advertising policy for the sporting goods department which you supervise? How shall this year's budget be allocated among the projects under your supervision? In cases such as these, choosing one alternative over another could make the difference between achieving or not achieving organizational objectives.

The Extent to Which the Supervisor Has Enough Information to Make a High Quality Decision Alone (B). If a quality decision is to be made, several courses of action must be identified and evaluated for their effect on the organization. Such a process requires a lot of information and expertise. The supervisor may or may not have enough of the information necessary to make a good decision. If not, obviously he or she will have to *get more* from other sources.

The Extent to Which the Problem Is Structured (C). Structured problems (as we saw earlier) are the problems whose solutions are known and probably described in a procedure. Problems of a routine nature can be solved by implementing specific, predetermined procedures *once all the necessary information has been gathered.* In other words, decision rules, such as reordering typing paper when supplies fall below four reams, are specified in advance. What is important is an accurate observation of the situation to determine whether the standard operating procedures apply.

If, on the other hand, the problem is unstructured, then specific procedures are not specified in advance and/or relevant information is not known. If the supervisor does not have all the relevant information then others who possess relevant information should be brought into the picture.

The Extent to Which Acceptance on the Part of Subordinates Is Critical to Effective Implementation (D). As we noted earlier, a high-quality decision can be ineffective because subordinates do not choose to support it. There are basically two situations in which acceptance does *not* matter in getting a decision implemented. One is when subordinates are not involved in the results of the decision. For example, the choice of firm to provide office supplies is of little concern to employees so long as paper, cartons, clips, and so on are of acceptable quality.

A second situation in which acceptance of a decision is not critical occurs when subordinates will be *required* to execute the decision, and their performance can be carefully controlled. When a supervisor is able to check the behaviors of subordinates and can reward and punish subordinates, it does not matter whether or not they accept a decision. They must do it! An example of such a situation is described in Block 13–3.

Being at work on time is a behavior you can check. Supervisors can see who is at their work stations at the beginning of a shift. Those who are tardy or absent can be disciplined.

Acceptance of the decision becomes important when initiative, judgment, or creativity on the part of the subordinates is involved; or when the supervisor is unable to observe or control rewards and punishments.

The Probability That a Decision Made Autocratically Will Be Accepted by Subordinates (E).   The decision feature above asked, Does it *matter* if employees accept the decision? This question asks, If you make the decision will they accept it? The issue involved is the supervisor's *power* or lack of it.

When subordinates have a high respect for authority, they will probably accept a supervisor's decision simply because they believe it is the supervisor's *legitimate right* to make such decisions. After all, he or she is the boss. This is the situation in military organizations, where decisions often must be made and carried out as swiftly as possible. Group decision-making techniques can hardly be applied on the battlefield. Therefore, it is necessary to have the leaders make the decisions and have them accepted.

Another situation that will probably result in subordinates going along with a supervisor's decisions occurs when the supervisor is seen as an expert. When the supervisor is the only one who has the necessary information and expertise to make the decision, subordinates are likely to go along with whatever he or she decides.

BLOCK 13–3   At Work on Time

The Quality Manufacturing Company produces wooden office furniture. The production operation is organized as an assembly line. Efficient production depends on everyone being at their work stations at the beginning of the shift. For example, when someone in the middle of the line is tardy or absent, all work from that station to the end of the line is delayed until the supervisor arranges for a replacement.

A third situation in which employees are likely to concur in a supervisor's decision occurs when they identify closely with the leader. Some supervisors have charisma—that is, they are strongly admired by subordinates and subordinates will go along with whatever they say.

In any of these three situations it is likely that the supervisor will be able to "sell" the decision. If these conditions are not present, however, decisions made only by the supervisor may not be supported by subordinates.

The Extent to Which Subordinates Want to Attain the Organizational Goals in This Situation (F).   The diagnostic question for this feature of the decisions situation is, Do subordinates share the organizational goals to be obtained in solving this problem? While employees or subordinates may have information and expertise that is useful in reaching a quality decision, their willingness to use that information depends on whether or not they want to achieve the goals or solve the problem.

For example, contrast these two situations: (1) Deciding on the size of raise to be received by each member of a work group; (2) deciding on how to improve a work group's safety record. In the first situation, a *supervisor's* prime concern would be to match good performance with size of individual raises. The members of the work group may not all share this goal. Some might rather use such things as individual need or seniority for setting raises. These factors are clearly unrelated to merit.

In the second example, trying to arrive at a way to improve the safety record, it is more likely that employees' goals will coincide with those of the supervisor. If subordinates *do not* share the supervisor's goals, it is not recommended that the supervisor give final decision making authority to the group.

The Extent to Which Subordinates Are Likely to Disagree over Solutions (G).   Subordinates may agree on a goal but disagree on how to achieve it. Conflict among members of a work group over how to implement a solution is relatively common.

There is a good deal of evidence from the field of social psychology that face-to-face interaction among people tends to reduce differences in attitudes and opinions. Group confrontation apparently has this "leveling" effect because of group pressures toward conformity.

Putting It All Together

The flow chart presented in Figure 13–6 summarizes our discussion on choosing a decision-making style. It combines parts of Figures 13–4 and 13–5 by incorporating both the quality of the decision and its acceptance by subordinates into the decision-making "tree." One significant factor

FIGURE 13–6 Decision Process Flow Chart

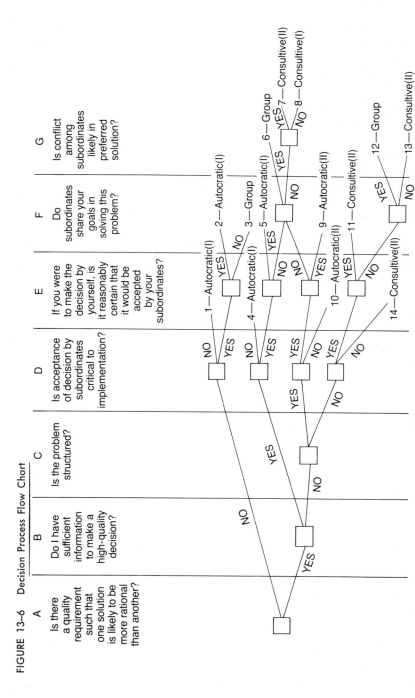

Source: Adapted, from "A New Look at Managerial Decision Making," Victor H. Vroom, *Organizational Dynamics*, Spring 1973 (New York: AMACOM, a division of American Management Associations, 1973).

that it omits is the amount of time required to make decisions. Whenever a group decision-making approach seems appropriate, expect to spend considerably more time in making a decision.

The starting point for using the flow chart is diagnostic question A, dealing with decision quality. If there is *no* quality dimension to the problem, skip situation features B and C and look at feature D. If acceptance is not critical, the supervisor should make the decision. However, if acceptance by subordinates *is* critical then the supervisor considers feature E (Will subordinates go along with a decision made by the supervisor?). If the answer is yes, it is also recommended that the supervisor make the decision himself or herself. However, if there are factors that suggest the subordinates will not accept the leader's decision, then turn the decision over to the group.

The flow chart also maps out a number of other possibilities. By tracing the decisional process through each of the seven steps, the supervisor can choose an approach based on known properties of the situation.

SUGGESTIONS FOR EFFECTIVE GROUP DECISION MAKING

If a supervisor is to use the group decision-making method effectively, he or she must know how to conduct a group meeting and how best to carry out the role of group leader. For group decision making to work, everyone in the group must feel free to participate without fear of pressure or reprisal from any in-group or from the supervisor.

It is also necessary to recognize group discussions are especially susceptible to pressure toward conformity. If this pressure goes unchecked, the group can be pushed toward making a poor-quality decision. We will now consider some suggestions for leading decision-making discussions as a supervisor.[2]

Avoid Defensiveness

As discussion leader, the supervisor must be able to phrase the problem so that it does not look like an attack on group members. Instead, you should try to emphasize that the problem is a shared one whose solution will affect both supervisor and subordinates. Block 13–4 provides examples of what to avoid and recommended approaches.

Provide Information

Effective group decision making requires the supervisor (1) to supply the group with all the essential information and (2) to indicate when a decision will be possible for the organization. In supplying information and specifying the range of freedom, it is critical that the supervisor maintain a neutral attitude.

One of the authors was rather amused at overhearing a conversation between two high-level executives. One, the president of a manufacturing concern, was commenting to a friend that he couldn't understand why some people had problems leading a group decision-making session. He said that in his experience it was a very simple process with very few problems. For example, in conducting a group decision meeting with the senior officers of his organization, there had been no difficulty in agreeing on a course of action. As a matter of fact, almost without exception the group would arrive at a decision which he had suggested was the best solution to the problem!

Maintaining a neutral stance during the discussion of alternative solutions is the key to using a group's talents effectively. If a supervisor reveals any hint of partiality toward a particular solution, members of the group will feel this immediately and arrive at what they think the superior wants.

Get Everyone Involved

An effective leader is able to draw out all members of the group. As discussion leader, you must convey the idea that everyone's viewpoint on the problem is wanted. An important rule is that members of the group must not criticize *each other*. Criticism will only result in shutting the door to opinions of those group members who are less self-confident.

One technique that can be used is to go around the room, asking each individual for his or her suggestions. These can be listed on a chalkboard or easel. To encourage a feeling of acceptance, you might begin by saying, "Early in the meeting, what we're trying to do is get everyone's ideas out on the table. We will come back at a *later* time and evaluate ideas." Do not evaluate any ideas until all ideas are out.

The supervisor can help the decision process along and avoid squabbles in the group by asking everyone to focus on ideas and issues and refrain from such comments as, "Gee, that's a dumb idea," or "How could you ever come up with something so ridiculous." Comments such as these reflect on the person who made them rather than the issue at hand. It might also be helpful to begin by stressing that differences of opinion should be *expected* in the course of any discussion, but that all participants should exercise self-control.

Learn to Wait

Another technique a supervisor as discussion leader can put to good use is to wait out long, quiet pauses. For example, when you are trying to get alternative solutions, group members who are unfamiliar with this process may be inclined to wait for someone else to make the first suggestion. A common trap for the leader to fall into when the silence becomes overwhelming is to suggest his or her own ideas. This results in the leader's dominating the discussion and discouraging further participation.

We are aware of one case in which a supervisor using this technique for the first time waited out an uncomfortable silence of three to four minutes before anyone would say anything. However, once the process of group discussion had started, ideas flowed quite freely. If the supervisor had given in to the silence, probably nothing would have been said later.

Summarize and Restate

A discussion leader should be able to *restate* accurately the ideas expressed by members of the group. In doing so, try to summarize the ideas in a form more abbreviated and more to the point. Restatement helps two things: (1) It clarifies any ideas that may have been fuzzy in some participants' minds; and (2) it shows that you are paying attention. One precautionary note: Be careful to avoid indicating agreement or disagreement or in any way evaluating the ideas. As the key figure in the decision process, any evaluation on your part will have an effect on the selection of an alternative. At various points in a group discussion a summarization of what has happened up to that point can be useful. It can get the discussion moving again if it has strayed from the central issues being discussed. It can also help in assessing the progress that has been made to that point. Summarizing at the end of a discussion also provides a final chance for members to disagree with a particular feature of the solution or to present evidence that had been overlooked.

SUMMARY AND CONCLUSIONS

There are five steps in the decision-making process: identify the problem; identify alternative solutions; identify the likely outcomes or consequences of the alternatives and evaluate them; select a course of action; and follow up to evaluate the effectiveness of the selected course of action. Involving subordinates in the decision-making process is a good idea because subordinates can often contribute valuable information at each step of the process.

Participation serves another function. When employees participate in decision making, they feel committed to the effective implementation of the decision. A decision of adequate quality to which people are committed is probably more effective than a higher-quality decision that meets a good deal of employee opposition.

Some decisions should be made by subordinates. Others are best left up to supervisors without any input from subordinates, and a third category is best handled by supervisors after subordinates have made an input. The decision model we presented helps supervisors choose which approach to use in a given situation. Following the guidelines of this model can make a supervisor a better decision maker.

Many decisions that do not have too tight a time limit can use the group decision-making method. When conducting group decision-making meetings, the supervisor should ensure that subordinates feel free to participate in the meeting. The group leader must also make sure that he or she does not bias the group in evaluating the suggested alternatives and in selecting a course of action.

QUESTIONS

1. Discuss the advantages of involving other individuals in the identification and evaluation of alternatives.
2. Contrast the role of judgment or intuition in programmed as opposed to nonprogrammed decisions.
3. Why is it important that a decision be accepted by those responsible for implementing it?
4. Describe five different decision-making approaches.
5. Describe the key questions to be considered in selecting a decision-making style.

6. Describe how to
    a. Avoid making subordinates defensive in a group decision-making session
    b. Get everyone to contribute ideas in a group decision-making session

---

THE CASE OF THE NEW VEHICLES

You supervise seven salespeople, each of whom covers a wide territory selling fertilizers, pesticides, and other chemical products to farmers and ranchers.

Every year one or two new vehicles are purchased by the company. Each salesperson is provided with a vehicle. This year two new Ford sedans are being purchased, and you again face the hassle of deciding whose vehicles will be turned in for the new Fords, and who will receive the new cars.

---

1. Select an appropriate decision-making style.
2. Outline the decision-making process within this framework.

NOTES

1 V. H. Vroom and P. W. Yetton, *Leadership and Decision-making* (Pittsburgh: University of Pittsburgh Press, 1973).

2 This discussion is based on the work of N. R. F. Maier, *Psychology in Industrial Organizations* (Boston: Houghton-Mifflin, 1977).

Supervising Change and Conflict, and Working with Other Supervisors

14   SUPERVISORY PROBLEMS

How can I handle conflict among my employees and make changes smoothly?

How can I best work with other supervisors?

LEARNING OBJECTIVES

When you have finished this chapter, you should be able to

1. Identify "driving" and "resisting" forces in change situations
2. Explain how changes in the work force have affected the supervisor's job
3. Discuss the idea that changes in work organizations are interrelated
4. Indicate predictable human responses to major change
5. List four common defense mechanisms and explain why people use defense mechanisms
6. Recognize a win-lose, lose-lose, and win-win conflict resolution situation
7. Specify the major issues in working with other supervisors

WHY CAN'T WE ALL JUST WORK TOGETHER?

As shop foreman at the state Maintenance Department, I am responsible for maintaining equipment for eleven different crews. My job requires me to interact with people on my own level, crew foremen, resident engineers, and state patrol division supervisors. Most of these working relationships over the past several years have been good, but a number of recent changes have caused difficulties.

In the first place, growth of industry in the state has meant the purchase of more equipment just to maintain the level of service we had in the past. And as operations have expanded, we have been forced to change our ways of doing things. In the past, we were fairly informal. Work orders were filled on a first-come, first-served basis, and I decided what the priorities would be on those rare occasions of conflict. However, the increase in work has resulted in our having to go to a formal priority system to schedule incoming work. Of course, each new foreman, resident engineer, and patrol division supervisor feels that his problems should have first priority, and tempers flare when the mechanics aren't able to complete someone's pet project.

I've attempted to get the crew foremen to give me their equipment at least a week before they need it so that I can schedule my people to work on it and also arrange for the purchase of required parts that may not be in stock locally. This works fine for routine maintenance, but when unscheduled breakdowns of emergency equipment occur—such as snow plows during a storm, patrol cars during holiday periods, or engineering vehicles carrying expensive instruments that must be transferred to other locations—tempers flare and requests are no longer turned in. Everything is treated as an emergency by these other supervisors when breakdowns happen. The changes that have been necessary to keep up with growth have resulted in conflicts among the other supervisors in the organization, and I'm caught in the middle.

If you want to avoid change, you're living in the wrong time period. Since the turn of the century, we have increased tenfold our speed of communication, our speed of travel, the speed of data handling, and our ability to control disease. These major changes, all of which have occurred within a relatively short time period, are representative of the many changes that have affected work organizations and supervisors.

Change affects not only the technology a supervisor must work with, but also the human resources at his or her disposal. Changes in the organization can lead to conflicts, and conflicts can lead to frustrations, fears, and many kinds of individual psychological problems with work force members. Change, as well as a host of other factors, can affect the relationships among supervisors in an organization. A supervisor's ability to get things done with other supervisors is an important factor in success or failure as a supervisor. These three topics—change, conflict, and working with other supervisors—are the subject of this chapter.

CHANGE

Successfully supervising change demands that we know something about the nature of change and the typical human reactions to change. Change is ongoing and continuous. In order to see this fact, try to imagine the dynamic nature of the forces in Figure 14–1—think perhaps of a tug of war.

There are two kinds of forces present in every situation: those forces in favor of change—the "driving" forces; and those forces that seek to maintain the status quo—the "resisting" forces. Figure 14–1 shows that so long as these forces are essentially equal in strength (top portion of the figure) very little change occurs. If the resisting forces are stronger, little change or negative change is likely to occur (bottom diagram). By contrast, if the driving forces prevail, some sort of progressive change will take place.

These forces are present in any situation, whether it concerns the organization as a whole or one of the supervisors in the organization. As an example, a supervisor who decides to delegate more effectively, faces

FIGURE 14-1   Forces for Change

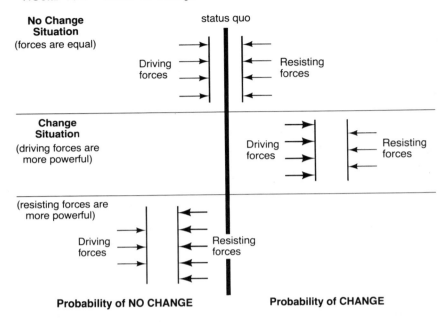

No Change Situation
(forces are equal)

status quo

Driving forces

Resisting forces

Change Situation
(driving forces are more powerful)

Driving forces

Resisting forces

(resisting forces are more powerful)

Driving forces

Resisting forces

Probability of NO CHANGE

Probability of CHANGE

a set of restraining forces and a set of driving forces, some of which are external (that is, outside the supervisor) and some of which are internal psychological needs. The restraining forces might be that the supervisor wants to retain control, or fears the risk of failure. Perhaps delegation isn't customary in this particular organization, or perhaps no one else has the experience to do the job, so that more delegation involves undertaking a major training program. But there are driving forces present as well: The supervisor needs more time for planning, the supervisor's boss firmly believes in the philosophy of delegation, workers need to feel that they are not stagnating on the job, and so on. As long as restraining forces and driving forces are in balance, there will be no change and the supervisor will *not* delegate more. When some of the restraining forces weaken or additional driving forces are added, however, the supervisor may find that he or she *can* begin to delegate.

Changes in the Work Force

There have been some fundamental changes in the nature of the work force supervisors have to deal with today. New attitudes among the labor force often constitute a driving force for change. For example, per capita income after taxes has increased 89 percent in the past decade in the United States.[1] Allowing for inflation, this gain is about 42 percent per capita. Never in the history of the world has fundamental economic change taken place so fast in a major country. As a result, the younger people in the work force aren't nearly so worried about having a job or enough to eat as some of the workers who have seen harder times.

Further, it has been suggested that the work ethic has declined markedly in this country. The term *work ethic* means a personal value system in which hard work is the key to "success" and material well-being. This devotion to hard work, thrift, and the competitive struggle, many feel, is being seriously challenged today. A recent study shows that 62 percent of the high school and college students surveyed believe it is immoral to ask an employee to work up to his or her capacity; 69 percent believe that hard work no longer pays off; and 64 percent feel negatively about being supervised.[2]

While such survey figures inevitably fluctuate according to socioeconomic conditions, the point remains that the work force of today is somewhat different from that of a generation ago. For the supervisor, the problem is getting performance and productivity from a work force that has at least partially cast aside the work ethic.

Such widespread changes affect the entire society, yet smaller changes are continually taking place within any organization. A certain amount of change is guaranteed simply because people "turn over." Husbands or wives are transferred to new jobs in different cities, people find better jobs, they die, they retire, and so on. Turnover changes old patterns of social relationships and often requires us to rethink some of the procedures we have used to deal with certain situations.

Change Is Interrelated

Possibly the most important thing for the supervisor to remember when dealing with change on an organization-wide basis is that change in one part of the organization always affects other portions of the organization as well. There is no such thing as a "self-contained" change. As Figure 14–2 shows, there are a great many interrelated things a supervisor must consider in proposing any new policy or change. If we think of the relationships among technological processes and people as one vast, interrelated network, perhaps we can imagine how changing one link in that network may cause many other links to combine in new ways.

It is a mistake to think, for example, that you can change work methods without affecting all of the other things involved, the people, the work groups, the authority relationships, and so forth. This is why

FIGURE 14–2   The Interrelated Nature of Change

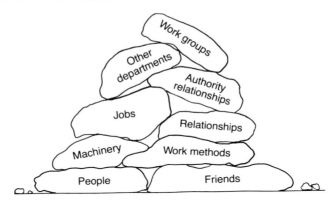

change can be successful only when a new proposal is considered in all of its ramifications. We have suggested that change is inevitable and that change in one part of the job affects all other parts of the job to one extent or another. Now let's consider human reactions to changes in jobs and organizations.

Human Reactions to Change

Most employees resist change. Any change in the status quo may arouse concern for their jobs, prestige position, or income. Employees may be concerned about whether they can do the new job and about whether they're going to have to be transferred or relocated. People typically fear the unknown, and in any change situation there are many unknowns.

To some extent, all change involves loss. Whenever people give up familiar ways of doing things, trusted relationships, routines, habits, and ways of seeing and doing things, they feel a real sense of loss. Even when change is clearly for the better, some sense of loss is inevitable. People typically experience sadness, anger, tension, or irritability in the face of changes. Gradually, however, they begin to "settle in" and the strange situation becomes more familiar.

One psychiatrist has suggested human beings go through a four-step process of adjustment to major changes either in their personal lives or at work.[3] *Step one is impact.* During impact, the individual feels somewhat numb, he or she is shocked to some degree, especially if the change is undesired and unexpected. This phase may last for a few hours or a few days. *Second, the recoil/turmoil phase.* This continues for one to three weeks. During this phase, a person may be very emotional about the change, may be very anxious, and depression may set in. *Third, the adjustment phase.* This may take two to four weeks. The painful feelings become somewhat muted and are gradually tempered with some hope about the future and growing optimism is likely. *Fourth, eventual reconstruction.* This phase may require many months. Time periods, of course, are subject to considerable variation. Specific times are influenced by the individual's personality and the magnitude of the change.

Resistance to Change

Resistance to change is inevitable in some form and may not be entirely bad. Resistance to change can be used by the supervisor very much as a body temperature reading is used by a physician. It can help to determine if there is something really wrong. Great amounts of resistance to what seem to be minor changes may indicate that there are problems you have overlooked in the proposed change.

Some resistance is good; it can help bring out opinions and concerns so that they can be dealt with in the open. An employee may resist change because of several unknowns: *how* the change will affect him or her; *when* the change is liable to take place; and *what* to do about the change. And, as we suggested earlier, uncertainty breeds resistance.

Why Do Employees Resist Change?

Employees may resist change not because the change itself is unwelcome but because they dislike the feeling of being compelled by a superior's "whims." If a supervisor calls for a change in methods, the employee may feel that the supervisor is *arbitrarily* trying to meddle with his or her situation. Change that is imposed from above doesn't always lead to positive motivation, cooperation, or smooth transitions.

Another factor is group pressure. If most of the group is against a particular change, those members who are on the fence or who perhaps don't mind the change are likely to hesitate about going along with it. Resistance problems are compounded if the supervisor sees the change one way and the employee sees it another way. Unfortunately, proposals for change often ignore the inputs from people closest to the work, yet these are the very people who might be able to contribute the most.

Third, employees may resist change because it is seen as a threat to their self-image. If a change in methods is opposite to the old way of doing things, the employee may feel that the vested interest he or she has in the old way is being criticized. It may even be that the employee developed the original method, and now here's somebody saying that the old way is *no good* or *inappropriate*. This type of change reflects badly on him or her as a person.

Employees may resist change because of what they feel will be a loss of status in the organization or in their work group. If the change is going to require them to do something different from what they've done before, and they are currently very good at what they do, the change may put them in the position of being an unskilled, unknowledgeable worker. The status of knowledge and expertise they have developed over the years might be lost.

Finally, the employee may see the change as simply an added burden. For an employee who has a number of problems outside work, the addition of problems related to a change at work may be enough to cause resistance. This situation is similar to the proverbial straw that broke the camel's back.

Overcoming Resistance to Change

With all the problems that can happen when making changes, what can a supervisor do to minimize these problems? Probably the most important thing to do is to *communicate* the change clearly. Make sure that it is understood, and address yourself to any false rumors that might be spread about the change. The more information people have about the need for the change and why the change is taking place, the less threatened they feel. In the absence of hard information, rumors and fantasies almost always occur.

Next, the supervisor should try to *create an open atmosphere* that allows for expresson of feelings. If people feel they won't be listened to, or will be punished for expressing their concerns about the change, they may bottle up their anxiety. Then it can escape and disrupt some other aspect of their lives. If not open, the supervisor might very well fail to get good information on how the change could be done differently. Honesty is very important here. Try to discuss openly the potential *problems* as well as the *advantages* of the change. By discussing the negative things, employees will know that the supervisor's eyes *are* open and that he or she appreciates the problems they will be facing.

Next, where it is appropriate, employees can *participate* in developing the change. People identify with what they help create, and group participation through opinions, suggestions, and so on can help people share in the plan's future success. This also helps recognize their needs and rights as employees.

Offering help and being available to give it are important for the supervisor too. People often need help in learning new ways, establishing new routines, and developing new skills. The ready availability of the supervisor during this period of time is desirable. The total time a supervisor invests may not be that much greater, but offering easy access of the employee to the supervisor is very important.

Finally, the supervisor might consider offering *tradeoffs* to reduce resistance to the change. If the change is an unpopular one, there might be some things that can be done to "sweeten it." For example, in one large plant, the installation of new equipment upset individual workers because they had to learn new procedures. Management announced that the employees would be allowed to do different jobs up and down the assembly line instead of staying in one spot as they had in the past. This appealed to many of the workers who were otherwise unhappy with the change, since they felt they were gaining something as well as losing something. Block 14–1 describes an actual case problem in which an employee demonstrates continued resistance to change.

CONFLICT

Conflict can result from changes in organizations as well as from a number of other sources. Regardless of the source, however, conflict is another inevitable fact of supervisory life. Contrary to management thinking in days gone by, conflict in work organizations *cannot* be avoided completely. In fact, to some extent, it is good, because it can lead to change. It may be that conflict is exactly what is needed either to add strength to the driving force or to reduce some of the pressure in the resisting forces.

A recent study shows that managers at all levels have a lively and growing interest in conflict resolution. The study found that managers spend an average 20 percent of their time dealing with conflict of one sort or another and that managing conflict has become a much more significant factor in successful management over the last ten years. In fact, conflict management was rated as of equal or higher importance than planning, communication, motivation, and decision making by managers in this survey.[4]

Conflicts can arise from many different situations. Let's consider some of the most common conditions for fostering conflict:

1. Conflict will be greater when the jurisdiction or "territory" of each party is ambiguous. When the actual boundaries between two work groups are unclear (who CAN or SHOULD do what), the potential for conflict increases.
2. Conflict is likely to occur when there is competition for scarce resources. If supervisors have to compete for skilled workers within the organization, we can almost surely conclude that conflict will arise.
3. The potential for conflict is greatest when barriers in communication exist. For example, if one party is physically separated from the other party—such as the day shift from the night shift—the opportunity for conflict is increased.
4. The opportunity for conflict is greater when one party is dependent upon the other party. For example, a supervisor who is dependent on a subordinate to make a marketing decision may monitor the subordinate's progress very closely, and close supervision can contribute to the potential for conflict.
5. Unresolved conflicts increase the likelihood of more conflicts. The suppressing of old conflicts by the use of power or compromise creates conditions which may lead to conflict later on.[5]

Conflict and Defense Mechanisms

Conflict can lead to frustration, and frustration to a number of different individual reactions called *defense mechanisms*. Defense mechanisms are psychological crutches *all* of us use to one extent or another. They are reactions to frustrating or unhappy situations.

These mechanisms are used to maintain our psychological balance, or self-image. When we are faced with some piece of evidence that is damaging to our self-image, we will probably use one or more of these defense mechanisms to help save face. Figure 14–3 gives examples of some of the most common defense mechanisms, reactions a supervisor

FIGURE 14–3   Common Defense Mechanisms

Overcompensation: Devoting oneself to something *completely* to overcome an imagined deficiency; for example, working hard in one area to overcome a handicap in another.

Fantasy: Daydreaming or imagining "getting back" at someone. Thinking of things you "should have said" to someone.

Negativism: Being unwilling to admit that a project one opposed is actually yielding good results; expressing only negative feelings about something.

Projection: Protecting oneself from one's undesirable traits or wants by seeing them in others; for example, the employee who loafs but is always catching everyone else loafing.

Rationalization: Finding excuses or "reasons" for everything that went wrong. These are usually socially acceptable explanations that clear the person doing the rationalization.

Repression: Excluding from your memory or suppressing things that are disturbing— "selective forgetting."

Resignation: Withholding any sense of personal involvement; simply not wanting to get involved because "what's the use?"

Withdrawal: Leaving a situation which you have found unpleasant; absenteeism from an unpleasant job.

will often encounter in dealing with subordinates, colleagues, and superiors. The use of defense mechanisms is perfectly normal, we all do it. In fact, you can look at the list of defense mechanisms and pick out the ones that *you* use most commonly. However, when defensive behavior becomes too common or when an employee ceases to be able to distinguish between reality and defensiveness, it can cause difficulties.

The most important thing to realize about psychological defenses is that people in this frame of mind are very difficult to deal with. Reasoning becomes impossible because the defensive person's view of reality is for the moment distorted. When a supervisor recognizes defensive behavior in a relationship, it is probably wise to adjourn the meeting and allow both parties time to reflect on the situation before resuming the discussion. So long as one or both parties continues to show a high degree of defensive behavior, there is a very low probability that much of anything will be accomplished.

Categories of Conflict Resolution

Basically, methods of resolving conflict fall into one of three categories.

1. Win-lose. Under this set of circumstances, two parties are "competing" and the conflict will be resolved by one party *winning* and the other party *losing,* as in an athletic contest. When a supervisor challenges a subordinate, "Do what I say because 'I am the boss' and if you don't I'll fire you," he or she is setting up a win-lose situation. If the subordinate chooses *not* to do what the supervisor says, he or she will lose and the supervisor will win. For some people, winning or losing is of primary importance. Winning may give such a person a sense of achievement. He or she feels that there *must be* a winner and there *must be* a loser in any conflict situation and he or she *must be* the winner regardless of the cost.

2. *Lose-lose methods.* This category of methods is called lose-lose because neither side really achieves its goals. Compromise is a kind of lose-lose situation if both parties have to give up their high-priority needs to reach the compromise. With both win-lose and lose-lose approaches to solving conflicts, energies are directed toward defeating the other party rather than toward solving the problem. Each party sees the problem only from its own point of view rather than trying to see it from the point of view of *mutual needs.* Conflicts tend to be personalized and focus on personalities rather than on issues.

3. *Win-win methods.* Win-win methods focus on ends or *goals* rather than on means. The most common strategy for a win-win method is *consensus,* or general agreement by all parties concerned. Consensus is difficult to reach; however, there are some guidelines that can be followed:

  a. Avoid *arguing* for your own individual judgment—approach the task as objectively and logically as you can.
  b. Avoid changing your mind only to reach agreement and avoid conflict; support only those solutions with which you can concur to some degree.
  c. Avoid conflict-reducing techniques such as majority vote, averaging, or trading to reach a decision.

In consensus, differences of opinion should be viewed as *helpful* and as *bringing new information* to bear on the problem rather than as a hindrance.

Classifying Conflict Styles

People usually prefer one conflict resolution strategy over the others. The person who enjoys the win-lose style and who wants to win at all costs might be dubbed the "tough battler." The individual who is overly concerned about the maintenance of relationships and doesn't worry very much about achieving his or her own goals can be thought of as the "friendly helper." This person wants to avoid trouble at all costs and feels that differences shouldn't be confronted if anyone is going to be hurt in the process. The third individual is the "problem solver." This individual tries to use consensus as a problem-solving technique to facilitate some sort of progress—perhaps social, perhaps organizational.

Figure 14–4 shows what happens in a conflict between people with these different styles. The win-lose battler does gain the advantage more often than not, yet bears the cost associated with the win-lose strategy: When there is a winner, there is also a loser. And where there is a loser, there's somebody who is unhappy, antagonistic, and perhaps defensive about the outcome. The best situation occurs when two problem solvers meet. They come to quick agreement and settle the conflict more easily than in any of the other situations depicted in Figure 14–4.

Some Conflict Is Good

We suggested earlier that conflict cannot be avoided. In fact, a certain amount of conflict is beneficial in that it can lead to change. An organization without any conflict is suspect. Human nature is such that people are not completely happy and satisfied all the time. If there is no apparent conflict, a supervisor would do well to check whether the atmosphere that has been created is chilling people's willingness to register protests and talk about what things might be wrong. To be useful, however, conflict must be managed—it must be kept in bounds and not allowed to reach the destructive win-lose state.

Conflict provides the challenging and questioning that is necessary to avoid stagnant thinking, weak decisions, and a general apathy. Resolving conflicts, however, can be frustrating, and supervisors must realize that they must sometimes play the role of *mediator* rather than decision maker in helping the parties work through their problems. In Block 14–2, for example, the supervisor should not make the decision herself but should help the parties work the conflict out.

In order to resolve a conflict successfully, all parties must come to realize that they have a vested interest in the outcome—that they share

FIGURE 14–4   Interaction of Different Conflict Resolution Styles

		Person A		
		Tough battler	Friendly helper	Problem solver
Person B	Tough battler	Stalemate 80% of the time	Battler wins 90% of the time	Battler wins over 50%
	Friendly helper	Battler wins 90% of the time	Stalemate 80% of time	Problem solver wins
	Problem solver	Battler wins over 50%	Problem solver wins	Quick agreement

Source: Adapted from A. C. Filley, *Interpersonal Conflict Resolution* (Glenview, Ill.: Scott, Foresman, 1975), p. 55.

At certain times during the year, I must be away from my office at various meeting and work assignments. I have a very good secretary and an excellent assistant supervisor. In my absence, they share the responsibility for ensuring that things run smoothly at the office.

Upon my return to the office, however, the secretary and assistant supervisor are generally upset with each other, and "at each other's throats" over various problems. Basically, the conflict seems to arise from uncertainty as to who is responsible for this or that task. I need to resolve this so it won't happen again, but I don't want either party to feel put down or to think that past assignments have not been up to par. I certainly wouldn't want to lose either one of them.

the common goal of solving the problem rather than "winning." The *problem-solving approach* avoids trying to determine who is "right" or "wrong," who "wins" and who "loses." Problem-solving approaches aren't appropriate for all conflict situations, especially those which arise as a result of different value systems, but for conflicts based on differences in *fact* or differences in *communication,* this technique can be quite useful.

WORKING WITH OTHER SUPERVISORS

Supervisors often find that some situation either in the organization itself or outside brings them into conflict with other supervisors. Since the bone of contention is probably some issue that must be resolved in the organization's best interest, the problem-solving approach is the best. By contrast, win-lose thinking might well sacrifice the larger goal to satisfy the ego of one or the other party.

As a member of the supervisory group in your organization, your performance and conduct affects the interests of fellow supervisors as well as other people in the organization. You *do* have certain obligations to other supervisors at your level. If you don't fulfill your obligations to them, they will disregard their obligations to you.

The *kind of work* a department turns out will affect the organization as a whole, and thus the other departments as well. *Promptness* is another telling factor that has repercussions on the efficiency, planning, and scheduling of other supervisors throughout the organization. Remember, too, that almost every supervisor seems to feel overwhelmed at times by the various tasks facing him or her. If you often feel that way, reflect for a moment on some of the difficulties other supervisors face—those known to you personally, those you have read about in this and other books, those you might imagine. A supervisor can develop nearsightedness with respect to difficulties under his or her jurisdiction.

A supervisor should occasionally ask, Am I *creating* problems with other supervisors? The things you do in your department can create problems for other supervisors. For example, if you permit bad management-employee relationships to build up in your department, this can lead to conflict in other departments. If you permit lax discipline in your department, employees in neighboring departments will want to follow suit, and their supervisors will have added difficulties. If you show favoritism, employees not under your supervision may clamor for special treatment. If you let substandard workmanship get by, it may add to the problems of the next department. If your workers are careless about safety, hazards may be created for other employees outside your department. If you permit grievances to pile up, you may be adding fuel to grievances in neighboring departments.

Supervisory Cooperation

Helping other supervisors can help you. Things that the supervisor can do to help fellow supervisors will work to his or her advantage in the long run. The most effective way to develop this kind of teamwork with other supervisors is to be a good "team player." Make constructive suggestions in a way that will be welcome, keep your promises to other supervisors, transfer good workers to their departments if you can't promote them in your own department. Ask for the other supervisors' advice and suggestions, and share your knowledge and experience with them.

There will often be some other supervisor who you feel is not cooperating or is openly "bucking" you. The best way to deal with such individuals is often to ignore them. Don't complain to others about the noncooperative supervisor; if you talk to anyone, talk tactfully to the individual who is giving you trouble. Avoid actions which may give the noncooperative person any reason for continuing his or her attitudes and behaviors. Block 14–3 presents a case in which a noncooperative person's behavior came back to haunt her later.

How Do I "Cooperate"?

Competition among supervisors for promotions is more severe than at lower levels in the work force. In fact, in some cases it is just this competition that attracts some people to supervision and seems to drive them to achieve one promotion after the other. However, there can be

BLOCK 14–3 The Problems Come Home to Roost

"Janet, we'll soon be expanding this department and one of the positions that needs to be filled is supervisor in the planning section. Now I realize that this is a promotion for you, and I'm confident you can do it. However, in the course of several conversations with some of the people you will be working with, it came to light that many of them are annoyed with what they think is "red tape" that you use to delay them. Others were quite hostile. I won't tell you who made these comments, but I'll give you a list of names of people whose good will you should cultivate. I suggest you go to each of them and put your cards on the table, explain to them that in the past things may not have been satisfactory, but that you're willing to work to see that these problems don't occur again."

After this conversation with her boss, Janet Wilson was understandably hurt, but she went to every person on the list and talked to them about the problems they had had in the past. By mending some fences, she was able to overcome many of the past difficulties. Several people gave her a bad time, but most were impressed by her sincerity. Some months after the discussion with Janet, another supervisor passed the information on to the boss that she had saved him from missing a critical delivery schedule. The boss knew he had made a good decision in promoting her.

friendly rivalry among supervisors. There is a middle ground between the extremes of pure competitiveness and selfless cooperation, and that is to balance ambition against possible danger to relationships with other supervisors.

Before taking a step designed to promote your own interest, ask yourself the following questions: Who is likely to be hurt if I take this course of action? How great will the damage be? Will the advantage coming from it be worth the loss involved?

Cooperation among supervisors is somewhat more complex than initially meets the eye. Real cooperation doesn't occur if it's obvious that one of the parties is motivated solely by a "what's in it for me" attitude. But a supervisor also owes it to himself or herself to avoid sacrificing personal goals for cooperation. There will be times when the cooperation you offer will probably never be returned, but then you will sometimes get aid and comfort from another supervisor which you will be unable to return.

Don't wait until you are asked to help if it is obvious that you are in a position to help another supervisor. If you offer your assistance freely, you will create more good will than if you wait to be asked. It is also a good idea not to make your assistance too blatantly obvious to the casual observer. Your concern should be the relationship between you and the person you're helping, not a matter of organization-wide gossip. Strangely enough there are those people who find it easy to cooperate but difficult to ask for cooperation.

In a well-functioning supervisory team, when the time comes (as it will) that a task is bigger than a supervisor's ability to get it done on time, he or she should not hesitate to ask for help.[6] Block 14–4 illustrates a case where supervisory cooperation was not present and ended up costing the supervisor involved his job.

How Does Coordination Work Best?

The supervisor is one of the most important links in the organization for achieving coordination. Personal contact is generally the most effective means for achieving coordination of activities with other supervisors. Group meetings can be very effective if their purpose is not to tell the group members something, but to permit the members to put their efforts together into a coordinated whole.

BLOCK 14–4   I'm Looking out for Number One

Jim Hettels would never admit a mistake. No matter what went wrong, he would go to great lengths to prove that some other supervisor was to blame rather than himself. Even in cases where defective workmanship was plainly traceable to his department, he would argue the point endlessly to the indignation of other supervisors.

It was only natural that there should be a great deal of antagonism between Jim and the others. It finally got to the point that they would deliberately gang up on him whenever they could. It was a continuous contest with Jim on one side and the rest of the supervisors on the other side. Recently, though, the situation came to a head when Hettels went to the district manager and complained that all the other supervisors in the organization were "bucking" him.

The district manager had been observing things himself and he realized that Jim Hettels had built up a reputation for poor cooperation and teamwork with the other supervisors in the district. He concluded that if they were all out of step but Jim, something would have to be done about Jim. It had gotten past the point where a cure was possible and the district manager decided that for the good of teamwork in the organization, Jim would have to be replaced.

Some organizations use "expediters" to coordinate products or projects. Expediters are people in charge of coordinating things. However, such a device on any but a temporary basis *may* be evidence of a poor organization structure. Putting an expediter on an occasional special project may be fine. But if an expediter is required to get coordination and cooperation from supervisors over a large number of situations, the level of cooperation among the supervisors isn't what it should be.

SUMMARY AND CONCLUSIONS

Change is inevitable. For this reason supervisors must be concerned with managing the human reaction to change. Change situations usually have both driving and resisting forces. It is often useful to try to identify these forces before implementing a plan for change. Planning is the key to successful change because there are so many interrelated factors that must be carefully considered before making a change.

In some cases, reaction to change may be quite severe, and a great deal of time may be needed to overcome the "shock." In general, however, resistance to change should be viewed as helpful and expected. People can usually be won over in time, and by maintaining an atmosphere open to communication and participation, when appropriate. Another useful technique is to include in the change package some trade-off item to satisfy employee wants.

Conflict is also inevitable in work organizations. When conflict helps clarify issues it can be useful, but it must be managed or controlled. Win-win conflict strategies are best where possible because unresolved old conflicts lead to conflict again later.

Defense mechanisms are self-image protections we all use. The supervisor should be able to recognize the most common of these and realize that someone who is on the defensive cannot be pushed to think and behave logically.

Cooperation and development of a teamwork approach among supervisors is essential to organizational well-being. The supervisor who examines his or her own contribution to teamwork from time to time is more likely to achieve smooth working relations with other supervisors.

QUESTIONS

1. What are the driving and resisting forces in improving air quality in major metropolitan areas?
2. Why is change "built into" a work organization's work force?

3. If work changes are truly interrelated, would a change in an X-ray department's scheduling process affect the rest of the hospital?
4. Think of a major change in your life. Now compare the four-step human reaction process to the way you reacted. Do the parts fit?
5. List three of your closest friends or co-workers. Which defense mechanism does each use the most often?
6. Why is compromise often a lose-lose situation?
7. If you don't get along well with some other supervisor but the business relationship has been cordial, what should you do?

WHAT DO I DO TO GET COOPERATION?

I work for a large Chevrolet dealership. The Parts Supervisor plays a very important part in the operation of our shop. Without his cooperation and assistance, we in the repair shop cannot get our work out in an orderly manner. Our Parts Supervisor has several years' experience and on good days he can be very helpful and cooperative. However, much of the time he is rude and grouchy, not only to the mechanics, but also to the other supervisors like myself. He takes his own time about getting the required parts when we ask for something. That keeps things from getting finished at the earliest possible time. Several of the other supervisors take every opportunity they can to get even with him. This is a major problem. Should I go to management with this problem and let them handle it, or should we try to work it out among ourselves?

---

1. What would you suggest before going to management?
2. If the supervisor has to go to the boss, how would you suggest he explain the problem?

NOTES

[1] A. L. Seelye, "Changing Social Values in Business," *The Personnel Administrator,* September 1975, p. 24.

[2] L. E. Tagliaferri, "Understanding and Motivating the Changing Work Force," *Training and Development Journal,* June 1975.

[3] R. G. Hirschowitz, "The Human Aspects of Managing Transition," *Personnel,* May–June 1974, pp. 12–15.

[4] Editorial Staff, *Personnel Journal,* "The Sources in Resolutions of Conflict in Management," May 1977, p. 225.

[5] This list is based on Allen C. Filley, *Interpersonal Conflict Resolution* (Glenview, Ill.: Scott Foresman, 1975), pp. 9–11.

[6] E. T. Reeves, "Dealing With Supervisors on Your Level," *Supervisory Management,* June 1973.

Supervising Your Time and Development

SUPERVISORY PROBLEMS

How can I get the most out of the hours of the day so that I can get my work done?

How can I identify areas in which I need to develop as a supervisor?

LEARNING OBJECTIVES

When you have finished this chapter you should be able to

1. Explain why supervisors run into time problems
2. Answer the question, How can I do a time analysis of my own time use?
3. Discuss the reasons for the "suggested best answers" on the supervisory time test
4. List four time-saving hints for supervisors
5. Make suggestions for saving time on paperwork, telephone calls, and meetings
6. Construct a chart showing how you would go about planning your own development as a supervisor

THIS IS GETTING TO BE TOO MUCH

Sheila Arnold was a good supervisor and she knew it. Since she took the supervisory job six months ago her department had shown more improvement in results than any other department. Currently it ranked among the leaders in most of the important production categories. But Sheila knew also that there was a cost associated with her effectiveness.

As she sat at her desk at 6:30 on a Friday afternoon trying to wrap up the unfinished business of the week, her mind wandered back over the last six months. She hadn't kept track, of course, but Sheila was certain she was putting in at least 55 hours a week, usually nine and a half hours a day during the week and a full day either Saturday or Sunday. It had been necessary at first because of the many adjustments and changes that had to be made. But now that things were running much more smoothly, Sheila wanted to be able to cut down on the actual number of hours on the job.

Most of the other top-producing supervisors were able to get their work done in a 40-hour week. Did they know something she didn't know? Maybe there were some tricks to utilizing the time she had more effectively. *But there never seemed to be enough hours in the day!* Just when she'd get started on a project, the phone would ring or someone would come into the office with a problem and she'd be thrown behind schedule. Then she would have to stay over late to get it done or come in the next morning. Weekends would almost always be devoted to planning.

Surely there must be another way! Sheila decided to talk with a couple of the other successful supervisors Monday morning and try to find out how they managed to get their work done in a 40-hour week.

Time waits for no one, and those people who don't realize or won't admit that they waste time should analyze for a moment just how they spend their time. One key to supervisory effectiveness lies in the elimination—or at least the reduction to a minimum—of all "nonessential" activities. The way employees on most jobs use their time can be rather accurately measured by periodical spot checking. The way managers and supervisors, in particular, allocate their time is somewhat more difficult to measure.

Each supervisor has his or her routine and often it is an effective one. Yet most supervisors can profit from checking their routine against some sort of standard. Such an analysis can often highlight those areas where supervisors need improvement. Most supervisors *know* what *needs* to be done, the problem is determining how long a time should be spent doing it.

When time pressure is especially strong, many of a supervisor's lower-priority items simply don't get done. Unfortunately, some important activities—for example, a supervisor's personal development—fall into this category. It is easy to rationalize that you don't have time to read a particular article which might help make you a better supervisor. It is also easy to put off going to a supervisory development conference on Wednesday when you have an important deadline to meet by Friday. Supervisory development is a topic that will be considered later in the chapter, but first we will try to determine how the supervisor can free up some time for these and other activities that are often neglected.

THE NATURE OF SUPERVISORY TIME PROBLEMS

A supervisor's busy schedule doesn't automatically allow enough time to do all the things that are (1) worth doing, (2) interesting, or (3) demanded. His or her conscience as well as pressure from above may dictate many tasks that aren't really necessary for effective supervision. One study rank-ordered how supervisors spend most of their time. In descending order, time is spent on activities which

1. interest them
2. they do well

3. are pleasurable
4. are forced upon them
5. are boring or unpleasant [1]

Another study found that a large portion of supervisory time is consumed by the following activities: (1) telephone calls, (2) meetings, (3) reports, (4) visitors, (5) procrastination, (6) special requests, and (7) delays and reading.[2] These items can take so much of a supervisor's time that it is very difficult to do the planning, controlling, and training that are demanded for effective supervision.

A key to increasing supervisory efficiency in the use of time is the elimination of nonessential but time-consuming activities. This can be accomplished through a *time analysis* study. Other keys are cultivating a time consciousness, developing the ability to "block" periods of time, and delegating more responsibility.

Using Your Time Well: Time Analysis

Formal time analysis is accomplished by recording your activities and the corresponding time expenditures in a daily log. Once this has been done, principles of work simplification (covered in Chapter 12) can be applied to reduce and eliminate some activities. It may be difficult to admit that you haven't been using your time very well, but accepting the fact is necessary before any change can be made.

Imagine, for example, one supervisor's surprise when he found from a daily log that he spent fully 25 percent of his day on the telephone. Further analysis showed that one-third of that time involved was *waiting* for the person on the other end. No wonder it seemed to him that he could never get anything done! For production workers, time use can be measured via formal time and motion studies. The efficiency of clerical workers can be measured by work sampling, a technique that can also be used by professional employees such as engineers and teachers. In work sampling, an electronic device can be used which beeps at random times. The person then stops what he or she is doing and records the activity. Of course, for the individual engaged in a number of short activities, a large number of observations may be required to obtain accuracy.

Unfortunately, neither formal work sampling nor time study provides a completely workable methodology for assessing the effectiveness of supervisors. A supervisor typically engages in many different tasks in the course of a day; for example, consider a supervisory meeting in which the participants are carrying beepers to allow them to measure their work. As the beepers sound off randomly for each individual at the meeting, discussion stops momentarily so that the person can record his or her activity at that point. Such interruptions may be accepted for the sake of the study, but they are nonetheless both annoying and distracting. A second problem is that the supervisor often cannot specify precisely what he or she is accomplishing at that moment.

An alternative to the work sampling and time study approaches consists of simply writing down once each hour, brief notes to yourself about what you have done during the last hour. Figure 15–1 shows some notes a supervisor made that can be used later to analyze that person's utilization of time. At the bottom of the figure is a summarization of time usage for the week.

Such summaries are often quite revealing. They can point up which areas need more or less time and indicate which might be rearranged so that they are done at the best possible times of the day.

Only by reviewing data on current time usage can a supervisor de-

FIGURE 15–1   Supervisory Time Analysis Notes

Monday

8– 9	Met with Jones about turnover problems
9–10	Planned next week's schedule
10–11	Phone call, mail, phone call
11–12	Visited shop floor
1– 2	Visited shop floor
2– 3	Talked to Mary Koperski about personal problems
3– 4	Read production report
4– 5	Visited shop floor

Tuesday

8– 9	Three telephone calls
9–10	Went to see Monroe in Accounting
10–11	Went to sales, talked to Mark Simmons about 120 model
11–12	Two phone calls, read mail, phone call
1– 2	
2– 3	Production meeting
3– 4	Phone call, visited shop floor
4– 5	Visited shop floor

Wednesday _____

Thursday _____   (continue to record)

Friday _____

Summary: For week
Mail and phone calls: 25 percent
On the shop floor: 30 percent
Meetings: 20 percent
Talking to other people: 25 percent

velop plans to become more efficient. Without data, good intentions generally result in very little happening. With data, supervisors can have a better idea of what changes should be made to increase their personal productivity. Block 15–1 is an example of one instance in which time analysis revealed some disconcerting facts.

Perhaps the most important result of the study reported in Block 15–1 was the profile made for each individual of his or her time allocation. Had the participants been asked by questionnaire to estimate their time use, the results undoubtedly would have looked nothing like the true profile shown by the work sampling technique. As the case in Block 15–1

BLOCK 15–1   We Talk A Lot. . . !

A time use study was undertaken in a chemical research organization, involving 142 individuals representing nonsupervisory employees, three levels of supervision, and several comparable levels of technical personnel. Each participant recorded his or her activities on a data collection form. Observation times were randomly selected and the observation continued for ten working days. Almost 6,000 observations were collected from all 142 participants.

When this information was analyzed, some interesting facts came to light. For example, 72 percent of the rank and file's time was spent on technical work, whereas this share declined to 43 percent for third-level management. This, of course, reflects the attention that supervisors and managers must devote to interpersonal matters as opposed to production per se.

A lot of time was spent communicating progress or results either formally or informally. Over half of the time spent communicating involved oral messages, and these amounted to an extraordinary 62 percent of the day for third-level managers. The breakdown of time spent on oral communications was as follows: telephone 4 percent; meetings 11 percent; informal contacts, gatherings, or bull sessions 20 percent. A great deal of this communication had little to do with work direction or objectives.

Obviously for nearly 20 percent of this communication the question should be asked, Was it necessary? An additional 11 percent of the work day (almost a full hour) was spent on communication that individuals considered to be of marginal necessity.

Source: Adapted, by permission of the publisher, from *Personnel*, July–August 1976, © by AMACOM, a division of American Management Associations, pages 46–47. All rights reserved.

indicates, analyzing time can result in many advantages, not the least of which is increasing time consciousness.

Using Your Time Well: Time Consciousness

Analyzing how you use your time can be quite helpful. However, before a supervisor can put this analysis to use, he or she will have to be motivated by an understanding of the *value of time*. Without a conscious realization of this dimension of the supervisory job, effective time use is very difficult.

Developing time consciousness can best be done by examining the hourly value of your time. In fact, any investment in supervisory time should be evaluated on this basis. Something that takes five hours of your time and pays back very little should be given lower priority than another task that requires three hours to complete but pays back more. With this perspective—basically setting one's priorities straight— the supervisor can allocate his or her time to those projects promising the greatest return, both personally and to the organization.

After doing a time analysis, supervisors typically are more aware of how they are spending their time even if they no longer bother to record it. The little internal clock that each of us carries around seems to be more important, and the supervisor is more conscious of how minutes of the day are spent. This time consciousness is very valuable for getting the most out of the time available at work.

Using Your Time Well: Blocking Time

The third key to getting more work done in the time you have available is to block out large periods of uninterrupted time to get those big projects done. If you estimate that it will take three hours to write a report, pick three hours that are your *best time of the day*. There are "morning people," who work best early and there are "evening people," who work best late in the day. Everyone is a little bit different in this regard so pick the time when *you* work the best. Then block out the three hours required so that you will be uninterrupted during that time period.

Interruptions on a large project involve more than just the time of the interruption. After having been interrupted, it may be difficult to pick up your train of thought again. Or you may have to reread certain things in order to reconstruct what had gone before. This is "wasted" time. The key to getting large projects such as report writing or scheduling done is the ability to block time.

Using Your Time Well: Delegation

We discussed delegation earlier as one of the ways supervisors can get more work done. The key to good delegation is making sure that instructions are given carefully and completely the first time. If you must explain again or correct mistakes, the savings from delegation may be lost. Delegation was covered in detail in Chapter 2 and giving instructions in Chapter 5.

Supervisors should plan ahead for times when they will be absent, such as vacations and out-of-town conferences. Their plans should include detailed instructions for those who will be acting supervisor during their absence. The authors have known supervisors who have not gone on vacation because they felt they had no one they could trust to carry on in their absence. Teaching at least one other person by delegating jobs to that individual would have resolved that problem. Planning ahead and delegating can save large amounts of time. If you feel you have no one to whom you can safely delegate, you should develop someone. Delegation is the key to getting more work out of the hours available.

After something has been delegated, the supervisor should be leery of getting wrapped up in things that other people *can do* or *are* doing. A supervisor should never have others do something which he or she can do more quickly alone. While the effective supervisor should delegate whenever possible, there are some jobs which *take more time to delegate than to do yourself.* The decision of whether or not to delegate should be based on how much of your time is going to be involved in each alternative.

SUPERVISORY "TIME TEST"

The time use test shown in Figure 15–2 can help you think through some of the most important issues in time management. If you have never supervised, answer the test in terms of the last job you held. Full-time students can answer in terms of how they manage their study time. In scoring the test, you should recognize that there will be deviations between the actual use of time and what we will term the "suggested best" use of time. This happens because not all principles of time management are universally applicable in all situations. Some jobs or special supervisory situations may require a response different from the suggested best answer because of differing needs. For example, item number 1 on the time test asks, "Do you keep a written log of how you spend the major portions of your working day?" An accountant or auditor may keep a very detailed log every day in order to accurately bill his or her clients and would therefore answer somewhat differently from the average first-line supervisor. Now answer the questions in Figure 15–2 before reading on.

FIGURE 15–2   Time Use Test

Listed below is a series of statements about various ways of supervising your time. Answer these items in terms of your characteristic habit patterns. Be honest. See how you rate in "the supervision of time" compared to others.

	Almost Never	Some- times	Often	Almost Always
1. I keep a written log of how I spend the major portions of my working day.				
2. I schedule my least interesting tasks at a time when my energy is at its peak.				
3. I review my job and delegate activities that someone else could do just as well.				
4. I have time to do what I want to do and what I should do in performing my job.				
5. I analyze my job to determine how I can combine or eliminate activities.				
6. Actions that lead to short-run objectives take preference over those that might be more important over the long pull.				
7. My boss assigns more work than he thinks I can handle.				
8. I attack short-time tasks (answering phone calls, reading correspondence, and so on) before projects taking a long time.				
9. I review the sequence of my job activities and make necessary improvements.				
10. I arrange task priorities based on the importance of task goals.				

PERSONAL SCORE _____

Scoring the Supervision of Time:
Self-Analysis

After answering the questions in Figure 15–2, score your answers with the suggested best answers in Figure 15–3. If your total score is above 25, you are using your available time very well. If your score is between 25 and 15, you are about average and should be able to pick up some helpful hints from the discussion that follows. If your score is below 15, your time is *not* being used as well as it could be and some corrective actions can be taken immediately to improve it.

Let's look at the logic behind the best answers in Figure 15–3.

Item 1: The suggested best answer to keeping a written log on activities is "sometimes." As we noted earlier, supervisors should recognize that this activity can be very useful when it comes to eliminating wasted effort. But they should also realize that it is not usually necessary to record *every single day of the work year.*

Sampling your own work habits, perhaps for one week three times a year, should be plenty. The time consciousness that you develop through formally analyzing your work habits in this way encourages an informal review of a continuing nature. It is possible to spend so much time accounting for how each minute is spent that you lose sight of the original purpose of the time analysis, which is to *become a more efficient supervisor.*

Item 2: The suggested best answer to scheduling the least interesting tasks when energy is highest is "almost always." As we saw earlier, supervisors tend to put off until last those activities which are least interesting. If you tackle the least interesting items first, you will usually find that you have enough energy left at the end of the day for the more

FIGURE 15–3   Scoring the Time Use Test

Item	Almost Never	Sometimes	Often	Almost Always
1	2	3	2	1
2	0	1	2	3
3	0	1	2	3
4	0	1	2	3
5	2	3	2	1
6	1	2	3	2
7	3	2	1	0
8	3	2	1	0
9	1	2	3	2
10	0	1	2	3

pleasurable tasks. All in all, this type of scheduling allows you to get more work done.

Item 3: The suggested best answer for delegating an activity is "almost always." The logic here is found in the words "someone else could do it just as well." The effective supervisor should not be concerned with doing the job *perfectly.* Rather the concern should be with doing the job "well enough." This involves a tradeoff between quality and cost.

An example of this is the so-called "Rolls Royce syndrome." Most people who *could* afford Rolls Royce automobiles don't drive them because they are "too good." The cost of obtaining such quality is too great for simple transportation needs. In the same vein, the supervisor who insists on doing all the work personally, because he or she is the only one who can do it to perfection, is wasting time and needlessly increasing the cost to the organization.

This does *not* suggest shoddy work. After all we are saying the job must be done well enough, but turning out Rolls Royces when a Chevrolet will do may be a waste of your time. If an employee can do the work at an acceptable level then he or she should be doing the work, not the supervisor.

Item 4: "Almost always" is the suggested best answer to having sufficient time to do what is needed. If the supervisor doesn't have time to do what he or she wants to do or what should be done, then some time analysis is certainly necessary. As we have seen, time analysis begins with recording your time, and results in increasing your level of consciousness as to how your time is being used. If the supervisor is complying with the principles in items 2 and 3, time should be available as needed.

Item 5: The suggested best answer is "sometimes" to job analysis and the combining of activities. As in item 1, recognizing the importance of time consciousness will help dictate that this activity be performed occasionally. Combining activities can help reduce time waste yet it is easy to slip into the habit of doing things a certain way and not think about the possibility of combining things. The old ways almost become habits, so occasional job analysis can be an effective way to change habits that are no longer appropriate.

Item 6: The suggested best answer regarding the preference of short-run objectives over long-term goals is "often." If planning has been done properly, the long-run goals will automatically take care of themselves *through a series of short-run goals.* The sum of the short-run goals and objectives should equal long-run goals and objectives.

Many people may feel that the long haul is the primary objective, and that the more immediate objectives should be held in abeyance to the long run. This is simply not true. Achieving the short-run objectives will carry you on toward the long-run goal(s) if you have planned properly. Nevertheless, from time to time one should check the direction being taken to make sure things are still on track. Long-run goals must be served but if the short run is not attended to, the long run will never happen.

Item 7: The suggested best answer to the assignment of an excessive work load by the boss is "almost never." Such behavior on the part of a superior would probably be taken as a personality quirk of some sort. Assuming that the superior is a "normal" individual yet often assigns impossible deadlines, we might interpret this to mean that the boss believes the supervisor is wasting time by doing unnecessary tasks. Perhaps the boss is trying to tell the supervisor that time is being wasted by assigning more work than the supervisor thinks can be done.

Item 8: "Almost never" is the suggested best answer to attacking tasks of short duration before lengthier assignments. From the research we cited earlier, the most common time problems are essentially *short, routine jobs.* Thus, it is quite possible for the supervisor to spend the entire day handling short-time details while trying to lay out blocks of time to do the big jobs. The catch is that the little jobs are *recurring:* The phone will always ring, the mail will always come in. These things simply do not go away.

Blocks of time are essential for completing large projects such as planning or writing reports. Understanding this is one of the keys to success in getting things done. The principle behind successfully handling the problem of competing demands on a supervisor's time is that little jobs tend to evaporate if ignored. Unread advertisements and unrewarded interruptions by subordinates tend to vanish without a trace. However, when confronted they take time and have the effect of encouraging subordinates to engage in future interruptions. There are obviously limits as to how far a supervisor can go in ignoring short-time interruptions, but the limit is much farther out than most supervisors realize.

The so-called *Ziegarnik effect,* discovered by a psychologist of the same name, applies to the short-time versus longer-time task issue. It suggests that once a job is *started* the human tendency is to want to *finish* it. Most people dislike unfinished work. Thus the supervisor is more likely to return to an unfinished job after an unavoidable interruption than to begin a completely new task. You can encourage more productivity from yourself by starting a job first thing in the morning and the Ziegarnik effect will help force you to finish it before the end of the day.

Item 9:   For reviewing the sequencing of job activities, the proposed best answer is "often." The proper sequencing of job activities is all-important for reaching goals. Without a frequent review of the order in which you are doing things, projects may be affected. The common use of PERT in industry today reflects this need. PERT, of course, is nothing more than a method for requiring the project supervisor to properly sequence the project activities. This kind of analysis can be useful in many instances. Since it can be done quickly and with relative ease, supervisors should do it daily.

Item 10:   The suggested best answer to arranging task priorities based on task goals is "almost always." A supervisor might be inclined to pursue those tasks which are of only middling importance unless he or she has a clear list of priorities. Since priorities can change with changes in the environment, a supervisor's priority list needs careful and constant review.

Summary of Time-Saving Hints

There are several time-saving hints of which you should be aware. Some of these were indicated in the answers to the time test, others were not. The summary presented here will help you pick and choose those that best fit your situation.

1. The supervisor should use all short cuts available, keeping in mind that *good enough* or "satisficing" is all that is needed in terms of quality performance on most aspects of most jobs.
2. Supervisors should be willing to tackle the tough jobs first. It is human nature to tackle the easy jobs first and put off the tough ones. If you tackle the tough ones first, you will be amazed at how much time is left to handle the jobs you find more pleasurable.
3. The supervisor can rely on the fact that unfinished business will be a stimulus to motivate him or her to complete the task. By contrast, something you have considered but not yet tackled holds no such compulsion. You can use the Ziegarnik effect to your advantage by starting a project early in the day so that you will feel the need to come back and complete it.
4. Supervisors must learn occasionally to relax, to "recharge their batteries." This means occasionally being willing to "goof off" in an effort to be more effective. This involves knowing your capacities, best work times, and to some extent, your emotional makeup. We all reach fatigue points at which we are too tired to get anything done effectively. That time may be better spent resting so that you can do a better and more efficient job after the rest.

5. The supervisor should be punctual. This is not only a matter of the effective use of your own time, but also the time of other members of the organization. When you are late you hold up yourself and at least one other person. Punctuality is a good way to improve time use.

6. The supervisor should keep trivial details handy for idle time performance. You can do such things as read your mail and return telephone calls while waiting for a subordinate to report. Such small time things usually do not require blocks of time. They can be used as fillers around the larger items.

7. The supervisor should have a plan for the work he or she must do first thing in the morning and ideas as to what must be accomplished before quitting time each day. When these are written on the calendar and attention is paid to getting them done each day, it makes managing your time much easier.

Although some of these points may be contradictory, a supervisory schedule that incorporates many of the time-saving hints will contribute to successful supervision.

TELEPHONE, PAPERWORK, AND MEETINGS

The use of the telephone, paperwork overload, and ineffective meetings can take large chunks of time. There are some ways to handle these three time robbers that will increase the time available for effective problem solving.

The Telephone

What can be done to improve telephone productivity? Many supervisors agree that the telephone is at best a necessary evil. A good secretary can screen calls and eliminate those that don't fall under the supervisor's highest priorities, as well as hold calls during blocks of time. But if you do not have a secretary, other techniques must be used.

Try jotting down notes concerning the points to be covered in a telephone conversation before you call. This tends to help keep you on track and get the important business taken care of more quickly on the phone. Calls should be kept as brief as possible.

Telephone calls can be saved and grouped together so that the supervisor can make as many calls as possible at one time. Some supervisors set aside two calling periods during the day, one in the morning and one in the afternoon, and accumulate calls until those times.

The key is to use the telephone to *your* advantage, not to allow it to enslave you. What happens, for example, if you *don't* answer the telephone when it rings? It eventually stops ringing! Again there are some obvious limits to such tactics, but if you are trying to get something important done such tactics are occasionally useful.

Saving Time on Paperwork

Paper handling is a real nuisance for many supervisors. As an organization grows, paperwork routines tend to become somewhat rigid and difficult to change, simply because no one takes time to analyze them.

Excessive paperwork is usually associated with larger organizations, but smaller ones are not exempt. Many organizations go on crash campaigns to eliminate reports and paperwork that is redundant or obsolete. This can be a worthwhile tactic but it is certainly not the only approach to the problem of "red tape."

We estimate that the average business letter now runs 120 words and costs $3.79. In 1953 the average letter was 250 words in length. This may reflect an increased understanding on the part of supervisors of the real costs of paperwork.

A good way to determine exactly how much paperwork can be eliminated is to bring together all of the forms, reports, and so forth that pass across your desk. Don't forget those that you require of your subordinates. Examine all of them and try to determine which ones can be simplified, which combined, and which eliminated altogether.

Using form letters or form paragraphs can minimize the amount of paperwork you have to deal with. Try writing your answer to a request of a routine nature in the margin of the original letter instead of writing a lengthy reply. This saves not only time but typing costs. Some experts suggest categorizing incoming paperworks into A, B, and C categories. "A" category pieces are important and need an immediate response. Items in the "B" category can wait, and paper in the "C" category is low priority and can be appropriately deposited in the waste can.

Many reports, forms, and routine mail pieces can be immediately re-routed to subordinates. In addition, every supervisor should schedule paperwork clean-ups occasionally. This includes weeding out from the files and from your in-basket the things that are no longer needed.

By paying attention to some of these simple hints, a supervisor can reduce his or her paperwork problems to manageable proportions. As with time utilization, only by inventorying what is currently being done and then determining what can be eliminated can any progress be made in this area. Many times more can be done away with than you might initially think. An excellent book on paperwork efficiency is *Fat Paper* by Lee Grossman.[3]

Conducting Efficient Meetings

Meetings can take up tremendous blocks of supervisory time. Although group discussion is necessary in many instances, certain techniques can be followed to make more effective use of everyone's time. Block 15–2, for example, considers a rather typical supervisory meeting format.

Reasons for Ineffective Meetings

There are many reasons for ineffective meetings. The following are some of the more common:

1. The task to be addressed in the meeting isn't made clear beforehand. If people have no idea what is going to be discussed when the meeting starts, they cannot prepare for it, so that a good deal of time is wasted in preparation that could have been done beforehand.
2. Lack of communication skills. If the leader or some of the members are unable to express their views well, or are poor listeners, meetings may take much longer than necessary.
3. Hidden agendas. Some participants may bring along certain "pet peeves" they want to discuss during the meeting. The signal may be a comment such as, "I just thought of something that . . ." The entrance of such irrelevant comments usually gets participants off the track.
4. No formal agenda. As in Block 15–2, when objectives remain unstated, things can really slow to a crawl.

BLOCK 15–2   Oh Those Monday Morning Meetings!

Robert Wilcox is a first-line supervisor who for years has held one-hour Monday morning meetings with his key employees. These meetings were originally held to discuss the upcoming problems of the week, but those issues were usually taken care of within 15 minutes. The remainder of the meeting degenerated into essentially a social gathering. Bob generally chatted for ten minutes or so about how he had spent his weekend, and two or three of the other individuals used the time to talk about things they were personally interested in. Bob was once asked by a friend why he continued to hold these weekly meetings. His answer was it "helped keep things running smoothly."

The five employees who attended these weekly meetings had an average salary of $18,000 a year. That represents between $45 and $50 total cost to the company for the one hour of nonproductive time each Monday morning. Considering the limited aims of the meetings and their questionable results, one wonders if this is sound use of supervisory time.

Making Meetings Effective

The key to making meetings effective is to develop a good formal agenda. It provides topics and an order of business for the group meeting. The agenda should be distributed well in advance so that people have a chance to consider the topics and think through their positions on them. The items on an agenda should be prioritized. Items on which the leader feels quick agreement can be reached should be considered first. This sets up a pattern of joint decision making and problem solving that will hopefully carry over to some of the more difficult items.

The person making the agenda should try to determine how much time should be spent on each item and indicate this on the agenda. Without a time budget it's possible to spend a great amount of time on minor items while major issues receive "a lick and a promise." An agenda serves another purpose as well. Although supervisory meetings should be kept rather informal, they shouldn't degenerate into just another bull session. With an agenda in hand, the discussion leader can ensure that only appropriate subject matter is presented for comments. If a participant gets too far afield, it is the leader's responsibility to bring the discussion back to the topic at hand.

Another way to make meetings more productive is to restrict attendance to those directly affected by the topic being discussed. Lengthy meetings often result from overattendance. If people aren't directly affected by the decisions being made or don't have something to contribute, then perhaps they shouldn't be attending the meeting.

In addition, every meeting should have a stated purpose. Routine weekly meetings *may* be beneficial, but if there isn't enough business to warrant the meeting being called, perhaps the time schedule should be changed to a meeting every two weeks, or a memo used instead.

Using charts at meetings can be quite beneficial. Some people are overwhelmed by numbers, and using visual aids can help overcome this problem. Bar graphs and simple line drawings can sometimes ease people's fears of numbers and too much time used in analyzing them.

One technique that some supervisors use to keep meetings within a stated time period is to start them at 11:00 so that they will end promptly at noon in time for the lunch break, or commence at 4:00 P.M. so that they will end promptly at 5:00 because people want to go home. This isn't always necessary, but when meetings often run on past the stated ending time, it may prove a useful device.

So You Saved Time—Now What?

If you are able to save some time with some of the foregoing time-saving hints, what are you going to do with it? Unfortunately, many supervisors don't use the extra hours that they can gain for useful activities. Often the result is just more routine work that expands to fill the time that has been saved. We would like to suggest that time saved in this manner be used to develop your personal supervisory skills. If you do not make a conscious effort to set some time aside for self-development, there is a chance that your good intentions will remain just that.

SUPERVISORY SELF-DEVELOPMENT

First-line supervisors typically have come up through the ranks and accordingly lack the formal knowledge of management that some of those higher in the organization may have. Further, supervisors do not always get adequate coaching on the job from second-level managers. This is why supervisory self-development is so important. You cannot always count on the organization or your immediate superior to develop your talents and skills as they should be developed.

Figure 15–4 shows the results of a study done in one organization with 805 first-level supervisors who described their own training needs and 716 second-level supervisors who described the needs of their subordinate first-level supervisors. Figure 15–4 shows that the first-level supervisors emphasized quite different things than did the second-level supervisors. Obviously, these groups differed greatly in their perception of development needs of first-level supervisors.

Company-Sponsored Development

For first-level supervisors the most common company-sponsored development activities are on-the-job coaching, tuition aid for college courses, and in-house training programs.[4] Of the organizations surveyed,

FIGURE 15–4   Different Perceptions of Training Needs for First-Level Supervisors

First-level supervisors felt they needed training on

Keeping up on new developments
Methods improvement
Making oral presentations
Job knowledge

Second-level supervisors felt first-level supervisors needed training to

Set goals for subordinates
Motivate subordinates
Check on subordinate performance
Encourage ideas from subordinates

Source: Adapted from R. P. Calehoon and T. H. Jerder, "First-level Supervisory Training Needs and Organizational Development," *Public Personnel Management,* May–June 1975, p. 197.

86 percent were found to use on-the-job coaching; 81 percent offered tuition aid for college courses, and 75 percent had in-house training programs. In addition, 54 percent of the organizations surveyed permit supervisors to attend professional or trade association meetings at organization expense, and about half of the organizations pay for self-training or correspondence courses for supervisors.

No organization can unilaterally decide to develop its supervisory talent. Individuals have to do much of this for themselves, simply because no two persons are alike. Supervisory self-development is based on an individual's current need for learning. Ideally, supervisory self-development actions and plans should be a shared responsibility between the individual and his or her superior. Self-development does not necessarily suggest advancement in the organization. The commitment is toward improvement and growth on the present job.

How Do I Develop Myself as a Supervisor?

The place to start is by analyzing the skills that you presently have and then planning to add or refine them in ways that would be most beneficial. Figure 15–5 shows six possible areas for supervisory self-development. You and your immediate superior can jointly decide on specific activities within each of these areas that could be improved.

Once you have completed an analysis of your work skills, you can build on your strengths and plan self-development actions for weaknesses. Select a specific development need, a skill that both you and your superior feel would be useful for you to improve upon. Then ask yourself the following questions:

1. What three persons are best qualified to teach me something about this skill area?
2. Is there someone I work with who is particularly skilled in this area?
3. Can I observe that person using this skill?

FIGURE 15–5   Possible Areas for Supervisory Self-Development

Working with subordinates
Organizing subordinates' work
Work planning and scheduling
Maintaining safe, clean work areas
Maintaining equipment and machinery
Compiling records and reports

Source: Adapted from B. E. Dowell and K. Wexley, "Development of a Work Behavior Taxonomy for First-Line Supervisors," *Journal of Applied Psychology, 63* (1978), 570.

4. What books can I read, and who else might know of some books that would apply in this area?
5. What new projects can I propose or work on to modify my current skills in this area?
6. Who is the best person to give me feedback on whether or not I am improving?

These few questions can help you pinpoint ways to develop or improve in a particular need area.

Like any good plan, your plan for supervisory self-development should consider several things. Two of the most important are timing and establishing priorities. Once you determine what you would like to improve, you must set some goals and specific objectives for improving it. Then set some time tables, and go about improving it.

Another important consideration is the stage of your career as supervisor. It has been suggested, for example, that early in their careers supervisors need to develop action skills, the ability to innovate, and a spe-

cialty on which to focus their main efforts. Mid-career supervisors may need to develop skills in training and coaching younger employees, as well as update their own skills and develop broader views of work in the organization. People in late career may be more interested in shifting to a role of consultation and in establishing themselves in various activities outside the organization.[5]

Remember there are some things that the company or the organization can do to help you develop as a supervisor, but you are the only one who knows exactly what you want, and you are the best source of information on how you should develop your talents.

SUMMARY AND CONCLUSIONS

Time use can be a major concern to supervisors—especially if they feel they are not accomplishing everything they should. Eliminating nonessential activities through time analysis and developing a time consciousness are two important steps in learning to manage your time more effectively. This chapter presented a test to help you analyze your use of time and how you might improve it.

Other important ways to save time are blocking time, time consciousness, delegation, and the use of various time-saving hints.

Telephone calls, paperwork, and meetings can consume much of the supervisor's time. Making notes before calling, grouping calls, or calling only twice a day can help the telephone problem. Paperwork needs periodic analysis. Using form letters or paragraphs, answering in the margin, categorizing, and routing can all help manage paper problems. Effective meetings save time. A good meeting has an agenda and a time limit; it should also limit participation to those who are directly affected.

If a supervisor succeeds in saving time we suggest he or she use it for supervisory self-development. The supervisor cannot always count on the boss to know what is needed or best for personal development. Areas that you should work on include (1) working with subordinates, (2) organizing subordinates' work, (3) work planning and scheduling, (4) maintaining quality and efficiency, (5) ensuring clean, safe work areas, equipment, and machinery, and (6) compiling records and reports.

QUESTIONS

1. What are the biggest supervisory time wasters?
2. If you were to analyze your own time use, how often and for how long should you do it?

3. Give the time use test to a friend or relative in a managerial job and compare that person's responses to each of the suggested best answers. Do you think your friend is using his or her time well?

4. Which of the time-saving hints would be most useful to your relative or friend?

5. Think of two additional time savers each for avoiding undue time spent on paperwork or on the phone and at meetings.

6. In what areas do you think *you* need the most development as a supervisor? Who can best help you develop in these areas? How?

WHAT IS GOING ON HERE?

I never envisioned all the problems first-level supervisors have to deal with. As a matter of fact, I'm swamped—I can't even find time to check out some of the faulty equipment that is constantly coming in. The major problem is that my manager expects me to do a million things at once instead of assigning me one thing at a time and allowing me to complete it correctly.

I know some managers have a tendency to push people too hard, but until now I had never known how frustrating such a situation can be. This is basically the only area in which he and I don't get along, though. Otherwise he is a very rational, logical person, and it is hard for me to understand why he is such a stickler on this point. He and I have talked about my performance and training needs and I think he wants me to "push things off" on my employees more than I want to. He's told me to delegate more of the work, but I am simply not comfortable doing it. Maybe if I just knew more about the job or if I knew more about how to improve some of the methods around here I wouldn't have these time problems.

---

1. Why do you suppose the superior is assigning so much work to this individual?

2. Are the items the supervisor rates important in terms of his ongoing development and the things the superior rates important the same?

NOTES

[1] Lee Danielson, "Management of Time," *Management of Personnel Quarterly,* Spring 1963, pp. 14–18.

[2] Leo B. Moore, "Managerial Time," *Industrial Management Review,* Spring 1968, p. 87.

[3] Lee Grossman, *Fat Paper* (New York: McGraw Hill, 1978).

[4] *Management Training and Development Programs,* PPF Survey No. 116 (Washington, D.C.: Bureau of National Affairs, March 1977).

[5] Douglas T. Hall, *Careers in Organizations* (Pacific Palisades, Calif.: Goodyear Publishing Co., 1976), pp. 64–90.

THE SUPERVISOR AND THE LAW

section four

Ignorance of the law is no excuse for making costly mistakes that can affect you personally and the organization as a whole. This section deals with three areas of law most pertinent to supervisory know-how: labor law, equal employment law, and safety requirements.

The Supervisor and the Union

16 SUPERVISORY PROBLEM

What role does the supervisor have in effective labor-management relations?

LEARNING OBJECTIVES

After finishing this chapter, you should be able to

1. Describe why organizations resist unionization and why employees form unions
2. Discuss the main provisions of the Wagner Act, the Taft-Hartley Act, and the Landrum-Griffin Act
3. Identify the union officials with whom a supervisor typically works and the issues for which they are responsible
4. Discuss key factors in meeting union organization campaigns
5. Describe the supervisor's role in preparing for contract negotiations
6. Indicate what supervisors should do to reduce the frequency of grievances

THE ORGANIZATION CAMPAIGN AT
BEST BUY DEPARTMENT STORE

John Hamilton was the owner and manager of the Best Buy Department Store. He had an assistant manager, but apart from these two, there were no other supervisors in the store. There were 23 additional personnel, all of whom shared in sales, stocking, and maintenance work.

John prided himself on his employee relations skills. He had an "open-door" policy. Whoever had a complaint could come to him and he would give that person a fair hearing. The wages and fringe benefits at Best Buy were good for a small operation. Of course, the big chain outfits paid better and had more fringes. On the other hand, John felt that Best Buy was like a family, he often said that "we have the personal touch and in the big operations you are just a number."

Last Thursday, John came across something that really took him by surprise. The day shift was leaving the store and the evening shift had already arrived. John was leaving early and noticed a gathering in the employee parking lot behind the store. Martha Adams and someone John did not know were passing out leaflets. John was in a hurry so he didn't stop to see what was going on.

The next morning he found one of the leaflets in the parking lot. It was union propaganda. "Join the Retail Store Employees Union. Best Buy Unfair." How could anyone believe this?

John didn't know for sure what to do. He thought he should talk to Martha. She had worked for Best Buy for five years. He looked for her but couldn't find her. About one hour after she was due at work, Martha arrived. She came to his office when someone told her Mr. Hamilton was looking for her. She said she had a flat tire on the way to work. John told her that irresponsibility would not be tolerated and she was discharged. Martha said, "You are doing this because you saw me passing out fliers last night." She yelled, "You won't get away with this!"

John decided he had better see that the fliers weren't distributed again, so he called Fred Martin, a pretty good handyman working for Best Buy. He told Fred to make a big sign saying, "No Solicitation—Violators Will Be Prosecuted." The sign was to be put up at the entrance to the employee parking lot.

Next, John decided to call a meeting after the store closed Saturday afternoon. Everyone employed by Best Buy would be requested to attend. At the meeting, John thought he would explain that Best Buy was a good place to work and a union would not make it better. Also, he would explain that if Best Buy paid the wages and fringe benefits of the big chain stores, it would be out of business within a year.

The Best Buy case describes a situation faced by thousands of organizations each year. Why has Mr. Hamilton reacted so negatively? Has he done anything that will make it difficult to stop a union campaign? These and other questions will be answered in this chapter.

What are the implications of one or more unions representing the various employees of an organization? The law requires that when a union represents the employees of an organization, the employer and representatives of the employees (union) must meet and confer in good faith with respect to wages, hours, and other terms and conditions of employment.[1] This means that management and the union reach a joint decision on how the organization will be operated and the personnel policies that will be followed. Because a union limits management's flexibility in making decisions, employers tend to resist the formation of unions within their organizations.

The presence of a union also strongly affects the authority of first-level supervisors. The frequency with which supervisors' decisions will be challenged when there is a union far exceeds what can be expected without a union. It was pointed out in the chapter on leadership that when a supervisor's power decreases, the ease of leadership is diminished. A union restricts and limits the supervisor's power, making a supervisor's job more difficult.

WHY EMPLOYEES JOIN UNIONS

Some employers believe that many, if not most, employees do not really want to belong to unions. They argue that employees join unions because they are compelled to do so by union shop agreements. A union shop agreement is an agreement between an organization and a union which requires new employees to join the union as a condition of taking a job. There may be some truth to this point of view. However, we feel that it is largely in error, because employees *can* vote to have a union removed yet it is not often that unions are voted out.

Unions Satisfy Needs

The reasons why employees join unions can be analyzed in terms of the Maslow need hierarchy. According to Maslow (see Chapter 3), the categories of needs are physical, safety or security, social, esteem, and development or self-actualization. Unions can contribute to the satisfaction of many of these needs. Most obviously, higher wages and more fringe benefits contribute to satisfying physical and security needs. A union also ensures that more importance will be given to seniority in making layoff and discharge decisions and that there will be a formal grievance procedure. These procedures contribute to security for employees.

Union membership can also help to satisfy social needs, and, as management is compelled to meet with union officials to discuss personnel practices, employees have an opportunity to participate in decisions affecting their place of work. This can contribute to the satisfaction of needs for esteem and self-development. In short, it can be argued that employees join unions because in so doing they can satisfy needs that would otherwise remain unmet.

Making Unions Unnecessary

If an employer wants his shop to remain nonunion, the employer must make unions unnecessary in the eyes of employees. In other words, nonunion employers who wish to prevent unionization must provide employees with those things that unions claim to provide.[2] An employer should establish a procedure for hearing employee complaints. Working conditions, wage and salary levels, and fringe benefits should be as good as those of unionized organizations. Inequities in compensation and unfair treatment by supervisors must be eliminated. Employees should be properly placed in jobs. Of primary importance is maintaining good communications between employees and supervisors and, second to that, allowing employees to participate in decisions affecting them and their jobs.

Supervisors play a key role in removing the need for a union. They have the greatest amount of contact with rank-and-file employees. As a result, they are most likely to know when, as well as why, employees are dissatisfied and frustrated. If the organization removes the causes of these problems, it removes the need for a union.

U.S. LABOR LAW: THE WAGNER ACT

The principal laws governing union-management relations in the United States have been passed since the 1930s. The Wagner Act, also called the National Labor Relations Act, was passed in 1935. The objective of this legislation was to encourage collective bargaining and to protect the rights of workers to form unions. There are three major provisions of the Wagner Act: the identification of unfair labor practices on the part of the employers; the creation of an agency to administer the law; and the establishment of a procedure by which it is decided if a union will represent a particular group of employees.

Unfair Labor Practices by Employers

The Wagner Act prohibits the following actions by employers:

1. Interference with employee efforts to form a union. For example, if an employer becomes aware that some employees are trying to form a union, management might fire the union activists; bribe them to stop their efforts; threaten them with discharge if they continue their efforts; or threaten to close the plant if a union is formed. All of these kinds of activities are prohibited by the Wagner Act.
2. Domination of a union. The term *company union* refers to a union that is under the control of the organization whose employees it is supposed to represent. The creation of a company union was a way some employers blocked the efforts of employees to form a union.
3. Discrimination against an individual because of union activities. This prohibits an employer from demoting, discharging, or in any other way discriminating against an employee because of union activities. Block 16–1 describes an action which violates this provision of the Wagner Act.

    We don't know if Jack will get away with his plan. Certainly his intent is in violation of the Wagner Act. If Millie is caught doing something that is grounds for dismissal, Jack will succeed. If Jack and Curt dismiss Millie without good cause, they will probably be found guilty of an unfair labor practice.

Millie Roering is a shop steward for the I. O. Steven Textile plant. Employees at this plant are represented by the Textile Workers of America (TWA). Millie is an effective steward. No contract violations escape her notice, and she pushes for fair settlement of all grievances.

Jack Sprat is the plant superintendent. Today he has an appointment with Millie's supervisor, Curt Clay. Jack is going to tell Curt to watch Millie like a hawk because he wants an excuse to fire her. The reason is that Millie is too effective as a steward.

4. Discrimination because of participation in National Labor Relations Board proceedings. The agency responsible for administering the law is the National Labor Relations Board. This provision of the law ensures that employees can make charges of unfair labor practices without being penalized.
5. Refusal to bargain collectively with a certified union. If an organization's employees are unionized, the employer *must* meet with union representatives and discuss wages, hours, and working conditions.

National Labor Relations Board

The National Labor Relations Board (NLRB) is the government agency which administers the law. The function of the NLRB is to hear charges of unfair labor practices and conduct elections to determine if a union will be the certified representative of a particular group of employees.

Representation Elections

The Wagner Act requires that elections be conducted to determine if a group of employees wants to be represented by a union. These are secret ballot elections, and are supervised or administered by the NLRB. The majority of employees voting determines whether or not there will be a union.

U.S. LABOR LAW:
THE TAFT-HARTLEY ACT

The Wagner Act resulted in a tremendous increase in union membership. Then, following World War II, there were a large number of strikes. In 1946, there were three times as many strikes as in any previous year in American history. Americans feared that unions were becoming too big and powerful. As a result, in 1947 Congress passed the Taft-Hartley Act, otherwise known as the Labor Management Relations Act. The intent of Congress was to curb union power.

The basic purposes of the Taft-Hartley Act were to specify unfair labor practices on the part of unions, to establish procedures that would facilitate the settlement of industrial disputes, and to set out guidelines for minimizing the effect of strikes threatening the national economy.

Unfair Labor Practices by Unions

The Taft-Hartley Act prohibits the following practices by unions:

1. Restraining or coercing employees in the exercise of their right to join unions of their own choosing or to refrain from joining the union. This prohibits unions from threatening and harassing employees during a representation election.
2. Discriminating against nonunion applicants. Prior to the Taft-Hartley Act, some unions were able to secure agreements from employers which required that job applicants be members of the union before they could be hired. This is called a *closed shop* security agreement. This kind of security agreement is no longer legal except in certain cases, for example, the building trades industry. However, the Taft-Hartley Act does permit the union shop security agreement, which makes it legal to require that new employees join the union within 30 days after employment.

    However, the Taft-Hartley Act does permit state legislation prohibiting the union shop security agreement. Such laws are called *right-to-work* laws. In 1976, there were 19 states which had passed right-to-work laws.
3. Refusing to bargain with an employer. Some unions had become so powerful that in contract negotiations no real bargaining took place. The bargaining consisted basically of the union presenting its demands and saying, "Agree to these demands or we'll close your organization down."
4. Participating in certain strikes and boycotts. A *primary boycott* is when a union brings pressure (for example, strike and pickets) against an employer with whom it is negotiating a contract. A *secondary boycott* is when economic pressure is brought against a neutral employer so that the neutral employer will encourage the primary employer to agree to union demands. Secondary boycotts are illegal.
5. Charging excessive initiation fees. Some unions charged excessive initiation fees and dues in order to restrict the supply of personnel in the particular occupation. This is an effective practice when the union has a union shop or closed shop security agreement with the employer. Deciding what are excessive initiation fees and dues is left to the Secretary of the U.S. Department of Labor.
6. Causing or attempting to cause an employer to pay for services which are

not performed. This provision was directed against "featherbedding," but it failed mainly because *make-work rules* are not prohibited. Make-work rules refer to unnecessary tasks that are performed in order to avoid the charge of featherbedding.

Efforts to Facilitate
the Settlement of Disputes

The Taft-Hartley Act created the Federal Mediation and Conciliation Service (FMCS). The function of this agency is to help labor and management reach agreement during contract negotiations. It is important to know the difference between arbitration and mediation. *Arbitration* occurs when a neutral third party hears the arguments put forth by labor and management and then makes a decision which is *binding* upon the two parties, that is, must be adhered to by both sides. *Mediation* occurs when the third party acts as a go-between and encourages the two parties to reach a settlement. A mediator cannot *require* that labor or management do what he or she thinks is best.

National Emergency Strikes

A national emergency strike is a strike which endangers the national health and safety. When such a strike is threatened or is actually in progress, the President of the United States can ask the U.S. District Court to issue an injunction prohibiting the strike for a period of 80 days. This 80-day injunction is called a "cooling off" period. During this time the two parties are expected to continue their negotiations and try to reach a settlement. One instance in which the President might invoke the national emergency strike provision would be in the case of a nationwide Teamsters strike. If such a strike were to take place, the nation would be crippled within several days' time.

U.S. LABOR LAW:
LANDRUM-GRIFFIN ACT

During the 1950s evidence was brought forward that in some unions, individual members were being denied the right to participate in union affairs. Evidence also came out that there were many cases of corruption and fraud on the part of union leaders. In response to this evidence, Congress passed the Landrum-Griffin Act, or the Labor Management Reporting and Disclosure Act, in 1959.

The Landrum-Griffin Act requires that union members be able to attend meetings and that these meetings be conducted in a democratic manner. The Act also requires the periodic election of union officials. With respect to union finances, the Act requires periodic financial reports to the U.S. Department of Labor. Also, union leaders who have financial responsibilities must be bonded.

COLLECTIVE BARGAINING IN THE PUBLIC SECTOR

Much of the growth of unions during the last two decades has been in the public sector. One reason is President Kennedy's Executive Order 10988. Although this order forbade federal government employees to engage in strikes, it did entitle them to join unions and bargain collectively with the executive agencies for which they worked. While Order 10988 pertained only to federal government employees, it had an influence on the formation of unions at state and local levels of government as well.

In 1969, President Nixon issued Executive Order 11491. This executive order resulted in greater uniformity among the policies federal agencies were developing to deal with union activities. Also, Executive Order 11491 established the Federal Services Impasse Panel, which has the function of settling negotiation disputes by final and binding arbitration if necessary. Many states have similar legislation concerning the settlement of contract disputes. This is particularly true in disputes involving fire-fighters and police personnel.

THE STRUCTURE OF UNIONS IN THE UNITED STATES

There are three union levels in the United States. One is the federation level, which is the American Federation of Labor and Congress of Industrial Organization (AFL–CIO). The second level is comprised of national and international unions, and the third is the local union level.

Figure 16–1 shows the relationship of these union levels to one another. The AFL–CIO is composed of member unions. This is represented by the dotted lines going to the AFL–CIO. The majority of members are national and international unions. When a national or international union is associated with the AFL–CIO, it is referred to as an *affiliated* national or international union. The other type of AFL–CIO member organization is an affiliated local, which bypasses the second level. Unions can choose to be independent of the federation. Examples are the Teamsters and the United Automobile Workers.

FIGURE 16-1   Structure of Unions in the United States

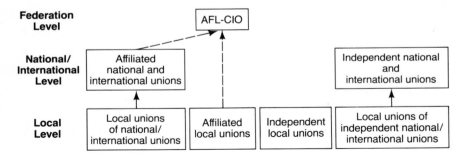

The national and international union does have a great deal of control over its member local unions. This is true whether the union is affiliated with the federation or whether it is an independent national or international union. For example, the national and international union will have a major say concerning dues charged by local unions, and it can determine the rules for membership in the local.

Functions of the AFL-CIO

The main purposes of the AFL–CIO are to lobby on behalf of unions and to serve as a mediator among member unions. The AFL–CIO lobbies in Congress for legislation favored by unions. In its mediator role, the AFL–CIO attempts to minimize conflicts among affiliated unions and tries to settle disputes which may break out among them. For example, two member unions at the national level may be attempting to organize the employees of the same company. The AFL–CIO may act as a mediator and try to get one of them to stop its efforts.

Functions of National/International Unions

The primary function of the national/international union is collective bargaining, or the negotiation of labor contracts. Typically, when a contract is being negotiated with an employer, the union side is led by a national or international representative. The reason for this is that negotiating skills are critical to success at the bargaining table, and the national/international representative is usually a specialist in this area. The second main function of the national/international union is to organize more locals, that is, bring more members into the union.

Functions of Local Unions

Approximately 98 percent of local unions belong to a national or international union. In such a case, the primary function of the local union is to administer the labor contract after it has been negotiated with an employer. Basically, this involves responding to grievances that union members have about the way their employer is applying the contract. (The grievance procedure will be described in detail later in the chapter.) Of course, if the local does not belong to a national/international union, then it will be responsible for negotiating the contract on its own. It should be noted that even when a local is part of a national/international union, local officials will play a role in contract negotiations.

Business Representatives

The local union is the level with which union members have direct contact. It is also the level with which supervisors have the most contact. Local union officers typically include a president, vice-president, secretary-treasurer, and business representative. The business representative is usually a full-time employee of the union. As such, he or she takes care of the day-to-day operations of the local union, plays a major role in negotiating and administrating the labor agreement, plays a key role in the grievance procedure, and may also be involved in collecting dues and recruiting new members.

Union Steward

The union (shop) steward is the union's counterpart to management's supervisor. When a union member has a grievance about the way he or she has been treated or about the way a contract has been applied, it is the union steward, along with the employee, who will contact the supervisor concerning the grievance.

UNION RECOGNITION: ORGANIZATION CAMPAIGN

The NLRB is responsible for conducting elections to determine if a union will represent a particular group of employees. Before the NLRB will conduct an election, the union must demonstrate that at least 30 percent of the employees in the organization are interested in joining a union. Consequently, the union will conduct a campaign trying to get employees to sign an authorization card. These cards can be used as evidence that the employees are interested in forming a union. Typically, a union organizer from some national or local in the area will coordinate the campaign. The employer can also be fairly certain that there are some employees within the organization interested in forming a union.

Supervisory Training

It is important that supervisors be aware of what constitutes unfair employer practices during a union organization campaign. These were mentioned briefly in our discussion of the Wagner Act. Basically, supervisors can do nothing that in any way resembles interference with an employee's right to form a union. Also, it is very important that supervisors do nothing that can be interpreted as discrimination against employees who have favorable attitudes about the formation of a union. Besides being illegal, such practices only serve to strengthen the union's claim that organization is necessary to protect employees from unfair and arbitrary treatment by their superiors. Block 16–2 is an example of another kind of unfair labor practice.

You should remember that *any* interfering with a union's attempts to organize is prohibited. Not only negative actions such as threats and discharge are illegal, but also promises of rewards are illegal.

COLLECTIVE BARGAINING

What is collective bargaining? The Labor Management Relations Act states that, "To bargain collectively is the performance of the mutual

---

BLOCK 16–2   You Will be Promoted

A union organization drive was on at the Bay City School District. Organizers from the National Federation of Teachers (NFT) were contacting the school district's teachers. Alice Wilson was principal of the Northside Elementary School. At Northside it was clear that Lois Cook was the union activist. Lois could be very persuasive. Alice was sure that if Lois could be sidetracked, at least at Northside the NFT would not have a majority. Alice arranged an appointment with Lois. After the usual pleasantries, Alice said, "Lois, you have the potential to be an excellent administrator. The assistant principal position here at Northside will be vacant next year. If you will stop encouraging our teachers at Northside to back the NFT, I guarantee that you will be the next assistant principal.

obligation of the employer and the representative of the employees to meet at reasonable times and confer in good faith with respect to wages, hours, and other terms and conditions of employment. . . ." Naturally, if an organization is involved in collective bargaining, a union has already been certified as the representative of the employees of the organization.

Preparations for Negotiation

From the employer's point of view, a thorough review of employee relations is needed to prepare for contract negotiations. The employer must try to anticipate the union's contract demands and then prepare counterarguments for the expected issues. When preparing for negotiations, a key source of information is the first-line supervisor. It is the first-line supervisor who has the most contact with employees. As a result, the supervisor is best able to identify the concerns of the rank-and-file employee. Key questions are: What are their gripes? What are their wishes? What seems to be most important?

You must remember that while contract negotiations will definitely deal with wages and fringe benefits, a wide range of other issues will often be included. Figure 16–2 lists subjects typically covered in a collective

FIGURE 16–2   Common Subjects Covered in a Collective Bargaining Agreement

1. Union security clause
2. Permissible union activities on company time
3. Equal opportunity
4. Decision-making rights of management
5. Conditions governing temporary and permanent transfers
6. Practices concerning probationary employees
7. Employee obligations under the agreement
8. Rules governing discipline and discharge
9. Grievance procedures
10. Arbitration procedures
11. Holiday and vacation rights
12. Wage structure
13. Overtime and premium pay
14. Shift differential
15. Rest and lunch periods
16. Determination of seniority
17. Procedures for layoffs and recall
18. Procedures for leaves of absence
19. Fringe benefit rights: Life and health insurance, long-term disability insurance, and pensions
20. Agreement concerning strikes, lockouts and boycotts during the life of the contract

bargaining agreement. Notice that wages, overtime pay, and various fringe benefits make up only four or five of the issues listed. The majority of items concern hiring, transfers, layoffs, and disciplinary procedures.

This emphasizes the problems involved in finding out what employees are really concerned about. It is bad judgment to assume that the *only* reason employees are interested in a union is wages and fringe benefits.

Contract Negotiations

Figure 16–3 shows contract negotiation positions once union and management representatives have actually sat down at the bargaining table. During the first stages of contract negotiations, the union's demands will seem rather excessive. On the other hand, management will offer counterproposals which are relatively far removed from the union's first position. The left side of Figure 16–3 represents what is called a *positive negotiating zone*. In this situation, the union's real position is somewhere below the employer's real position, so that there is some overlap between the two sets of demands.

The right side of Figure 16–3 represents what is called a *negative negotiating zone*. This is a situation in which the best offer the employer is willing to make is below or less than the smallest offer the union is willing to accept. Negotiations that fall into this zone usually result in a deadlock, leading to a work stoppage (strike).

Why do both labor and management take extreme positions at the beginning of negotiations? This tactic results mainly from the kind of

FIGURE 16–3   Contract Negotiations and the Bargaining Zone

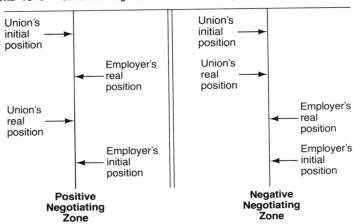

labor legislation we have in this country. The law requires that the two parties get together and negotiate concerning wages and other conditions of employment. Both sides are required to "bargain in good faith." In the eyes of the NLRB, bargaining in good faith means that each side is willing to make compromises. To be able to make compromises, both sides start out in positions far removed from their real positions so they are able to make compromises without giving up what they really want.

ADMINISTERING THE CONTRACT

After a contract has been agreed upon, it becomes a part of the personnel rules of the organization during the time period covered by the contract. The mechanism for administering a contract is known as the *grievance procedure*. About 99 percent of all agreements have a grievance procedure.[3] The grievance procedure serves many functions. It provides a means for controlling conflict that arises during the contract. Without a grievance procedure, if disputes arise over the application and interpretation of the contract, about the only thing that can be done to settle these disputes is to strike. It provides a means for an employee to complain about what he or she thinks is unfair without fear of retaliation. It also serves as a means for interpreting and clarifying the meaning of the collective bargaining contract. Finally, the grievance procedure provides a means to identify sources of dissatisfaction and potential problems *and* a communication channel to facilitate conflict resolution.

The Grievance Procedure

A typical grievance procedure is presented in Figure 16–4. It is initiated by an employee who has a complaint about the application of the contract and begins with a meeting between the employee, the shop steward, and the immediate supervisor. This stage is handled verbally. The employee or the shop steward explains the employee's complaint. After checking on the complaint and thinking it over, the immediate supervisor responds to the grievance. If the supervisor's answer is not satisfactory, the grievance is reduced to writing.

At the next level in the grievance procedure, higher-level officials in both the organization and the union are involved. A department or plant manager may represent the employer, and the union's business representative or a grievance committee designated by the local union might be the union's representative. These parties discuss the grievance and try to reach an agreement. If negotiations at this level also fail, then the complaint goes to higher levels in both the organization and the

FIGURE 16–4 A Typical Grievance Procedure

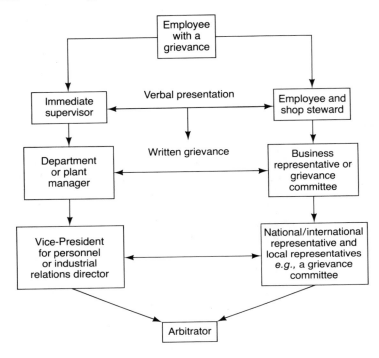

union. On the organization's side, a vice-president for personnel or direc-tor of industrial relations might be involved. On the union's side, a national or international representative will probably be called on. If discussions at this level are unable to reach a satisfactory solution to the grievance, then the last step will be arbitration. Ninety-four percent of all collective bargaining agreements specify that the final step of the grievance procedure is arbitration.

If there is provision in the contract for arbitration, after both sides have presented their cases to the arbitrator, he or she makes a decision that is binding on the union and the employer. In this example, there are three levels before the grievance goes to arbitration. The number of levels varies. Some organizations have four or five levels and others have only two levels before the grievance goes to arbitration.

Usually specific time limits are set for all steps in the grievance procedure. For example, a common limit is two or three days for the first step and then somewhat longer periods for subsequent steps, perhaps five to seven days for the second step and 10 to 15 days for the third and fourth steps. This means that if an individual has a grievance, it must be submitted within two or three days; management will then have two or three days to respond to the complaint, and so on with each of the subsequent steps.

What Specifically Is a Grievance?

The answer to this question depends on the particular collective bargaining agreement. There seems to be a 50–50 split in defining a grievance: [4] In roughly half of all collective bargaining agreements, a grievance is *any employee complaint* regardless of whether or not the topic is covered in the contract. In the other 50 percent of agreements, the complaint must pertain to *disputes in interpretation and application of the contract.* Block 16–3 presents a sample grievance form with the employee's complaint.

What should Denise DeMarco do? The remainder of this chapter will recommend a general approach supervisors should follow in dealing

---

BLOCK 16–3

Grievance Form

Employee: Sally Howard

Job Classification: Secretary: Level I

Supervisor: Denise DeMarco

Department: Marketing

Statement of Grievance

I completed six months service since ending my probationary period last Friday. The labor agreement states that I am entitled to a 25 cent per hour raise after six months on permanent status if my work is satisfactory. I *have not* received the raise. My work is as good as the other secretaries in my department, and most of them have been here two or three years.

Employee _____   Steward _____
                Signature   Signature

Received by _____

Time _____

Date _____

with grievances. We will also outline the specific steps to be taken in handling a grievance.

Issues Going to Arbitration

A recent study of issues going to arbitration found the following: [5]

1. The most prevalent issue involved discharge and disciplinary action.
2. Next most common were grievances involving seniority; for example, promotion, layoff, recall, and transfer decisions.
3. Third were grievances concerning job evaluation or determining the classification of jobs.
4. Fourth were grievances having to do with overtime: determination of overtime pay, distribution of overtime among employees, and compulsory overtime.

This information gives us clues as to what issues are most troublesome or most difficult to settle.

Factors Affecting the Frequency of Grievances

The incidence of grievances seems to depend in part on the nature of labor-management relations in the organization. If the relationship between the union and the employer is one in which each side is out to get the other, then it can be expected that the number of grievances will be high. On the other hand, if the relations between union officials and management are cordial and union and management cooperate to solve problems, then the number of grievances is usually low. Also, those grievances that do occur are more likely to be settled at the first step.

The kind of relationship we are talking about here is described in Block 16–4. Charlie Bragg is a steward for the Ford Motor Company.[6]

BLOCK 16–4   Charlie Bragg: Shop Steward

When asked about what a shop steward does, Charlie said, "The main function of a committeeman (shop steward) is to settle problems right on the floor." During an average day, Mr. Bragg handles 20 individual problems. In addressing complaints and problems, his prime goal is keeping the union members happy. However, he says that he must have a good working relationship with their supervisors. He tries to use his ultimate weapon, the written grievance, sparingly. Charlie states, "What I want to do is take care of the problem and do it quickly."

We suggest that supervisors follow the same approach in dealing with shop stewards. Try to solve employee problems without magnifying them and at the same time accomplishing your work goals. The nature of supervisory behavior in relationship to the frequency of grievances has been studied.[7] Recall from the chapter on leadership that two dimensions of leadership are consideration and structure. Consideration includes trust, respect, and rapport between the supervisor and his subordinates, as well as giving subordinates a say in decisions affecting them and encouraging two-way communication. Figure 16–5 reports the results of a study which shows that a supervisor low in consideration has high levels of grievances. This is true regardless of the level of leadership structure. Looking at the lower line in Figure 16–5, you can see that those supervisors who were high in consideration, even when they placed a good deal of emphasis on goal attainment (structure) had low grievance rates.

Preventing Grievances

Two key factors in preventing grievances are that (1) supervisors know in detail the provisions of the labor contract [8] and (2) they have a cooperative relationship with the union steward. If a supervisor views the steward as a troublemaker who is cutting his or her authority, the relationship will be filled with hostility and conflict. In such a situation, grievances will be frequent and settlement at the first step, infrequent.

FIGURE 16–5   Leadership Behavior and the Incidence of Grievances

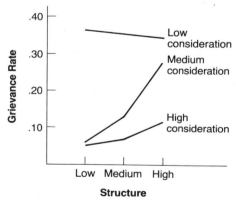

Source: E. A. Fleishman and E. F. Harris, "Patterns of Leadership Behavior Related to Employee Grievances and Turnover," *Personnel Psychology, 15* (Spring 1962), 50.

Besides these two, there is a third preventative tactic: the amount of consideration a supervisor shows the employees.

We are not suggesting that the supervisor give away the candy store. It is essential for any person in authority to enforce and apply the rules specified in the contract. But in so doing it is critical for the supervisor to apply these rules and provisions in a consistent and fair manner. The supervisor cannot afford to play favorites or allow bias to enter into decisions concerning employee matters.

Adjusting Grievances

What should the supervisor do when an employee and shop steward come forward with a grievance? Here are some suggestions: [9]

1. Listen. Get the grievant to describe the problem that is bothering him or her. It is important for the supervisor to hear the grievant's story. Don't interrupt, let the grievant talk the problem out. The objective here is to let the individual know there is no reason to fear retaliation and to communicate to the employee that you are sincerely interested in the problem.

2. Discuss the grievance. The objective is to ensure that you, the supervisor, understand the grievant's point of view. At this stage it is possible that an argument could develop. The supervisor should see to it that the discussion remains calm.

3. Get input from other relevant individuals. Usually the incident will involve at least one other person. The supervisor should question these individuals about their perception of the situation. When gathering information from others, the supervisor should emphasize that facts are being gathered to insure fairness to all involved. The supervisor should avoid giving the impression that he or she is checking up to make sure the grievant didn't lie.

4. Look at the situation from the grievant's point of view. The supervisor should not assume that the employee and the steward are always wrong. The supervisor must try to look at the situation in an objective manner. In doing so a supervisor is demonstrating to the employee that an effort is being made to be fair.

5. Evaluate the facts and opinions relevant to the situation. A fact is something that is not in dispute. For example, objective records concerning the situation. An opinion, on the other hand, is someone's judgment. The supervisor should consider whether or not the relevant opinions are objective. In evaluating facts and opinions, it is important to avoid snap decisions.

6. Make the decision. In making the decision, try to be logical and equitable and avoid letting bias enter into the decision. When considering grievances

involving discipline, it is very important for a supervisor to consider the following factors:

a. Distinguish between major and minor offenses. The general point of view is that the punishment or disciplinary action must fit the nature of the offense. Appropriate discipline for various offenses is discussed in detail in Chapter 10.

b. Distinguish between long-service employees and recent hires. A disciplinary action that is appropriate for a recently hired employee might be too severe for a long-service employee.

c. Except for major offenses, the proper disciplinary sequence is (1) oral warning, (2) written warning, (3) disciplinary suspension, and (4) discharge.

d. Impose similar penalties for similar offenses. This means that the supervisor must be consistent across individuals.

e. The intent of the disciplinary action should be to correct undesirable performance or behavior rather than to punish the employee.

7. Communicate the decision. There are two factors to keep in mind in communicating the decision. One is timing. A supervisor shouldn't act too quickly. On the other hand, don't delay too long. If a supervisor acts too quickly and the decision is favorable to the employee, the perception might be, "The supervisor knew I was right all along so why didn't he say so in the first place." Alternatively, if the decision is unfavorable to the employee and the supervisor acts too quickly, the employee could reach the impression, "The supervisor didn't give me a chance, he didn't take enough time to consider all the factors about my case."

If the decision is unfavorable to the employee, it is recommended that the supervisor make a straightforward statement to the employee, indicating the reasons for the decision. A supervisor should never try to rub the nose of the steward or employee in a decision if it is unfavorable to the union member. Neither should a superior gloat over being right in his or her original action. Instead, phrase your decision so that both the steward and the employee have an opportunity to save face—perhaps, "I can understand the way you feel, but you just didn't have all the facts that were available to me in making my decision," or "I hope this incident has made one thing clear to all of us—that in the future we will have to work harder at avoiding misunderstandings of this nature."

If the decision is favorable to the employee, it is important for the supervisor to try to avoid showing any feelings of resentment. A supervisor should realize that everybody makes mistakes. The important thing is to avoid the same error in the future.

If supervisors implement these suggestions, they will have a high probability of handling complaints at the first level of the grievance procedure. What we are really talking about is developing good communications between employees and supervisors and using a leadership style that is appropriate to the situation. It should also be apparent that handling grievances effectively is a topic that overlaps with handling the problem employee. Fair and consistent disciplinary action is the key factor.

THE GRIEVANCE PROCEDURE
IN NONUNION ORGANIZATIONS

In nonunion organizations, the traditional way to handle employee grievances is the "open door" policy. This means that if an employee has a complaint or grievance, he or she is free to discuss the matter with the supervisor at a mutually convenient time. The effectiveness of this approach depends on the fairness of the immediate supervisor. If supervisors "get even" or retaliate against employees who come forward with grievances, the open door policy will be a failure.

However, some nonunion organizations have adopted a grievance procedure similar to those found in unionized companies. The major difference is that in the nonunion setting there is seldom any provision for binding arbitration. Obviously, then, the final decision will rest with some higher-level manager in the organization. In our opinion arbitration is a necessary final step, because it ensures that employees will have a fair hearing in any disputes they bring for settlement.

Last but not least, if grievance procedures in the nonunion organization are to be effective, there must be *written* personnel policies. The rules of the organization must be specified before a grievance procedure will work.

SUMMARY AND CONCLUSIONS

A supervisor should be aware of the various provisions of our labor laws. Of primary importance is the fact that an employer cannot bribe, discriminate against, or in any way threaten an employee because of union activities.

A supervisor is a key figure in preparations for contract negotiations. It is important for management to know what employees are concerned about most, and, in their intermediate position, supervisors are best qualified to judge these concerns.

The immediate supervisor is also the key figure in preventing and handling grievances. The key factors in doing so are a thorough knowledge of the labor contract and a good working relationship with the shop steward and the employees under his or her supervision.

QUESTIONS

1. What can an organization do to make unions unnecessary?
2. What are some unfair labor practices employers can engage in?
3. Describe the structure of American labor unions.
4. What are the duties of business representatives and shop stewards?
5. Describe a typical grievance procedure.
6. What can a supervisor do to minimize the number of grievances?
7. Describe how a supervisor should handle a grievance.

WHO IS SENIOR?

The union contract states that overtime will be assigned on the basis of seniority, assuming ability to do the job. A list of employees under your supervision in order of seniority is provided by the personnel department. You use this list in drawing up schedules for overtime, which is normally on a voluntary basis.

Last Saturday you needed three people, so Friday afternoon you made the rounds to find out who would work. The three most senior people who wanted the overtime came in Saturday.

Monday morning, Ivan Dilski and Steve Bartin, the shop steward, wanted to know why Ivan hadn't been asked if he wanted the overtime. Ivan claimed that he had been with the company about three or four months longer than Mark Milkovich who did work on Saturday.

Your recollection of the list from personnel is that Milkovich is the next more senior employee to Dilski. Both were in this department when you were transferred here, so you personally don't know.

1. What should you do to respond to Ivan's complaint?

Assume you checked and found that in terms of continuous service, Ivan is three months senior to Mark. However, Mark's employment was interrupted by three years in the Army, and he had worked here for a year prior to military service. The union contract states that seniority will be based on continuous service. However, if one's employment is interrupted by sick leave, pregnancy, military service or layoff, time with the company prior to the interruption will count in computing seniority.

On the other hand, assume your investigation found that Ivan was correct. You had reversed the order of their names in your mind. In fact, the list from personnel showed that Ivan was more senior than Mark.

1. Plan two interviews with Ivan and Steve to tell them about your findings: one for when they are wrong and one for when you are wrong. Be prepared to role play both interviews with other members of the class.

NOTES

1 Taft-Hartley Act (Labor Management Relations Act) of 1947, as amended in 1959 by Public Law 86–257.

2 C. L. Hughes, *Making Unions Unnecessary* (New York: Executive Enterprises Publications, 1976).

3 A. W. J. Thomson, *The Grievance Procedure in the Private Sector* (Ithaca, N.Y.: State School of Industrial and Labor Relations, Cornell University, 1974).

4 J. F. Power, "Improving Arbitration: Roles of Parties and Agencies," *Monthly Labor Review, 95* (November 1972), p. 21.

5 Ibid.

6 W. S. Mossberg, "On the Line: As Union Man at Ford, Charlie Bragg Deals in Problems, Gripes," *The Wall Street Journal,* July 26, 1973, p. 1.

7 E. A. Fleishman and E. F. Harris, "Patterns of Leadership Behavior Related to Employee Grievances and Turnover," *Personnel Psychology, 15* (Spring 1962), 43–56.

8 M. S. Trotta, *Handling Grievances: A Guide for Management and Labor* (Washington, D.C.: The Bureau of National Affairs, 1976).

9 Ibid.

Equal Opportunity
Is
the Law

SUPERVISORY PROBLEMS

What are the equal employment laws and regulations which
a supervisor must understand?
How do they affect the supervisor's job?

Courtesy of A. T. & T. Co.

LEARNING OBJECTIVES

When you have finished this chapter, you should be able to

1. Identify the principal equal employment opportunity laws and regulations and describe their basic provisions
2. Discuss the first-level supervisor's role in adhering to and implementing these laws and regulations
3. Describe the impact of these laws and regulations on personnel practices and on employment opportunities for members of minority groups and females
4. List the main problems in supervising EEO programs
5. Identify questions commonly asked during employment interviews or on application blanks that are illegal
6. Describe characteristics of effective supervisors of minority employees
7. Explain the steps to be followed in discharging a female or minority group employee whose performance is substandard

---

DO YOU KNOW WHAT IS ILLEGAL JOB DISCRIMINATION?

Before reading this chapter, take this short test to see how well you understand the concept of job discrimination.

An Employer	True	False
1. as a general policy, can refuse to hire an applicant because of his/her arrest record	_____	_____
2. can pay men more than women doing the same job, if the men have families to support and the women are single or have husbands who are employed	_____	_____
3. can refuse to hire a 60-year-old qualified applicant because that person would only be able to work a few years before retirement	_____	_____
4. can refuse to hire women because they have small children at home	_____	_____
5. can require all pregnant employees to take a leave of absence at a particular time before the expected birth date	_____	_____

6. may hire only males for a job if state law
   prohibits employment of women in such a job   _____   _____
7. must hire minority applicants, even if
   they are not qualified, if the percentage
   of minority employees is less than the
   percentage of minority workers in the
   local community   _____   _____
8. must adjust work schedules to permit
   an employee time off for religious
   services, regardless of how inconvenient
   for the organization   _____   _____
9. must permit a person to work till age
   70 if they want to, regardless of
   job performance   _____   _____
10. can require that everyone hired has a high
    school diploma, even when level of edu-
    cation makes no difference in job
    performance   _____   _____

The objectives of this chapter are to familiarize you with the laws on equal employment opportunity and the administrative agencies involved in enforcement of these laws. In addition we will discuss the implications of these laws and regulations for the supervisor. It is important that supervisors understand the legal climate in which they must function, as well as the reasoning behind the regulations with which they must comply.

The first part of the chapter attempts to set straight the facts on equal employment opportunity. We can begin by noting that the answers to all the questions in our introductory quiz are false. However, most answers were different prior to 1963. Beginning on that year, legislation in the field of equal employment opportunity gathered momentum. The last part of the chapter focuses on what the supervisor has to do or has to avoid doing to be in compliance with the law. In addition, suggestions are made that might be helpful in supervising female and minority group employees.

The supervisor should realize the importance of his or her actions in this area. The supervisor is considered a part of the management group and his or her actions reflect the organization's compliance with the law. Recent settlements with some major companies illustrate just how costly errors in this area can be. Some examples include

Anaconda Aluminum Company had to pay $190,000 in back wages to 276 women.

Virginia Electric Power Company paid $250,000 to black workers.

Lorillard Corporation paid $500,000 in back pay to black employees.

Household Finance Corporation paid $125,000 to white-collar female employees who were denied promotion.

AT&T paid approximately $15,000,000 to thousands of employees who suffered from discriminatory employment practices, plus an estimated $50,000,000 in yearly payments for promotion and wage adjustments.

WHAT ARE THE EQUAL EMPLOYMENT OPPORTUNITY LAWS AND REGULATIONS?

The Equal Pay Act (1963)

The Equal Pay Act, passed in 1963, was the first federal legislation dealing with equal opportunity passed in this century. It is an amendment to the Fair Labor Standards Act. The intent of the Equal Pay Act is "equal pay for equal work." The law prohibits different pay scales for men and women doing essentially the "same" work. Jobs requiring substantially equal skills, effort, and responsibility performed under similar working conditions in the same establishment constitute the "same" work.

The objective of this legislation is to eliminate situations in which men are paid more than women doing essentially the same job. As of July 1, 1979, enforcement of the Equal Pay Act was taken over by the Equal Employment Opportunity Commission (a federal agency that will be discussed later in the chapter). Block 17–1 describes a violation of the Equal Pay Act.

Some might argue that on humanitarian grounds, Nussbaum *might* be justified but what he has done violates the Equal Pay Act. Wage and salary differences based on differences in job difficulty or on merit are legal, but differences based on sex roles are not.

The Civil Rights Act (1964)

The 1964 Civil Rights Act prohibits discrimination in employment because of race, color, religion, sex, or national origin. This law has had a major impact on employment patterns in the United States. It covers all private employers, state and local governments, educational institutions, and labor organizations with 15 or more members. It, too, is administered by the Equal Employment Opportunity Commission. The law pertains to all aspects of employment: hiring, promotion, demotion, transfer, layoff, selection for training programs, and rates of pay.

The Civil Rights Act is sometimes misinterpreted to mean that mem-

Gene Nussbaum, principal of the Green River Elementary School, was faced with a difficult decision. He was deciding how large the raises should be for each of the teachers in the school. The school board had decided that the raises should average 5 percent, but could range from 3 to 7 percent. The board felt that one-third should receive 7 percent raises, one-third 5 percent raises, and one-third 3 percent raises. The decision as to the size of each teacher's raise was to be made by Mr. Nussbaum.

The grouping of teachers into above-average, average, and below average had gone fairly well. Mr. Nussbaum was comfortable with his performance appraisals. What he was uncomfortable with was that John Samuels, one of the teachers at Green River, was clearly an average teacher but really needed the 7 percent raise. John is married, has three small children and his wife does not work. Most of those in the above-average grouping are married women whose husbands have good jobs. Some of them are older and no longer have children at home.

Mr. Nussbaum decided to "move" Samuels into the above-average category and "move" Denise Birch into the average category. Her children are finished with school and settled. Besides, her husband has a good paying job.

bers of minority groups or females are to receive preferential treatment in employment. This is not true (see Block 17–2), as is evident in the Supreme Court's ruling in the case of *Griggs* v. *Duke Power Company*. In this case Griggs questioned the company's requirements for employment of a high school diploma and a predetermined IQ score. Griggs argued that these hiring requirements were not necessary to perform lower-level jobs within the organization. The Supreme Court ruled against Duke Power Company. In discussing the case, the Supreme Court made the statements quoted in Block 17–2.

In *Griggs* v. *Duke Power Company*, the company was unable to show that, for the jobs in question, the requirements of a high school diploma and "successful" completion of the intelligence test were associated with higher levels of on-the-job performance. These requirements did, however, screen out a higher proportion of minority group applicants, because (1) a higher percentage of whites had completed high school and (2) on the average, whites scored higher on the intelligence test administered by Duke Power Company.

There are other aspects of the Griggs ruling which are important for supervisors to understand. First, to be in violation of the Civil Rights

BLOCK 17–2 Comments of the Supreme Court on *Griggs* v. *Duke Power Company*

Congress did not intend by Title VII (The Civil Rights Act), however, to guarantee a job to every person regardless of qualifications. In short, the Act does not command that any person be hired simply because he was formerly the subject of discrimination, or because he is a member of a minority group. Discriminatory preference for any group, minority or majority, is precisely and only what Congress has proscribed [forbidden]. What is required by Congress is the removal of artificial, arbitrary, and unnecessary barriers to employment when the barriers operate invidiously to discriminate on the basis of racial or other impermissible classifications. . . .

. . . Congress has not commanded that the less qualified be preferred over the better qualified simply because of minority origins. Far from disparaging [lower the importance of] job qualifications as such, Congress has made such qualifications the controlling factor, so that race, religion, nationality, and sex become irrelevant.[1]

Act, it is not necessary to prove that the employer is *intentionally* discriminating against minorities or females. If a hiring requirement screens out minorities at a higher rate than whites and *is not related to success on the job,* then it is illegal. The employer's *intentions* or motives make no difference. Second, if a hiring requirement results in the rejection of a higher percentage of minority group applicants than whites, or a higher percentage of females than males, it is up to the *employer* to prove that the hiring requirement is related to success on the job.

Figure 17–1 presents an example which indicates the kind of evidence an employer is expected to be able to present in order to justify a hiring requirement. The example considers the requirement of a high school diploma. Figure 17–1 shows that for this job 80 percent who have completed high school are satisfactory performers, but among those who have not completed high school only 40 percent are satisfactory performers. In such a situation, having a high school diploma is clearly

FIGURE 17–1 Association Between High School Diploma and Job Performance: *Hypothetical Example*

	Job Performance	
High School Diploma	*Satisfactory*	*Unsatisfactory*
Yes	80%	20%
No	40%	60%

associated with satisfactory job performance, and the employer *would be* justified in requiring job candidates to have a high school diploma. This requirement would be legal even though it might result in the rejection of members of minority groups more often than whites.

The supervisor is a key figure in gathering evidence to prove that hiring requirements are related to job success. This is because the usual measure of job success is performance ratings, and the immediate supervisor is generally the person best able to evaluate employee job performance.

In some cases an employer can use the results of job analysis to justify certain hiring requirements that screen out minorities or females at a higher rate. The immediate supervisor also plays a key role in job analysis.

Equal Employment Opportunity Act (1972)

The Equal Employment Opportunity Act is an amendment to the 1964 Civil Rights Act. This law reemphasizes the concern of Congress for ensuring equal employment opportunity. The principal change brought about by the Equal Employment Opportunity Act is the increase in enforcement powers of the Equal Employment Opportunity Commission (EEOC). As a result of this law, the EEOC is now permitted to take employers accused of discrimination into U.S. District Court.

Figure 17–2 describes the steps followed in responding to complaints made by an employee or a job applicant to the EEOC. After receiving a complaint, the EEOC investigates. For example, the EEOC might contact the employer, discuss the circumstances surrounding the case, and review employer records relevant to the complaint. Following the investigation, the EEOC representative will make a judgment: Is there evidence that the complaint is justified, that is, evidence of discrimination? If the EEOC finding is that there is no discrimination, the person making the complaint can, on his or her own, take the complaint into the U.S. Federal District Court.

If the EEOC finds that there is evidence supporting the charge of discrimination, the next step will be an attempt to gain the voluntary compliance of the employer. If the employer voluntarily agrees to stop the practice causing the complaint or is willing to otherwise satisfy the person bringing the complaint, the issue is settled. If not, then one of two actions can be taken: Either the EEOC or the person making the complaint can go to U.S. District Court.

The reason behind passage of the Equal Employment Opportunity Act was that large organizations, with their legal staffs, were able to intimidate or bluff their way out of many valid complaints. Because of

FIGURE 17–2   Processing a Charge of Discrimination by the EEOC

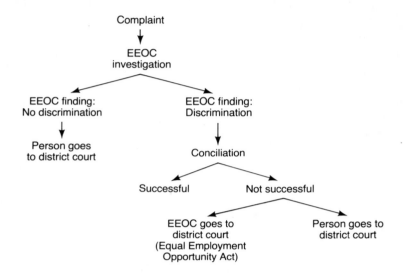

their substantial financial resources, organizations were able to get away with continuing discriminatory practices, despite the fact that the EEOC found evidence of discrimination.

Conflict Between State and Federal Laws

Many states have legislation designed to protect working women. Examples include laws prohibiting women from being employed on jobs which

1. Are thought to be especially hazardous
2. Involve lifting heavy objects
3. Require working a night shift
4. Involve working long hours (usually in excess of 10 to 12 hours per day)

The Civil Rights Act overrides such state laws. As a result, such laws now apply equally to both men and women. For example, a law that no one can be required to work more than 12 hours per day or lift objects weighing more than 75 pounds would not violate the federal law.

This means that an employer cannot refuse to hire a woman qualified to do a particular job because such employment is prohibited by state protective labor legislation. For example, if a state law prohibits women from working in jobs which require regular lifting of an object weighing more than 50 pounds, an employer cannot refuse to hire a woman for such a job because of the state law. The employer would have to determine if specific applicants, both male and female, have the strength and endurance to perform the job.

Executive Orders 11246 and 11375

Presidential Executive Orders on equal employment opportunity apply to those organizations which have contracts with the federal government. Executive Order 11246, issued in 1965, prohibits discrimination on the basis of race, creed, color, or national origin by those organizations doing business with the federal government. Executive Order 11375, issued in 1967, prohibits discrimination based on sex. The principal requirement of these executive orders is a written *affirmative action plan* for those organizations with 50 or more employees and a contract with the federal government of $50,000 or more.

The terms *equal employment opportunity* and *affirmative action* are sometimes confused when the topic of discrimination in work organizations is discussed. *Equal employment opportunity* assures all job applicants and employees of an equal chance in employment based on their qualifications to perform the job in question. Discrimination is prohibited in *all* areas of employment, including recruiting, hiring, training, promotion, benefits, discipline, and discharge.

Affirmative action, on the other hand, goes beyond equal employment opportunity. It requires the employer to make an extra effort to hire, train, and promote members of minority groups and females. An affirmative action plan specifies the steps an employer is taking, or will take, to guarantee equal opportunity to members of minority groups and to women. For example, the employer might plan to recruit job applicants from schools in predominantly minority neighborhoods or from women's colleges. The plan not only specifies goals and objectives, but also includes a timetable for improving the employment opportunities for members of minority groups and for women.

Executive orders are administered by the Office of the Federal Contract Compliance (OFCC). Compared to the EEOC, the OFCC has a big enforcement club that it can hold over the head of an employer. It can cancel a contract with the federal government and disqualify the organization from further federal contracts.

Evidence of Discrimination for EEOC and Affirmative Action

Basically, the evidence that the EEOC and the OFCC seek is whether minority groups and women are "underrepresented" in the organization's work force. They compare the percentage of minority group members and women in the given organization with the percentage in the local labor force. If, for example, Mexican-Americans make up 20 percent of the local labor force it would be expected that the employing organization would have about 20 percent Mexican-Americans on its payroll.

Another item to be checked in equal employment opportunity or affirmative action analysis is the *level* at which members of minority groups and women are employed in the organization. For example, are women or members of minority groups employed at the supervisory and managerial levels of an organization or only in lower-level jobs? An organization will have trouble explaining why all its women employees are in clerical positions or why minority group employees hold down the majority of unskilled jobs. Block 17–3 describes an organization in which job level was thought to be an irrelevant factor.

Age Discrimination Act (1967)

The Age Discrimination Act of 1967 prohibits not hiring, firing, or in any way discriminating against an individual because of age. When the Act was passed in 1967, it applied to those between the ages of 40 and 65. An amendment passed in 1978 prohibits mandatory retirement prior to age 70.

This law was designed to remedy the higher rates and longer terms of unemployment commonly found among older workers. Evidence concerning productivity and accident rates suggests that older workers are

---

BLOCK 17–3   The Bank of Albany

At the time this incident took place, the Bank of Albany employed 67 people. There were five officers in the bank; all were men. The remaining 62 employees (all women) filled customer service and clerical positions. Some of these women were in first-level supervisory positions.

Ivan Fox, one of the junior officers, received a job offer he could not refuse and resigned. The bank informally put out the word that there was an opening for a recent college graduate majoring in business, preferably with an MBA. Allison Baker learned of the opening and applied for the position. She had an MBA, was interested in a banking career, and wanted to live in the Albany area.

Jack Adams, president of the bank, spoke to Allison after reviewing her application. He informed her that while her credentials met the requirements of the job he was unable to offer her employment. He pointed out that 92 percent (62 of 67) of the bank's employees were women; therefore, the bank had to hire a man for this position, because equal employment opportunity laws prohibit sex discrimination, and the bank already had an overrepresentation of female employees.

equally effective as younger workers, so the reasoning was that such a law would protect the rights of deserving, older workers.

The Age Discrimination Act covers employers with 20 or more employees and pertains to all aspects of employment—promotions, demotions, vacations, sick leave, access to training programs, job assignments, transfers, seniority, and compensation and fringe benefits. As with other EEO legislation, if it can be proved that youth is associated with better job performance, an employer who uses age as a selection criterion is not guilty of age discrimination. For example, in the case of *Hodgson* v. *Greyhound Lines,* it was found that Greyhound's right to impose a hiring cutoff at age 35 for bus drivers was justified. Greyhound convinced the Court that the age limit was a reasonable occupational qualification, because after age 35 speed of reflexes and reaction time begin to slow down.

An employer is always permitted to discharge or otherwise discipline an individual for unsatisfactory job performance regardless of age. For example, if an individual's job performance deteriorates with advancing age and the employer can show the reduction in performance, then the employer can either discharge the individual or transfer the person to a job he or she can perform satisfactorily.

Vocational Rehabilitation Act of 1973

This Act requires all employers with federal contracts of over $2,500 to take affirmative action to recruit, hire, and promote handicapped persons who meet reasonable qualifications for jobs. The objective of this legislation is to remove artificial barriers to employment of the handicapped.

Contractors are required to hire qualified handicapped individuals who, with reasonable accommodation to the handicap, can perform a job at the same level expected of a nonhandicapped employee. Both the Age Discrimination Act and the Vocational Rehabilitation Act are administered by the Equal Employment Opportunity Commission.

WHAT HAS BEEN THE IMPACT OF EQUAL EMPLOYMENT OPPORTUNITY LEGISLATION?

A recent survey on the impact of equal employment opportunity legislation points up some of the problems encountered by employers in supervising equal employment opportunity and affirmative action programs. Figure 17–3 presents the highlights of this survey.

FIGURE 17-3   Impact of Equal Opportunity Legislation

Section I	Percentage of Employers Who Have
Recruiting, Selection, and Layoff Policies	
Specific recruiting programs for minorities	69
Specific recruiting programs for women in traditionally male jobs	61
Changed selection procedures	60
No special treatment to minorities or women in layoffs	88

Section II

	Percentage of Employers Who Have
Programs for Implementing EEO Policies	
Communications on EEO policy	95
Follow-up by personnel or EEO officer	85
Training sessions on EEO	67
Periodic publication of EEO results	48
EEO achievements included in performance appraisal	33

EEO Program Results	1967	1975
Highest position held by minority		
Executive	2	24
Middle management	12	43
Highest position held by a woman		
Executive	13	32
Middle management	24	39
Women employed in positions previously held only by men	43	84

EEO Results		
Men employed in positions previously held only by women	10	49
Minority group members employed in positions previously held by whites only	not available	69

Section III

Most Difficult Problems in Administering EEO Programs

One-third: Finding qualified minorities and women for the job categories in which they are underrepresented

One-fourth: The reluctance of managers and supervisors to accept and adhere to EEO policies and guidelines

One-tenth: Record keeping and reports

Source: *Equal Employment Opportunity: Programs and Results,* Personnel Policy Forum Survey No. 112 (Washington, D.C.: Bureau of National Affairs, March 1976).

Concerning recruiting programs, 69 percent of the employers surveyed indicate that specific programs focusing on the recruitment of minorities have been developed, and 61 percent indicate such programs have been developed for women applicants. In recruiting minorities, the most effective techniques have been found to be:

1. Direct contact with community agencies and interested local groups
2. Recruiting through present employees
3. Contacting educational institutions (colleges, high schools, and trade schools) which enroll a high proportion of minority group members

In recruiting women, advertising is reported to be most effective, while contacting educational institutions and recruiting through present employees are auxiliary methods.

One effect of the 1964 Civil Rights Act has been to alter or eliminate selection procedures which might result in discrimination against minorities or women. Sixty percent of the responding organizations report some such changes, for example, eliminating tests shown to be irrelevant to job success, revising educational requirements that screen out minorities unnecessarily, and deleting from application blanks questions about a candidate's arrest record.

Concerning layoff policies, among those organizations having had layoffs prior to the survey, nearly nine out of ten companies (88 percent) did not give special treatment to minorities or women in deciding which employees were to be laid off. In most of these companies, the layoffs were made on the basis of seniority.

Those surveyed were asked, "Have any measures been taken to ensure that equal employment opportunity policies are followed by supervisors and others making hiring and promotion decisions?" Ninety-six percent of the responding companies answered yes to this question.

The different forms of action taken to ensure compliance with EEO policies are highlighted in the second section of Figure 17–3. The most common practice is some form of communication with supervisors on EEO policy, for example, written documents outlining the organization's EEO policy. About two-thirds of the responding organizations conduct training programs for supervisors which emphasize the importance of equal employment rules.

This survey suggests there has been an increase in employment opportunities for minority group and women employees as a result of the civil rights legislation. A comparison of the responses made in 1967 with those made in 1975 shows that the proportion of organizations having minority group members at middle and executive management levels has increased significantly. Perhaps more important, automatic stereotyping of jobs as male or female jobs is also decreasing.

The most common problems reported in administering EEO are indicated in the last section of Figure 17–3. The number one problem is finding qualified women and minority group applicants for jobs in which they are underrepresented. The second major problem is the reluctance of management and supervisory personnel to follow equal employment opportunity and affirmative action programs. Organizations reported having trouble convincing first-level supervisors of the serious consequences of noncompliance with EEO regulations. They did not understand that the company is responsible for the actions of individual supervisors.

WHAT ARE THE IMPLICATIONS OF EQUAL OPPORTUNITY REGULATIONS FOR THE SUPERVISOR?

As a result of the civil rights legislation, a number of changes in organizational personnel practices have occurred. The changes have focused on eliminating loopholes that can restrict equality of opportunity. Ways of changing rules and policies to improve equal opportunity include:

1. Open posting of job opportunities in the organization
2. Recruiting programs that advertise job opportunities to all types of schools and individuals
3. Development of a performance appraisal system for identifying promotable or high-potential employees within the organization
4. Validation of selection and promotional criteria
5. Review of organizational practices to ensure that they do not have a discriminating effect on women or minorities (for example, height or weight requirements)
6. Discussion of results of performance appraisal and career development plans with employees at all levels within the organization

All of these ideas for overcoming barriers to equal employment opportunity affect the job of the supervisor to some extent since the supervisor is the key source of information. For example, identifying high-potential employees, validation of selection procedures, and discussion of performance appraisals with employees, all rely on the supervisor as the primary source of information concerning an individual's performance and potential.

The importance of the supervisor in implementing effective equal employment opportunity programs cannot be overemphasized. The supervisor is the organization's representative to the employees. And it is the supervisor who must effectively implement the plans and programs. For these reasons training in the area of equal employment opportunity is crucial.

What Can't Be Asked in an Interview or on a Job Application Blank

Block 17–4 shows a case that is not all that unusual. Criteria for hiring and the reasons behind them have evolved in the department store over many years and have never been questioned.

Although the thinking behind Mr. Allen's standards is undoubtedly still widespread today, the fact is that these criteria discriminate against women or against members of minority groups and are illegal. The law prohibits the use of all selection criteria or rules which disqualify a larger percentage of members of minority groups or persons of one sex. To use such hiring criteria, they must be valid predictors of successful job performance. Specific issues which have been addressed by court and EEOC decisions include: [2]

 1. *Height and weight.* Minimum height and weight requirements are illegal if they disproportionately screen out members of minority groups (for

---

BLOCK 17–4   The Arrow Department Store

Robert Allen, manager of the Arrow Department Store, had been in that position for many years. Over the years he had developed a list of several characteristics and requirements he looked for in hiring people to work in the store. The following is a partial list of his selection criteria and a brief indication of his reasoning.

1. Among applicants who have served in the military, hire only those who have an honorable discharge. If one can't get along well enough to get an honorable discharge from the Army, he/she probably won't work out here.

2. Hire only men for supervisory positions. Usually women don't like that kind of responsibility, and they don't have the right temperament for making decisions and leading. Also, women typically aren't as committed to a work career. They get married and quit work to raise a family, or their husbands get transferred or get better jobs somewhere else. In any case, the outcome is the same.

3. Never hire anyone with an arrest or conviction record, regardless of job.

4. When hiring someone who will often interact with customers, give preference to those who are good-looking and of average height and weight. Customers prefer to deal with good-looking people. They don't like to deal with unusual people.

5. Give preference to those applicants who own a home and have kids. These characteristics are a sign of stability and maturity.

---

example, Asian-Americans and Mexican-Americans) or women, unless the employer can show that these standards are essential for safe or effective performance of a job. Examples which have been ruled illegal include height and weight requirements for police officers and guards at a correctional institution.

2. *Marital status, number of children, and provision for child care.* Questions about marital status, pregnancy, future childbearing plans, and number and ages of children have been frequently used to discriminate against women. The Supreme Court has ruled that preemployment inquiries about child care arrangements *that are asked only of female applicants* are in violation of the law. An employer may not have different hiring policies for men and women with preschool children. Thus, asking such questions only of women in job interviews or on application blanks is illegal. Also, it is illegal to refuse to hire a woman because she is engaged. Information about these issues which may be needed for tax, insurance, or social security purposes can be obtained after employment.

3. *Educational requirements.* The requirement of a high school education is illegal if the employer is unable to furnish evidence that the diploma is related to successful job performance. This applies to all levels of education where there is no direct evidence to show that education is related to job success.

4. *English language skills.* Where English language skill is not related to performance of the work in question, such a requirement is in violation of the Civil Rights Act. It has a discriminatory effect on members of certain minority groups.

5. *Arrest record.* Members of some minority groups are arrested substantially more often than whites. The courts have held that without proof of "business necessity," an employer's use of arrest records to disqualify a job applicant is unlawful.

6. *Conviction record.* An arrest is only an accusation. A more appropriate question is, "Have you been convicted of a serious crime?" Even here, however, this question is in violation of the Civil Rights Act unless the applicant would have responsibility for money or security in the performance of the job in question.

7. *Discharge from military service.* Because the number of less than honorable discharges from military service is higher among minority group members, the criterion of an honorable discharge has been ruled illegal. Generally, you may ask about an individual's job experience and training while in military service but not about the applicant's military discharge.

8. *Citizenship.* The law protects all individuals, both citizens and noncitizens, living in the United States. A person legally living in the United States may not be discriminated against on the basis of his or her citizenship except in the interest of national security. Where states have enacted laws prohibiting the employment of noncitizens, these have been superseded by the Civil Rights Act of 1964.

9. *Credit ratings.* Rejection of applicants because of poor credit ratings

results in higher rates of rejection of minority group members and has been found to be unlawful by the EEOC, unless the employer is able to demonstrate that credit ratings are associated with successful job performance or business necessity.

10. *Availability for work on weekends or holidays.* Questions concerning a person's availability for work on Friday evenings, Saturdays, Sundays, or holidays are not automatically violations of the law. However, employers have *an obligation to try to accommodate* the religious beliefs of employees.

11. *Car or home ownership.* Unless the applicant is applying for a job in which a car is a necessity, as in some sales positions, this may discriminate against minority group members and consequently should be avoided.

SUPERVISION
OF MINORITY GROUP EMPLOYEES

A common problem among minority group employees is that turnover may be quite high during the first year. The first-line supervisor plays a key part in ensuring that such workers make a smooth adjustment into the job situation. The supervisor must walk a thin line in this process—a hard-nosed approach probably won't work with a minority worker.

Supportive behavior on the part of the supervisor seems to be critical. An attitude of *empathy* is most appropriate: Putting oneself into the minority worker's position and trying to see the situation as the new hire sees it seems to be the most effective technique in improving communications with the person. However, we strongly recommend avoiding such "openers" as, "I went to school with blacks," or "Some of my best friends are Mexican-Americans." These may be well intended but often create a negative impression.

One survey identified those qualities and attitudes a first-line supervisor should demonstrate in order to be successful with minority group employees.[3] Figure 17–4 summarizes the results of this study.

Supervision of Female Employees

There has been very little space in the literature devoted specifically to supervision of female workers. In our opinion, however, many of the traits that have been given special emphasis with respect to minority group employees apply just as well to the supervision of female employees (actually to *any* group of employees). Male supervisors should be careful to avoid stereotyped thinking about women, especially when they occupy

FIGURE 17–4   Qualities of the Successful Supervisor
                of Minority Group Employees

Conveys ideas well to others
Is willing to listen to others
Works well with others
Goes out of his or her way to help others
Is considerate of other people
Shows respect for all
Is willing to learn new methods of supervision
Is alert to ways and means of gaining cooperation

positions traditionally staffed by male employees. General rules of fairness and objectivity as we have outlined them elsewhere are appropriate. Give the female employee a chance to prove herself, provide appropriate training, and attempt to be objective in evaluating the quality of job performance.

An area which *has* received some notice is the problems encountered by women in supervisory positions.[4] Some of these problems are

1. The expectation that women supervisors will do their own filing and clerical chores
2. The reluctance of female subordinates to recognize that a female supervisor is not just another "one of the girls"
3. The reluctance to send women on business trips alone
4. The difficulty some women have in paying the meal tab
5. The intolerance of any display of emotion or ambition by women in the office, even though the same behavior is accepted of a male employee
6. The expectation that women who are supervisors will take notes and serve the coffee at a meeting of supervisors

Central to this list of problems is an idea that is hard to dispel, even among women themselves. It is that to be feminine, a woman must be dependent or subservient. Subservient, in this case, means that women are capable of handling *details,* such as filing or recording minutes of a meeting, but that positions involving *real responsibility* are beyond their capabilities. To generalize about any group of persons, to project group "traits" onto the individual, is one of the most serious—and common— human failings. In Block 17–5 one supervisor gives this issue some thought.

Discharge of a Female
or Minority Group Employee

With equal employment opportunity legislation, there is pressure on an organization to increase the proportion of the work force composed of minority group and female employees. As a result, there is an under-

Ralph Smith was giving some thought to the rationale behind the equal opportunity laws and regulations. In essence he thought it boiled down to one basic idea. Within any group of people, there are differences among individuals in the capacity to perform a given job. Some people have the ability, given appropriate training, to be successful physicians, others can be successful machinists, supervisors, engineers, teachers, what-have-you. What the law prohibits is stereotyped employment decisions, or employment decisions which do not consider differences in individual abilities. Employers are expected to hire, compensate, promote, and discharge on the basis of ability and performance, without regard to race, religion, sex, national origin, age, or handicap. Ralph thought to himself, "Put in those terms, the laws seem reasonable and fair."

standable reluctance in some organizations to discharge a minority group or female employee whose job performance is poor. What should be done in such a situation?

The best approach is to be fair. After the individual has had ample opportunity to overcome poor performance, has received the necessary training, has been formally informed of the substandard nature of his or her job performance, such an employee should be discharged. The recommended procedures are discussed in detail in the chapter on discipline. The critical point for the supervisor is to make sure that the employee has been given ample opportunity to learn the job, and that formal records are maintained to demonstrate that the individual has been given a fair chance. We are certainly not suggesting that such records need only be kept for minorities and female employees—such information should be kept for all employees! Everyone should receive a fair chance to perform on the job. If someone fails to measure up to the established standards then the employer is justified in terminating employment. Again, the successful implementation of procedures falls mainly on the shoulders of the supervisor.

SUMMARY AND CONCLUSIONS

The Equal Pay Act, the Civil Rights Act, the Equal Employment Opportunity Act, the Age Discrimination Act, and the Vocational Rehabilitation Act are the principle laws concerning equal employment opportunity. The laws prohibit discrimination in all phases of employment, hiring, promotion, access to training, compensation, lay-off and discharge, on the basis of race, religion, sex, national origin, age, or physical handicap. Employers must make employment decisions based on an individual's ability and job performance, and not on the basis of stereotype.

In addition, employers doing business with the federal government are required by Executive Orders 11246 and 11375 to go beyond providing equal employment opportunity by engaging in affirmative action— that is, they must make an extra effort to hire, train, and promote members of minority groups and females.

As a result of these laws and regulations, most employers have changed recruiting and selection procedures and attempt to attract minority group and female applicants. These programs appear to have had a good measure of success judging from the increase between 1967 and 1975 in the percentage of companies reporting women and minorities in middle-management and executive positions, women employed in positions previously held only by men, and men in positions previously held only by women.

In an effort to implement EEO programs, most companies have training programs for supervisors and also engage EEO specialists to follow up on the implementation of EEO policies. Implementation is crucial. Yet one-fourth of the organizations in a recent survey report that the most difficult problem in administering EEO programs is *the reluctance of managers and supervisors to accept and adhere to these programs.*

The first-level supervisor is the key figure in implementing EEO programs. In interviewing applicants for jobs under his or her supervision, the first-level supervisor must exercise care in avoiding certain questions. To validate selection criteria and to identify promotion potential and training needs, performance appraisals are necessary. Again, the immediate supervisor is best able to provide these performance appraisals. This person is typically also the one called on to discuss the results of the appraisal with the employee.

The successful supervisor of minority group and/or female employees possesses effective communication skills and is empathetic and understanding. The supervisor must recognize individual differences in abilities and job performance and avoid stereotyped thinking.

QUESTIONS

1. Explain the principle underlying equal employment opportunity legislation.
2. Equal employment opportunity legislation requires that preferences be given to minority groups and females. Do you agree or disagree? Explain.

3. What is the difference between equal employment opportunity and affirmative action?
4. Describe the type of evidence the EEOC will look for when investigating a charge of race or sex discrimination.
5. Suppose state law prohibits the employment of women in hazardous jobs such as mining. Can an employer refuse to hire women for such jobs because of state law?
6. Explain how the supervisor can be the key figure in determining whether or not an organization's EEO programs will be effective.
7. Describe the behavior of a supervisor who is effective in supervising minority group and female employees.

AJAX MANUFACTURING

Peter Garcia was hired as a machinist three months ago. During the first month both his job performance and attendance were satisfactory. However, during the last six weeks, there has been a noticeable change for the worse. It is your recollection that he called in sick on one occasion and failed to show up for work without explanation on another. You have noticed that he is absent from his work station quite often lately. Also, the number of units he produces that are rejected by quality control seems to be increasing and the number of satisfactory units seems to be decreasing.

You are trying to decide what to do. An important consideration in your decision is that Juanita Rodriguez, the Ajax EEO officer, announced at the supervisors' meeting last week that Ajax is falling behind on its affirmative action plan. Miss Rodriguez said that the specific problem was underrepresentation of minority group members and females in skilled production jobs.

This is critical because the principal product of Ajax Manufacturing is replacement parts for field artillery, and the principal customer is the U.S. Army.

1. Should action be taken which could result in Mr. Garcia's discharge? Why or why not?
2. Can you identify any problems in the way you, the supervisor, have handled this situation so far?
3. List the steps you should take in dealing with Mr. Garcia.

BACKGROUND AND GOALS

On the next page are pictures of four young people. After studying their photographs, write a paragraph describing what you would expect is the background, current work situation, and future career plans of each one of the individuals pictured.

NOTES

1 *Willie S. Griggs et al. v. Duke Power Company,* March 8, 1971, 401 U.S. 424.

2 U.S. Equal Employment Opportunity Commission, *Preemployment Inquiries and Equal Employment Opportunity Law.*

3 Robert L. Finkelmeier, "The First-Line Supervisor Who Directs the Disadvantaged Worker," *Training and Development Journal,* February 1973, pp. 26–30.

4 "New Answers to An Old Question: Women's Place Is in the What?" by Richard Allen Stull. Reprinted with permission *Personnel Journal,* copyright January 1973.

The Supervisor and Safety

 SUPERVISORY PROBLEMS

What can I do to keep the work place safe?
What are my responsibilities under the Occupational Health
and Safety Act?

LEARNING OBJECTIVES

When you have finished this chapter, you should be able to

1. Construct a plan for an effective safety program in a particular supervisory work unit
2. Discuss the pros and cons of discipline for safety violations
3. Explain ways to make the most common safety administration devices more effective
4. Identify the psychological conditions in a work situation that are likely to be related to accident rates
5. Answer the question, Is there such a thing as accident proneness?
6. Teach someone about OSHA and its effect on work organizations and supervisors

---

WHICH COMES FIRST, SAFETY OR PRODUCTION?

While looking over the monthly reports, the superintendent noticed that the two safety meetings scheduled to be held by foreman Ann Dalton in her department had not been held. The superintendent also recalled that Dalton's regular monthly safety inspection report had come in nearly two weeks late. The superintendent called Dalton in and asked for an explanation. Ann's answer was that production pressure had kept her completely snowed under. The situation had been doubly difficult because two of her most important employees were out with injuries.

"Do you think the safety program we have set up will reduce injuries if it is properly carried out?" the superintendent asked. "Yes, I'm sure it would," Dalton answered. The superintendent then pointed out that if Ann had pushed an active safety campaign in the department, the injuries to her two critical people might not have happened. "Maybe so, but in times of rush production, I feel I have to put the work ahead of routine meetings and reports," Ann answered.

In the discussion that followed, an agreement was reached that Ann could carry on an effective safety program in the department by using only a very small percentage of the total available working time. Ann admitted that most of the effective things a supervisor can do to keep workers interested in safety can be done at the same time she is making contact with individual workers on other matters pertaining to the job.

Immediately following the conversation with the superintendent, Ann

Dalton made a very careful plan for the weekly safety schedule and found that she *could* give closer attention to safety. This could be done by setting aside 15 minutes at the end of the first hour of the day for such things as systematic equipment inspection, follow-up on safety, contacts with individual workers, and inspection of work hazards. Ann decided that the necessary precautions to prevent accidents could be taken during the course of her routine supervisory duties.

A good safety record doesn't just happen, it requires a number of people doing a number of things properly. More organizations are showing greater interest and concern over safety than they did just a few years ago. Safety clauses are making more frequent appearances in union contract agreements, and safety is being viewed as an important factor in overall job satisfaction.

No organization, however small, can afford to overlook the issue of job safety. Developing safe working conditions requires the involvement of many people. Top management, for example, must demonstrate its concern about safety for any such program to work. In some organizations, staff people are involved, perhaps as safety supervisors or safety managers. Most important of all, however, is the supervisor. Most safety experts see the supervisor as the critical link in promoting a safe work environment and work habits.

It usually falls upon the supervisor to enforce safety procedures on a daily basis. If the supervisor doesn't do his or her job, the efforts of top management or of staff simply won't make much difference. The supervisor typically (1) investigates all accidents to determine why they occurred, (2) inspects the work area routinely for unrecognized hazards, (3) coaches the employees on safe work methods, and (4) instills among his or her subordinates a *desire* to work safely. It is also up to the supervisor to (5) enforce safe job procedures, (6) set the example for safety, and (7) deal with those employees who *can't be trained* to work safely on the job.

One study attempted to determine which factors were most important to a successful comprehensive safety program.[1] Over 140 companies took part in the survey and completed a questionnaire rating the importance of various safety activities. *Supervisory participation* was found to be the most important single aspect of making a safety program work.

WHY IS SAFETY SO OFTEN NEGLECTED?

Safety often gets lost in the shuffle because so much of a supervisor's work is *scheduled* and must be completed at a certain time of the day. Thus, despite good intentions, many supervisors keep putting off doing anything about safety. Further, some supervisors fail to recognize the very real importance of safety, including the effects neglect of safety precautions has on the other results in the department. There is also a tendency on the part of many supervisors to "take a chance" on safety, perhaps because it is one of those activities whose effects are more felt in the *absence* than in the careful adherence to duty.

Interestingly enough, a supervisor really doesn't need to spend a great deal of time making most departments safe. Fifteen minutes a day at a regular time, if used effectively, can produce some amazing results. After all, the supervisor that is in charge of the work is the one who has to prevent accidents. No one else can do very much about it. He or she is in the best position to do the many small things necessary to prevent accidents on the job.

Prevention Is the Key

It has been argued that 98 percent of all accidents are of a preventable type. Accident prevention is an area in which supervisory effort really pays off, because the methods that prevent accidents are much the same as those which control quantity, cost, waste, efficiency, and good employee relations. Let's think through a practical six-step plan for preventing accidents.

Step 1: Budget Some Definite Time for Safety

The supervisor must first commit himself or herself to budgeting a definite amount of personal time, perhaps 15 minutes a day, to the consideration of safety matters. This does not mean that you shut your mind to matters of safety for the rest of the day. It does mean, however, that you should develop a habit of close, daily personal attention to safety. This is very important. If it is neglected, your departmental safety record will not be nearly as good.

Step 2: Make a Thorough Survey of All Hazards

There are three direct causes of all accidents: unsafe conditions, unsafe acts, and unsafe attitudes. The purpose of the hazard survey is to detect not only the hazards, but the unsafe conditions in any work area. The real starting point of accident prevention is to *know* about unsafe conditions and unsafe acts and to correct them before the accident happens.

The first move in making a hazard survey is to set up a simple card file for each piece of machinery or potentially unsafe condition in the department. This will help you make sure that you have covered all of them and will at the same time serve as a checklist for later inspections. Next, if a safety code is available from either OSHA (the Occupational Safety and Health Administration) or from the manufacturer of the machinery, this should be read and reviewed. Then, carefully check each piece of machinery and its condition against the standards. Make a notation on your file card showing the date you inspected the equipment, the conditions found, and what action, if any, was taken to fix unsafe situations.

Hazards may be discovered in many different areas:

1. *Work area hazards:* Check housekeeping, storage, piling, cramped corners, stairways, inclines, aisles, blind exits, holes, excavations, illumination, exposed electrical heat, or obstacle hazards. Most office accidents occur from falls. Slippery floors, rugs, and poor lighting are some of the things to be watched in office situations.
2. *Material handling hazards:* Ask yourself, Are materials handled on the job heavy, rough, sharp, hot, slippery, long, poisonous, explosive, fragile, flammable, or acid?
3. *Machine hazards:* Consider point of operation, cutting, forming, power transmission, line shaft, belts, gears, pinch points, projections, or flying pieces.
4. *Hand tool hazards:* Consider proper tools for jobs, proper use of tools, proper place for tools, proper condition of tools.
5. *Clothing hazards:* Watch for improper clothing: loose, ragged flammable clothing; neckties; jewelry; high heels or thin soles. Consider need for protective clothing for head, feet, hands, or body.
6. *Poor ventilation:* Is the ventilation sufficient that dust and other particles or odors from chemicals are removed so that the workers don't have to breathe them?

Eighty-nine percent of all accidents result from human failure. However, we can't underestimate the importance of checking machinery to prevent injury. Injuries resulting from mechanical causes are usually serious.

Step 3: Make a Thorough Survey of Work Methods

The purpose of the work methods survey is to detect and correct the second direct cause of accidents—the unsafe acts of workers. Most accidents are caused by unsafe acts, and a plan that does not include continuous safety education with systematic follow-up to detect and correct unsafe acts is not complete. The following unsafe acts are common:

1. Operating machines or equipment without authorization or instruction. All workers, both long-time employees and new hires, should receive instruction on new assignments.
2. Oiling, cleaning, adjusting, or repairing a machine or equipment while

it is in motion. This unsafe act is especially dangerous if a worker wears clothing that is likely to be caught in the machine.

3. Failure to wear personal protective equipment. Goggles, helmets, safety shoes, and so on should be carefully chosen for the hazards involved and should be maintained in good condition.

4. Failure to keep safety devices in place. Mechanical safeguards are injury preventers only when they are kept in place and in operation. They should be properly designed and kept in place.

5. Taking an unsafe position. Standing on chairs, descending ladders improperly, working on high ladders which are not secure, lifting improperly, and so forth are unsafe acts that will develop into accidents when the unexpected happens.

6. Distracting or startling a person and horseplay often result in accidents. For example, the standard shop "practical joke" of directing compressed air against any part of another person's body has caused many serious and even fatal injuries.

7. Operating at unsafe speed is an act that has resulted in numerous accidents.

8. Improper use of equipment. Using wrenches for hammers, ladders for working platforms, file cabinets for ladders, and so on, are unsafe acts that can, and do, result in frequent accidents and injuries.

These are among the most common unsafe acts. The supervisor who makes a habit of looking for unsafe acts and conditions on the job before an accident happens is progressing well toward decreasing accidents in his or her department.

Step 4: Train Your Employees

Complete cooperation on the part of your employees is absolutely necessary. When the hazards and work methods surveys are completed, the supervisor is ready to enlist the support of his or her employees. The request for full cooperation in safety can be made at departmental meetings or through personal, individual contacts.

The safety instruction of every new worker and every worker assigned to a new job is the most important single factor in making a departmental safety plan effective. The development of positive attitudes toward safe behavior begins there.

Having removed every possible hazard and unsafe condition, the supervisor must now see to it that dangerous conditions which cannot be eliminated are covered by thorough safety instruction. Effective safety instruction does not take the form of merely warning the employee to "be careful." It must consist of a specific statement and *information* given to the employee that will teach him or her the safe way to do the job. You can do this by (1) preparing the learner (putting him or her at ease and arousing his or her interest); (2) presenting the instructions slowly, carefully, and completely so that the information registers; (3) testing the employee's understanding by having him or her perform the operation or restate the directions; and finally, (4) following up on the instructions to see that they are observed.

There are some questions you can ask yourself about each of your employees to help determine what might be needed in individual cases: Is he or she properly instructed? Does he or she make safety suggestions? How many accidents or near accidents has he or she had in the last three months? Does he or she take chances? Is his or her eyesight good enough for the job? Is he or she alert? Answers to these and other such questions will help determine what further instruction the worker might need or whether he or she may need to be transferred to another job, given safety discipline, or closer supervision.

Step 5: Deal with Unsafe Attitudes

Unsafe attitudes invariably affect employee behavior patterns and may be particularly dangerous in the work environment. Lack of responsibility, lack of motivation, and disregard for safety instructions are some common examples of unsafe attitudes.

The supervisor is usually not an expert in advertising techniques or skilled in devising signs, posters, charts, films, contests or games. However, simply supplying information on safety is often not enough. Employees must be motivated to apply safety procedures to their own job practices.

To emphasize the importance of accepting safety as a personal goal, the supervisor should watch a worker's safety performance just as he or she does individual job performance. This means training employees in the proper way of doing things and following up to *make sure* that they are done.

The supervisor's attitude toward safety is reflected in the extent to which he or she is willing to enforce safety requirements. What should the supervisor do when an employee is found breaking a company safety rule for which disciplinary action is required? Many supervisors face real dilemmas when a good worker commits a safety violation. They know that formal warnings or laying the worker off often creates hard feelings and destroys friendly relationships. Yet they also know that they can get into real trouble if a safety violation results in a serious accident.

Some companies go so far as to have their safety experts "police" on-the-job conditions. When they do this, they in effect remove safety from the supervisor's list of responsibilities. Yet, as we have seen, the supervisor is the most critical element in the safety process and *should not be removed* from the safety process.

When supervisors fail to invoke penalties that are required for safety violations, they may give such excuses as (1) the violation was in doubt; (2) the penalty is too strict; (3) the worker cannot afford the penalty; (4) the employee will resent the discipline.[2] Supervisors typically do not feel comfortable with a legalistic stand of determining guilt and handing out punishment in cases of safety violations. They are inclined to recognize the feelings of the employees and to believe that future precautions will be taken.

Obviously, workers don't want to have accidents, so punishment may fall wide of the mark in adjusting attitudes. This means that discipline for repeated safety violations is not appropriate. For example, a supervisor may have to transfer or dismiss an employee who is unable to perform his or her job in a safe way, both for the employee's safety and in the long-run interest of the organization.

Step 6: Follow up on Your Safety Program Regularly

Follow-up is an essential part of any supervisory action. This is especially true of a safety program. Safety cannot effectively be run on a "campaign" basis—it must be continuous. Indeed, a distinguishing characteristic of an effective safety program is this nonstop feature.

To ensure proper follow-up, you must do the following things:

1. Maintain a personal interest in safety and continue to devote 15 minutes daily to safety activities. This is important and it is a responsibility that *cannot be delegated* without reducing its effectiveness. A quarter hour daily does not constitute a serious problem to the supervisor who plans his or her work carefully. Remember, good safety programs not only prevent accidents, but also promote work efficiency, reduce waste, and so forth.
2. Recheck machinery and conditions on a regular schedule to see that those needing repair or correction have been taken care of. Employees are quick to detect any apparent lack of supervisory sincerity in the program, and failing to recheck is a sign of failing interest.
3. Contact one or two employees daily and while observing work methods, talk to them briefly to stimulate safety thinking. This doesn't have to be obvious. Just let safety enter your informal conversations with your employees. They will catch on.
4. Maintain the necessary records so that no equipment or worker is overlooked and contacts are made in a systematic, rotating manner but with a minimum of red tape.

THE ADMINISTRATION OF SAFETY

A recent, large national study found that more than 82 percent of all organizations responding had a formal safety program. Such programs are found in nearly all of the manufacturing companies (97 percent), in 66 percent of nonmanufacturing businesses, and in 61 percent of the nonbusiness organizations.[3] The responding organizations that did not have formal safety programs were mostly in the finance industry (banking and insurance), trade (wholesale or retail trade), or education, usually considered relatively safe industries.

Figure 18–1 presents some interesting information about safety programs from that survey. Less than half of the companies responding budgeted the safety program separately, which means that these companies probably did not have a separate safety "department." The survey also indicates wide usage of safety committees, a topic we deal with next. Most importantly, in a majority of the organizations, both supervisors and employees receive safety training. In a high percentage of these organizations, training is mandatory, and employees must pass a proficiency test in handling hazardous equipment, before they are allowed to use it.

FIGURE 18–1 National Safety Program Profile

	Percentage of Companies					
	By Industry			By Size		
	Mfg.	Non-mfg.	Non-bus.	Large	Small	All
Companies with formal safety programs	97	66	61	88	76	82
Safety program has separate budget	48	19	43	49	31	41
Safety program involves a safety committee	94	76	93	88	93	90
Supervisors are given safety training	84	59	91	86	71	79
Employees are given safety training	80	63	70	88	58	73
Training is mandatory	84	75	94	77	94	84
Employee must pass proficiency test in handling hazardous equipment	67	80	44	65	68	66

Source: Adapted from *Safety Policies and the Impact of OSHA*, PPF Survey No. 117 (Washington, D.C.: Bureau of National Affairs, May 1977), pp. 2–7.

Safety Committees

Safety committees are typically appointed by top management, often on the basis of one representative from each department or unit. There are often union representatives on the safety committee as well.

Safety committees' responsibilities vary widely from one organization to another. In about half of the organizations with committees, the safety committee is primarily an advisory body and seldom has the authority to stop operations because of hazards.[4] There are two problems associated with safety committees. They can become stale and they often don't work.[5] It has been suggested that for safety committees to make any kind of impact, they should be chaired by a management person. By becoming directly involved in the work of the committee, management can demontrate its sincerity to workers and set the proper example.

It has been suggested that the membership on the committee should rotate every three to six months so that all members of the organization, and especially all supervisory personnel, have been actively involved in correcting accident situations.

The committee should be regularly involved in inspections. Every member should inspect a part of the work place looking for hazards. This is best done in pairs. The emphasis should be on preventing accidents rather than on analyzing accidents that have already taken place. Certainly those should be examined in detail, but prevention should be the main concern.

Safety Posters

Safety posters have been, and continue to be, rather widely used communication methods to promote safety awareness. Eighty-five percent of the companies surveyed in the BNA survey referred to earlier use safety posters as a method of communication. Posters and slogans *can be* quite useful. However, as with all advertising, these devices should be kept simple, reasonable, and constructive. Unreasonable, untrue statements are worthless.

Emotional appeals made in posters may have a temporary value, but if they arouse fear, they may do more harm than good. A frightened employee is not a safe employee, and although a gruesome picture attracts attention, it may not have the desired effect. Posters showing the agony of an injured worker or a pair of hands dripping with blood probably arouse fear more than they educate.[6] Safety posters should be approached from an educational perspective and, as such, it is best to provide a positive rather than a negative message.

FIGURE 18–2   Safety Equipment

| | Percentage of Companies | | | | | |
| | By Industry | | | By Size | | |
	Mfg.	*Non-mfg.*	*Non-bus.*	*Large*	*Small*	*All*
Employees wear special safety equipment*	100	59	91	89	86	88
Equipment Required						
Safety glasses or goggles	99	84	90	95	94	94
Face shields, masks, or welders' helmets	87	58	81	83	78	81
Safety shoes or boots	86	68	62	81	75	78
Hard hats	75	63	81	79	67	74
Respiratory equipment	70	42	62	71	55	63
Protective clothing such as jackets or overalls	65	47	67	67	57	62
Hair nets	41	32	57	55	27	42
Safety belts	39	47	43	50	31	41
Ear plugs	16	21	0	16	12	14
Other	7	16	14	12	8	10
Safety equipment is mandatory	96	79	95	93	92	93
Company pays entire cost of safety equipment	43	63	57	43	57	50

* Percentages are of total sample. The percentages in the remainder of the table are of companies with safety equipment for employees.

Source: *Safety Policies and the Impact of OSHA*, PPF Survey No. 117 (Washington, D.C.: The Bureau of National Affairs, May 1977), Table 6, p. 9.

Safety Equipment

As Figure 18–2 indicates, nearly nine out of ten of the companies surveyed require employees to wear some type of personal safety equipment. This may be nothing more than safety glasses or goggles, or it may include such items as ear plugs, safety belts, protective clothing, and so forth. About half of the companies that require safety equipment pay the entire cost of that equipment for the employee. Block 18–1 shows how one company handled mandatory safety equipment.

THE PSYCHOLOGY OF SAFETY

Being aware of the psychological reasons for accidents can help us understand successful safety programs. Both mental and physical fatigue, working conditions, individual susceptibilities, and outside activities are important concerns in looking at the psychology of safety.

At R. J. Reynolds Tobacco Company, manufacturing process changes had resulted in noise hazards. After engineers had pinpointed the dangerously noisy areas, personal protection devices were provided to the workers in the noisy areas while engineering solutions were being devised. Yellow and black noise warnings signs were posted wherever personal hearing protection was *required*.

When the employee picked up a personal hearing protector, he or she received some information reviewing the facts on noise and hearing loss, and reminding the employee to wear ear protection in all areas marked with yellow and black signs. Ninety percent of the employees required to wear hearing protectors comply with the requirement.

R. J. Reynolds' program is a mandatory program, but one in which management has tried to use education and salesmanship rather than discipline to make it work. The evidence of the program's effectiveness is that the annual hearing checkups show no appreciable change in employee hearing levels since the program began.

Adapted from "How R. J. Reynolds Protects Workers' Hearing," *Management Review*, July 1973, pp. 64–66.

Fatigue

Fatigue is closely related to accident proneness. The connection between fatigue and accidents isn't purely physical, but includes such psychological factors as absent-mindedness, inattention, daydreaming, and so forth, all of which arise from being tired or bored. Both the beginning and the end of the work week generally show higher accident frequencies, as do lengthy periods of overtime. A tired worker generally becomes inattentive to details of the job, *including the hazards*. As he or she becomes less alert, motions tend to slow down and become somewhat clumsy. Tired people react less quickly to any sudden danger.

Common causes of fatigue are

1. long hours
2. unfavorable working conditions
3. heavy or monotonous work
4. illness
5. unfavorable mental conditions
6. off-the-job activities

When long hours are unavoidable, every effort should be made to keep working conditions as comfortable as possible; favorable seating, additional rest breaks, and elimination of wasted motions or awkward work positions can all help. Job rotation can also help by reducing monotony. Extremes of temperature or light, poor ventilation, excessive noise, and dirty or unpleasant working conditions—anything about the job which makes it uncomfortable or disagreeable—will cause a worker to tire much more rapidly than normal.

Working Conditions

Good lighting can lead to a reduction in the accident rate. It has been estimated that as many as 25 percent of all industrial accidents are caused by poor lighting. The temperature at which work is performed also affects the accident rate. Studies of factory workers have shown that the accident rate is lowest when the temperature is between 68 and 70 degrees Fahrenheit. Accidents increase when the temperature varies in either direction and are particularly frequent under extreme conditions. Evidence suggests that older workers are more affected by temperature extremes than younger workers. In hot work environments, older employees are much more likely to have accidents than in cooler environments.

The type of industry involved also affects the accident rate. In general, construction, mining, lumber, and quarry work have high accident frequencies. Aircraft, automobile manufacturing, rubber warehousing, and communications are unusually low. Typically, fewer accidents occur during night shifts than during comparable day shifts. This may be related to lighting.

Individual Factors

Workers with physical handicaps are usually *good* accident risks. If handicapped persons are in good general health and are assigned to jobs equal to their ability, accident rates are usually found to be lower than those for more able-bodied workers.

Generally, older workers and those who are relatively experienced have *lower* accident rates than younger, more inexperienced workers. Older people's reaction time and hand/eye coordination may not be as good as that of younger workers, but by virtue of their greater experience, they may have a better approach to the job. Older employees tend to have a more serious attitude toward safety than younger employees as well.

Another important factor is the emotional state that an employee brings to the job. Studies have shown that fewer accidents occur when workers are happy and content than when they are angry, frustrated, or worried. In one study, more than 50 percent of the accidents observed took place during negative emotional periods. Thus, temporary emotional states *can be* factors in accidents.

Workers subjected to an unhappy home life or personal or job-related problems are more susceptible to accidents. Lack of interest, uncertainty about the job, fear of his or her boss, antagonism toward fellow workers, fear of the dangers on the job, worries about outside problems, all of these increase worker fatigue on the job. Knowing that these mental causes of fatigue are detrimental to safety, supervisors should maintain as close contact and understanding with each worker as possible in order to ensure a positive attitude toward the job.

Outside Activities

Outside activities can present a major stumbling block for supervisors to contend with. An employee usually resents interference with his or her activities off the job. However, sometimes outside difficulties *can be* reduced by a supervisor's help. Perhaps he or she could be helped with transportation and housing difficulties through some personal counseling or advice. If a supervisor is personally close enough to his or her workers, such friendly advice and suggestions may be taken seriously by the worker.

However, the supervisor's influence on outside activities will depend upon his or her ability to win employees' confidence and respect. A good rule of thumb is that when outside activities reach a point at which they are affecting the job, it is then time for the supervisor to discuss such things with the employee. If outside activities continue to interfere with job performance, at some point dismissal may be advisable. Block 18–2 illustrates a case in which both physical and psychological problems were involved in accidents.

ACCIDENT PRONENESS

The idea that some people are more likely than others to have accidents has been popular for some time. A person who has been termed *accident prone* has significantly more accidents than others who are exposed to essentially similar dangers on the job. It has been hypothesized that the accident prone person behaves or thinks in some special way to create accidents.

A survey of 27,000 industrial accidents and 8,000 nonindustrial acci-

Joe Kern had been having one minor accident after another. Fortunately, none of them were serious enough to cause any major problems, although any one of them was potentially catastrophic. The quality of Joe's work had also fallen down, and his output was not what it should have been. His supervisor, Bill Dunn, had warned him several times that he would have to improve. Then Kern spoiled a batch of work and Dunn told him he would give him one more chance, but the next one would mean his job or a transfer to other work.

A few days later, Kern made another mistake and he was immediately transferred to a materials handling job in another department. Fred Tybert, Joe's new supervisor, soon noticed that he wasn't working very effectively on this job either. He watched him closely and decided that the man was not well, so he had a friendly talk with Joe. Their discussion indicated that Joe had been losing weight for the last six months, that he had been getting weaker and his eyesight had been getting poorer.

Tybert made arrangements immediately to have him examined by the company doctor. The examination showed that Joe was indeed ill. However, the illness was treatable, and within six months Joe had regained his former healthy physical condition, although he had to watch his diet to prevent the illness from happening again. He has a higher skill level than is being used at the present time in Tybert's department, and arrangements have been made to transfer him to another department. However, Joe has specifically requested not to be transferred back to Dunn's department.

dents indicated that the accident repeater contributed only 0.5 percent of these accidents, while 74 percent could be attributed to relatively infrequent experiences of a large number of persons.[7] Further study has suggested that the relatively small percentage of the population that could be considered accident prone is essentially a *shifting group,* with new people constantly entering and leaving the group.

It has also been suggested that during the course of a life span almost any normal individual under stress or in periods of conflict may become temporarily accident prone and may suffer a series of accidents at fairly rapid succession. Most people, however, solve their problems and leave the highly accident prone group after a few hours, days, weeks, or months.[8]

Despite these data, a fair number of organizations, according to a recent survey, do attempt to identify accident prone employees. Nearly two-thirds of those surveyed said that they do. Figure 18–3 shows the

FIGURE 18–3   Handling Accident Prone Employees

	Percentage of Companies					
	By Industry			By Size		
	Mfg.	Non-mfg.	Non-bus.	Large	Small	All
An attempt is made to identify "accident prone" employees	72	50	65	65	66	65
Measures taken to help accident prone employees work safely*						
Counseling	68	81	80	74	72	73
Given increased supervision	56	63	67	57	62	59
Transferred to less hazardous jobs	54	38	20	40	49	44
Given special training	34	38	46	33	41	37
Other (including discipline)	24	25	13	29	15	22

* Percentages are of companies identifying "accident prone" employees.
Source: *Safety Policies and the Impact of OSHA,* PPF Survey No. 117 (Washington, D.C.: The Bureau of National Affairs, May 1977), p. 13.

results of that survey on accident proneness. The data show that in those companies which attempt to identify accident prone employees, the problem is generally approached through counseling. A lesser number of organizations provide increased supervision and 44 percent of the respondents consider transferring employees.

Although the accident proneness idea still has many supporters, it no longer enjoys the credibility it once did. Current research suggests that some people may have a tendency to have more accidents *in certain situations* but that this does not necessarily carry over to other types of situations. In other words, accident proneness may be specific to a given situation.

THE OCCUPATIONAL SAFETY AND HEALTH ACT

As part of the nation's labor law, the Occupational Safety and Health Act (1971) has greatly influenced most organizations' and most supervisors' behavior and thinking about safety and safety programs. The purpose of the act is to "assure so far as possible every working man or woman in the nation safe and healthful working conditions and to preserve our human resources." Every employer engaged in commerce who has one or more employees is covered by the act. The act authorizes the establishment of the Occupational Safety and Health Administration known as OSHA.

Background on OSHA

OSHA is empowered to set mandatory standards for conditions in the work place. Examples are (1) that moving parts on machines be guarded, (2) that forklift trucks have overhead protection against falling objects, (3) that airborne concentrations of chemicals, dusts, gases, or fumes be kept below certain levels, and so forth. At the time the act was passed, about 14,000 people were dying each year in industrial accidents in the United States, and 100,000 were being permanently disabled. The average member of the labor force had more than one chance in forty of being temporarily or permanently disabled from an accident. For industrial workers, the risk was even higher. Another survey suggested that 31 percent of the illnesses identified in a sample group of workers probably were *caused by their jobs* and another 10 percent were suspect.[9] There obviously was a need for improved measures to deal with employee safety.

Effect of OSHA

OSHA has had some tremendous effects on safety and health in American organizations. One of the most noticeable effects has been work place safety, which had previously been a low priority item for many organizations. A Lou Harris poll has estimated that six out of ten companies who now have a safety and health program did not have one prior to OSHA.[10] OSHA has also had a marked effect on the behavior of supervisors, who are now much more likely to survey the work place for hazards and measure their operation against some kind of safety standard than they were before the federal law.

OSHA established a standard national system for recording occupational injuries, accidents, and fatalities. Employers are required to maintain an annual detailed record of various types of accidents for inspection by OSHA representatives. The act also provides for on-the-spot inspection by OSHA agents. These agents, known as compliance officers or inspectors, usually *do not* give prior notification of an inspection.

Criticism of OSHA

OSHA has definitely increased the safety consciousness of employers. However, criticism of OSHA has emerged for several reasons. One is that some standards are not explicit enough to be able to recognize easily whether one is complying. Another complaint is that many rules are so complicated and technical that small businesses without a safety

399

specialist are strapped for the know-how to apply them. Finally, many have been concerned about the buildup of red tape that results in too much noneffective time to be spent on complying with unimportant details.

OSHA's Change in Direction

Recently, OSHA has experienced a change in direction. There is an increased emphasis on occupational health and a deemphasis on many of the complicated safety rules. OSHA says the purpose is to get tough on health hazards in the work place that cause irreversible injury, cancer, nerve damage, leukemia, lung disease, and all of the rest.

OSHA is currently combing through the more than 5,000 "consensus standards" to eliminate the "mickey mouse" rules that burden employers without really protecting workers. Recently, OSHA dropped 928 of these rules. Among the rules being dropped are those covering the design of toilet seats, the kind of wood to be used in building portable ladders, the height for mounting fire extinguishers, and the location of certain exits in buildings in relation to public thoroughfares.

Some of these regulations were incredibly detailed, for example, section 1910.141 had to do with toilet facilities. It stated, "Every water closet shall have a hinged seat made of substantial material having a nonabsorbent finish. . . ." The regulation ran on and on for *over a thousand words* detailing the requirements for such facilities. After the editing job, the revised regulation reads, "Except as otherwise indicated in the subdivision, toilet facilities shall be provided in all places of employment."

OSHA's emphasis on health has resulted in one of the heaviest civil fines in history. At the N. L. Industries plant in Beach Grove, Indiana, OSHA found the air in the lunchroom contaminated with lead. OSHA charged that employees were not trained in the use of respirators, and were not given adequate medical treatment. These violations were described as "repeated and serious" and the combined penalties to the company added up to $154,000. The issue will be contested before OSHA's review commission and then in the courts, but it shows that the agency is concerning itself with serious and significant matters of employee health and safety, and not worrying quite so much about the composition and shape of toilet seats.

How Does OSHA Affect Me?

OSHA directly affects supervisors, since supervisors play a strategic role in attaining the goals for which the act was created. Supervisors are responsible for safety, and the law does not excuse ignorance in this regard. All supervisors are required to know what their responsibilities are under the law.

Generally speaking, there are four supervisory responsibilities:

1. Reporting Requirements

As we suggested earlier, there are certain record-keeping and reporting requirements under the act. Different organizations require the supervisor or, alternately, the personnel department to fulfill these functions. In addition, OSHA requires a daily log in which the employer must enter certain reportable injuries and illnesses. This form can be obtained through your local OSHA office, and must be available to the OSHA compliance officer if he requests it.

There is also a detailed form that must be completed on each separate reportable injury or illness. The information required parallels the data requested on the state workman's compensation form. It must be kept on file and available to any compliance officer who might be doing an audit. Then there are annual reports that must be made and retained in the event of an OSHA inspection. These generally will not be done by the supervisor. However, the keeping of the daily log and the investigation of circumstances surrounding an injury or illness are things that supervisors typically are required to do.

2. Hazard Identification and Explanation Requirement

The law does not require that hazards be totally eliminated, but it does require that they be identified and explained to the worker. It is usually up to the supervisor to identify such hazards and develop methods of working safely around them. All hazards must be identified by appropriate labels or signs.

3. Awareness of Hazard Monitoring Requirements

If equipment is used to monitor the level of gases in a particular work location, or the level of x-rays being distributed in a room, the supervisor will have the responsibility for seeing that the monitoring equipment is working properly. The supervisor will be responsible for reporting any unmonitored excesses, and helping subordinates become more aware of the danger.

4. Notification of Employees About Provisions of the Act

The supervisor is typically required to train employees in all aspects of safety pertaining to their job. There are many good reasons for a supervisor to want to carry out his or her duties of training and safety

Tim Kent had a crew at a marine terminal loading cargo on a freighter that had berthed the night before. A stranger stood watching the loading operations for a few minutes, then he walked over to Tim, pulled out a card, and introduced himself as a compliance officer from OSHA. Tim barely glanced at the card; he felt he wasn't doing anything wrong so he said, "Go right ahead." He sent a crew member with the inspector.

Later Tim was approached by the inspector who asked, "Do you know what these men are loading, and what could happen to them if any of it leaked out of the drums?" "Of course," Tim replied, "It's Toluene Diisocyanate, a dangerous chemical." "Do the men working here know that?" the inspector asked. "They certainly should," Tim answered. "Every drum is clearly labeled with a warning." "You mean you haven't explained the hazard to them?" said the inspector. "I'm writing this one up, it's a violation."

The OSHA judge pointed out that some of the men might not bother to read the labels and, in fact, an occasional worker might not be able to read. "It's not enough," he said, "to rely on the labels alone." Tim should *specifically* have told *every* worker about the potential damage to his health and safety if the drum leaked any of the toxic substance. The company (and Tim) lost the decision.

education regardless of any legislation that requires them to do so. However, the law *is* present and provides a push for those supervisors who for some reason have had difficulty training their employees in safe methods of doing their work. Block 18–3 describes a case that illustrates the importance of OSHA for supervisors.

SUMMARY AND CONCLUSIONS

Successful safety programs require the work of many people, but the supervisor is clearly the key. Prevention of accidents is the best way to approach safety. A six-step plan for setting up a supervisory accident prevention system includes these actions: (1) Budget definite time for safety; (2) make a thorough hazard survey; (3) make a thorough work methods survey; (4) train your employees; (5) deal with unsafe attitudes; (6) follow up on your safety program continually.

Administering safety in work organizations can include using safety committees, posters, safety equipment, and so on. Surveys presented in

the chapter show the extent to which these are used in work organizations, and methods for making them more effective are discussed.

Fatigue is an important psychological factor that contributes to higher accident rates. Working conditions such as light, temperature, the nature of the industry, and the specific work shift affect accidents, as do characteristics of workers and their outside activities.

Accident proneness among certain individuals is a widely accepted idea that research is beginning to question. It may simply be a temporary condition for some employees.

The Occupational Safety and Health Act has brought some significant changes in the ways organizations deal with the problems of safety. Organizations *and* supervisors now place safety on a higher priority than before OSHA was created. The supervisor is especially involved in *reporting, hazard identification* and *monitoring,* and *notification* or *training* of employees.

QUESTIONS

1. What are typical hazards in a work place?
2. Contrast safety problems at an office with safety problems in the textile manufacturing industry.
3. Why don't supervisors deal with safety violations more severely?
4. Pick an organization you are familiar with. What could be done to improve their safety program?
5. If you have ever known someone who you felt was accident prone, analyze the conditions or personal elements that might have contributed to that state.

6. Make a list of the positive and negative things you know about that are associated with OSHA. What suggestions do you have for making OSHA more effective?

BURT'S ACCIDENT RATE

The frequency of accidents in Burt Lauden's department had risen to a point where the superintendent felt that some action needed to be taken. He called for all the "minor injury" and "lost time" accident reports that had been turned in during the past six months by Lauden. There were eight.

On each injury report slip there was a question that had to be answered by the supervisor regarding the injury. The question was, "How can this injury be prevented in the future?" As the superintendent went over Lauden's reports, he paid particular attention to the way Lauden had answered this question in each case. He found that the answers were generally similar and usually vague such as "be more careful," "do the job correctly," "watch out for hazards," or "think before acting."

In looking at these answers to the question, the superintendent came to the conclusion that Lauden probably limited his instruction on safety to just such remarks. Later when he talked to Lauden, he found that it was true, that his idea of giving safety instruction was to warn workers about getting hurt and advise them to "be careful." He also found that after having given the worker a warning to "look out so you don't get hurt," Lauden had little sympathy with the person who had the accident.

---

1. What's wrong with Burt's approach to safety instructions?
2. What would you do about it if you were superintendent?

NOTES

1 K. Planik, G. Driesen and F. Volardo, "Industrial Safety Study," *National Safety News,* August 1967.

2 N. R. F. Maier, *Psychology in Industrial Organizations,* 4th ed. (Boston: Houghton Mifflin Co., 1973), p. 472.

3 *Safety Policies and the Impact of OSHA,* PPF Survey No. 117 (Washington, D.C.: Bureau of National Affairs, May 1977), p. 1.

4 Ibid.

5 R. Wilkinson, "Keep that Safety Committee Moving," *Supervision,* March 1978.

6 N. R. F. Maier, *Psychology and Industry,* 3rd ed. (Boston: Houghton Mifflin Co., 1965), p. 565.

7 Maier, *Psychology in Industrial Organizations,* p. 461.

8 Morris Schulzinger, *Accident Syndrome* (Springfield, Ill.: Charles C Thomas, 1956).

9 S. Kelman, "OSHA Under Fire," *The New Republic,* May 21, 1977, p. 20.

10 R. E. McClay, "Professionalizing the Safety Function," *Personnel Journal,* February 1977, p. 73.

Index

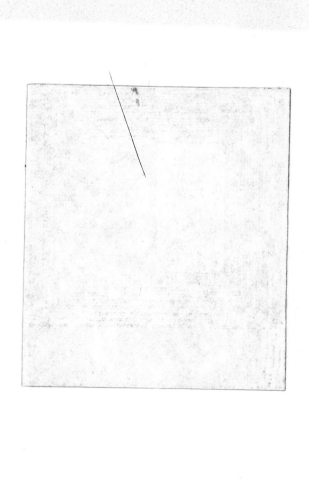

1

Af